THE DEVELOPMENT
OF THE NOTION OF SELF

Understanding the Complexity of Human Interiority

William S. Schmidt

Studies in the Psychology of Religion
Volume 5

The Edwin Mellen Press
Lewiston/Queenston/Lampeter

Library of Congress Cataloging-in-Publication Data

Schmidt, William S., 1950-
    The development of the notion of self : understanding the
complexity of human interiority / William S. Schmidt.
        p.   cm. -- (Studies in the psychology of religion ; v. 5)
    Includes bibliographical references.
    ISBN 0-7734-9341-7
    1. Self (Philosophy)--History.   2. Self--History.   3. Soul-
-History of doctrines.   I. Title.   II. Series.
BD421.S38   1994
126--dc20
                                                                93-20925
                                                                CIP

This is volume 5 in the continuing series
Studies in the Psychology of Religion
Volume 5 ISBN 0-7734-9341-7
SPR Series ISBN 0-88946-247-X

A CIP catalog record for this book is available from the British Library.

The Edwin Mellen Press
Box 450
Lewiston, New York
USA 14092-0450

The Edwin Mellen Press
Box 67
Queenston, Ontario
CANADA L0S 1L0

The Edwin Mellen Press, Ltd.
Lampeter, Dyfed, Wales
UNITED KINGDOM SA48 7DY

Printed in the United States of America

To my Father, William Schmidt

And my Mother, Erna Schmidt

CONTENTS

INTRODUCTION   **1**

Chapter I   THE GREEK PARADIGM   **8**

Plato: Pioneer of Selfhood   9
The Aristotelian Challenge   17

Chapter II   THE JUDEO-CHRISTIAN CHALLENGE   **32**

The Foundation to Human Identity   33
The Biblical Self as Dynamic Process   37
The Spirit/Flesh Polarity   42

Chapter III   EARLY EXPLORERS OF SELFHOOD   **55**

Augustine: First Guide to the Study of the Self   56
The Human Self as Reflection of the Divine Image   57
The Augustinian Legacy   65
Aquinas and the Aristotelian Resurgence   66
The Nature of the Thomistic Self   67
The Thomistic Inheritance   73
The Self in Meister Eckhart (1260 - 1328)   75
God and the Self   76
The Process of the Self's Life   83
A Revised Dualism?   88
Conclusion   90

Chapter IV THE TRANSITION TO THE MODERN PERIOD   97

Rene Descartes (1596 - 1650)   98
The Challenge of David Hume (1711 - 1776)   104
Immanuel Kant (1742 - 1804): Answer to Hume and Descartes   109
J.G. Fichte (1762 - 1814) and the Ego-Self Relation   115

**Chapter V   G.W.F. HEGEL (1770 - 1831) AND THE UNIFIED
          SELF   131**

Survey of the Hegelian Paradigm   132
Hegel's Path to Selfhood   144
Preliminary Responses   181

**Chapter VI KIERKEGAARD (1813 - 1855) AND THE
          SYNTHESIZING SELF   189**

The Kierkegaardian Self   189
Kierkegaard's Path to Selfhood   202
Hegel and Kierkegaard Revisited   221

**Chapter VII SIGMUND FREUD (1856 - 1939) AND THE
          PSYCHOANALYTIC PATH TO SELFHOOD   234**

Freud's Historical and Philosophical Background   235
Freudian Models of the Psyche   237
The Freudian Structure of Personality   238
The Topographic Model   238
The Tripartite Model   245
The Psyche and Its Energy   250
The Limits of Freud   261

**Chapter VIII CONTEMPORARY PSYCHOANALYTIC
           PERSPECTIVES: THE BRITISH SCHOOL   267**

Melanie Klein   269
Ronald Fairbairn   273
D.W. Winnicott   279

Chapter IX THE PSYCHOANALYTIC MODEL CONTINUED:
            AMERICAN OBJECT RELATIONS THEORY   293

Heinz Hartmann   294
Edith Jacobson   299
Margaret Mahler   305
Otto Kernberg   313
Heinz Kohut   321
The Adequacy of Self Psychology   331

Chapter X   C.G. JUNG (1875 - 1961) AND THE
            TRANSPERSONAL SELF   339

Jung's Philosophical Inheritance   340
The Bi-polar Psyche   341
The Ego as Seat of Consciousness   342
The Unconscious and Its Archtypes   343
The Archtypes Identified   347
The Self: Alpha and Omega of Personhood   355
The Adequacy of the Jungian Self   363

Chapter XI THE FULFILLED SELF   370

The Self Defined   371
The Structure of Self   373
The Process of Self   381
The Phases of the Life of Self   389

BIBLIOGRAPHY   399

INDEX   408

Acknowledgements

I am delighted to be able to thank the many persons and institutions whose supportive efforts helped make this book a reality. The seed for this book was planted during a 3 month sabbatical at the Claremont School of Theology in Claremont, California during the spring of 1986. I am grateful for the support offered to me as a Visiting Scholar and the kindness shown by Howard Clinebell and the staff of that institution.

Above all, however, my gratitude extends to the Royal Alexandra Hospital in Edmonton, Alberta particularly its staff and administration. Not only did my primary employer grant me the initial gift of time to begin this effort, they encouraged the process of research and writing throughout my 10 year term as Director of Pastoral Care and Counseling. A special thanks is directed to the Administrators under whose leadership I was privileged to serve. This indebtedness extends from Mr. Bud Casey, to Mrs. Margaret Johnson, and to the current President, Dr. Tom Noseworthy, whom I feel privileged to call colleague and friend.

I also wish to express my particular appreciation to my departmental colleagues at the Royal Alexandra Hospital. They include Neil Elford, Doug Cossar, and Jeannette Martin who all graciously tolerated my philosophical meanderings.

Further indebtedness extends to my colleagues at St. Stephen's College, Edmonton, Alberta, in particular Bill Close and the members of the Doctor of Ministry Committee. They along with members of the Edmonton Theological Colloquium and the Edmonton Supervisors of the Canadian Association for Pastoral Education helped provide the intellectual, spiritual, and clinical environment within which my search for deeper meaning could be actualized.

My deep gratitude extends to Dianne Fedorak and Kathy Siemens whose diligence with transcription was indispensable. Thanks also to Ann Forde and Dennis Phillips, Loyola University of Chicago graduate assistants, whose help with the index, bibliography, and with proofreading was invaluable.

My deepest appreciation is felt toward my family. My wife Margita maintained her intimate companionship in the face of the solitariness of the writing viii

endeavor. She sustained my selfhood through my serious illness in 1989 and believed that the project could find completion even when my faith faltered. Furthermore, she provided editorial support, and carried the manuscript through the tedious final stages of preparation.

My three sons Michael, Thomas and Matthew have hardly known a time when I was not working on this book. Yet rather than divide us it has perhaps made the interactions among us more direct, more intense, and more loving.

Finally, this book is dedicated to my parents William and Erna. It has been 40 years since we immigrated from Germany to Canada and a scant 50 years since they left their respective homes in Hungary and the southern Ukraine. I trace my love of history and the seeking of the spiritual links among humanity to the history I share with them. We know the pain of homelessness but we also know that the journey can be trusted.

Spirits Song over the Waters

Johann Wolfgang von Goethe

The human self
is like the water,
from heaven it comes,
to heaven it rises,
and again down
to earth it must go,
eternally changing. . .

Human self, how like water you are,
Human destiny,
how like the wind!

Translation: W. S. S.

INTRODUCTION

This book is an attempt to apply the conceptual resources of philosophy, theology, and psychodynamic psychology to a most pressing contemporary issue: the phenomenon of human self-identity. I believe there is a special urgency to this task because of the erosion of constructs which historically have carried the agendas of human interiority and subjectivity. Among the most noteworthy of such developments is the collapse of the soul construct.

For previous eras the notion "soul" was the primary representation of human essence, the fullness of subjectivity which defined persons as human. For reasons I will uncover in this study "the soul" became increasingly understood in static, otherworldly terms, cut off from flow, movement, and the dynamism necessary for a full subjectivity.

The final and fatal step for the soul construct was reached when soul became fully identified with rationality, that power which separates reality into its constituent parts by means of mental representation. This separation generated by thought fit nicely with transcendent and largely dualistic religious and philosophical constructs of various epochs. Inevitably, soul became locked into an otherworldly realm sharing eternal and timeless serenity with its maker, the Deity. This static, removed-from-life basis for human subjectivity has collapsed into dust.

In this era of soul-death a deep hunger has emerged for establishing a basis for human identity which is **not** (1) static, (2) otherworldly, or (3) externally defined. My hope for this study is to reclaim the lost dynamism of the soul construct thereby enriching our evolving understandings of self. Self, in my estimation, is the most viable contemporary formula for representing human identity and "subject"-ivity.

I carry numerous assumptions with me into this task. A first assumption is that important constructs are best understood from an evolutionary vantage point. That is, I operate from a broadly - understood developmental framework which holds that subsequent developments rest upon prior formulations and adaptations. The multiple adjustments visible along the way are not only interesting for vague archeological reasons, but provide a foundation from which further developments emerge either to grow and flourish or wither and die. I believe this study confirms that the development of self-representations in the Western world reveals a traceable lineage of great achievements and destructive dead-ends.

Unfortunately, there is much historical ignorance in our modern world leaving us vulnerable to short-sighted and thinly sustained conclusions about ourselves as subjects. I therefore strongly affirm a corresponding assumption, that historical analysis is vital for contemporary viability.

A third assumption is that such an expansive historical effort must of necessity be interdisciplinary. The analysis of the structures and patterns of human self-consciousness has historically been carried out by philosophy with numerous methodologies and vantage points being used in this effort. Operating concurrently alongside the philosophical disciplines have been numerous theological frameworks which sought in various ways to root the operations of the human agent within the life of Deity, however understood. The most noble visions for human subjectivity seem to require this theological parallel.

Finally, the emergence of psychological paradigms (within those schools which allow for human interiority), has significantly increased our ability to understand human subjective life and identity development. Our ability to talk about self would be fatally compromised if the psychological window were not available.

But there is an even more important factor which supports an interdisciplinary effort, namely, the corrective action of one discipline upon another. For instance, theological frameworks do offer necessary ontological supports for self-construction, but often suffer under the orthodoxy requirements of their respective belief systems. Furthermore, their assumptive worlds often tend to exclude the experiential crucible so absolutely vital for self-definition.

Similarly, certain psychological frameworks offer rich models for honoring the historical and contextual necessities for self-construction, but flounder when it comes time to inquire as to the meaning of what they observe. Furthermore, I would argue that the philosophical disciplines provide a means of uncovering the assumptive worlds which frame every inquiry. The corrective action of philosophical, theological, and psychological worlds upon one another allows us not only to see their respective assumptive roots, but provides us with the tools for discerning the presuppositions and potentials of all contemporary self-models. Without these historical resources we risk collapsing the emerging dynamism of self. In short, a comprehensive analysis of the self-construct requires the engagement of all three disciplines in a mutual accountability.

Finally, historical analysis is needed for more than quaint archival purposes. Our contemporary solutions to the pressing identity problems of today are strengthened by an awareness of previous dilemmas. Contemporary solutions are not separate from their historical heritage. In fact, ownership of these historical roots allows our contemporary quest to remain grounded even as we leave behind the deadened portions of our inheritance. For instance, the feminist indictment of solipsic selfhood is strengthened by the discovery that subject-object reciprocity was held to be vital by numerous philosophers including Kant and Hegel. Not only did their philosophical efforts prepare the way for future developments, the resonance (or challenge) of contemporary feminist concerns with prior questions and proposals lets us appreciate the deep and abiding quality of feminist presuppositions beyond contemporary expediency.

When we discover that a question has been asked before, and that certain answers did or did not work, we become linked in a profound way with the larger human quest beyond the confines of our own day and age. We come to discover that our questions are not necessarily new nor are our answers always that novel. But hidden in the past are found both the sources of our frequent bondage to outmoded models, as well as the inspiration for the transformative possibilities yet to be found. Only a full acquaintance with our past opens us to transforming possibilities in the future.

I therefore intend to make ancient and contemporary texts and notions of self accessible to the modern reader. I proceed in this task by dealing with key representative figures within decisive historical epochs, in depth. My criteria for

4

inclusion or exclusion is a scholarly judgement about the subsequent impact of a contributor toward the self-construct. The closer one moves to the contemporary era the riskier this becomes since the sifting of history has not yet occurred. In such cases I opted for those perspectives which seem to have greater potential for human interiority and subjectivity. The reader will need to assess whether my choices are worthy of the task I have set for them.

This book is essentially divided into three major sections. Chapters 1 through 6 are largely philosophical and theological, surveying the primary contributors to the evolving self-concept for the Western world from the Greek classical period through to the modern era.

Chapter 1 begins this effort by presenting the Platonic and Aristotelian contribution as foundational for Western self-consciousness. Not only did their efforts propel us toward the particular path upon which we currently find ourselves, their thought has rebirthed itself in myriad forms. Whether in Augustine and Aquinas, Freud or Jung, the Platonic-Aristotelian tension continues to play itself out. Their primary question concerns the conflict between permanence and change as these elements impact human self-construction. The historical record reveals extreme reactions to both factors with few models able to maintain balance and reciprocal engagement between stability and change, between structure and movement.

Chapter 2 illustrates how another vital assumptive world, the Hebraic, came into contact with the Greek and took on a certain form within the early Christian context. This Judeo-Christian framework did not simply collapse its Hebraic inheritance but found a way to recast the Hebraic vision into forms palatable for the day. The relationship between inner and outer, the dynamism between finitude and transcendence, or the relation between freedom and bondage persist as inevitable questions within self-construction. I propose that the early Judeo-Christian vision makes a vital contribution toward contemporary self-definition.

Chapter 3 covers the span from the Patristic to the Medieval periods by presenting a primary representative for each period. This great chronological span becomes less problematic as I demonstrate how the Platonic and Aristotelian threads of previous eras were rewoven into the intellectual and spiritual fabric of the day, with this conflict continuing to impact us today. Augustine and Aquinas are the respective inheritors of the Platonic and Aristotelian streams with each enriching the self-construct even as they imposed further burdens which continue to trouble our contemporary quest. Finally, in the medieval mystic paradigm of Meister Eckhart a bold step beyond both Augustine and Aquinas was taken which again offers us possibilities and pitfalls for our modern quest for identity.

In Chapter 4 I embark upon the transition period to the modern era. In this period from 1500 to 1800 A.D. there emerged four great scholars who forever changed the way we understand the phenomenon of human selfhood. They are Rene Descartes, David Hume, Immanuel Kant, and J. G. Fichte. The fact that each of them "failed" to resolve the dilemmas of human identity is less important than understanding the problems they were seeking to address. In their grappling with the central self-dilemmas, whether it be the divine-human link, the ego-self relationship, or the time-less/time-bound factors within self, we are being reminded that we too will not be able to side-step the problems they first addressed.

Chapters 5 and 6 conclude the first section of the book by presenting the self models of the two intellectual giants who frame the modern understanding of self: Hegel and Kierkegaard. It is impossible to claim to understand the self without grappling with the polarity they represent. In Hegel we will find a grand, unifying vision for dynamic selfhood, unsurpassed in its comprehensiveness, yet seriously challenged by its Kierkegaardian opposite, the self standing alone within the existential givens of its life. Held together, Hegel and Kierkegaard represent profound possibilities for self.

In section two the psychological paradigm emerges by focusing on the two primary perspectives which intentionally pursue human interiority, the Psychoanalytic and Analytic frameworks. Beginning with Sigmund Freud in Chapter 7, the psychoanalytic path diverges into the British Object Relations school in Chapter 8, and its American counterpart in Chapter 9. From Freud through Heinz Kohut the archaic substructures and patterns of human selfhood have been uncovered in their richness and complexity. Our selfhood has thereby been inextricably rooted within the historical, social, and cultural givens of our lives. This is not to suggest that a simple continuity exists through the vagaries of psychoanalytic thought. However, the intriguing drift from Freud's instinctive forces, through ego processes, to an embrace of self-like unifying operations reveal a growing compatability with comprehensive models of selfhood.

Chapter 10 offers a counterpart to a self driven by historical necessity, namely, a self infused by trancendent possibilities. In the transpersonal claims of C.G. Jung's Analytic psychology a sharp contrast to Freud's historicism is offered. Just as neither Hegel nor Kierkegaard could stand alone, with their tension offering us a comprehensive vision, so too do Freud and Jung represent the outer limits of psychological approaches to self.

This is not to suggest that other psychological models are irrelevant. William James, Gordon Allport, Margaret Mead, Alfred Adler, and Erik Erikson, among others, all have useful things to say about self, but none approach the depth nor complexity of the Freudian and Jungian inheritance.

As each philosophical, theological and psychological vantage point is offered it is presented as fully as possible on its own terms. In each instance, however, critique is offered by asking the following questions:

(1) How does the model in question deal with the factor of movement or more precisely, development, within the life of self?

(2) How does the model understand the subject-object bi-polarity of selfhood?

(3) Are the structures of self fluid and open to process, flow, and reciprocity, or is structure artificially maintained for whatever reasons?

(4) How does the perspective being examined honor the tension of universality - particularity for self? Is the tension collapsed, ignored, or integrated into the self system?

(5) What meanings for self are offered by the model in question, and what depth and fullness does self attain?

As the historical journey unfolds I offer not only analysis and critique, but an emerging perspective, a cumulative vision, which will reveal both outer limits and common centers for the notion of self in the Western world. In my final section, Chapter 11, I offer suggestions for a dynamically comprehensive model of self. It is only at this point that I risk proposing a definition for self. From my working definition I proceed to a structural model for self depicted in fluid i.e. dynamic terms. This is followed by an analysis of the movements visible for self, an examination of its living process. Finally, I offer a model for the phases of the life of self, a proposition concerning the meaningful possibilities available for self.

I have written this book as a reminder to the reader that the possibilities for self are rooted in an intellectual and spiritual past. It is my hope that our quest for fulfilled selfhood will be strengthened as we re-engage our philosophical, theological and psychological self-inheritance. Only as this task is undertaken can we gain the confidence necessary to leave behind what we must.

CHAPTER I

THE GREEK PARADIGM

Our inquiry regarding self begins at a point generally attributed to be the great dawning of Western civilization: the Greek classical period. With the arrival of Greek civilization revolutionary methodologies as diverse as mathematics and introspection became available which resulted in a quantum leap in the human ability to classify the world and conceptualize the place of the human therein. Self-reflection as mediated by myth and ritual gained a depth and sophistication which even today has not been mined of all its treasures.

I must of necessity limit my review of Greek contributions to the understanding of selfhood to the most formidable intellects of that era: Plato and Aristotle. Together they set the tone for human self-understanding for subsequent millennia and the doors they opened are our only viable point of entry into the issue.

Other Greek thinkers are not without merit: Pythagoras, Heraclitus, Socrates, Hippocrates all contributed to Greek cosmology, metaphysics and psychology. None, however, reach the depth of analysis or influence of Plato and Aristotle. For this reason these two pioneers will be our exclusive focus beginning with Plato, the teacher, followed by his most famous student.

PLATO: PIONEER OF SELFHOOD

The task of summarizing Plato's understanding of selfhood is made more difficult by the fact that his theories of the human "soul" are neither consistent nor systematic. But to ignore Plato is not an option. Not only did Plato's metaphysics and anthropology become determinative for the first 1000 years of Christian thinking, contemporary psychological perspectives as diverse as the Freudian and Jungian cannot be discussed without a sense of their linkage to him.

In order to bring some coherence to my efforts at presenting Plato's concept of soul I will direct our attention toward three basic issues: (1) a definition and description of the Platonic Soul, (2) an analysis of the soul as unified or divided and (3) the nature of the tripartite soul.

Plato lived from 427 to 347 B.C. and experienced in his lifetime of over eighty years not only the flowering of Greek culture but its unraveling as occurred through the decay of the city state.[1] From his teacher Socrates he received a method of self-examination or introspection which allowed the "mind" to be used as a tool for discovering the real, i.e. the abiding, permanent realities behind the changeable flow of life. As indicated, Plato was confronted with the deteriorating nature of change, particularly in its bodily, social, and political manifestations. This inevitability of decay caused him to conclude that the meaningfulness of reality was not to be found in the decaying processes of the material world. Only eternal and abiding entities could provide certainty and reveal the true nature of reality. These eternal and immutable structures Plato found in the universal forms.

Universal forms or "ideas" are not simply human thoughts, but the very patterns which undergird the world of objects. All material including the human body are inevitably crushed by the decay and deterioration which comes with all change. But behind all this decay are eternal patterns which are visible in the sensate world. The sensate manifestation of a universal form is not reality, but a reflection of its underlying, abiding form.

There have been many attempts to describe and classify the Platonic forms with the general consensus being that they include both "qualities of being" such as beauty, goodness, justice, as well as "properties" such as hot and cold, odd and even numbers, life and death, etc.[2] In general, any tangible object will have its own "form(s)", namely, the properties by which it is what it is. Thus a rock will have certain properties such as size, (largness or smallness), texture (hard or soft), weight (heavy or light), and even beauty (it may be a sculpture or a simple stone). What is most noteworthy, however, is that these properties exist separately from objects. The presence of an object may reflect certain properties but the absence or non-existence of the object does not in any way cancel out the properties which would define the object should it come to exist. We could say for instance that an automobile reflects universal forms of size, weight, beauty, and function etc. even though Plato knew of no such object. A Platonist insists that:

> properties exist timelessly, and no property ever comes into existence or goes out of existence. Consequently we should recognize too that there also exist many properties which **we** never think of and **we** have no words for, and which perhaps no one will ever think of or speak of ... properties, can be thought of as 'possible meanings', but they would still exist even if there had never been any human beings, or any language to have those meanings.[3]

This separation of Universal meaningfulness from its objective representation in the world is the heart of the famous Platonic dualism. Plato's well-known cave analogy illustrates this conclusion. Plato insists that human beings are chained in a cave with their backs to the only opening. As light streams into the opening it casts shadows against the wall. These shadows represent the fleeting sensate images which bring only an indirect knowledge of appearances, not what is real. Real knowledge is knowledge of the forms which is available only through the soul.[4] But what is this Platonic soul?

The Platonic Soul Defined

Simply put, the soul is the agency which apprehends eternal forms. It is by definition immortal and characterized by self-motion. The following excerpt from **Phaedrus** elaborates.

> The soul through all her being is immortal for that which is ever in motion is immortal; but that which moves another and is moved by another in ceasing to move ceases also to live. Only the self-moving, never leaving self, never ceases to move, and is the fountain and beginning of motion to all that moves besides ... For the body which is moved from without is soulless but that which is

moved from within has a soul, for such is the nature of the soul.
But if this be true must not the soul be the self-moving, and
therefore of necessity unbegotten and immortal?[5]

If the essence of soul is motion, self-motion to be exact, how is such movement to
be understood?

The movement of soul is a movement requiring no other cause, in other
words, it is self-directed. As inner motion, it is both spontaneous and directional
having its source and goal within itself. Plato's "list" of movements of the soul
includes such diverse "motions" as will, attention, deliberation, joy, sorrow, fear,
hatred, and love etc. [6] As a list these processes have little in common, but Plato's
point is that such movements "guide all things to growth and decay, to composition
and decomposition, and to the qualities which accompany them."[7] These
operations are the movements of life process, the motions or energies by which
soul accomplishes its purposes.

Central to the intentionality of soul is the issue of the soul-body
relationship. It is commonly known that for Plato body and soul are separate
substances. While this understanding is correct, it tends to overlook the
relationship Plato attempts to maintain between the two. Plato's understanding of
sensation serves as a good illustration.

Plato claims that a body is the "exterior environment" of the soul, with the
motion of the one interacting with the motion of the other, allowing reality to be
apprehended.[8] A body's sense organs are not simply a "passive screen" picking up
what is "out-there"; rather, the soul as "inner activity" acts upon the motion
(sensations) received from the external world, with soul giving these sensations the
qualities which allows them to be distinguished. Soul, then, provides **patterns of
perception** by which reality becomes ordered based upon the movement occurring
internally and externally. A contemporary interpreter of Plato writes:

> Plato too seems to have conceived of the world-soul (energy) and
> the world-body (matter) as inseparable, so that the dichotomy
> between soul and corporality is not between two separable beings
> but between motion in terms of its sensible manifestation
> (corporeality) and in terms of its inherent rationality of pattern and
> purpose (soul) in accordance with the forms.[9]

The idea that an inner process provides a meaningful pattern or cohesion to external movement did not die with Plato. Whether in the form of Augustine's "knowing" soul, Kant's transcendental ego, Fichte's Absolute Self, Hegel's Absolute Spirit, or Jung's collective unconscious, we will discover numerous variations of this theme of the meaningful and directional unfolding of soul. Not even Freud in his use of eros and thanatos could escape this Platonic influence.

The Soul: Uniform or Divided?

Variations in Plato's descriptions of the soul's makeup can leave one with the impression that his conclusions contain gross contradictions. I would suggest on the contrary that these variations are not so much contradictory but reflective of shifts in purpose for Plato.[10] The primary question concerns whether the Platonic soul is (1) simple (uniform), (2) dual (divided), or (3) tripartite (a composite of forms)? Said another way, is the Platonic soul a complex entity or a simple unity, or somehow both, implying that it contains both unity and diversity?[11] Evidence for the unitary oneness of the soul is readily available in Plato's **Phaedo:**

> ...of all which has been said is this not the conclusion? -- that the soul is in the very likeness of the divine, and immortal, and intellectual, and uniform, and indissoluble, and unchangeable; and that the body is in the very likeness of the human, and mortal, and unintellectual and multiform, and dissoluble, and changeable.[12]

Because of its immortality and distinction from the transient body, the soul is held to be undivided and whole within itself. It needs nothing other than itself for its own completion.

On the other hand, the Platonic soul exhibits a division with one dimension reflecting rationality or the capacity for apprehension of forms, and the other dimension reflecting non-rationality as manifested in appetite and desire.[13] We find this duality of soul highlighted in the **Republic:**

> Then we may fairly assume that they (soul's capacities)* are two, and that they differ from one another; the one with which a man reasons, we may call the rational principle of the soul, the other, with which he loves and hungers and thirsts and feels the fluttering of any other desire, may be termed the irrational or appetitive, the ally of sundry pleasures and satisfactions?[14]

While this duality within soul amounts to its partitioning, Plato understands this division as a reflection of higher and lower modes of functioning when soul is in relationship with body.

The example Plato uses to illustrate the operation of this division is that of a thirsty man who desires to drink, but who is held back from drinking by some other factor. This "other factor" which negates the impulse to drink must be another internal principle which clashes with the urge to drink. So, surmises Plato, these dual elements in the soul must be the **rational** principle with which the soul reasons, and the **irrational** principle through which the soul expresses its inclination as governed by pleasure and satisfaction.[15] Because these two capacities of soul consistently clash Plato must somehow explain how a soul so divided can find a larger unity. To understand this larger capacity of soul we must therefore turn to Plato's most developed framework: the tripartite model.

The Tripartite Soul

In describing the soul from the vantage point of its tripartite operations, Plato is attempting to overcome the **dualism** between body - soul, reason - irrational desire, which is so dear to him. To maintain a linkage (even as its dualism is maintained) Plato proposes a three-dimensional soul containing the elements (1) reason, (2) spirit, and (3) appetite (desire).

Reason is the highest form or manifestation of soul in that it most fully represents the principle of motion. The motion of reason as found in thought is a motion requiring no cause other than itself. Reason provides the capacity to know the forms or **frameworks of experience** and in its pure form as abstract thought, it is distinct from the body which it illumines.[16] Reason, given its lofty position of equivalency with the eternal and immutable forms, serves to guide and control the lower functions of the soul which tend to be distorted by the demands of the finite and decaying body.

The second element within tripartite soul Plato calls **spirit**. Spirit is very much caught in the middle between the higher Reason and the lower appetite and therefore reveals characteristics of both. Spirit is the force or energy by which the directives of Reason or appetite are carried out. Spirit can express the intensity of appetite just as it can channel the directives of Reason.

Plato's example of the function of spirit draws upon the experience of a man Leontius who comes upon a place of execution and is drawn by a desire to see the dead bodies even as he is repulsed by his inclination to do so. After an internal struggle Leontius' desire wins out, but as he runs up to the bodies to look he reproaches himself for doing so.[17] Plato's conclusion is that raw desire and the spirit or energy which animates it are not the same thing. The force by which an inclination is lived out can vary greatly: as a matter of fact there can be a direct clash between an appetite and the spirit or energy which would accomplish this intent. Plato's point is that an internal division can occur within soul, a division revealing split inclinations not necessarily related to the capacity for Reason. It is, however, also possible for spirit to align itself with Reason to accomplish the more ordered purposes of the highest level of soul.

Plato's own synonym for spirit is "passion", which represents the factor of Eros within soul as it seeks either higher or lower goals.[18] Since soul is never at rest and consistently seeks the new, soul as spirit surfaces in human experience as ambition and goal-directedness, just as it arouses indignation and aggression when one's inclinations are thwarted.

The third and final dimension within soul Plato calls **appetite** or raw desire. This form of desire is strictly bodily-based and runs on the pleasure-unpleasure equation. It represents the simplest state of awareness where one's concern is strictly for bodily self-preservation. A soul seeking body-maintenance alone is a soul in bondage as far as Plato is concerned, a soul "riveted" to the body with its only truth the particular demands of the body.[19] Since raw appetite governs this level of awareness, Reason is only implicitly present through patterns of organic fulfillment such as hunger or thirst. Appetite alone knows no other unities or fulfillments other than the satiation of its immediate need.

The stark contrast between these various operations of soul raises the question of its potential for harmony and/or disunity. How does Plato envision the soul's coming to some consistency and unity of purpose given its very fragmentation? To answer this question Plato draws upon an analogy we will find again in this study (most notably in Sigmund Freud). The particular analogy chosen by Plato is that of a charioteer who is attempting to drive two winged horses. The one horse is a pure breed (spirit), full of vigor and power who needs no whip but responds to the wishes and commands of the driver (Reason). The other horse (appetite) is an unruly beast only controllable through the use of force and punishment. Only through great effort can the charioteer guide this juxtaposed team to the sought goal (finding the beloved), a goal which only the driver can understand.[20] Only when the guidance of the charioteer (Reason) is maintained can the genuine harmony of union with the beloved be gained. If this highest function of the soul is suspended the goal might still be reached but when accomplished through the appetite-driven striving of the horses alone, it cannot lead to fulfillment since they do not have "the approval of the whole soul."[21]

We can safely conclude that Plato's use of both dual and tripartite models of soul are efforts at explaining the need for balance between appetite (desire) and passion (energy) as both are controlled and harmonized by a soul seeking certain purposes or forms (reason). Only a soul in step with the eternal forms of truth and beauty, claims Plato, will be able to find the happiness which comes with the attainment of the purest of forms, wisdom.

The Platonic Legacy

My purpose in tracing the Platonic thread is not to establish its rightness or wrongness; rather, my intent is descriptive, guided by the necessity of understanding the evolution of the construct called soul or self as it has developed through the ages. In Plato, then, we have reached our first waystation, one which attempts to understand selfhood by dissociating it from historical process. In separating that which changes from that which does not, Plato was attempting to validate selfhood by grounding it in abiding and eternal forms. By infusing the soul with substantiality or permanence, Plato hoped to unify the soul within itself in keeping with the principle of self-motion.

Plato was seeking certainty, and nothing but the underlying unity provided by the self-contained flow of thought could survive the test of non-decay. In this fashion human subjectivity was given immortality, thereby touching the gods, even as it became distanced from history and the material confines of the body. This soul/body, soul/history division became a useful device for elevating human identity, although regretably, only the "rational" portion qualified.

In insisting upon the soul's self-containment Plato did not assume that the soul is static. As pure thought, soul is governed by the movement which seeks its own completion, in other words, it seeks itself. It seeks the beauty (patterns or forms) of which it is already full. The principle of movement in which a linkage is assumed between inner and outer, higher and lower, is an idea which has persisted throughout history, finding particular psychological development in Freud and Jung among others.

But perhaps the most abiding of Plato's contributions is his insight regarding duality within selfhood. Although we cringe at the Platonic blaming of the body for this division, the fact remains that Plato insisted that even a uniform soul can be a house divided. His insistence upon the power of the non-rational factor within soul opened the door to the exploration of the hidden forces which operate within selfhood. Plato's insight regarding "unconscious" processes allowed him to begin to describe the inevitable "conflicts" within soul even as it seeks its harmony and fulfillment.

In addition, Plato paved the way for greater ownership of so-called drives or inclinations within selfhood including an emphasis upon desire, a theme which will become more fully developed in Hegel and Kierkegaard. In short, Plato ensured that the uncovering of human identity could not occur without an acknowledgment of the deeper forces which operate within selfhood; namely that selfhood reflects larger unities within its operations.

Nevertheless, Plato's contributions cannot obscure the great handicaps through which he contaminated the search for selfhood. The divorce of the soul from matter and historical process left it floating in an ethereal, timeless sea, cut off from the very life it was supposed to guide. Given the soul's immortality, all developmental relevance became lost. This not only destroyed any real meaning to soul's self-contained movement, it split the developmental process from the larger unity which soul supposedly reflects.

Even though 1500 years of Western thinking drew its inspiration from the Platonic framework it did not take long for corrective efforts to emerge. To find the first and perhaps strongest challenge to Plato's system we need only look to his most famous pupil for a formidable critique.

THE ARISTOTELIAN CHALLENGE

Plato was 44 years old when Aristotle was born in 384 B.C. into a physician's family which served the king of a Northern Greek Province. At the age of 18 Aristotle arrived in Athens and became a pupil of Plato, a relationship which continued for almost twenty years until Plato's death at the age of 80. It is impossible to appreciate Aristotle's genius without recognizing the Platonic soil out of which his thought emerged. As was true with Plato, no uniform or static reflections upon soul can be found in Aristotle. He too adjusted his conclusions as his thought matured, although in directions away from his original Platonic indebtedness.

The seeming contradictions in Aristotle which have been so problematic for Aristotelian scholarship are no doubt accentuated by the inevitable development of his thought as he increasingly left behind his dualistic inheritance. I will, however, only present the most mature Aristotelian reflections upon soul, since these later models became absorbed into Western thought beginning with Aquinas and remaining visible through to our encounter with Freud. But first I must clarify the similarities and differences between the Platonic and Aristotelian vision of soul.

Plato and Aristotle Differentiated

Without a doubt the early Aristotle was thoroughly dualistic, holding to a largely Platonic theory of forms, and insisting upon the immortality of the soul and its primacy over the decaying body. With the death of Plato and Aristotle's departure from Athens and the Academy, his own independent thought emerged, most readily visible in his challenge of the Platonic theory of forms.

Aristotle came to strongly oppose Plato's doctrine that reality only belongs to the forms which exist independently of the objects they illumine. His thought became increasingly monistic in the sense that all physical objects in the universe reflect a union of two essential factors, the material content of the object and the form or structure which makes the object what it is?[22] What prompted this shift toward an integration of the material and immaterial elements?

Perhaps the most important factor which nudged Aristotle in this direction was his shift in vantage point. The lenses through which Plato had viewed reality were the disciplines of mathematics and astronomy. This inheritance was a carryover of the Pythagorean methodology which held that the universe is an eternal oneness which functions according to mathematical principles. This Pythagorean legacy negated the knowing attainable through the senses and insisted that reality can only be known by recognizing the rational and harmonious patterns of the universe as revealed in geometric forms and ratios.

In contrast to this mathematical lens which prompted Plato to see the universe in abstract and global terms, Aristotle approached reality from the vantage point of **biology** in which **particular** phenomena and **individual** material entities were most important.[23] It is ironic that the very factor which had driven Plato more and more toward the eternal and immutable forms became the factor which pushed Aristotle in the opposite direction: this factor is the phenomenon of change.

It was impossible for Aristotle to study the life of particular objects in the universe without appreciating their changeableness and incorporating this essential feature into his framework. For Aristotle form only has meaning in light of the changes occurring in an objects' material manifestations; furthermore, unless a form is embodied it does not exist. In contrast, Plato demands the primacy of forms **separate** from any object. For Plato as we recall, a property such as blackness exists whether or not a black object can be found. This Aristotle clearly rejects: "if all become healthy there will be health and no disease and again, if everything turns white, there will be white but no black."[24]

With form now connected to matter and not separate from it, Aristotle was in a position to wrestle with the changes he observed in the universe from a more unified vantage point. How then did this incorporation of change into the nature of reality impact the search for knowledge and ultimately, the understanding of soul?

Although Aristotle distinguishes three types of change which he describes as (1) qualitative (shift in likeness); (2) quantitative (growth or decay); and (3) spatial (change in location) these classifications are less important in themselves than the particular operations or **functions** which Aristotle believes the change serves. The overriding concern which Aristotle brings to the question of change focuses upon the "causes" of change in objects and the ends which are thereby served.

The Soul as Changing

In turning my attention to Aristotle's efforts at understanding the factors behind change I am still laying the groundwork for presenting his definition of soul which will emerge shortly. In good Aristotelian fashion I am thereby following his methodology which determines the form or meaning of an entity by virtue of the "purposes" which it serves.

Aristotle assumes four "causes" which bring about change which he calls (1) the material cause (the substance out of which something is formed), (for example, the bronze from which a statue is shaped); (2) the form (archtype) or essence of an object, i.e. that which defines a statue as statue, (3) the agent or source of the change (the power which causes it to take shape and (4) the aim or goal for which something changes.[25]

It may seem odd to have the material substance of an object and its identifying characteristics considered as "causes", as having anything to do with explaining change. It is here, however, where Aristotle's monism can be most clearly recognized in contrast to the dualism found in Plato. Aristotle cannot conceive of an object changing separate from those particular agents which bring about the change. In other words, the conditions necessary for change include the very matter and form of an object since without those elements nothing could change.

Thus, the most important factor which informs Aristotle's notion of change is the end which everything serves. This teleological emphasis holds that everything, including soul, moves toward some goal depending upon the functional capacity for which it is designed. The change undergone by any object or organism is not only determined by its originating impulse but by the form (function) for which it is intended. Aristotle is not simply referring to conscious intention, although so-called "higher" forms of soul do exhibit a conscious seeking of the good for which they are intended.[26] His point is that all matter, whether simple or complex, seeks to complete its functional capacities. In Aristotle, then, we find a creative blending of structure and function as factors which determine change. An

organism will be so structured and follow its developmental path in accordance with
the function for which it is designed.

The Aristotelian Soul

If in Plato the soul is the disembodied and self-sufficient agency which
apprehends the eternal forms, how might the Aristotelian soul differ? To begin
with, the Aristotelian soul is not divorced from matter but is the very **form** of
matter which allows an organism to function in a particular way. This soul does
not hang between the eternal forms and decaying matter where it tries to mediate
one to the other as was true in Plato, but in a much more intimate sense gives matter
which it organizes the capacity to act in its intended ways. Thus, says Aristotle,
"soul is an actuality or formulable essence of something that possesses a potentiality
of being besouled."[27]

What is so noteworthy about this Aristotelian viewpoint is not that the
organism is the actualization of the potential of soul, but its opposite, that soul is the
actualization or realization of the potential of a natural body.[28] Soul is the
structural and functional accomplishment or completion gained by an organism. No
longer is organized matter simply a poor reflection of a separate eternal essence, but
the functioning of a material body **is** the essence of soul.

This revolutionary shift opened up all manner of new possibilities for
understanding nature, human development, and the body-spirit relationship.
Among the more noteworthy implications is that soul is not simply "given" as was
true for Plato, but "develops" as it "becomes" the form of the body. While Plato
can at best only allow for a static and uneasy relationship between soul and body,
Aristotle can affirm a psychosomatic unity with soul serving as source, goal, and
essence of its bodily manifestation. In Aristotle, a first step is taken away from
soul as "thing" toward a notion of soul as dynamic entity which develops itself
along functional lines. An opening is thus created for the possibility that
organisms' contain adaptational capacities, a thought reintroduced into the
biological arena by Darwin. Freud drew from this same source to explain the
adaptive dynamics of the psyche just as he would find highly useful the Aristotelian
developmental motif that higher levels of soul carry within them the capacities of the
lower levels even as they develop beyond them. The Freudian genetic emphasis

which ties later development to its etiological or genetic foundation has its roots in this revolutionary adjustment created by Aristotle. But what are the capacities of this "soul" and how does Aristotle organize the soul along functional lines?

The Soul's Functions

As indicated, there is a hierarchial gradation to the Aristotelian soul with functional capacities determining where on the hierarchial grid a given object might reside. Soul, we must remember, is both the source and goal of all operations, with all living process seen from the vantage point of the potentiality---actuality continuum.

The first "level" of soul described by Aristotle is the **nutritive** or **vegetative** function. This function has to do with the capacity for growth, not simply the expansion of material substance, but the differentiation and maturation of an organism.[29] Plant life best represents this level of functional organization; as a matter of fact, plants are only capable of this level of soul. Even at this rudimentary level, soul reveals the capacity not only to multiply itself by gaining greater mass, but to transform itself in its nutritive efforts.[30] Aristotle's point is that the very act of nutrition requires a relationship between organism and environment. While an organism is fully dependent on an environment for its very survival, its use of the environment's resources will be determined **by the organism.**[31]

The second functional level of soul Aristotle calls the **sensate** which describes the capacity to receive and respond to data received through the senses which include touch, sight, hearing, smell, and taste.[32] This sensate factor distinguishes higher organisms such as animals from those exhibiting the lower function of nutrition only (plants).

Aristotle argues that sensation offers organisms a direct linkage to the objects of the world, but in their form, not in their matter. He writes:

> By a 'sense' is meant what has the power of receiving into itself the sensible forms of things without the matter.[33]

As a body senses, it is absorbing the form of an external object without devouring the material substance of the object as was true for nutrition. When an apple is seen or touched, its forms of color and texture are being absorbed without its mass being annihalated. Conversely, if an apple is being eaten, its taste, texture, color and odor are not being eaten but only its mass. An objects' forms are received by an organism based upon Aristotle's assumption of the interactional nature of form and matter. Senses serve as "channels" or pathways of encounter with an environment, with movement or change the linkage between a form and its material receptor in the sense organ.

As Aristotle understands it, sensing only occurs as activated by the qualities of a particular object. The stimulus provided by an object activates a movement which must proceed through the medium of a sense organ where it is transformed into consciousness.[34] Aristotle believes that an organ and its object of sensation become **unified** into one in the act of hearing, for instance, even as they maintain a separation not found in nutrition. Sensation, then, brings a subject-object quality into the soul-concept with both unity and distinction necessary for sensation to proceed.

This conclusion raises important questions. How can an object with multiple properties be perceived as one particular object? How do sensory qualities coalesce to allow for an object to be recognized with its compound characteristics? Furthermore, how do "qualities" such as motion or rest, quantity, or unity-over-time, become recognizable when they are not mediated by a particular sense but arise out of a common unifying capacity.[35]

To resolve this question Aristotle proposes what he calls the **common sense**, not as a separate sixth sense, but the activity which synthesizes the operations of all senses. This synthesizing capacity not only ties sensations together to allow for the perception of units, but unites in a rudimentary way a receiving subject. All senses functioning together as a "common sense" must include the capacity for memory and imagination. Just as memory "ties together" the movement of senses over time, imagination names the movement generated by the sense itself.[36] In suggesting that memory and imagination are activities of a perceiving subject, Aristotle pioneered the study of human identity in a manner not unlike the efforts of William Hume 2000 years later.

The third function of soul which Aristotle calls "**appetite** or **desire**" should not be thought of as somehow separate from the rest, but as a hierarchial continuation of the functions examined thus far. The critical capacity which

Aristotle attempts to explain at this point is motion, the power which actualizes movement between an organism and its environment.

For Plato as we recall, soul is self-moving or self-contained, having both cause and effect within itself. The Platonic soul is the **cause of motion** in matter which cannot move itself. For Aristotle, on the other hand, soul **infuses** matter which allows movement to be explained by virtue of the **relationship** between the **organism** and its **environment**. Aristotle claims that the environment and organism are linked through the functional capacity of the organism which causes it to seek a particular kind of relationship to its environmental objects. The "directed-by-soul" organism can now maintain itself in its world and interact in various ways with the objects it needs and seeks.

Desire is the engine of this movement for Aristotle, with a direct linkage to sensation and its by-product, the pleasure-unpleasure tension. The following passage elaborates:

> If any order of living things has the sensory, it must also have the appetitive; for appetite is the genus of which desire, passion, and wish are the species; now all animals have one sense at least viz. touch, and whatever has a sense has the capacity for pleasure and pain and therefore has pleasant and painful objects present to it, and wherever these are present, there is desire, for desire is just appetition of what is pleasant.[37]

The movement brought about by soul has a magnetic attraction-repulsion force based upon the pleasure - unpleasure qualities of the sensation. In its less developed form such reactions to an object operate in simple stimulus-response fashion, while in its higher versions desire takes the form of wish and volition.[38]

Movement, then, is initiated by a separate but desired object which triggers the motion of the organism. The "gap" between subject and object creates the tension which activates the organism into action. The desire for or seeking of the object is present because the organism seeks to complete its functional intent i.e. accomplish its intended purpose for which it needs its object. Thus the object "gets the ball rolling" so to speak, although it is not necessarily affected by desire as is the subject.[39]

The fourth and final capacity of soul Aristotle calls the **rational** or **reasoning** faculty. Here as elsewhere gradations are found with criteria for ranking again the intended purposes of the various functions. Reasoning soul is divided by Aristotle into two main faculties called **practical reason** (thinking) and **speculative or theoretical reason** (knowing). The first function always calculates toward some end and in so doing, is always engaged in movement which is either pursuing or avoiding an object.[40] The second seeks after "truth" or universals i.e. the indivisible concepts true in all times and in all places.

Thinking is a process intimately linked with all of the functions of soul already identified, including sensation and desire. Without sensate data and the images and memory which allow such data to be collected and organized into meaningful patterns, no thinking could occur. The simple organization of data into patterns through images is still not thinking, however, but simply perception. True thinking involves **anticipation** of the **future** which allows another level of response with regard to an object of desire.[41] Desire alone is stuck in the present moment and can assess an object only for its pleasure/unpleasure capacities. Thinking on the other hand incorporates the factor of judgment into its response to what the environment presents and calculates the rightness or wrongness of a desired goal or object.[42] The images which arise out of the thinking process allow for a "larger picture" to be obtained which can anticipate outcomes and assess the correctness of a particular path of action. Because of the calculative nature of thinking it must divide the object from the thinking subject in order to prove the validity of the linkage. This kind of thinking arrives at truth in a "mediated" or synthesizing way by asserting the likeness and/or distinction of the images it uses to re-present reality to itself.[43] This necessary division of the subject from the object in time and space is what leaves such thinking prone to error even as it allows for errors to be corrected.

It is also possible for thinking to be at odds with desire giving rise to a further division within the human organism. Action can be hindered or enhanced depending upon its "rightness" for a thinking soul. Thus even though thinking is a higher, more encompassing function it does not exist apart from the lower and can even be overcome by the lower.

A very different dynamic is envisioned by Aristotle when it comes to the capacity called **knowing**. Knowing operates with an immediacy and directness not possible with thinking. Aristotle writes:

The ground of this difference is that what actual sensation apprehends is individuals, while what knowledge apprehends is universals, and these are in a sense within the soul.[44]

Knowing (nous) is the capacity to receive the pure forms. This is not "mediated" knowledge but immediate in the sense of an intuitive grasping of truth. But is this not a throwback to the Platonic eternal forms which Aristotle had left behind? To answer this question we must take note of the fact that for Aristotle the eternal forms are **not separate** from material reality as was true for Plato. In Plato the material realm is but a poor imitation of the abiding eternal forms; for Aristotle the forms **are** the very patterns which allow an object to be what it is. A further elaboration is in order here.

Aristotle assumes a linkage between every object and that which comes to know the particular object. Just as every organism is in intimate interaction with its environment through nutrition and sensation, so too is every thought in intimate connection with the universal form which allows a thought to recognize the object for what it is. Just as sensation, perception, and thinking pick up the **particular** features of objects, knowing receives their **universal** characteristics. One could even say that knowing is the process of soul knowing itself since the soul is the place of forms.[45]

For Aristotle the knowing of whiteness, straightness, numerical "truth", or the recognition of human or animal form is given. His point is that the knowing soul is in identity with the object known. This does not mean that objects are superfluous but that the **actual** appearance of an object arises out of the **potentiality** of the universal forms present in soul as knowing. Such knowing is a universal capacity, the sum total of all the actualized possibilities of nature. If anything exists, it can be recognized by us through the affinity our soul has with the objects' form since our soul is "the place of forms".[46] Whenever we exercise the faculty of reason, our soul takes on the form of the object and becomes identical with it. This does not make the subject the same as the object; rather, the receiving subject is identical with the **object's form**.

The process of coming-to-identity of a subject as it relates to an object will be encountered throughout our study. However, in this early form as understood by Aristotle, this engagement remains contaminated and severely limited by his own sharp dualism. Upon what basis can such a judgment be made?

While it is helpful to declare that form is embedded in particular objects and does not exist apart from them as was the case for Plato, it is also true that Aristotle insists upon the imperishable and eternal quality of soul:

> It (mind or knowing soul) seems to be an independent substance implanted within the soul and to be incapable of being destroyed... mind is no doubt something more divine, and impassible. That the soul cannot be moved is therefore clear from what we have said, and if it cannot be moved at all manifestly it cannot be moved by itself.[47]

Soul, then, contains not only the ability to know the frameworks through which reality is structured, it is an immortal and eternal substance, unmoved in itself. How did Aristotle arrive at this conclusion?

The Unmoved Mover

Aristotle proposed that all material motion has its source in an Eternal Mover that is itself unmoved.

> For everything is moved by pushing and pulling. Hence just as in the case of a wheel, so here there must be a point which remains at rest, and from that point the movement must originate.[48]

All movement must have a cause and this cause must be eternal since movement is eternal. Since matter is not self-activating, the movement of matter (including that of organisms) needs a cause outside of itself to spark its movement. This motion has its source in the eternal Unmoved Mover.[49]

> There is, then, something which is always moved with an unceasing motion, which is motion in a circle; and this is plain not in theory only but in fact ... There is therefore also something which moves it. And since that which moves and is moved is intermediate, there is something which moves without being moved, being eternal, substance, and actuality. And the object of desire and the object of thought move in this way; they move without being moved.[50]

The Unmoved Mover is the source of all life and movement, and is itself not actualized by anything else. Rather, it is what actualizes; it is "pure actuality", i.e. without matter or potential for change, but the still point around which all movement flows. In fact, the Unmoved Movers' only activity is thought, pure thought (knowing) to be exact. The Unmoved Mover does not direct, guide, or activate motion but "elicits" motion by being the perfect object of desire - the ideal form which the universe seeks.[51] For this reason Aristotle is able to say that the Unmoved Mover is the object of its own thought. In turning in on itself in pure thought it knows itself completely and immediately and thereby acts as the object of desire which moves all things.

The relevance of this point becomes clearer when seen against the backdrop of the Platonic forms toward which these Aristotelian challenges are directed. In Plato, the world of forms or pure thought is a completely separate entity with soul the **mediator** between the eternal transcendent ideas and the world of change. In Aristotle by contrast, a **direct link** exists between ideas (forms) and the particular elements of the universe. Thought, in Aristotle, remains connected to sense experience in that the very seeking of a desiring soul involves the accomplishment of its intended purpose, the "thought" which it attempts to complete. Thus in Aristotle there is a clear link between changing nature and its ultimate cause, a link we do not see in Plato.

Nevertheless, even this connection cannot overcome Aristotle's final dualism. Aristotle's metaphysical foundation, his Unmoved Mover, is transcendent and remote, suggesting that the "linkage" is realized only in the eternal transcendent realm. Aristotle can incorporate change into his paradigm, can even acknowledge the meaningfulness of change, but can only leave the essence of soul unchanged as an Unmoved Mover.

The impact of this conclusion for the search for self in subsequent centuries cannot be overstated. While Aristotle brilliantly laid the foundation for empirical science, including the inquiry into the nature of human self-awareness, his ideas led to a split in the search for a meaning and wholeness to human subjectivity, a split that I suggest was only overcome in G.W.F. Hegel and Soren Kierkegaard. How did this split evolve in the course of human self-inquiry?

On the one hand, Aristotle's adjustment of the Platonic dualism allowed for the activity of the human psyche to be empirically studied along functional lines, a "faculty psychology" approach to human organism. This stream eventually emerged as a full-blown empiricism in John Locke, William Hume, and the wider British Empirical School. A wide range of contemporary psychologies including

Behaviorism, Clinical Psychology, and even certain strands within humanistic psychology can be traced to this lineage. Even the psychoanalytic path to selfhood can trace its inheritance to this strand of Aristotle's genius, through its recognition of subject-object factors as building blocks of selfhood. If various versions of empiricism are the child of one portion of Aristotle's "soul" where did the other portion become lodged?

The remaining split-portion of the Aristotelian soul, the **Eternal**, as represented by the Unmoved Mover, was gladly appropriated by theological scholars from the Middle Ages onward who were most happy to attribute the workings of the universe to a transcendent deity, itself unmoved, but nevertheless the cause and paradigm of all things including the human soul. For this group the essence of human selfhood became locked into an eternal, static prison, an immortal soul, mirroring the static transcendence of its transcendent author. Many giants of human intellectual activity followed in these footsteps including the grand sweep of the medieval period culminating in the static soul of Rene Descartes. For virtually 2000 years of human self-reflection this state of affairs of split selfhood has persisted with certain noble efforts at resolution.

However, another profound influence was evolving during the ascendancy and eventual decline of Greek culture, a paradigm I will call the Judeo-Christian. It offered sharply different perspectives from the Greek, but also easily borrowed from the Greek models which had preceeded it. In order to allow the Judeo-Christian paradigm to present itself on its own terms I will temporarily leave the Platonic and Aristotelian models behind until arriving at the first great scholar of the Christian era, Augustine, who drew on Greek models as containers into which he could pour his Christian content.

As we leave Plato and Aristotle certain thorny questions begin to take shape. What in fact grounds human identity? Is it given through a universal "world-soul" with its human equivalent simply broken off bits of this encompassing Oneness? What place then remains for the body, for history, and the entire developmental process including death and decay? Or, is human identity grounded only in its capacities? Does function satisfactorily reflect the unity of change and stability-over-time which seems intrinsic to human subjectivity? What is the relationship of "God" and "persons", of the finite and the infinite, matter and spirit, the One and the many? For a radically different vision of reality which might well provide other answers concerning the coalescense of these factors within personhood we now turn to the Judeo-Christian vision of selfhood.

1. Robert I .Watson, *The Great Psychologists: from Aristotle to Freud,* (Philadelphia: J.B. Lippincott Company, 1963), p.21

2. David Bostock, *Plato's Phaedo,* (Oxford: Clarendon Press, 1986), p. 196

3. Ibid., p. 209

4. Plato, "Republic (514-521)"; "The Dialogues of Plato", Tr. by Benjamin Jowett, *Great Books of the Western World,* Vol. 7, (Chicago, 1952).

5. Plato, *Phaedrus,* 245

6. Plato, *Laws,* 897

7. Ibid.

8. Plato, *Timaeus,* 34

9. Kenneth Dorter, *Plato's Phaedo: An Interpretation,* (Toronto: University of Toronto Press, 1982) p. 183

10. Support for this position can be found in Watson, 1963, p. 29, as well as Zakopoulos, 1975, p. 57-67. See also Bostock, 1986, p. 40-41

11. Zakopoulos, 1975, p. 57

12. Plato, *Phaedo,* 80

13. Plato, *Timaeus,* 69-72

14. Plato, *Republic,* 439

15. Ibid.

16. Plato, *Timaeus,* 29

17. Plato, *Republic,* 439-440

18. Ibid., 441

19. Plato, *Phaedo,* 83

20. Plato, *Phaedeus,* 253-257

21. Ibid., 256

22. Runes, Dagobert D., Ed. *Dictionary of Philosophy*, (Littlefield, Adams and Co.; Totowa, New Jersey, 1980) p. 21

23. Watson, 1963, p. 39

24. Aristotle, *Categories*, 14a 5-10. See also Edwin Hartman, *Substance, Body, and Soul*, (Princeton: Princeton University Press, 1977), p. 12, 15

25. Aristotle, *Physics*, 195a 15-35

26. Aristotle, *Metaphysics*, 983a 25-30

27. Aristotle, *De Anima*, 414a 25

28. Ibid., 412a

29. Clarence Shute, *The Psychology of Aristotle*, (New York: Russell and Russell, Inc., 1964) p. 19

30. Aristotle, *On the Generation of Animals*, 723b

31. Shute, 1964, p. 20

32. Aristotle, *De Anima*, 424a 20

33. Ibid., 424a 15

34. Watson, 1963, p. 56

35. Aristotle, *De Anima* 425a 15

36. Aristotle, *On Memory and Reminiscence*, 450a 20-30; see also *De Anima*, 429a 1

37. Aristotle, *De Anima*, 414b 5

38. Notice should be made that these conclusions are a direct forerunner to Freud's libidinal theory.

39. Watson, 1963, p. 61

40. Aristotle, *De Anima*, 432b 25

41. Ibid., 433b 5

42. Watson, 1963, p. 64

43. H. Wijsenbeekk-Wigler, *Aristotle's Concept of Soul, Sleep and Dreams*, (Amsterdam: Adolf M. Hakkert, Publisher), See also *De Anima*, 430a 25; 431a 15

44. Aristotle, *De Anima*, 417b 20

45. Ibid., 429b 5

46. Ibid., 429a 25

47. Ibid., 48b 15-25

48. Ibid., m 433b 25

49. Peter A. Angeles, *Dictionary of Philosophy*, (New York: Barnes and Noble Books, 1981), p. 306

50. Aristotle, *Metaphysics*, 1071b 20-25

51. Peter Angeles, 1981, p. 306. See also W. T. Jones, *The Classical Mind: A History of Western Philosophy* (New York: Harcourt Brace Jovanovich, Inc. Second Edition, 1970), p. 230-232

CHAPTER II

THE JUDEO-CHRISTIAN CHALLENGE

All surveys of the great historical streams of human self-discovery run the risk of relying upon simplified generalizations which err either toward the obscuring of distinctions or their artificial sharpening. However, the necessity of understanding the evolution of the self-concept makes this a risk worth taking. Without such an understanding no foundation to human identity can be given. The evolution of Greek, Hebraic, and Christian thought-forms did not occur in a vacuum nor in isolation from a prior inheritance. This was demonstrated most decisively in the movements which were plotted from Plato to Aristotle. As was documented in the previous chapter, the prevailing Greek tendency was to see the operations of human selfhood in dualistic fashion. Whether the dualism took the form of a Body/soul or rational/nonrational division, the dynamics of the human organism manifested a hierarchy of operations semi-unified in non-historical terms. Even the efforts of Aristotle could not completely overcome the matter/spirit, time-bound/time-less divisions of human selfhood. While Aristotle's functional viewpoint brought a limited unity to the soul question by virtue of the unifying paradigm of purposive activity, he could not grant ontological status to the operations of soul. The movement of soul in the end remained the perogative of the Unmoved Mover.

Running parallel to this Greek perspective but developing on a separate track, so to speak, is the Hebrew vision of human personhood. The predominant factor which distinguishes Hebraic anthropology from the Greek is the unity of humanness. In the ancient Hebrew world there is no dualism between body and soul, matter and spirit, but each points to a unified human being as seen from a particular point of view or unified in a particular way. There is a certain duality to be found within Hebraic selfhood, but no separation of the bodily from the psychial or the spiritual from the material.

These two tracks began to converge in the Hellenistic period beginning in the era after Alexander the Great, from 320 B.C. onward. Hellenized Judaism was not simply a syncretized amalgamation of two very diverse thought forms, but primarily a process whereby Hebraic content was recast within the prevailing intellectual frameworks of the day. With the arrival of the Christian vision and its articulation in Paul and John this process was intensified. In other words, the Hebrew vision of reality and personhood remained foundational for the Christian paradigm even as Greek language and thought forms became the vehicle for the articulation of the new message.

Before we proceed to search out the relevance of the Biblical paradigm for the understanding of human selfhood a word of caution is in order. First of all, this portion of the study intends to uncover **Biblical** perspectives with regard to selfhood. This betrays my underlying assumption of a basic continuity between the Testaments with regard to their respective anthropologies. Secondly, my focus must of necessity be narrow and precise, namely, an uncovering of those Biblical themes most relevant to an understanding of the dynamics of selfhood. For these reasons I will focus on three limited tasks: (1) The Biblical understanding of the God-self relation; (2) Dynamic processes within selfhood, and (3) The flesh/spirit polarity to selfhood and its potential resolution in (a) the law or (b) Christ realities.

The Foundation to Human Identity

For both Plato and Aristotle the operations of human personhood demand a metaphysical grounding by virtue of the fact that material and non-material elements are interacting in some way to bring about the sophisticated possibilities which come with being human. In Plato this linkage is provided by the **Demiurge** which serves as the impersonal force energizing the perfect ideal forms (including soul), as these forms shape decaying matter into its particular patterns. For Aristotle the **Unmoved Mover** takes on the task of acting as transcendent cause of all motion including the many functions of soul. As we approach the Biblical tradition we find that human personhood gains an even greater metaphysical foundation, in that **the very structure of human personhood** reflects deity.

Without any doubt a most radically divergent position from the Greek is found in the Hebrew Scriptures. Genesis 1:26, 27 illustrates:

> Then God said, "Let us make humanity in our image, according to our likeness ... And God created humanity in God's own image, in the image of God they were created; male and female God created them.

No longer is humanity a by-product of eternal ideas or forms, but the very nature of human identity mirrors divine life. No longer is there a higher and lower division to the human organism but its basic life shares the power of that which called it into being.

> Then the Lord God formed the human being of dust from the ground and breathed into the nostrils the breath of life; and the earthling became a living being(Gen. 2:7).

Soul as "Living Being"

The Hebrew word **Nephesh** as found in the passage just cited is among the most basic anthropological terms in the Old Testament. It occurs over 750 times and was translated in the Latin Bible as **anima** or **soul**.[1] Its most basic meaning is life or life principle. This meaning of Nephesh as life or animating principle does not refer to an indestructible core of being in the sense of a substantial i.e. eternal soul, but to unified personal existence. .It is not a question of **having** Nephesh as a possession, but the fact that one **is** Nephesh.[2] For the Old Testament, personal being manifests itself as a centered unity whether as a volitional center (Ps. 24:4), emotional center (2 Kings 4:27; Exodus 23:9), or desiring center (Gen. 34:2f). In each instance we are not dealing with separate psychological or physical activities, but with unified human beings directed in a particular way. The desire, appetite, volition, or emotiveness of an individual is not the action of an autonomous soul but the particular orientation of a total human being, i.e. a self. While Nephesh is the most basic Hebrew term conveying unity of personhood, other closely-related terms are used by the Old Testament to represent further nuances of unified personal existence. Ruah (spirit), for instance, expresses the energy or direction of a self as it lives its life in a particular way. Ruah (spirit) is the God-given vital power which gives human selfhood its thrust, force, or intensity. It becomes visible in human feelings, will, and interior life, with the possibility that one can have a despondent spirit (Job 21:4), a seeking spirit (Isaiah 26:9), a patient or arrogant spirit (Eccl. 7:8), a jealous spirit (Numbers 5:14), a decisive spirit (Ezekiel 36:26), or an erring spirit (Isaiah 29:24). This human spirit or "energized selfhood" is inseparable from the breath (Ruah) of God as vividly portrayed in Ezekiel's vision:

> Thus says the Lord God to these bones, behold I will cause breath (spirit) to enter you that you may come to life. And I will put sinews on you, make flesh grow back on you, cover you with skin, and put breath (spirit) in you that you may come alive; and you will know that I am the Lord (Ezekiel 37:5-7).

Not only is the life of human beings interwoven with the God who calls it forth, but this life is marked by creaturely i.e. finite, existence. The fleshness (bashar) of human existence is the Hebrew acknowledgment of human transience but even this bodily basis of human identity is not separate from one's personal unity. Like spirit, flesh is used as a personal pronoun, as another way of expressing a particular feature of one's life.

> "My soul (nephesh) thirsts for thee, my flesh (bashar) yearns for thee" (Ps. 63.1).

For the Hebrew, the body (as bashar) is never a lower-order shell housing some higher principle, but it reflects one's unity with the entire created order, the creatureliness through which we are dependent upon God for our existence (Job 34:14).

How then is Ruah (spirit) distinguished from nephesh (personal being/soul) for the Hebrew? Simply put, spirit is the energy by which soul (self) lives out its life as flesh. It would be even more accurate to say that Nephesh (soul) refers to human existence as a unified self, a center of being which is continuously shaped by Ruah (spirit) as it lives itself out as Bashar (flesh). We must be careful, however, not to see these factors as separate entities acting upon one another, but as manifestations of the operations of selfhood when seen from the vantage point of the self's dependence upon God.

Evolution of the God-Self Relation

Even at this early stage in our journey it can be declared with some certainty that the prevailing metaphysical climate of any age will determine the limits of the self-representations one finds therein.[3] Although I am oversimplifying the point, it is quite possible to demonstrate parallels between the capacities and operations of deity and the depth and breadth of human self-reflection. G.W.F. Hegel brilliantly accomplished this task in the *Phenomenology of Spirit* and *History of Religion* as we will discover more fully later. Suffice it to say that the evolution of the God-concept directly impacts the possible range of meanings to be discovered for selfhood.

For instance, the plurality of gods in the Greek pantheon serves as a useful projective device mirroring the vast range of possible patterns to be found in the operations of selfhood. It is no accident that 20th Century Psychological Science has looked to Greek myths to uncover the subtle movements of human interiority. Myths, of whatever era or cultural ground, reveal the internal architecture of selfhood. For the Greek, however, human participation in the divine drama is tangential at best. The affairs of humanity are directed by the gods, the human self simply a stage upon which divine forces clash. There is no autonomy to selfhood, only a process dictated by, and at the full mercy of, the gods. Selfhood is not yet able to see itself as self, as subject in direct encounter with object and with itself.

With the birth of Hebrew monotheism a completely new quality of relationship between the human and divine became possible. The one God and the individual human being now stood face to face. They had achieved a one-to-one relationship, a partnership, as symbolized by the lofty capacities achieved by the first Adam. The management of the earth and its life became the mandate of God's partner even as Adam's creatureliness and dependence upon God was reasserted. But rather than diminish the value of selfhood this factor of dependence cemented the earthling into a position of unsurpassed value. The uniqueness of God established the uniqueness of personhood by virtue of the image which they now shared.

As religious consciousness evolved within the Hebrew framework a further development called apocalypticism again nudged the capacities of selfhood forward.

God, as eschatological judge, weighs all things including the motivations of one's heart, those hidden factors normally obscured from view.[4] Individuals thus became ethically accountable for themselves in a fuller way. Even one's interior life now becomes an open book to the God who will weigh all things. Self-exploration is thus moved to a new and deeper level.

Even though this Hebrew eschatological God of future reckoning is very remote and transcendent by virtue of his Lordship over the future, this God also facilitates a deepening of human interiority. An unconscious realm becomes established where deeper impulses reside. The apocalyptic possibility of a future reckoning expands the call of God first given to Adam in the Garden of Eden. Only now the call of God is not an accountability for a single action but for the fullness of who one is. This enhancement of the otherness of God as judge strengthens the human capacity to become ."other" to oneself, to enter into fuller relationship with oneself, a step vital for coming to selfhood. The heightening of sin-consciousness which occurs in the Hebrew tradition thus serves to deepen the human capacity for self-understanding.

With the arrival of the Christian paradigm a further step is taken. The God who is "other" is also internally present, becoming visible in the inner movements of the self's life. The fullness of God must be also visible in human interiority in order for the complete mirroring of the divine image to be maintained. The second Adam of the New Testament becomes the vehicle for drawing selfhood toward a more comprehensive union of the human and divine. The distant image of the divine which initially grounds human identity (first Adam) has now given way to a new pattern. The eternal and historical, the one and the many, the material and spiritual, have become interwoven in a mysterious fusion. This mystery will require a more detailed treatment. But first we must grapple with the dynamics of selfhood as understood by the Judeo-Christian tradition.

The Biblical Self as Dynamic Process

We have already become acquainted with the possibility that selfhood contains internal operations. The life of self has something to do with how the elements contained therein come into harmony and/or disunity. In Plato, we discovered an acknowledgment of an inner battle between spirit and desire as both are harnessed to serve the purposes of a charioteer (Reason). For Plato this remained a non-historical process with the "portions" of personhood autonomous and related to one another along hierarchial lines. This first vision of selfhood depicts the operations of self as a clash of dualistically separate entities. Even the functional monism of an Aristotle could not overcome the limits contained within the Greek approach.

With the ascendancy of the Judeo-Christian world-view a new paradigm emerges which allows for fluid operations within the self, but without the dualistic divisions noted for Greek selfhood. This is not to say that there are no sharp divisions to be found within the Biblical self, only that there is an overriding oneness to human personhood even as divisions occur and are overcome.

The Inner/Outer Dynamic

An inner/outer dynamism is evident throughout the Biblical anthropological framework. The word heart (Leb) for instance, is used 858 times in the Old Testament making it the most common anthropological term to be found there. Its patterns of usage reveal that heart is the primary indicator of inwardness. As the organ of interior life it reveals deep, often unconscious impulses.

> If you say "See, we did not know this," does not He consider it who weighs the hearts? (Proverbs 24:12)

The creator-God is not only aware of human externality but is intimately acquainted with the secret recesses of our innermost being. The Psalmist writes:

> Our heart has not turned back, and our steps have not deviated from your way ... if we had forgotten the name of our God would not God find this out? For he knows the secrets of the heart (Ps. 44:18-21).

The heart as metaphor of inwardness speaks of the internal cognitive, emotive, and spiritual impulses of the self, keeping in mind that these cannot be artificially separated for the Old Testament. In the heart reside emotions such as sadness (I Sam.1:8), joy (Psalm 13:15), courage (II Sam. 17:10), or fear (Gen. 42:28). Not only do emotive currents stir the heart but it represents all inner desires of the "highest" or "lowest" order, whether desire for a neighbor's wife (Proverbs 6:25), the desires of pride (Is. 9:19), or one's deepest hopes (Proverbs 13:12).

Not only does the heart represent the nuances of emotion and/or desire, it also reflects the rational and volitional capacities of reason and will.[5] The human capacity for insight and discernment is not separate from the inevitability of choice which propels selfhood on its way. The heart is the instrument of insight (Isaiah 6:10) and wisdom (Psalm 10:12). Whether as organ of thinking, emoting, discerning or choosing, heart always refers to the human being in some sort of direction, some sort of relationship to oneself, one's neighbor, and one's God.

For the Hebrew there exists no separation of the functions of feeling, desire, or judgment from one's subsequent actions. Even as a heart understands it chooses, even as it desires it directs itself on its way. It is at one and the same time an instrument of engagement with the world and of encounter with itself. The heart allows the human individual to be subject to herself even as the person interacts with the otherness of her world.

It would be incorrect, however, to see the heart as a uniform entity without internal tension. A heart can change its mind (Hos. 2:16), can be tested to determine its true impulse (Deut. 8:2), and can even require transformation from a heart of stone to a heart of flesh (Ezekiel 11:19). In short, I as human being am a unified whole even as I live out a multiplicity of dynamics within myself.

But how, it can be asked, is this duality actually different from the Greek? Did the Greeks not allow for conflict between drive and reason, a division of motivation at the most interior levels?

Indeed, the Bible shares the Greek emphasis on a division within selfhood, particularly in Paul who picks up the theme of conflict between willing and doing (Rom. 7:15). Yet in Paul the conflict is not simply between knowledge (reason) and emotion (desire), as would be true for the Greeks, but extends much deeper to include levels of inclination below and beyond a cognitive challenge to the inclinations of desire. For Paul there exists a division at the very foundation of selfhood even as such a self continues to operate as a structural unity.

The Fall as Paradigm of Divided Selfhood

Few other images capture the Biblical vision of divided selfhood as sharply as the story of the Fall. It remains a highly ambivalent image in the late 20th Century with many still chafing under notions of original sin which hurls them out of the Garden into God-forsakeness. Others have come to see the Fall as a "fall-upward", a positive step essential for the birth of self-consciousness, without which human selfhood would be impossible.[6]

I would propose that the Fall motif of necessity carries both possibilities within it; both are perhaps stations along the path to selfhood. On the one hand it is impossible to conceive of true human personhood without the positive awakening brought about through the otherness of the object - a process I will examine from numerous angles. On the other hand, the Biblical tradition assumes that this process has an inevitable disorienting and fragmenting component to it. Selfhood is internally divided, claim the scriptures, and it is our task to understand why this claim is made, and what possible relevance this has for us in the late 20th Century.

According to the Genesis account, the human creature prior to the Fall is a two-dimensional entity living out what one might call a simple subject-object duality .As a conscious creature such a being is capable of two-dimensional existence, of interacting with an environment as is any higher life form, but without the capacity to know itself. Such a two-dimensional "self" is not divided in the full sense of the word but is "divided" only with regard to its orientation toward the world and its place therein.[7]

Such a "self" runs on a pleasure/unpleasure engine and orients itself to the world accordingly. It is seeking or avoiding, manipulating or structuring the objects of the world in ways which serve its organismic needs. But the very otherness of the world drives a wedge between this "self" and its world, an otherness which activates the desire for that which is separate (Gen. 3:6). As will be rediscovered throughout the search for the self, desire is the doorway to self-consciousness, not only because it reinforces the presence of the desired object but because it awakens the insufficiency of the desiring subject. Adam and Eve's desiring of the fruit proceeded hand in hand with the discovery of an insufficiency in themselves which the fruit would fill. This insufficiency brought them into relationship with themselves in the form of a narcissistic trauma, an insight rediscovered by contemporary psychoanalytic theory. This injury and the shame it aroused had to be covered up, the beginnings of a self relating to itself.

For the Old Testament (the Fall account in particular) desire is the doorway to self-consciousness. We see here the beginning recognition that selfhood is a triadic process of coming to oneself through the otherness of the object and the subsequent otherness (neediness) discovered in oneself. Selfhood, then, seeks the otherness through which it comes into encounter with itself. As self encounters the otherness of the object. it awakens a gap within itself, from which it becomes divided based upon the negative relationship it takes to this third element. But how did this divided self come to the unity so central to the Hebrew vision? And what did the Christian tradition add to this process?

Law vs. Spirit as Forms of Reconciliation

It has already been made clear that the Old and New Testaments give human interiority a central place in the operations of selfhood. The awakening to one's insufficiency brings all manner of attempts at coverup with it, whether through the hiddenness with which one tries to hide one's true self, or in the form of covetousness, that out-of-control desire which consumes all otherness thereby hoping to obliterate it.

For the ancient Hebrews, the path to reconciliation takes the form of adherence to the law, the divinely given parameters toward which selfhood is to be oriented. The mosaic law is the external norm of conduct by which selfhood can measure itself and find its security. One could say that this form of selfhood seeks its otherness in law (the social norm) as supported by the transcendent deity. Restoration of relationship to the divine other who validates selfhood is sealed for the community through the act of circumcision. A covenant is thereby established with each new generation (at least for its male members), but which nevertheless needs to be actualized or lived out according to the parameters of the divine law.

For the Christian community there emerges a radical shift away from legal/behavioral means of validating selfhood toward what one might call the spiritual. No longer is the sign of restored relationship placed upon exterior factors, whether body or behavior, but is present within the deepest reaches of human interiority. As Paul suggests it in 2 Cor. 3:7, the mosaic law is only carved on letters of stone, but not written in the human heart.[8] The Old covenant given to Moses transformed him alone as depicted by his radiance upon descending from Mt. Sinai. This glory of Moses, his transformed self, forces him to veil himself before his people who are unable to share in his glory given the veil covering their hearts.

The central claim of the Christian community is that a second Adam models direct access to the Spirit of God thereby validating and grounding selfhood in its complete fullness. No longer does the exterior dimension alone validate selfhood, but its most interior reaches lives out the tensions and reconciliations of every self. But how does the New Testament envision these tensions and by what means does the reconciling action occur?

The Spirit/Flesh Polarity

No other terms capture the dynamic richness of New Testament selfhood as fully as do spirit and flesh; together they constitute the two primary centers around which Biblical selfhood organizes itself.

The New Testament's justification for this duality is the human capacity to develop a relationship to one's self and to God. Human beings are on a path of becoming **subject** and **object** to themselves, an inevitable differentiation process which allows persons to shape themselves for better or for worse, and to develop or reject a relationship with God, the final criterion for selfhood. To the extent that human existence is an "on the way" existence involving the forming of selfhood, then certain forces will impact the direction human selfhood takes. Flesh and spirit thus stand as factors which shape the particular quality of relationship which will be taken toward oneself and toward God.

Flesh as Factor of Finiteness

Flesh (Sarx) carries several meanings in the Pauline and Johannine corpus. It can refer to simple physical existence as an alive body with instinctive and sensate capacities. In this form flesh means "natural humanness" or creatureliness, an affirmation of one's continuity with nature. There is nothing sinful about flesh when understood in this manner. Flesh includes the various critera for existence which created beings have in common, even when these features are specific to various life forms:

> All flesh is not the same flesh but there is one flesh of men, and another of beasts, and another of birds, and another of fish (I Cor. 15:39).

But by far the most noteworthy use of the term is its identification with finite, transient existence. Even in this form flesh is not to be understood as an attempt at dividing human beings into a higher or a lower part, with flesh somehow further from God than another "higher" portion. Flesh is rather used synonymously with "world", the **context** of one's natural, earthly existence through which one is sustained and toward which one can develop a healthy or twisted relationship.[9]

To live "in the flesh" is to live in the natural earthly realm as the context within which the self determines its shape. But this still does not tell us what distinguishes flesh from spirit nor what makes flesh potentially sinful.

Flesh becomes sinful when it takes itself to be the norm of selfhood with the direction of such a self set toward the pursuit of fleshly (transient, finite) ends to the exclusion of larger purposes and larger unities. This "fleshly self" is not the sensual or instinctive self, but rather the lopsidedly **autonomous** or **self-depreciating** self.[10] Its sin is that of narrowness and self-deception which either negates otherness and thereby itself, or swallows otherness up thereby artificially inflating itself. Such a self remains blind to itself preferring the darkness of non-transparency to the light of self-knowledge. A "fleshy" self can manifest itself in a zealous fulfilling of the law (Gal. 3:3-11); in narcissistic pride in one's special spiritual endowment (2 Cor.10: 12-18); or in the out-of-control desire which seeks itself only in the narrow thereby losing its full self (Rom. 1:25). An "in the flesh" self can thus refer to human beings who stand in some sort of misdirected relationship toward themselves and their creator, with the primary manifestations thereof a distorted narcissism and/or a misguided dependence (Gal 5:16-26).

Nevertheless, as twisted as a "fleshly" self may be, all existence - even when transformed - is an "in the flesh" existence! Paul writes:

> I have been crucified with Christ and it is no longer I who live but Christ who lives in me; and the life which I now live **in the flesh** I live by faith in the Son of God who loved me, and delivered himself up for me. (Gal. 2:20).

Just as the created universe is good, so is flesh a positive manifestation of divine activity. Persons are not called to abandon the flesh or the world to live in some ethereal realm, but to develop a different relationship to themselves and the world. Persons are not sinful because of their earthly finiteness, but because they end up dealing with this finiteness by loving the darkness and rejecting the light (John 3:19).

The New Testament claims that human finiteness leads individuals to run from their ontological dependence upon God and to turn only to their finiteness for a center to their universe. Rather than live out a fullness of selfhood as children of God, human beings turn to the narrow to define themselves, (John 1:10-14). In this fashion humanity creates a world standing over-against God, a self separated from itself. Rather than recognize its divine origins such an autonomous self becomes its own self-referent, one which defines itself via itself. This, according to the New Testament, is the source of the enmity between God and the world and the basis for the flesh/spirit polarization.

Spirit as Factor of Freedom

How, then, is spirit another factor determining selfhood? I must make it very clear that for the New Testament spirit is not some higher mental or spiritual principle within human beings, but a self oriented in a particular way. In contrasting spirit from flesh we must be careful not to think only in structural but also in dynamic terms. Spirit is a process, a source of power, and as a form of energy it allows a self to be oriented in a particular manner.

For both Testaments, the related words pneuma and ruah carry similar meanings referring to an animating, dynamic force. Human striving, willing, and intention are all products of spirit, the attitudinal and volitional thrust which gives direction to one's self.[11] But how is spirit's direction different from the inclinations of flesh?

Perhaps the sharpest contrast one can draw is to be found in Romans 8:6 where Paul writes:

> For the mind set on flesh is death, but the mind set on the spirit is
> life and peace.

Spirit is a consciousness-expanding power which opens up the possibility of freedom for the self. Just as flesh closes the openness self needs for itself thereby killing it, spirit provides a new orientation for the self expanding its horizons, offering it a new and infinitely enlarged vision of what it in fact is, Paul writes:

> For you have not received a spirit of slavery leading to fear again,
> but you have received a spirit of adoption as sons (and daughters)
> by which we cry out "Abba! Father!" The Spirit himself bears
> witness with our spirit that we are children of God (Romans 8:16,
> 17).

Spirit not only allows selfhood to claim its divine inheritance, it provides the self with a mysterious freedom which mirrors divine life.

As a new orientation for the self, spirit takes on a special role in the lives of those who are open to the unique manifestation of spirit as revealed in Christ.

> And if Christ is in you, though the body is dead because of sin yet
> the spirit is alive because of righteousness. But if the Spirit of Him
> who raised Jesus from the dead dwells in you, He who raised Christ
> Jesus from the dead will also give life to your mortal bodies through
> His Spirit who indwells you. (Romans 8:10, 11)

Even if one's being has taken on a deadness through the activity of sin, nevertheless, the renewing power of Christ's spirit will reanimate dying and decaying selfhood. Not only is spirit a transforming power which renews human existence, spirit is implicitly present as a power which awakens persons to God. Paul writes:

> For us God revealed them (spiritual thoughts) through the spirit; for
> the spirit searches all things even the depths of God. For who
> among men knows the thoughts of a man except the spirit of man,
> which is in him? (I Cor. 2:10, 11).

There is an implicit kinship between the human and Divine Spirit which allows the human spirit to orient itself toward the fullness of personal being, a fullness which is possible only because of this affinity. Spirit, then, refers to the empowering capacity which allows for transformed selfhood, for the formation of a purposive center, a center which chooses and pursues some goal. Because spirit is not "above" the sin which arises out of a twisted flesh-orientation, this goal can be either for or against God, for or against itself.

But the New Testament is not content with a simple flesh/spirit dichotomy. We must direct our attention to an additional element which, one might say, attempts to unify the flesh and spirit aspects of self. This factor is the **law**.

The Law as Negative Third

It has already been proposed that Biblical selfhood finds its unity in relationship to a third element, an element which in some fashion unifies or transforms a subject stuck in a state of tension or overagainstness with an object. Furthermore, we know that the Bible affirms the raw instinctive and earthly factors which we have come to know as flesh. We could even say that Biblical selfhood appreciates and affirms the presence in flesh of factors which psychoanalytic thought calls **drives** or **instincts.** This "id-like" flesh must be unified in some way, must be channeled into the norms of community so that a cohesion of personal identity can occur. This "coalescing of identity" so necessary for selfhood is first attempted through the law.[12]

The law emerged as the factor of mediation between instinctive impulses of personhood and the parameters of community within which selfhood comes to life. In so reconciling individual inclination with corporate/communal constraints, selfhood was given a reference point, one which had a divine covenant as its background (Mt.Sinai). Law, we might say, became the third leg of selfhood which reconciled the individual with the social norm thereby providing self with a certain level of organization. Identity could now be established as a self aligned itself with the parameters of community behind which stood the validation of the transcendent law-giver.

In Paul, however, the law itself is indicted as a form of bondage, the very agent of the death of the self. In order to understand this radical shift it is necessary to acquaint ourselves with Paul's lengthier analysis found in Romans 7:5-11.

For while we were in the flesh, the sinful passions, which were aroused by the Law, were at work in the members of our body to bear fruit for death. But now we have been released from the Law, having died to that by which we were bound, so that we serve in newness of the Spirit and not in oldness of the letter. What shall we say then? Is the Law sin? May it never be! On the contrary, I would not have come to know sin except through the Law; for I would not have known about coveting if the Law had not said, "You shall not covet." But sin, taking opportunity through the commandment produced in me coveting of every kind; for apart from the Law sin is dead. And I was once alive apart from the Law; but when the commandment came, sin became alive and I died; and this commandment, which was to result in life proved to result in death for me; for sin taking opportunity through the commandment, deceived me, and through it killed me (Romans 7:5-11).

The above passage is critical for our appreciating the revolutionary nature of New Testament anthropology and may serve to be useful as we assess models of selfhood throughout history. To begin with, Paul assumes a tripartite structure to selfhood within which certain operations become visible.

Between the primary antithesis of flesh and spirit stands "I", the conscious center of being (ego) which must unify these polarized orientations. The Pauline ego is an ego in relationship to the flesh and spirit elements within itself and as it relates to these elements it either finds life or it dies, either finds its self or loses its self.

As we have already seen, Paul is too sophisticated to see this struggle as a cognitive choosing, as if a simple "decision" for spirit and against flesh could "save" a self from itself. The means by which an ego might unify itself thereby becoming a self has a deeper duality to which can either suffocate the emerging self or give it life.

An inevitable occurrence according to Paul is that fleshy "I" and spiritual "law" will come to oppose one another. Every "I" carries flesh elements (instincts and impulses) within it and these in and of themselves cannot provide the unity of purpose necessary for selfhood. A "flesh-only" I operates on the pleasure/unpleasure equation only and therefore cannot find "life" beyond its immediate need satisfaction. The God-given law emerges as a first form of spirit which provides an ego with the parameters of conduct and frameworks of security which attempt to "save" the instinct-driven ego from itself.

But even though the law is opposed to sin (ego twisted by finiteness) the law itself joins with sin to condemn the "I". Law, as the inherited norms of community and transcendent ideals, kills, because it sets individual inclination **over-against** absolute norms. Sin was dead without the law, the law being the factor which awakens the self to the parameters of conduct as they have evolved in the history of the human race.[13]

Every self is awakened through its encounter with the demands and constraints of family, one's social group, and the "absolute" norms mediated by one's religious traditions. But, claims Paul, this "superego factor", as vital as it is to awakening selfhood, **kills**! It does so through the guilt and anxiety which surface as by-products of the inevitable transgressions an ego will incur. In the end an ego can only condemn itself because it will consistently fall short of the ideals held before it as its normative criterion.

Paul furthermore claims that there is a seductive and/or aggressive quality to the allure of the law, that sin (the inclination to define selfhood by finite means) uses the law to attempt to provide a false unity for the self.[14] It is possible for a self to seek to unify itself by aligning itself completely with the law, an identification of itself with the ideal norm which it zealously seeks (Pre-conversion Paul). Or, rather than take a libidinous approach toward the law, a self can take a hostile-aggressive attitude toward it by rejecting any norm, by rebelling from the demands placed upon the self by the prevailing social and religious order. Either way, the self is in bondage by being unable to transcend the internal otherness (self-alienation) brought about by its alienation from, or collapse into, the norms of the world.

In summary, law reveals the Pauline vision of self as dialectic process. A self is of necessity divided within itself and in attempting to overcome this division a self will either find itself or lose itself. Law (the social and religious norms of the world) therefore acts as a wedge which opens up the subject-object division within the self, even as it fails as an adequate mirror to allow the self to come to reconciled relationship to itself. It fails because it can only offer the self an unreachable ideal which will either crush the self under its unattainable goal, or fool it through the seduction of scrupulous adherence to the law.

Christ as Positive Third

If Biblical selfhood is a triadic process in which a tension between two internal elements is overcome by a "new" third, and if in the case of "law" this third element eventually "kills", how is even this death transcended?

All prior reconciliations attained by selfhood are externally mediated in the sense that the "environment" presents new possibilities of behavior and patterns of identification allowing "identity" to be formed. In the case of law this results in an "adaptational self" accommodating itself to the social and religious norms within which it moves. But a self oriented only toward external sources of validation will never be at peace with itself because it is always seeking itself outside of itself.

The profound claim of the New Testament is that Christ, the God-person, allows this final alienation to be overcome. By what criterion does the New Testament make this claim?

As far as the New Testament is concerned, Christ becomes a new image for the self, a new model of what selfhood in fact is. The basis for this assertion is the identification of Christ as the second Adam, the prototype of the fullness of what it means to be human. Even though the first Adam is created in the image of the divine (Gen. 1:27), this relationship was marked by distance, a relationship which required an external mediator (Moses) whose mirroring of the "glory" of the divine could only take veiled form. Now in Christ the veil is removed:

> But whenever a man turns to the Lord the veil is taken away. Now the Lord is the Spirit; and where the Spirit of the Lord is, there is freedom. But we all, with unveiled face beholding as in a mirror the glory of the Lord are being transformed into the same image from glory to glory just as from the Lord, the Spirit (2 Cor. 3:16-18).

Through Christ direct access to the Divine is provided, an image which transforms the beholder into the same pattern of being. Not only does Christ reveal God, he reveals the fullness of what it means to be human. Just as personhood bears the image of the first Adam so too are persons capable of being transformed into the second Adam:

> So also it is written, "The first Man, Adam, became a **living soul**." The last Adam became a **life-giving spirit**. However,

the spiritual is not first, but the natural; then the spiritual. And just
as we have borne the image of the earthly, we shall also bear the
image of the heavenly (I. Cor. 15:45, 46, 49).

As fully human and fully divine, Christ unifies in his own being the finite and the
infinite, the particular and the universal, the natural and the spiritual. He is a union
of opposites and reconciles all alienated fragments within personhood. Most
noteworthy of all, this Christ overcomes the self's separation from God, the author
and paradigm of selfhood. As far as the New Testament is concerned, Christ thus
represents the ultimate norm of the self.

But the New Testament recognizes that identification of Christ as **image
only** is potentially as suffocating as the law which he transcended. If Christ
remains only an external reference point then this very image can kill through its
supreme loftiness, its "perfection". Or, this external-only image can kill by virtue
of its serving as a fetish which a self tries to imitate even as it devalues itself. A
Christ present as idealized image only can be used by an ego to maintain its self-
depreciation thereby killing the self.

For the New Testament, then, Christ must be more than a **representation**
of idealized patterns of selfhood but must **be** the very **pattern of selfhood**. Paul
claims in Col. 3:9-11 that the Christ reality permeates all selfhood - selfhood which
is in an ongoing process of being renewed:

> Do not lie to one another, since you laid aside the old self with its
> evil practices; and have put on the new self who is being renewed to
> a true knowledge according to the image of one who created him, - a
> **renewal** in which there is **no distinction between** Greek and
> Jew, circumcised and uncircumcised, barbarian, Scythian, slave and
> freeman, **but Christ is all and in all**.

The grand sweep of Christ's life it seems cannot only serve as a **model** of the
self's path to wholeness, but the **very living of selfhood** is the story of the
divine interfacing with the human.

As we are about to discover, subsequent centuries often collapsed one story
into the other, rather than maintaining the tension of one serving as mirror for the
other. Some perspectives gave primacy to the Divine by allowing only for a
Universal Ego (Subjective Idealism) with individual selfhood collapsed into the

Absolute, while other perspectives offered legitimacy only to the individual human in isolation from the Universal (Empiricism).

But the very point of the Biblical paradigm is that the God-human relationship is just that - a relationship - which is why we cannot allow ourselves the luxury of overcoming the polarity by collapsing one into the other. Both the human and the divine remain determinative for the unfolding of selfhood. Christ, it seems, serves as far more than a **reference point** for the self, but the story of the God-person remains the on-going story of God, just as the Christ-process defines the life of the self, at least as far as the New Testament is concerned. What, then, is this Christ-process and what does it have to say about selfhood?

Christ takes on the full form of sinful flesh (Rom. 8:3) as one of us and places himself under the conditions of finiteness. He fully shares our capacity to seek self-denying solutions to this dilemma (Hebrews; 3:6; Luke 4:1-13). But as a spiritual being fully integrated with fleshness he lives out a harmony toward his finiteness without being determined by the demands of flesh. A freedom is therefore available to him which allows him to transform the limits which accompany being a self.

The point must be underscored that the pattern of Christ's selfhood does **not** mean a vaulting over the conditions of selfhood but their transformation **by virtue of the redemptive possibilities** he brings to the self. Every developmental step, every life crisis, carries an element of tension within it as a prevailing state of selfhood is challenged by a demand which tries to overcome that which preceded it. Allow me to give an example from Jesus' life.

The adolescent Jesus in the Temple is awakened to the claim of the Ultimate upon his life which forces him to differentiate himself from his parents and their framework for his life. This step needed to be repeated more than once as we know through Jesus efforts to separate himself from his mother's agenda for his ministry. Jesus must deny his parents' control over his life even as he remains their child, although now in new form. Jesus "new" identity transcends the former without the rejection of the old or avoidance of the new.

But perhaps the most relevant motif of all for the story of selfhood is Christ's pattern of crucifixion and resurrection. Christ too became caught in the jaws of the "law" - the law which claims to unify selfhood but eventually kills. Christ was condemned as sin as is all selfhood:

> He made him who knew no sin to be sin on our behalf that we might
> become the righteousness of God in him (2 Cor. 5:21).

As the condemned one Christ stands as the internal representation of all patterns of
judgment, whether parental, social, or internal (superego). The rejection and
"death" which accompanies the violation of any norm - is placed upon him - the
negation which accompanies any living self is a negation known by him, received
by him.

Conversely, Christ not only represents the ever-present factor of
negation/condemnation, within the self but he actualizes the factor of renewal,
transcendence, and transformation. The resolution of alienation so necessary for
wholeness requires both transparency and acceptance, two additional features of
Christ's action within selfhood.[15]

Christ's revelatory function reveals what is hidden and secret within human
interiority. Christ will "bring to light the things hidden in the darkness and disclose
the motives of human hearts" (2 Cor. 4:5, 2 Cor. 4:6). Christ eliminates the
boundary between conscious and unconscious, between me and not-me, and allows
the full range of otherness within selfhood to become known to itself.

In so revealing all otherness to itself, Christ does so with such a radical
acceptance that no further displacement or denial is possible. For the New
Testament Christ is the new internal judge and as a new guiding center Christ draws
the split-off portions of selfhood into Christ's self. The enmity between flesh and
spirit, the contradiction between personal uniqueness and communal demand is
overcome in a new unity which transcends them both. Christ thus becomes not
only a "symbol of liberation" from internal condemnation, but becomes the very
impulse of the "restructuring" of one's inner and outer world.[16]

Christ therefore acts as an integrating reality within the self, transforming
and renewing the self even as Christ joins it in its multiple "deaths". Christ does
this through the radical love which allows itself to be broken for the world.

> For the love of Christ controls us, having concluded this that one
> died for all therefore all died; and He died for all, that they who live
> should no longer live for themselves, but for him who died and rose
> again on their behalf. Therefore from now on we recognize no (by
> what he is in the flesh); even though we have known Christ (by
> what he is in the flesh), yet now we know him thus no longer,

therefore if anyone is in Christ, he is a new creature; the old things
passed away; behold new things have come (2 Cor 5: 14-17).

Christ as "new" unifying third carries for the self the reconciling Spirit of God
which eternally unifies that which is broken (2 Cor.5: 18-19). There is no
condemning forum on heaven or earth which can drive a wedge between the self
and its internal love object which is its very self. (Romans 8:31-39).

It seems there is no end to the newness and otherness confronting every
self. A self will always encounter internal or external otherness, but the New
Testament suggests that the pattern of Christ provides a way for this otherness to be
overcome - not eliminated - but honored and reintegrated into the self system.

This possibility allows the self to be free. It is now free to be itself, to
move into the differentiation required of it even as it embraces with the over-
againstness and tension which comes with this process. In so finding itself through
otherness it lives out the image of the one whose life it mirrors, claims the New
Testament.

This brings us to the culmination of the Biblical vision of selfhood.
Whether the models of selfhood which evolved over subsequent centuries match the
Biblical in terms of its ontological grounding and psychodynamic relevance remains
to be seen. The words of Paul in 2 Cor. 3:17,18 cited earlier in this chapter will
serve as a formidable measure of the supreme value claimed for the Biblical self:

Now the Lord is the Spirit; and where the Spirit of the Lord is, there
is freedom. But we all with unveiled face beholding as in a mirror
the glory of the Lord, are being transformed into the same image
from glory to glory, just as from the Lord, the Spirit.

---

1. Hans Walter Wolff, *Anthropology of the Old Testament*, Trans. by
Margaret Kohl, (Philadelphia: Fortress Press, 1974), p. 10

2. George Arthur Buttrick, et. al. Editor, *The Interpreter's Dictionary of the
Bible*, Vol. 4, (New York: Abingdon Press, 1962), p. 428

3. Support for this position can be found in Gerd Theissen, *Psychological
Aspects of Pauline Theology*, translated by John P. Galvin, (Philadelphia:
Fortress Press, 1987), p. 107-111

4. Theissen, 1987, p. 108

5.   Wolff, 1974, p. 46ff

6.   Matthew Fox, *Original Blessing*, (Santa Fe, New Mexico: Bear and Company, 1983), p. 46

7.   In actuality, a dydadic process is not a self but an ego - the conscious capacity to interface with an environment in adaptive ways.

8.   I am indebted to Theissen, 1987, p. 139-143 for his excellent comparison of Pauline and Mosaic criteria for personhood.

9.   Rudolf Bultmann, *Theology of the New Testament*, Vol. I, translated by Kendrik Grobel (New York: Charles Scribner's Sons, 1951), p. 235

10. Gunther Bornkamm, Paul, (New York: Harper and Row, 1971), p. 133

11. Bultmann, 1951, p. 205, 206

12. I am following the general sweep of Theissen's argument in my discussion of the dynamics of the law.

13. Theissen, 1987, p. 229

14. Ibid., p. 245-246

15. Ibid., p. 103-104

16. Ibid., p. 386

Chapter III

EARLY EXPLORERS OF SELFHOOD

In seeking to understand the evolution of thought concerning selfhood in the post-Biblical era we must stretch our historical vision to cover a virtual millennium of time. The early centuries of Christian thinking known as the Patristic period were concerned with the establishment of Christian truth-claims in the face of a hostile pagan world, and as such, scholarly efforts were directed largely toward the apologetic task of legitimizing the Christian faith. Reflection upon human subjectivity was at best an adjunct to this overriding task.

The major exception to the above is the towering figure of Augustine (354-430). He is without a doubt the most influential theologian of the early church and his efforts are so expansive that they include significant contributions toward the understanding of selfhood. He has in fact been called the founder of the study of the self for the Western world.[1]

With the collapse of the Roman Empire came the period of stagnation known as the Dark Ages with little psychologically useful material emerging during that 500 year period. It was not until the birth of Aquinas (1225-1274) that new impetus was given to the inquiry regarding selfhood. The Aristotelian framework which became available to Aquinas opened all manner of opportunities for the growth of knowledge in science, philosophy, and psychology. While Aquinas emerged as the premiere thinker of the Medieval period, another movement, the mystic, was evolving in the background only to be driven underground due to the challenge it presented to both the Platonic and Aristotelian perspectives as they fought for intellectual supremacy. In the person of Rhineland mystic Meister Eckhart (1260-1327), a noteworthy step beyond both Augustine and Aquinas was taken, one which became vital for the search for selfhood in the Eighteenth Century and beyond.

I would be so bold as to suggest that it is impossible to understand the full meaning of selfhood without entering into dialog with the vision and limitations these great scholars bring to the quest. Their inclusion in this chapter is not because of any particular affinity with one another but because each has earned a central place in the unfolding of the story of the self.

Augustine: First Guide to the Study of the Self

Augustine lived in a world decaying all around him. The crumbling of the Empire and the eventual sacking of Rome by the Goths all occurred in his lifetime and likely contributed to the heightened emphasis upon subjectivity one finds in his thought. In being driven toward introspection Augustine was not simply being nudged by social/political factors, but also by the turmoil of his own personal life. Factors such as his ambivalent relationship to his mother, the death of his son Aderatus, and the seemingly insurmountable conflict with his own sensuality all contributed to Augustine's interest in human interiority. The Platonic world-view described in Chapter One found great affinity in Augustine given his decaying personal and communal world. This dualistic Platonic framework which placed stability/permanence at one pole and destructive decay at another became increasingly determinative for Augustine.

Another critical development directed Augustine toward the study of personhood, a factor not directly related to an interest in the self, but having to do with a far more pressing theological need which preoccupied much of Augustine's scholarly life. The backdrop for this overriding concern was the tremendous religious upheaval which occurred in the fourth Century A.D. as Christianity underwent a sudden transformation from persecuted sect to virtual state religion under Constantine. With this sudden shift into prominence a search for orthodoxy, for stability, created strong pressure to preserve the purity of Christian belief. The dogmatic and political challenges facing the early church intensified the need for doctrinal clarity. This necessity brought about the various ecclesiastical councils which attempted to define the faith against its many internal and external challenges.

Among the thorniest issues debated in the fourth century was the nature of the Trinitarian God as Father, Son and Holy Spirit. The great Trinitarian councils of Nice and Constantinople faced a difficult question. How God could be three "persons" yet maintain oneness and indivisibility?

The primary challengers of the Trinitarian formula were the Arians who denied the full divinity of Christ for the reason that God must be of one substance i.e. without qualities, contingencies, or properties. Since the Son is begotten and the Father unbegotten they cannot be of the same substance or have the same identical nature.

Into this fray jumped Augustine with the contention that God's nature is not distinguished by static uniformity, but by **relation**. In other words, the "inner" workings of God are not a static oneness but an eternal relatedness within the Godhead. Augustine's proposal is that there is something dynamic and relational about God - God's essense must be reflected in all three "persons" of the Trinity.[2]

It is one thing to propose a new model for resolving the Trinitarian dilemma, and quite another to spell out what it **means** for Father, Son and Holy Spirit to be One yet distinct; what it **means** for the Son to be eternally begotten of the Father, or the Spirit eternally proceeding from the Father and the Son. This is the task to which Augustine directed himself in his book **The Trinity** and where we find his clearest pronouncements about the self.

Augustine's reflections about selfhood were prompted by his assumption that God cannot be known directly; the best we can do is examine God's image, the most accurate reflection available to us being **the human self**. The words of Genesis 1:26 had cleared the way for Augustine: "Let **us** make humans according to **our image**."

The Human Self as Reflection of the Divine Image

The problem confronting Augustine was a thorny one indeed. How can the three Trinitarian "persons" each possess the divine nature in their fullness without "needing" one another thereby diminishing their completion in themselves? How can it be one and the same thing to be Father, Son, and Holy Spirit with each being fully God? Of course, Augustine's assumption that personhood is defined by autonomous self-sufficiency already hints at a fatal flaw which we will explore shortly. Augustine answers the above questions by developing several images of the Trinity as he finds them in the human self. As Augustine examines human subjectivity he finds various patterns of triadic process which he discards as deficiencies surface within each model. Our task is not to become bogged down in understanding the details of each model, but to follow the general sweep of his argument with our primary concern a comprehension of the movement within Augustinian selfhood.

The First Image: The Phenomenon of Self-knowledge and Self-love

Augustine begins his analysis with this simple pronouncement: since God is love, to see the Trinity is to see love. But love is not some static thing, but a process which contains the elements of lover, beloved, and the love itself. Augustine writes:

> So then there are three: the lover, the beloved, and the love. What else is love, therefore, except a kind of life which binds or seeks to bind some two together namely, the lover and the beloved?[3]

Since, however, the lover and the beloved are the same thing when I love myself, there remain only two elements, my self and the love. But where then, asks Augustine, is the Trinity if the internal relation within the self only contains a duality?

Augustine's answer is to introduce the element of self-knowledge into the equation.

> The (self)* cannot love itself unless it also knows itself for how can it love what it does not know ... But just as there are two things, the (self) and its love, when it loves itself, so there are two things, the (self) and its knowledge when it knows itself. Therefore, the (Self) itself, its love and its knowledge are a kind of trinity; these three are one, and when they are perfect they are equal.[4]

In attempting to see God mirrored in the self Augustine looks at the self's processes of knowing and loving and discovers there what he wishes to see: a confirmation of the "substantiality" or eternal unchangeableness of the self. The attempt to illustrate the **unity** of the Trinity through the **unity** of the self forces Augustine to give the self a wholeness and indivisibility through the factors of self-love and self-knowledge he finds there. In other words, as far as Augustine is concerned, there is no self if there is not knowledge and love of self. But how does this in any way explain the Trinity?

Augustine suggests that as the self loves and knows itself it generates an idea or concept of itself. This Augustine calls the self's "word".[5] This knowledge is not just a knowledge mediated by the senses but an immediate knowledge of itself, an inner awareness of itself. This allows Augustine to confirm that the Son is indeed the Divine "Word" or Logos, the immediate and eternal manifestation of God's self-knowledge.

Just as the self conceives or gives birth to ideas and concepts of itself and the world, so the Son, the Word of the Father, eternally proceeds from the Father. The divine Word is the image of the Father just as our inner word or self-knowledge is the image of what the self knows. Augustine elaborates:

> And since knowledge has a likeness, to that thing which it knows, namely, that of which it is the knowledge, then in this case it has a perfect and equal likeness, because the (self) itself, which knows, is known.[6]

Thus the eternal begetting of the Son is imaged by a self knowing itself.

Furthermore, just as love supposedly proceeds from knowledge, the Spirit eternally proceeds out of the Father and Son. In the generating of the love which follows knowledge, the self in its capacity for self-love mimics the eternal Spirit in its spontaneous loving of what is known. But even with these admittedly creative linkages Augustine was forced to reject this model.

The Breakdown of the Analogy

For what reason did Augustine abandon this first analogy? A careful reader will have noticed that the three elements of the self called upon to reflect the Trinity included: (1) the self, (2) self-knowledge, and (3) self-love. The difficulty with these elements is that they are a mixture of substance and **relation**. The

Augustinian self, as we recall, is supposed to be "substantial" i.e. complete in itself. The latter two factors, self-love and self-knowledge, are relational and highlight the self's actual relationship to itself in loving and understanding, while the first factor, the self, is fully "self-contained" so to speak. This means that the first analogy is really a reflection of **God**, Son, Holy Spirit, not **Father**, Son, Holy Spirit.[7]

God must be "**substance**" (completely self-sufficient) as far as Augustine is concerned, but the Trinity highlights relationship, not the independent substantiality of each "person" in the Trinity. Augustine's dilemma is that selfhood always needs to be actualized: self-knowledge and self-love are not automatically given.[8] Augustine could appreciate that the human self knows and loves itself only as it relates to itself, but this observation he could not extend toward the Godhead since the "persons" of the Trinity are not supposed to find completion only upon relating to the others. Augustine's rampant dualism forces him to banish the factor of movement from the Godhead.[9] What Augustine could not allow is that the "persons" of the Godhead might find completion **in** their inherent relatedness.

The Second Image: Remembering, Knowing and Loving

The shift which Augustine undertakes in his second effort is to characterize the dynamics within the self using the triad: (1) remembering itself, (2) knowing or understanding itself, and (3) loving/willing itself. This allows Augustine to work with the following distinctions:

1. The "substance" or "structure" of the self;
2. The self's dynamic openness or "potential" which allows it to give shape to itself;
3. Its actual relating to itself in remembering, understanding, and loving/willing.[10]

Augustine assumes that the three acts of remembering, understanding and loving are **relational** and refer the self to itself and the world. Furthermore, these acts reflect or **arise out of** the unity of a particular structure of selfhood. To use his own words:

> Since these three, the memory, the understanding and the will are
> therefore, not three lives but one life, not three (selves) but one
> (self), it follows that they are certainly not three substances, but one
> substance.[11]

Selfhood, then, reveals a unity of structure and purpose even as it engages in the triadic operations which define its life.

Given Augustine's search for the eternal i.e. for a permanence to selfhood, he shows a surprising sensitivity to the developmental necessities of selfhood. Augustine asks himself:

> What does the (self) love, therefore, when it ardently seeks to know
> itself while it is unknown to itself? Behold! the (self) seeks to know
> itself and is inflamed with this desire. Therefore, it loves, but what
> does it love? Itself? But how, since it does not yet know itself, and
> no one can love what he does not know.[12]

Augustine suggests that the self of an infant, for example, becomes gradually known to itself through the data, the stimulation with which it is awakened.[13] Since to be a self requires the capacity to be present to itself, even when undeveloped, it is present to itself through whatever minimal "knowledge" it has. Even though this "knowledge" is highly "imperfect" as Augustine calls it, more like a vague "sense" or "feeling", it is nevertheless a complete or "whole" unit even in its rudimentary organization as he tries to argue:

> Does that which knows itself in part not know itself partially? But it
> is absurd to say that it does not know as a whole what it knows. I
> do not say that it knows wholly, but what it knows it knows as a
> whole. When therefore it knows anything about itself, which it can
> only know as a whole, it knows itself as a whole.[14]

It does not matter to him if the self is not fully known to itself because even in its desire or seeking it shows that it is already aware of itself through its very seeking. Augustine can therefore claim that when the self seeks to know itself it does so because it is already aware of itself through its implicit presence to itself.[15]

In short, Augustine takes the three elements of memory, understanding, and love/will, and uses them to illustrate the **structure** and **dynamic** flow of the self. Having analyzed the self and given it shape through the terms memory, understanding, and loving/willing, he claims to have painted a picture of the eternal unity of the Godhead. But again the analogy breaks down for Augustine.

While the human self is changeable, the Divine (according to Augustine's dualistic assumptions) must be permanent and unspoiled. The problem Augustine faces is that the self can relate to itself in a wide variety of ways - for better or for worse. As suggested, Augustine uses the concept of the "word" to describe the particular shape a self can give itself as it relates to itself. The image which the self gives itself becomes its "word" with the possibility that this image will be flawed and tainted. This is not the case with God since God's internal relating is always one of truth and purity.

Selfhood, insists Augustine, shapes itself through its unity of love and thought (word).[16] Said another way, the particular "word" which defines a self (that by which it becomes known) is a blending of its thought (i.e. its memory or "sense" of itself) with the "pleasure" or attachment it derives from this "thought". Or, more simply, the self becomes attached to that which it loves (seeks) and in attaching itself to its objects it becomes like them. In other words, the particular shape of a self will be determined by the unity it finds. This profound truth will be "rediscovered" many times in the centuries to come.

The Self and Sin

In suggesting that selfhood involves a process of mirroring as it seeks itself, Augustine concludes that a self can become confused about its identity in the process. Augustine elaborates:

> But because it (the self) is in those things of which it seeks with love, and it had grown accustomed to thinking of sensible things, that is, of bodies with love, it is incapable of being in itself without the images of those things. From this arises its shameful error, that it can no longer distinguish the images of sensible things from itself, so as to see itself alone. For they have marvelously cohered to it with the glue of love, and this is its uncleanness that, while it endeavors to think of itself alone, it regards itself as being that without which it cannot think of itself.[17]

Augustine's point is that a self through its pattern of identification either identifies exclusively with its sought objects thereby losing itself, or it sees its self as an autonomous agent generating itself.

Augustine therefore tends to think of the breakdown of the self in two ways. On the one hand he claims that selfhood is inclined to identify with the **particular** rather than the **universal** in defining itself, leading to an exclusive identification with narrow and specific "things" to the neglect of one's larger dependence - i.e. upon God. As one might expect, this conclusion is linked to his Platonic framework in which the perversion of selfhood involves a twisting or inverting of the higher and lower, with the seeking of the lower or finite becoming a substitute for à seeking of the infinite. Sin, says Augustine, involves "an immoderate inclination towards those goods of the lowest order (while) the better and higher are forsaken."[18] In seeking only "the particular" or the narrow, the self drifts from its inner knowledge of itself and directs its love (desire) only toward the sensate impressions through which it is so powerfully impacted.[19] As is well known, Augustine regrettably equates "the particular" with the sensate and bodily, thereby heightening the body/spirit dualism which will remain so persistent through the centuries.

Secondly, Augustine suggests that sin goes beyond simple entanglement with the sensate products of experience, and involves a particular quality of seeking which resides in the very structure of selfhood. Augustine labels this deeper factor within sin "concupiscence" as follows: "that (love) is base with which the (self) pursues what is less than itself; it is more correctly called cupidity which is the root of all evils."[20] While the first form of sin, the inverting of the higher and the lower remains important, it is largely symptomatic of this deeper division within selfhood.

What prompts the inversion in the first place is an orientation toward oneself and the world which Augustine calls **pride** or **appetite**. In the **City of God** Augustine describes this deeper manifestation of sin as follows:

> Moreover our first parents only fell openly into the sin of disobedience because, secretly, they had begun to be guilty. Actually, their bad deed could not have been done had not bad will preceded it; what is more, the root of their bad will was nothing else than pride. For pride is the beginning of all sin. And what is pride but an appetite for inordinate exaltation? Now exaltation is inordinate when the soul cuts itself off from the very source to which it should

keep close and somehow makes itself and becomes an end to itself.[21]

For Augustine the root of sin is an inner distortion within the self visible as the narcissism which makes itself the center of its universe. Sin arises out of the supposedly inordinate desire of a self to be the center of reality. Such egocentricity is inevitably in a state of tension with any rival claimant upon its identity which leads such a self into tension with God.

It is perhaps impossible to salvage Augustine's view of sin from its dualistic contamination, but one or two points can be summoned in its favor. First of all, Augustine attempts to integrate the sin phenomenon into the very structure of selfhood. This allows sin to be understood in an operational sense as a phenomenological occurrence within selfhood. This structural approach is in contrast to those who see the root of sin to be unbelief. When seeing sin primarily as disbelief or disobedience, the phenomenon can become limited to a function of cognition, leaving open the possibility that sin itself becomes an article of belief.[22]

In contrast, Augustine insists that sin is a built-in factor within the dynamic unfolding of selfhood: it describes an inherent tendency in human beings to develop a distorted relationship to themselves and the objects of their world. What is interesting about this aspect of Augustine's thought is its possible parallel with 20th Century empirical conclusions about selfhood as represented by Heinz Kohut's psychoanalytic insights, for example. In describing the narcissistic thread as a central infrastructure for the self, Kohut has hinted at the inevitability of narcissistic injury as selfhood is born, with various successful and/or unsuccessful efforts at resolution.

Augustine allows for narcissistic fulfillment of the self, but acknowledges that such seeking can break down into destructive detours as the seeking for the essence of selfhood is denied. Regretably, Augustine's relevance for the contemporary quest for selfhood is totally undermined by his persistent use of sexual desire as his vehicle for demonstrating selfhood's running away with itself in concupiscence. If we can momentarily look beyond this serious limitation, a positive kernel can perhaps be found. Namely, Augustine gives us the possibility of seeing **the very relationship the self takes to its defining objects** to be the basis for its distress, its sinfulness, not simply some cognitive denial of divinity or the violation of codes of conduct.

The Augustinian Legacy

The greatness of Augustine cannot be overestimated. Not only is he the first great scholar of the post-biblical era to systematize the operations of selfhood, his conclusions are determinative for the first thousand years of Western thinking and continued to reverberate in the evolution of understandings of selfhood through to the modern era..

As noted, Augustine is called the founder of the study of the self by virtue of his being the first post-classical scholar to describe the internal operations of selfhood. He establishes a trust toward internal experience and affirms the legitimacy of subjective ways of knowing. He highlights the self as seeking agent through the desires and inclinations which nudge it forward, and the freedom of will by which such seeking is actualized. Augustine insists that it is only our very own selves that we can know directly, that all other knowing is a knowing mediated by the senses (via sense perception), and finally, that all operations of selfhood are intimately interrelated.

But after all is said and done one cannot shake the impression that Augustine lived with a contempt of the human self, a rejection of its life due to its very finiteness and interwovenness with the body he so despised. For Augustine the life of the human self and the Divine can never overcome their static opposition. His dualism forces him into a static transcendence with one set **over-against** the other even as they mirror each other.

Augustine's triadic formulas are at best "still photographs" of the divine-human relationship. By giving the human self permission to develop while at the same time denying this possibility to the Divine, it forces Augustine to separate the one from the other at their very core - the movement through which the fullness of selfhood is attained. The human self for Augustine is at best an imperfect mirror separated by an insurmountable gulf with the changeable self on one side and the changeless God on the other. Divine and human nature remain intrinsically and tragically separate with "union" only possible in a timeless, static way cut off from the flow of life. This is the self Augustine envisions. As we turn our attention to

Aquinas it will be important to consider whether Aquinas helped correct the limitations imposed onto our search by Augustine.

Aquinas and the Aristotelian Resurgence

In turning from Augustine to Thomas Aquinas (1225 - 1274) I am not arbitrarily overlooking 800 years of scholastic activity but am honoring the fact that the Platonic foundation which guided Augustine remained the operational paradigm for virtually the entire era under question. By the beginning of the thirteenth Century a new intellectual wind was blowing prompted in large part by the recovery of Aristotle in the Arab world and his translation first from the Arabic and eventually from the Greek into Latin.

This influx of Aristotelian ideas gave Aquinas a superior vantage point from which to address a burning issue of the day, the reconciliation of faith with the pronouncements of human reason. This task did not emerge out of idle speculative interests but as an attempt to correct departures from theological orthodoxy.

The threats toward which Aquinas directed his efforts came from two directions. On the one hand he felt compelled to challenge the Neoplatonism which had grounded Christian theology for 1000 years. From Augustine onward this perspective artificially separated selfhood from the body, elevated "will" at the expense of intellect (nous), and locked the self as "soul" into a static, non-material, non-historical unity.

The second major challenge facing Aquinas came from the Avorrists who with Aquinas drew their inspiration from Aristotle. The Avorrists, however, insisted on (1) the eternal viability (self-sufficiency) of matter, (2) the universal identity of intellect (nous) in all persons, and (3) the duality of truth, i.e. that truth comes in two forms with a proposition therefore able to be true philosophically but false theologically.[23] These claims not only challenged the Christian insistence upon God as agent of creation, they threatened to split "truth" into two separate camps.

These developments were deeply troubling for Aquinas for whom faith and reason were not separate truths but diverse paths to one truth.[24] The faith/reason dichotomy was not the only issue confronting Aquinas, however. The split between the material and spiritual world also became highly problematic for him.

Form and matter are separate in a Platonic universe and this state of affairs became completely unacceptable to Aquinas as it had for Aristotle 1600 years earlier.

In discovering Aristotle, Aquinas gained a "new" vantage point which offered him the opportunity to overcome these troubling divisions much along the lines of his mentor. Aristotle, as we recall, attempted to bridge the gap between permanence and change by proposing the Unmoved Mover. That is, all motion (which is eternal), finds its cause in the still centerpoint which is itself unmoved but which gives matter its particular developmental path. This construct allowed Aquinas to incorporate a teleological perspective into his metaphysics. Change gained meaning in that change has an intention, direction, and destination inherent in it. This new meaning was used by Aquinas to reconcile change with Christian beliefs about an unchanging God and God's relationship to a changeable universe. How in particular did Aquinas envision this reconciliation?

Aquinas, as has been suggested, insisted upon the inseparability of form and matter which in the case of human beings means the unity of body and soul. And yet every human being perishes, implying that the soul too must perish. To resolve this dilemma Aquinas follows the footsteps of Aristotle by regarding a certain operation of self (namely mind or nous) as higher than the rest in that mind is the most complete actualization of the possibilities inherent in selfhood. Since the operations of mind are supposedly complete in and of themselves and therefore (eternal) it provides Aquinas with a bridge which unifies the soul **and** links it to the life of the divine. In nous (as the highest fulfillment of soul) Aquinas believes he has found the construct which fulfills the criteria of **stability** and **change**. But before we pass judgment on the adequacy of the construct we must wrestle with the larger picture concerning the Thomistic self.

The Nature of the Thomistic Self

The key elements of Aquinas' self can be identified in three ways: (1) the self as rational, (2) the self as self-sufficient (substantial) and (3) the self as immortal.[25]

The Self (Soul) as Rational

With the re-discovered Aristotelian perspective in hand, Aquinas is able to incorporate all functional capacities into selfhood, arranged in a hierarchial grid. For Aristotle, the rational soul operates at a higher level than the sensate, which operates at a higher level than the nutritive and so forth. For Aquinas this same hierarchial vantage point allows him to classify the operations of self according to their ability to "grasp" the objects they seek. As one moves up the grid and approaches the higher levels, the self's capacity to "know" the objects for which it is intended grows because of its increasing affinity for them. The highest level, intellect, transcends all lower faculties because of its ability to grasp the nature of all bodies in their universal essence i.e. their form and function. Aquinas elaborates:

> For the nature of each thing is shown by its operation. Now the proper operation of man as man is to understand, because he thereby surpasses all other animals ... But the species of anything is derived from its form. It follows therefore that the intellectual principle is the proper form of man.[26]

Even though Aquinas insists that this highest level of self (intellect) is fully united with the body because it is the body's actualization, it is detached from matter and does not "need" matter to actualize itself. Aquinas continues:

> But we must observe that the nobler a form is, the more it rises above corporeal matter, the less it is merged in matter and the more it excels matter by its power and its operation ... For, in order that man may be able to understand all things, by means of his intellect, and that his intellect may understand all things and universal, it is sufficient that the intellectual ower not be an act of the body.[27]

The intellectual capacities of self demand a transcendence of the constraints of matter even as the self (soul) remains the form of the body (the actualization of the body's potential). Aquinas argues that the intellect cannot be bound to a bodily organ since that would preclude the self's knowledge of all bodies. The intellect's loftiness is both its ability to apprehend non-material realities (ideas, etc.) as well as its capacity to apprehend material objects in their universal, as well as their particular form. This is the basis of the self's spirituality for Aquinas. In seeing its operational capacity for grasping "universals," Aquinas is able to infer that the soul's nature is the **eternal** ability to **actualize** all those potentialities rooted within it.

The boldness of this step is that it allows Aquinas to elevate human rationality into an **organizing principle** thereby forging a greater unity between the material and spiritual constituents of reality. In Augustine primacy had been given to feeling (will), to subjective process, which for Augustine remains handicapped through its proximity to the body. With Aquinas, **Reason** unifies the operations of human personhood. The material and non-material factors of personhood are brought into harmony through the intellectual operations of self.[28] One could even say that the operations given to self through **Reason** makes Aquinas the forerunner of modern understandings of **ego**, understood as the organized and conscious patterns of response to an environment.

The Self (Soul) as Self-sufficient

A second characteristic of the Thomistic self is its self-sufficiency (or substantiality) which means that it is not reducible to any other factor. This somewhat obscure point requires further explanation. By definition, every quality which is not considered to be essential to the being or essence of a thing is considered to be **accidental**. The redness of an apple, for instance, is an accidental factor not essential to the nature of the apple. Correspondingly, the true nature of a thing is often called its **substance**, namely, that factor without which something would not exist, i.e. would not reflect its essential nature. From a Thomistic vantage point the essential factor which defines selfhood is mind (nous) or Reason. This highest capacity within self is what defines the human being as human.

A difficult question now emerges for Aquinas. How can each individual human being be unique if self is but a "mold" defining the highest human possibilities? If self is a "form only" how does it provide for individuality? If the self is truly self-sufficient, then its relationship to a particular body is accidental as Plato had taught.[29] Upon what basis does it remain the **form** of the body if a **particular** body is of no consequence to it? Furthermore, how can individuality be maintained after death (since the self is supposedly immortal) if the self or soul is the essence of persons in a generic sense only?

Aquinas arrives at a solution to these problems by describing the self's self-sufficiency in two ways.[30] On the one hand the self as animating capacity contains the full range of possibilities which come with being human as Aristotle had taught. All capacities of the human species are contained in this aspect of self (soul) as the actualization of potentialities. This would imply that there is but one self, with this self "individualized" only upon actual union with matter, as was the claim of the Avorrists.[31] How did Aquinas overcome this dilemma?

There is a second feature to soul's self-sufficiency insists Aquinas, namely, soul and body are an **essential**, not an accidental unity.[32] Every self is individualized by its relation to its **individual** body and even if that body dies and decays this relation remains because its natural inclination is to be united with its own body. Aquinas elaborates:

> The soul communicates that being in which it subsists to the corporeal matter, out of which, combined with the intellectual soul, there results a unity of being so that the being of the whole compositor is also the being of the soul ... For this reason the human soul retains its own being after the dissolution of the body though this is not so with other forms.[33]

In short, the self as soul is both self-sufficient (complete in itself) as the form of all human potentiality, but at the same time finds its **particular completion** when in union with its own body. Aquinas can therefore claim that self (soul) is both a **universal** form **and** the actualization of that which is **particular** and **unique**.

The Self (Soul) as Immortal

It is but a small step from Aquinas' position that the self as soul is the eternal form of the body to the conclusion that it is incorruptible, that is, not subject to decay. In coming to a declaration of the self's immortality Aquinas must nevertheless explain the self's relationship to change, in this instance the deterioration that seems inherent in all life forms.

Aquinas suggests that a thing can decay in one of two ways, either accidentally or as a constituent of its being.[34] All objects which decay when a factor which they require is removed are said to decay accidentally. For instance, the withholding of water from a plant causing its death is considered to be an accidental form of decay. On the other hand, decay can also be a built-in factor within objects, a disintegration consistent with their nature. The death of an animal without the action of some other agent is considered to be the end of its substantial form or soul. It has naturally completed its functional purpose.

With the human self, however, a very different end is envisioned. Since the human self is pure form for Aquinas, it cannot cease to exist because it cannot be separated from itself. Aquinas writes:

> For it is clear that what belongs to a thing by virtue of itself is inseparable from it; but to be belongs to a form, which is an act, by virtue of itself. Therefore matter acquires actual being as it acquires the form, while it is corrupted (decays) so far as the form is separated from it. But it is impossible for a form to be separated from itself and therefore it is impossible for a subsistent [substantial] form to cease to exist.[35]

Self (soul) cannot cease to exist because it does not depend upon its body for existence; that is, its very act of existence is pure knowledge (form) from which it cannot be separated. Since the human self is not an amalgamation of parts it cannot be dissolved or dissociated from itself. This is what renders it immortal.

The argument Aquinas uses to establish his case rests in large measure on the means by which the self "knows." Sense knowledge, claims Aquinas, is organically mediated which allows for a knowledge of particular objects in the here and now.[36] But the senses can only operate through a material distinction between the recepter organ and the source of the impulse. This subject/object distinction necessary for sense knowing is overcome in **understanding** or **intellectual** activity as Aquinas declares:

> Now every bodily organ possesses a sensible nature but the intellect, by which we understand, is capable of apprehending all sensible natures. Therefore, its operation, namely, understanding, cannot be carried out by a bodily organ. Thus it is clear that the intellect has an operation of its own which the body does not share.[37]

For this reason, claims Aquinas, the intellectual principle by which persons "know" has its own mode of existing superior to the body and not dependent upon it.

Because it operates with non-material realities, it itself must be non-material and able to abstract independently of material constraints.

The Self as Image of God

As I noted earlier, Augustine became the first to formally propose that the self reflects the image of God through its operations of memory, self-understanding, and self-loving. While Aquinas echoes these Augustinian conclusions he adds another feature to Augustine's analysis by suggesting that the image of God must reflect not only the Trinity of persons but the **one divine nature** since "in God Himself there is one nature in Three Persons."[38]

As one might expect, Aquinas sees this "one nature" of God best represented in human intellectual capacities (Nous). He writes:

> Since man is said to be the image of God by reason of his intellectual nature, he is most perfectly like God according to that in which he can best imitate God in his intellectual nature.[39]

These intellectual capacities which "imitate" God are represented for Aquinas by the natural capacity or potentiality for knowing and loving God, a capacity common to all persons even when not actualized. It would not be possible to know God at all if it were not for this affinity between intellect and God's nature.

Secondly, a "deeper" level of imaging is attained as persons **actually** come to know and love God which Aquinas calls a reflecting of the image of God as **grace**. Finally, as persons come to know and love God fully or perfectly, they reflect the image of God as **glory**. This three-layered imaging of the nature of God in the self Aquinas calls (1) creation, (2) recreation and (3) likeness, with all persons sharing the first image, the "just" sharing the second and only the "blessed" sharing in the third.[40] In short, it is only when a self fully knows God that it approaches a more perfect likeness; until then it is an imperfect image only.

How, then, can we assess these Thomistic conclusions? What helps or hindrances are provided for an understanding of selfhood, and do they nourish a sense of self as dynamic, living process or drive selfhood even further into a static rationality?

The Thomistic Inheritance

The influence of Aquinas cannot be overstated. His genius has impacted Western thinking for 700 years and the critiques I am about to direct at his pronouncements about self do not obscure the impetus he gave to Western scholarship. Perhaps the most formidable legacy given by Aquinas is his attempt at unifying the search for **knowledge** with the search for **God** through the integrating construct of intellect (mind). Through mind Aquinas attempts to unify the operations of self and link it to the life of God. In giving **Reason** such lofty status great impetus was provided to the quest for knowledge. The affirmation of rational process, including the legitimacy of trusting the knowledge gained through the senses, not only reopened the door to empirical inquiry, it re-established a vital unity between soul and body in contrast to the Platonic stream which denigrated sense-knowing and split soul from body. Regrettably, however, this very reliance upon Reason as the factor of integration imposed a new dualism upon the self..

The Self as Hierarchial and Intellectual

In attempting to unify the material and non-material aspects of personhood Aquinas sought a viable metaphysical agent through which the structure and operations of the self could operate. This metaphysical factor is nous (intellect), the non-decaying, self-sufficient capacity of self.

Because the Thomistic metaphysic values permanence and unchangeability over decay and contingency, the various operations of selfhood become hierarchically arranged according to their relative closeness to the factor of non-changeability or substantiality. The capacities of nutrition, locomotion, and sensation have a body-based distortion inherent in them and operate at a lower order than those which allow more direct access to the universals, namely mind or (Reason) itself. Even intellect, however, as the capacity to recognize the forms remains "clouded" for Aquinas through its association with the body, since it operates through the indirect processes of fantasy and cognition.[41] Since the self is in union with its body, its knowledge of itself is always handicapped by the sensate and cognitive processes which "come between" the self and its forms.

Not only is the burden for this separation placed onto the material realm, Aquinas must conclude that the self is unknowable in itself because of its dependence upon its sensate and cognitive operations. While the self must of necessity be united with the body to complete its intellectual operations, when separated from the body it will be able to "know" without the intermediate action of sensation and cognition.[42] Upon what basis could Aquinas make such a claim?

Human and Divine Natures

Aquinas makes his knowledge-claims for self based upon God's knowledge of God's self. God, from Aquinas' vantage point, must be free of all potentiality, in other words, free of any need to still actualize God. Since the eternal God must be separate from decaying matter, this non-material God can only be represented by complete knowledge. Aquinas writes:

> Since therefore God is in the highest degree of immateriality, it follows that He occupies the highest place in knowledge.[43]

In elevating rationality as a unifying paradigm for self, Aquinas believes he has found the means by which the human and divine natures share a common image.

But in connecting the human and the divine at the level of intellect or understanding only Aquinas moves the point of contact between God and persons away from subjectivity, away from experience, toward objectivity, that is, the pure intellectual operations by which self knows objects in their universal form. God and the human do not touch in their inwardness but only reflect one another in the actualization accomplished by the self-contained operations of mind.

In turning away from human subjectivity as a source of data about the divine, Aquinas eliminates the path of experience as a means of contact between God and persons. Perhaps it was his fear of simply identifying God with the events of the universe (Pantheism) which prompted Aquinas to insist upon this radical difference between God and the world.

While it would be unfair to suggest that Aquinas sees human and divine natures as completely alien, even in their affinity they remain radically separate because God dare not be reduced to a process of becoming.[44] The divine must remain unchanging which inevitably drives a wedge between God and the changing self.

Thus, in the end Aquinas can only provide us with a model of self as a static mirror of God's eternal self-sufficiency, with this God in an absolutely transcendent relation to the human self.

What began in Augustine as a dualism of **body** over-against **self**, of **matter** over-against **spirit**, has become in Aquinas a dualism of **thinking** over-against **feeling**. What began in Augustine as a valuing of **human subjectivity** and **interiority** to the **neglect of object-relatedness**, has swung in Aquinas toward a valuing of **objectivity** and **rationality** to the neglect of **subjectivity**. In both instances God and self remain in static opposition to one another.

But this is not the only vision of the medieval period. Another model was evolving as a possible resolution to this unfortunate split and it is to the mystic paradigm as represented by Meister Eckhart that I now direct our attention.

The Self in Meister Eckhart (1260-1328)

The person and work of Meister Eckhart defies easy classification and can thwart the most ambitious newcomer to his preaching and teaching. The unitive vision he brought to his ministry sees such an intensity and intimacy to the God-self relation, that it can leave one quite bewildered in the face of such a paradigm shift.

Eckhart's radicalness left much controversy in its wake which even today challenges the metaphysical assumptions we bring to our anthropological task. However difficult it might be to classify Meister Eckhart, there is no doubt that he operated within the larger Christian mystic tradition wherein he became known as the founder of Rhineland mysticism.[45] Mysticism has been defined as:

> the mysterious desire of the soul - felt to be sacred, preceding any rational justification and sometimes unconscious yet profound and irresistible - which urges it to enter into contact with what it holds to be the absolute [46]

Whatever else one might say, this pithy statement captures the state of selfhood envisioned by Eckhart.

Indeed, Eckhart's work is permeated by a unitive vision which provides him with an encompassing framework within which he views the operations of human selfhood and its participation in the life of the Divine. As a Dominican,

Eckhart was grounded in the Platonic-Augustinian tradition even as he came under the influence of radical new Aristotelian ideas through his own teacher Albert the Great, and Albert's most famous pupil, Thomas Aquinas.

A great scholastic war had erupted in the fourteenth century between the proponents of a Platonic position which gave primacy to subjective operations of **love** and **will**, and those who insisted upon the superiority of **reason** and **intellect** as primary means of knowing reality and knowing God. In many ways Eckhart became a victim of this battle through the charges of heresy brought against him, primarily by those resisting the Aristotelian influence. However, Eckhart's challenges to the prevailing theologies of the day are not what warrant his inclusion as a guide to the discovery of selfhood, nor would it be accurate to suggest that Eckhart acted as a synthesizer of Augustinian and Thomistic ideas somehow reconciling one to the other. Rather, Eckhart demands inclusion because of his very transcendence of both perspectives through his mystic vision of the union of God and self.

God and the Self

What makes Eckhart's perspective unique is not so much that he brings a dynamism to the life of self but that its very dynamism is the story of the self's journey into God and God's journey into the self. Eckhart is therefore the first scholar to look at the life of selfhood from the vantage point of its sharing in the life of God.

According to Eckhart, the fundamental impulse of human existence is to fulfill itself by gaining an **identity**.[47] The final form of this goal is to become "identical" with God. But how does Eckhart envision this identity of God and self? To answer this question we must grapple with three components contained within the question, these being (1) the meaning of "identity", (2) Eckhart's understanding of God, and (3) the nature of the self's participation in the life-process of God. Once these questions are understood we will be in a position to comprehend the life of self from the vantage point of the Absolute which is Eckhart's primary intent.

The Meaning of Identity

It has already become evident that identity implies relation, as having something to do with how an element finds self-definition by virtue of its relation to something else. In the case of the ancient term soul, its metaphysical nature as a unity of material and non-material factors caused its "identity" to be determined through its relation to an eternal factor, this being its Absolute criterion (whether known as Unmoved Mover, Demiurge or Divine Other). For the classical and medieval periods such a metaphysically-given identity is based upon the relation of non-changeable substances.

The billiance of Eckhart's vision is that he is not content with seeing divine-human identity either as sheer absorption or as utter separation. The former sees the human and divine as "identical" (pantheism); the latter insists on God's absolute difference (transcendence) which leaves God and self in static stalemated opposition. Meister Eckhart in contrast, is committed to revealing their dynamic and living relatedness.

Identity as Process

As far as Eckhart is concerned the fundamental objective of human existence is to achieve oneness with God, not as an identity of substances, but as an identity of operations.[48] What might Eckhart mean by such an identity? An operational identity is a "living together," or more literally, a "being thrown-together" of the divine and the human in which they live out a radical (eternal) unity undergirding **all difference and separation.** The following citations from Eckhart are illustrative:

> The Father gives birth to his Son without ceasing (John 1:1) and I say more: He gives me birth, me, his Son and the same Son. I say more: He gives birth not only to me, his Son, but he gives birth to me as himself and himself as me and to me as his being and nature. In the innermost source, there I spring out in the Holy Spirit where there is one life and one being and one work.[49]

On another occasion he writes:

> Where the Father gives birth to his Son in me, there I am the same Son and not a different one. We are of course different with respect to our humanity, but there I am the same Son and not a different one. "Where we are Sons, there we are true heirs" (Rom. 8:17).[50]

Eckhart's claim is that "underneath" any division into so-called separate substances lies the activity of God and the becoming of humans united in an identical event.[51] The perceived gap between God and persons is the result of a process by which distinction emerges out of a prior unity. Distance and difference from God are subsequent by-products of a deeper unity for Eckhart.

I must offer a reminder that this is **not** a collapse of identity into God, a swallowing up of the self in a primordial sea. Rather, Eckhart is searching for the ground **and** goal of the self. In searching for a God/human identity he is not seeking some eternal soul as many before and after him have done, but he is searching for a resolution of the tension between the time-bound and time-less which seems to play itself out within human personhood. But in order to understand how God and self attain such a fullness of identity as **process** one must first come to grips with the nature of Eckhart's God.

A Living God

In arriving at a conception of God as a living and encompassing reality, Eckhart borrowed widely from neoplatonic themes of **emanation** and **return** along with an emphasis upon **intellect** as the "ground" of the soul and of the "inner life" of God. These Platonic and Aristotelian themes which he inherited from Albert the Great and Aquinas became wedded into a framework which reinforced the intellectual nature of union with God.[52]

Eckhart's particular approach is to take the Augustinian vision of the **Trinitarian God** and blend it with the Thomistic emphasis upon the **unity** of God, thereby developing a model of God's life as a movement from **unity** to **differentiation** to **return**. In so doing Eckhart did not repeat the simple Augustinian formula in which the functional activities of remembering, knowing and loving reflect the life of God, but rather that the very dynamics **within** God **are** the story of selfhood. This radical idea requires careful unpackaging.

It is impossible to understand Eckhart without understanding his distinction between God and the Godhead. By God, Eckhart means the Trinitarian God known as Father, Son and Holy Spirit. God's creative activity takes the form of thoughts and their emergence in time, space, and matter. Every particular thing goes out from and returns to God upon whom all things are radically dependent. But all these creative "externalizations" or manifestations of God do not reveal the Divine essence, which can only be referred to by the term Godhead. The Godhead is the God beyond God, the ineffable essence beyond any distinction. If God were only a particular being, suggests Eckhart, such a God would be finite and have a status as a particular being alongside other beings. A particular God must always end as separate other - albeit a being from whom one might expect favor, reward, or even salvation. But to speak of the Godhead, claims Eckhart, is to name the God beyond differentiation where all boundary whether inside or outside of God must be surrendered.

In the Godhead nothing is separated from itself which includes all that the Godhead subsequently pours forth. Eckhart's words are at his provocative best when he suggests that this becoming of God requires the emergence of the creature without which God could not exist.

> God becomes; where all creatures enunciate God, there God becomes. When I still stood in the ground, the soil, the river, and the source of the Godhead, no one asked me where I was going or what I was doing. There was no one there to question me. But when I went out by (breaking open into identity) all creatures cried out: "God." If someone were to ask me: "Brother Eckhart, when did you leave home?" this would indicate that I must previously have been inside. It is this that all creatures speak of God. And why do they not speak of the Godhead? Everything that is in the Godhead is one and of this nothing can be said.[53]

This is no narrowly pantheistic vision but an affirmation that all created things retain a linkage to their divine origin even as they emerge from the seedbed of the Godhead. As "separate" as the corporeal world of time and space might seem, every facet of this world is a living image of God. Eckhart continues:

> God is unseparated from all things, for God is in all things and is more inwardly in them than they are in themselves.[54]

The Father as primordial source of all thought and being is not "God" to the Son, just as Spirit is not "God" to the Father. God, as far as Eckhart is concerned, is an articulation only used by what is not-God, by what is separate from God.

Eckhart is quite clear that even as my being is given by the God from whom all things flow, my very creatureliness is also separation, a separation which causes me to cry forth "God"! Eckhart's own words are quite clear:

> When I stood in my first cause, I then had no "God," and then I was my own cause... I was an empty being and the only truth in which I rejoiced was in the knowledge of myself ... But when I went out from my own free will and received my created being, then I had a "God," for before there were any creatures, God was not "God" but he was what he was ... But when creatures came to be and received their created being, then God was not "God" in himself, but he was "God" in the creatures.[55]

The becoming of God is tied to the becoming of creatures but in their very becoming a separation is inflicted upon a prior unity. This inevitable separation is behind Eckhart's quest for the seeking of a unity **beyond** the particular God. But why seek such an encompassing unity? What relevance can this possibly have for the self? Eckhart's answer concerns two vital features of the self's life: (1) its process and (2) its destination. I will deal momentarily with both.

As noted earlier, Eckhart sees the goal of human personhood to be that of fulfilling itself in identity - an identity with that which alone is capable of reflecting the fullness of selfhood. The home which the self seeks is its divine authorship of which it is not a fragment but a complete reflection.[56] If, however, God is seen only beyond humanness, as the perfect being beyond human imperfection, then the birth of God in the self can only be realized by negating one's connection with the divine and highlighting the vast difference.

A second possibility is to deny the self's distinction from the divine and affirm only its unity. This swallowing up of all distinction amounts to the absorption of the self by the divine. While I must reserve final judgment whether Eckhart truly avoids either extreme, I can restate that his primary objective remains the discovery of unity **with** distinction. How then does Eckhart find such a unity without sacrificing identity or autonomy?

Identity as Process of Understanding

To again restate the goal, Eckhart sees the fundamental thrust of human existence to be that of fulfilling itself in identity. The task of human existence is to achieve oneness with God, not as an identity of substances but as an identity of operations. Eckhart claims that the movement of God and human becoming reflects a mutual process actualized through knowing and loving. The following sermon fragment illustrates:

> God and I, we are one. I accept God into me in knowing: I go into God in loving. There are some who say blessedness consists not in knowing but in willing. They are wrong; for if it consisted only in the will, it would not be one. Working and becoming are one. If a carpenter does not work, nothing becomes of the house. If the axe is not doing anything, nothing is becoming anything. In this working God and I are one; he is working and I am becoming.[57]

The struggle between the neo-Platonists and Thomists regarding the primacy of **loving/willing** over-against **knowing** is the primary background for Eckhart. He tries to overcome this tension by suggesting that both are necessary for human becoming; furthermore, both describe the life of God.

At the same time, Eckhart leaves little doubt that he gives priority to understanding (intellect) as the highest form of the image of God, the operations of which reveal the true identity of God with selfhood.

> Intellect (understanding) is the temple of God. Nowhere does God dwell more properly than in his temple, in (understanding), as the second philosopher said: "God is (understanding) living in the knowledge of himself alone" ... God in the knowledge of himself knows himself in himself.[58]

What makes God - God, as far as Eckhart is concerned, is God's capacity for Pure Understanding. God is fully known to God without mediation by some other agent or activity. God is supremely and infinitely self-conscious.

By shifting the nature of God from God's being toward self-understanding, Eckhart tries to avoid the danger of seeing God as a being alongside other beings. In so doing he reinforces the transcendence of God while at the same time claiming

that in the immediacy of self-knowledge the essence of God becomes visible. This
very essence of God is mirrored as the essence of the self. Eckhart summarizes:

> There is a power in the soul, namely, the intellect. From the
> moment it becomes aware of God and tastes God, it has within itself
> five properties. The first is that it separates from here and now.
> The second that it is like nothing. The third that it is pure and
> unmixed. The fourth, that it is operating or seeking within itself.
> The fifth, that it is an image.[59]

What is Eckhart attempting to declare in this citation?

In the first instance, Eckhart insists that the heart of self (and by definition
the inwardness of God) is only known as one gains a detachment from the flow of
time and space. Time acts as an artificial boundary which must disappear, just as
all attachment to a "here" must be overcome if the eternal presence of God is to
become known. Secondly, the self is like no-thing in the sense that it is not
ultimately defined by a particular object but only by the universality of its own
essence. All of nature, claims Eckhart, seeks this encompassing God who serves
as the principle of operations of all things.[60] God is the ultimate impulse of all
seeking and striving.

Thirdly, Eckhart claims that the self is pure and unmixed, suggesting that at
its core a unity of purpose and harmony of operations must manifest itself.
Fourthly, selfhood as pure understanding is always seeking itself **internally** in
contrast to the will which seeks what it loves outside itself. As noble as such desire
is it does not lead to God who is seen only through "that in which God sees
himself," namely, pure understanding.[61]

Finally, the self is an image of God but "without any distinction between
image and image." Eckhart elaborates:

> But the soul he made not just according to an image in himself, nor
> according to something coming forth from him, as one describes
> him. Rather, he made it according to himself, in short, according to
> all that he is in his nature, his being, his activity which flows forth
> yet remains within, and according to the ground where he remains
> within himself, where he constantly gives birth to his only begotten
> Son, from where the Holy Spirit blossoms forth. God created the
> soul in accordance with this out-flowing, inward-remaining
> work.[62]

The life of self, then, is not only a **reflection** of the life of God but a **re-enactment** of the divine life-process which pours itself out and in so doing remains true to its inwardness.[63]

Eckhart uses the analogy of a hinged door to illustrate his point.[64] The swinging of the door Eckhart compares with the outer person in movement to and fro. The hinge is identified with the inner person intimately connected both to the swinging door and the solid frame. Even as the door swings the hinge remains connected. It is this state of **connected detachment** which best expresses the inner reality of the self as it images God.

Eckhart's development of the notion of non-attachment attempts to move the dynamics of self away from our experience of "things" into the realm of the **non-attached heart** as the deepest ground of our identity with God. Detachment transcends love for Eckhart since love is still seeking "something", perhaps even God. To the extent that it contains residues of grasping, holding, or seeking, it is looking for God and its self "out-there". Rather, the object of a non-attached self is nothing; it makes no claim upon anyone or anything but simply wishes to be.[65] As the essence of letting-be it reflects the self as **freedom**, that is, in its infinite openness to what is.

Thus the spiritual ground of the self for Eckhart is the **self without appetite**. It is a self incessantly living in a non-clinging freedom. It is the alchemy of the soul, a transformation of self into God-likeness.

The Process of the Self's Life

Any attempt to describe Eckhart's vision of the self's transformations must be careful not to impose a chronological or hierarchial structure onto his insights. Eckhart's understanding of the self's journey is **not** that of an ascending ladder, nor are suggested replacement images such as "spiral(s)" of expanding consciousness particularly helpful.[66] It is true that expanding awareness is central to Eckhart's developmental paradigm, but to think in terms of upward-downward retains counter-productive notions of hierarchy, of discarding or leaving behind prior "levels" of selfhood.

As noted, it would be a distortion of Eckhart's insights to envision the self's path as a form of skin-shedding as one ascends up ladders or spirals toward God. A more Eckhartian image might be a pebble thrown into a pond. As the self sinks into its ground its expanding ripples suggest an ever-wider circle of self-discovery even as it remains in a dynamic relationship to its center. Eckhart's intent is to describe the relation of the self to its ultimate object (God) via **four phases of non-attachment**. In so doing Eckhart claims to have described the on-going birth of God in the self.

Again restated, Eckhart's overriding goal is to describe the self's transformation into God. This goal of oneness does not refer to a reawakening of some eternal component within the self to be reunited with its divine author, nor to a pantheistic metamorphesis of self as God, but to a dynamic dance in which an emerging oneness holds distinction within itself in a creative tension. Such oneness is found in the radically non-attached person who can release all partial attachments in a growing openness to all that is and ultimately to the totality of what is. This path of release has four phases to it which Eckhart calls **Dissimilarity, Similarity, Identity**, and **Breaking-through**: they mark the way-stations of the path toward the self's God-consciousness.[67]

Dissimilarity

By beginning with dissimilarity Eckhart is declaring a radical discontinuity between God and persons, a discontinuity which extends to the entire material realm. Only God possesses Being while humans do not in the sense that they are created or contingent beings. As contingent we do not possess ourselves but derive our being from another. Eckhart is quite clear as he exclaims:

> All creatures are a pure nothing. I do not just say that they are insignificant or are only a little something: they are a pure nothing. Whatever has no being, is not. Creatures have no being because their being depends upon God's presence.[68]

Just as Eckhart's sharp, even absolute division separates God and creature, it also underscores the absolute dependence of the creature upon God. And yet one cannot help but notice what will become a fatal flaw in Eckhart, namely a devaluing of the material realm. As I have already hinted, this devaluation is part of a larger devaluation of temporality and uniqueness which Eckhart seems destined to sacrifice to his vision of encompassing Oneness.

Similarity

A second mode of the divine-human relationship Eckhart calls **similarity**. It represents the first movement toward identity, not as sameness, but via a process of letting-go. All those features which stamped personhood as separate must be "released" with a corresponding transformation into God-likeness. Eckhart uses an image of wood transformed into fire to describe the process by which all dissimilarity must be "chased out" of that which is separate.[69] Each phase of this process involves a letting-go of prior artificial or surrogate identifications. At any step along the path of its life a self reflects its identifications and in being ever-moving, it lets-go of one identification even as it anticipates another. This on-going journey involves a dying to an old self and a rising to the new.

Eckhart borrows Augustine's analogy of an image to illustrate the tension contained within similarity. He states:

> Every image has two characteristics. The first is that it takes its being immediately and of necessity from that of which it is an image. It issues from it naturally, coming forth from its nature like a branch from a tree. When a face is placed opposite a mirror, the face has to be reflected in it whether it wants to be or not ... The second characteristic of an image can be learned by concentrating on the image's similarity [to its object][70]

Within the notion of image Eckhart attempts to harmonize the tension between human finiteness in contrast with the human capacity to show likeness with the divine. An image has no being of its own but derives its being from that which projects it - it exists only as it goes out! However, the very existence of the image depends upon its reflecting that which it represents. In this manner, persons (as an image of God) remain distinct from God, not yet "in" God, although able to reflect God.

Identity

Eckhart again draws on the metaphor of flame to illustrate the overcoming of both dissimilarity and similarity in identity. The end result of combustion is identity, what I will call "identity in operation." Eckhart elaborates:

> God is not found in distinction. When the [self] reaches the original image [of which it is a reflection] and finds itself alone in it then it finds God. Finding itself and finding God is one single process outside of time. As far as it penetrates into him, it is identical with God, ... not included, nor united, but more: identical.[71]

Eckhart claims that this identity of God and self is more than a living "with" God, but a living "in" God. This ground of the self is the region of such intimate communion that it is filled only with divine presence. Here we arrive at the "spark of the soul", the completion of a God-consciousness so radical that it is beyond all distinction.

As I have suggested earlier, this "spark" of identity is the intellect, pure understanding, completely unmediated and not simply a rational process. It is a contemplative awareness of oneness with God and not the product of inductive or deductive thinking. It is fully detached from any here and now, space and time process.

Such understanding is not a power or faculty of the self such as thinking, feeling, or willing, but is **the capacity for awareness in the fullest sense possible** - a capacity which is open to know all of reality. Because it is like no particular "thing" in the universe it is open to everything or better said, to the cause of every-thing. It is open to the infinite possibilities of knowing and as such to knowing God.[72]

This identity "in" God becomes the ground of the self's freedom for Eckhart, a freedom which "lets-be" and invites all things to their true identity. Again, non-attachment is the hallmark of this identity which has let go even of its attachment to God to join in a universal chorus of dynamic becoming which Eckhart calls breaking-through.

Breaking-Through

Breaking-through is the culmination of the eternal process of letting-be, the opening of the fruit allowing its seed to be scattered. In letting-be, the identity of God and self pour themselves out without a why. To live without a why is to live with reckless abandon, with no investment in outcomes, no responding to artificial exterior motivations, even those as noble as loving or serving God more fully. One finds no seeking of God here since there is no God outside the self to be found. One looks for nothing but lets whatever is, be!

To level the charge of fatalism or determinism at this notion of identity would reveal a misunderstanding of Eckhart for whom such distinctions require that God and self be object to one another. In a provocative sermon on "Spiritual Poverty" Eckhart summarizes this culmination of the journey of the self into the God beyond God:

> When I flowed out from God, all things said: "God is." And this cannot make me blessed, for with this I acknowledge that I am a creature. But in the breaking-through, when I come to be free of will of my self and of God's will and of all his works and of God himself, then I am above all created things, and am neither God nor creature but I am what I was and what I shall remain, now and eternally ... then I neither diminish nor increase, for I am then an immovable cause that moves all things. Here God finds no place in man for with this poverty man achieves what he has been eternally and will evermore remain. Here God is one with the spirit, and that is the most intimate poverty one can find.[73]

Eckhart has painted for us a picture of the self's breakthrough into the eternal inwardness of God. As the self finds its radical detachment, its total poverty, it discovers its identity in God. This is a self which pours itself out and in pouring itself out is transformed into the divine essence. As such a self moves through its temporal life, its self-emptying of any narcissistic investment in the objects of the world, including even the God-object, allows the eternal to be born within.

Grace, claims Eckhart, is what brings this process to completion as he echoes the words of Paul: "All that I am, I am by God's grace." (I Cor. 15:10).[74] Grace becomes the bridge between the temporal and eternal thereby creating an opening for the self to be what it is. Every self, insists Eckhart, needs time and space to become itself, to be what it has been since eternity. Grace brings to eternal completion the self's at - homeness with God through an increasing release from all that is less than God, God being its very own self.

The very ebullience of Eckhart's vision increases the risk of our being swept away by this tide of eternal oneness which the self shares with God. As sublime as Eckhart's vision may be we cannot allow ourselves the luxury of overlooking the deficiencies and problems left in its wake. Before the final verdict on the Medieval period can be given I must direct our critical scrutiny toward Eckhart.

A Revised Dualism?

Certain formidable questions present themselves as we attempt to come to terms with Meister Eckhart and his unitive vision for selfhood. Among the thorniest is the question whether Eckhart in fact resolves the bi-polarity factor within selfhood, this persistent nemesis which consistently threatens to split selfhood asunder. Does Eckhart resolve the tension between the temporal and eternal, between the material and the spiritual, between body and psyche? Does he artificially unify the human and Divine in ways which in the end negate history and becoming in the service of an encompassing, but ultimately artificial unity?

Before answering these questions, I must assert that whatever verdict is directed at Eckhart, we cannot overlook the refreshing dynamism he brings to the quest for selfhood. Not only is his God a **living** God, this vibrant, creating God is in such intimate engagement with human selfhood that any "division" between them is but an artificial abstraction imposed upon their unity. Just as the remote and transcendent lawgiver God of the Old Testament (Chapter II) provides a certain grounding and worth for self given the image they share, so too does the very dynamism of God provide a profound validation for the self as operational, creative agent. No longer can a static image of God or self satisfy. But here our problems with Eckhart begin.

As noble as Eckhart's divine-human connection may be, it is regrettably actualized only as three barriers are overcome, these being (1) the **material** or corporeal (that which is subject to decay), (2) the **multiple** or the varied nature of the universe, and (3) the **temporal** or transitory nature of things.[75]

As much as Eckhart can grant the self a dynamism and provide a legitimacy to its developmental life, in the end the unity so essential for Eckhart is gained only by stripping the self of the three encumbrances just mentioned. Only the fully non-attached self enters the kingdom of the Divine and finds itself therein. This is the fatal flaw which persistently appears in Eckhart: his self is only unified through **negation** or **kenosis**. Eckhart grossly empties self of all its contents in a complete detachment from matter, from the flow of time, and from the particular, in order to give it an "eternal" unity. He does so to the neglect of the absolutely necessary process of **attachment** also vital for the fullness of self to be realized.

To use an analogy from the life of Christ, Eckhart's way is a way which recognizes Golgatha to the exclusion of Bethlehem as part of the process. Eckhart's eternal unity negates incarnation, a negation which swallows all particularity. His "process" of identity formation is an identity realized outside of time resulting in an identity which excludes a primary factor which distinguishes the human as human - **finiteness and particularity**.[76] Said another way, the identity gained by the self in Eckhart is indeed lofty, but in its very "loftiness" becomes separated from its humanity.

This limitation in Eckhart is a direct outgrowth of his placing the essence of self within **pure intellect**, the capacity self supposedly shares with God. It will be remembered that Aquinas made the first strong move in this direction by making intellect the central feature of the life of God. In Eckhart, however, this gulf is made larger by his **unhooking the material being of creatures** from the **Being of God**. Eckhart rejects the linkage to material being which had been maintained by Aquinas, in favor of a primordial oneness realized in the eternal realm of pure thought, separated from its concretization in the visible universe. The "thinking" process within God is complete in and of itself, separate from the being of creatures who strictly speaking have no being of their own. Eckhart therefore insists:

> God is something that of necessity must be above being. Whatever has being, time, or place does not touch God. He is above it. God is in all creatures, insofar as they have being and yet he is above them.[77]

Since God is God by virtue of the purity of thought which understands itself fully, God needs no actualization other than God's own self-knowledge of which God is eternally full.

And so the promise which we first found in Eckhart ends in a sharpening of the very dualism he hoped to overcome. While the medieval mystic vision flourished for perhaps a century at best, the challenges it presented to orthodoxy caused it to be perceived as a dangerous threat forcing it underground and into virtual oblivion. The opening it created for process, for movement, and for a **living** divine/human identity was soon closed with even more ominous clouds appearing on the horizon which were destined to bury the possibility of a fully living self for many centuries to come.

Conclusion

What are the overriding impressions we take with us as we leave the Patristic and Medieval periods? To begin with, a great legacy was given to us through the genius of Augustine, enabling us to see the operations of selfhood as an internally-rich process of self-relatedness. The subjective life of self took on a quality and depth by virtue of its seeking of multiple internal unities. The relationship of human inwardness to the objects which define its existence is an Augustinian insight absolutely vital for any viable model of selfhood, an insight which will only become fully developed as we arrive at the end of the 20th Century.

Yet Augustine did great harm to the quest for selfhood through the rampant dualism he imposed onto reality and thereby onto the self. Augustine's massive body/self, matter/spirit split separated selfhood not only from the material and contextual frameworks of its life, but just as tragically from the God whose life the self was supposed to reflect.

What began as a rampant dualism in Augustine became a subtle but no less dangerous dualism in Aquinas. Matter and spirit became linked again as was true for Aristotle, but now in a hierarchy of operations actualized through intellect. Aquinas' efforts to unify body and spirit, self and history, were noble but fell short of his intended resolution for the reason that matter remained empty of spirit other than through the functional animation accomplished within organisms. Only to the extent that matter becomes animated to that extent does it reveal the capacities of soul.

Because of his hierarchial vantage point, Aquinas assumed that the closer the operations of self come to intellect the less necessary matter becomes. Self is only itself in the self-contained operations of pure thought. In the end, intellect (nous) remains over-against matter as it had been for Aristotle. And so human personhood with its manifold joys and traumas is again left to drift in separation from any validation to its process.

Given this state of affairs, the emergence of Meister Eckhart came as a breath of fresh air. There was now allowance given for development, for becoming. Even God could be allowed to share in this dangerous possibility. But in order to protect God from full exposure to the ravages of time and space, Eckhart ensconced God and thereby the self behind the invincible wall of intellect, the purity of self-contained operations. Such a God and such a self could only find unity by negation, by stripping themselves of the temporal and material in order for their sublime oneness to be attained.

It is worth noting how far we have departed from the Biblical vision of selfhood which insisted on (1) **embracing** or **desiring** the world, time, and history ("For God so loved the world ...") as well as (2) the necessary letting-go (Phil 2:7) which together seem to define the life of God and perhaps the self. This is not to suggest that the Greek thought-forms which became so quickly wedded to the Judeo-Christian vision only contaminated of the latter. On the contrary, Greek sensitivity to the dualities inherent in reality served as a necessary supplement to the Judeo-Christian message even if that message tended to align itself with either the Dionysian or Apollonian viewpoints.

In short, the challenges which the Greek vision directed toward the Judeo-Christian world-view did not subside with the Middle Ages but took on new forms in subsequent centuries with new attempts at resolution. Our next task is to determine whether the "solutions" of subsequent centuries were any more successful than were Augustine, Aquinas, or Eckhart.

---

1.   Paul Henry, *Saint Augustine on Personality*, (New York: The Macmillan Company, 1980), p. 12

92

2.   Augustine, *The Trinity*, translated by Stephen McKenna, The Fathers of the Church, Vol, 45 (Washington: Catholic University of America Press, 1963), Book 5, Chapter 3

3.   Ibid., Book 8, Chapter 10, p. 266

4.   Ibid., Book 9, Chapter 3,4; p. 273-274 *The translation of self as (mind) is incomplete given our narrow contemporary understanding of mind as intellect or rationality. Rather, self is preferred since it carries the meaning of identity or encompassing subjectivity more in keeping with Augustine's intent. (See also Hill, 1984, p. 211).

5.   Ibid., Book 9, Chapter 7, p. 281

6.   Ibid., Book 9, Chapter 11, p. 286

7.   Hill, 1984, p. 211

8.   Eugene Te Selle, *Augustine the Theologian* (New York: Herder and Herder, 1970). p. 302

9.   Augustine has been given the distinction of being the primary source of the denial of polarity of God.
C.G.Jung, *Aion,* C.W. Vol. 9ii; translated by R.F.C. Hull, (Princeton: Princeton University Press, 1978), p. 46

10.   Augustine, *On the Trinity*, Book 14, Chapter 8, p. 426

11.   Quoted in Te Selle, 1970, p. 302-303. Augustine has at this point combined loving and willing since mature love is for him a volitional act.

12.   Augustine, *On the Trinity* (Book 10, Chapter 11), p. 311

13.   Ibid., Book 10, Chapter 3, p. 297

14.   Ibid., Book 14, Chapter 5, p. 419

15.   Ibid., Book 10, Chapter 4, p. 299

16.   Ibid., Book 9, Chapter 8, p. 282

17.   Ibid., Book 10, Chapter 8, p. 305

18.   Augustine, *Confessions*, II, 5, 10. See also Wolfhart Pannenberg, *Anthropology in Theological Perspective*, trans. by Matthew J. O'Connell, (Philadelphia: The Westminster press, 1985), p. 87-91 for an excellent analysis of the Augustinian position regarding sin.

19.   Augustine, *On the Trinity*, (Book 10, Chapter 8) p. 305

20.   Augustine, *De div. quaest*, 83(396)

21.   Augustine, *City of God*, Book 14, Chapter 13

22.   Pannenberg, 1985, p. 93

23.   Runes, 1980, p.16

24.   Watson, 1963, p. 115

25   I am generally following the thematic outline offered by H.D. Gardeil, *Introduction to the Philosophy of St Thomas Aquinas*, trans. by John A. Otto, (St. Louis: B. Herder Book Co., 1956), p.224. Note also the equivalency between self and soul as the terms defining human subjectivity and identity.

26.   Aquinas, Summa Theologica, I, Q76, Art. 1

27.   Ibid.

28.   Reason at this juncture refers to the principle that nothing happens in the universe without there being a Reason (functional accomplishment) for it happening that way.

29.   Gardeil, 1956, p. 226

30.   Aquinas, *Summa Theologica*, I Q.75, Art II

31.   Reginald Garrigou-Lagrange, *Reality: A Synthesis of Thomistic Thought*, Trans. by Patrick Cummins, (St. Louis: B. Herder Book Co., 1958), p. 192

32.   Aquinas, *Summa Theologica*, I Q. 76. Art. 2

33.   Ibid., I Q. 76, Art. 1

34.   Ibid., I Q. 75, Art. 6

35.   Aquinas, *Summa Theologica*, I Q. 75, Art. 6

36.   Ibid.

37.   Aquinas, *Commentary on De Anima*, a. 14 corp.

38.   Aquinas, *Summa Theologica*, I Q. 93, Art.5

94

39. Ibid., I Q. 93, Art. 4

40. Ibid.

41. A.D. Sertillanges, *Foundations of Thomistic Philosophy* Trans. by Godfrey Anstruther, (Springfield, Illinois: Templegate Publishers), undated, p. 229

42. Ibid., p. 284

43. Aquinas, *Summa Theologica*, I, Q. 14, Art. 1

44. Hans Kung, *The Incarnation of God*, Trans. by: J.R. Stephenson, (New York: Crossroad: 1987), p. 531

45. Richard Woods, *Eckhart's Way*, Wilmington, Delaware: Michael Glazier, 1986), p. 11-14

46. Jeanne Ancelet-Hustache, *Meister Eckhart and the Rhineland Mystics*, Trans. by Hilda Graef, (New York: Harper Torchbooks, 1957), p. 5

47. Woods, 1986, p. 154

48. Reiner Schurmann, *Meister Eckhart: Mystic and Philosopher*, (Bloomington: Indiana University Press, 1978), p. 104

49. Eckhart, D.W.I., Sermon 6; cited in *Meister Eckhart: The Essential Sermons, Commentaries, Treatises, and Defence*, Trans, by Edmund Colledge and Bernard McGinn (New York: Paulist Press, 1981), p. 183

50. Eckhart, D.W.I. Sermon 4; Cited in *Meister Eckhart, Teacher and Preacher*, Bernard McGinn, Ed. (New York: Paulist Press, 1986), p. 251

51. Schurmann, 1978 p. 106

52. Woods, 1986, p. 88

53. Eckhart, Sermon "Nolite timere eos"; cited in Reiner Schurmann, 1978, p. 115

54. Eckhart, Sermon D.W. 77; Cited in Woods, 1986, p. 94

55. Eckhart, Sermon 52 II D.W.; cited in *Meister Eckhart Essential Sermons*, 1981, p. 200

56. Eckhart, D.W. I Sermon 6

57.   Meister Eckhart, D.W. I; Sermon 6, cited in Meister Eckhart, *Essential Sermons,* 1981, p. 188-189

58.   Eckhart D.W. I; Sermon 9, cited in MeisterEckhart, *Teacher and Preacher,* 1986, p. 257. The translators note that "understanding" may be a more acceptable translation of Vernunftigkeit rather than the word intellect with which I strongly agree. There is an immediacy and directness implied in understanding not present in the more cognitive, differentiating process known as intellect.

59.   Ibid., Sermon 69, D.W. III, p. 313

60.   Ibid., p. 314

61.   Ibid.

62.   Meister Eckhart, D.W. I; Sermon 24, cited in *Meister Eckhart, Teacher and Preacher*, 1986, p. 284-285

63.   The notion that the operations of self serve as a living mirror of the Absolute was to remain dormant for almost 500 years until resurrected by G.W.F. Hegel as will be discussed in detail in Chapter 5.

64.   Meister Eckhart, "On Detachment" cited in *Meister Eckhart, Essential Sermons,* 1981, p. 291

65.   Ibid., p. 287

66.   Matthew Fox, *Breakthrough*, 1980, p. 9

67.   Reiner Schurmann, 1978, p. 59

68.   Eckhart, D.W. I Sermon 4; cited in *Meister Eckhart, Teacher and Preacher*, 1986, p. 250

69.   Schurmann, 1978, p. 93

70.   Eckhart, D.W. I Sermon 16B; cited in *Meister Eckhart, Teacher and Preacher*, 1986, p. 276-277

71.   Eckhart, Sermon "Et ecce homo erat in Ierusalem," cited in Schurmann, 1978, p. 107

72.   Woods, 1986, p. 61

73.   Eckhart, D.W. II, Sermon 52; Cited in *Meister Eckhart Essential Sermons,* 1976, p. 203

74.   Ibid., p. 202

75.   Woods, 1986, p. 111

76.   See footnotes 51 and 69, particularly noting Eckhart's sermon D.W. I,
       Sermon 4

77.   Meister Eckhart, D.W. I, Sermon 9; cited in *Meister Eckhart, Teacher and
       Preacher*, 1986, p. 256

CHAPTER IV

THE TRANSITION TO THE MODERN PERIOD

The predominant legacy of the post-Biblical era from Augustine through the Middle Ages was an ever-deepening split between personhood and the historical process. What had begun in the Biblical era as a rich duality **within** selfhood had become a pervasive dualism **around** the self. The more the self (as soul) was safely left in the hands of a transcendent, eternal God, the more it became a static "thing", itself timeless and eternal, cut off from the life of the universe in which it must participate.

As we reached the end of the Middle Ages, personhood found its validation through the static identity of God and soul. This was not an identity gained through any historical process, but a **given**, timeless union of eternal substances. Not only did this cut self off from its own history, it removed selfhood from a changing and becoming universe. And so the outcome of the seeking for a foundation to human identity was the creation of an autonomous, timeless self placed in the care of a remote, largely unreachable God.

Even the noble efforts of Aquinas and Meister Eckhart could not overcome these limitations, the one because of his exclusive reliance upon Reason-based forms to describe the life of self, the other because of his exclusive reliance upon the path of negation through which he hoped to unify personhood. Be that as it may, the tidal wave of scientific inquiry was about to wash over this medieval arrangement leaving in its wake problems which are still with us today.

Our task in this chapter is to understand the search for solutions to this breaking-up of an artificial divine-human unity, a process begun by the Renaissance. In the transition to the modern era (1500 to 1800 A.D.) there are four great scholars who represent the most notable attempts at resolving this problem of human identity. These four individuals are Rene Descartes, David Hume, Immanuel Kant, and J.G. Fichte. Each in his own way was searching for truth about the self, God, and the divine/human relationship, with sharply different conclusions in each case.

Rene Descartes (1596 - 1650)

Of all the contributors to human self-definition in the post-medieval era, Descartes is without a doubt among the most notable. He is a pivotal figure in our Western understanding of identity and self-consciousness, and in a sense everything we say today about selfhood, about the so-called subject/object split, and about the self-world relation has been impacted by his dualistic conclusions. Although Descartes is much maligned these days, his perspective remains alive within Western thinking, particularly his division of matter from spirit and his emphasis upon the primacy of mathematical thinking for discovering what is real.

The Cartesian Method

It is correctly said of Descartes that he is one of the founders of modern epistemology, the science of knowledge.[1] Descartes gained his epistemological breakthrough by virtue of a truly revolutionary approach. His hope was to develop a methodology whereby unconditional certainty and security could be provided for human beings concerning what is real. The burning questions for Descartes are "What can I really know?" and "Upon what can I really depend?" To gain such certainty persons must be able to discover an unshakable foundation of truth for themselves.

Methodologically, Descartes took the novel approach to trying to negate or doubt anything which is open to the least bit of questioning, "to see if afterwards there remained anything in my belief that was entirely certain."[2] It turns out that nothing offers such certainty, that all the **contents** of human consciousness can have their "reality" eroded via doubting negation. In other words, all data entering human awareness can be disputed based upon the inevitable human capacity for error, distortion, and the non-reliability of sense impressions.

But at the very apex of such doubting Descartes stumbled across his great solution:

> But immediately afterwards I became aware that while I decided thus to think that everything was false, it followed necessarily that I who thought thus must be something, and observing that this truth: **I think, therefore I am**, was so certain and so evident that all the most extravagant suppositions of the skeptics were not capable of shaking it, I judged that I could accept it without scruple as the first principle of the philosophy I was seeking.[3]

In the very act of thinking Descartes finds his abiding, indestructible foundation. Certainty has come in the form of the "I" which thinks.

By identifying human essence with the process of thinking, Descartes gives formal birth to the human ego as the center of consciousness. The basis of human identity becomes the capacity to think. Descartes elaborates:

> I thereby concluded that I was a substance, of which the whole essence or nature consists in thinking, and which, in order to exist, needs no place and depends on no material thing; so that this "I", that is to say the mind by which I am what I am, is entirely distinct from the body, and even that it is easier to know than the body and moreover, that even if the body were not it would not cease to be all that it is.[4]

It is painfully obvious as we read these words that the dualism which became so problematic in earlier centuries has taken an even sharper form in Descartes. Even Aquinas, who gave primacy to the operations of knowing, allowed for an intimate union of body and soul, but in Descartes the matter/spirit split has been pushed beyond what even most Platonists - the champions of dualism - would allow. Why, then, is this so-called "contribution" of Descartes not simply overlooked as a massive leap backwards and dismissed outright? What could possibly have been accomplished to be of any value to us?

The Primacy of the Ego

Until Descartes, all particular beings including human beings were largely considered to be objects "supported by an abiding God who gave them their reality."[5] By proposing that the thinking ego is the source of its own permanence, Descartes replaces both the Greek metaphysical and Christian theistic solutions to the identity problem with his abiding and transcendent human ego. This thinking ego now becomes the reference point against which reality must be measured. The conscious ego becomes the supreme object with everything else subject to it. Descartes has found his Absolute!

It is most ironic that Descartes' intent was in fact quite the opposite of what he accomplished. His hope was to rescue faith and thereby God from the creeping tentacles of the skeptics who were increasingly tearing down the theocentric universe of the Middle Ages. Descartes thought he could provide sufficient "proof" for God's existence by first establishing the certainty of mental process, and by concluding that if this irrefutable "mind" has the idea of God within it, surely God must exist![6] But in spite of this "proof" a great reversal occurs: God is now at the mercy of the doubting but supreme ego. The tables have been turned on God.

In the midst of universal doubt, one item of certainty emerges - the ego which knows it doubts. This Cartesian ego "doubts" or better said, "thinks itself" into existence. By thinking itself into being, real ontological status is granted to this ego which is capable of grasping its own reality. Because this ego which doubts sees itself, the ego as object is identical with the ego as subject. Or, said another way, the ego is its own subject and object because (1) its reality i.e. its thoughts are immediately available to it (thinking and being are one), and (2) no reality has validity outside of it (the ego is the center of the universe). In short, the thinking ego becomes the carrier of human identity. Again restated, ego and self are one.

Great implications leap out of this Cartesian conclusion that ego and self are one, an assumption persisting through to our day and age. The "thinking" ego becomes a fixed and permanent structure, tying together the flow of consciousness, thereby seemingly supplying the desperately sought-after unity of human identity. For some who followed Descartes this unity of ego and self was seen in a purely "objective" way, as the simple continuity provided by memory (John Locke and David Hume); for others, the unity took on more "subjective" form as the

permanent "I" or subject which ties together all experience (Immanuel Kant).[7]
Twentieth Century Ego Psychology including the later Sigmund Freud and Heinz
Hartmann among others, adhered to the latter approach by seeing the ego as the
organizing capacity of consciousness, with all other "facets" of human identity
brought into unity by this ego. While 20th Century Ego Psychology has granted
the ego far more complexity and richness than did Descartes, even Freud could not
fully grasp that an ego is not only in relationship with an objective world but also
with itself. Nevertheless, we must acknowledge that Freud did open the door to the
ego's encounter with itself through (1) the concept of narcissism and (2) the
superego which served as a forerunner to the later psychoanalytic self construct.

Be that as it may, Descartes' doctrine of personhood makes the ego the
subject and object of human consciousness in the sense that the ego is given
automatic unity and structural cohesion independent of any experiences it may have.
This "solution" is of course not unique to Descartes. The Platonic tradition had
long proposed a constant and abiding subject, a self or soul which is self-contained,
ensuring permanence within the passing flow of time. What makes Descartes so
noteworthy is the pivotal role he gives to the **human thinking subject** as the
abiding entity which holds together human identity. In so giving birth to the human
ego, Descartes gives a powerful and legitimate boost to the search for selfhood,
even as he divides the universe into two completely separate realms: the material
and the spiritual.

The Consequences of Cartesian Dualism

The abiding permanence of the ego, its so-called "substantiality", has had
great appeal throughout the centuries for the reason that it seemingly eliminates
ambiguity at the very heart of human identity. A modern dualist can therefore offer
a very "comforting" definition of selfhood:

> The self or person is not the particular mental events that make up
> his life, or any shape or pattern of them but the being or the entity,
> or subject who has them and remains **Identical*** in the varied
> course of them.[8]

The persistence of these notions of permanence and substantiality reveals a deep
yearning for stability and certainty, a searching for an unshakable foundation to

reality and personhood. With the continuing advance of science the old theistic foundation was eroding, forcing Descartes to find a new foundation for identity, in this case the self-contained ego whose thinking-capacity could not be denied. Perhaps now, thought Descartes, God and ego could share the ontological status of substantiality and unchangeableness.

But how did Descartes understand this notion of substance and how did it help ease his anxiety about change and God's relation to a changing universe? Descartes explains:

> By substance, we can understand nothing else than a thing which so exists that it needs no other thing in order to exist. And in fact only one single substance can be understood which clearly needs nothing else, namely God ... Created substances, however, whether corporal or thinking, may be conceived under this common concept: for they are things which need only the concurrence of God in order to exist...[9]

For Descartes, God alone is substance, although certain created or finite substances are also self-sufficient in the sense that they need only the support of God in order to exist. The created ego (or immaterial soul) is such a created substance whose essence (to think or have thoughts) it never loses. If it lost this ability it could not know or be known, hence it would no longer exist.[10]

Substance, then, is that which is indivisible, uniform, and self-sufficient. God, as suggested, serves as the primary substance, with body and mind (ego) derived but separate substances. The essence of spiritual substance is thinking (ego) while the essence of the material substance (body) is extension in space and time. All other properties of spiritual "substance" such as imagining, willing, or reflecting are modes of its one essence, namely, thinking.[11]

The appeal of this formula is its simplicity, its neat separation of the material and immaterial realms, and its uniformity. By eliminating developmental and time/space criteria from mind, the thinking ego gains a static unity with God while at the same time being able to transcend the ravages of the material universe. Eternal unity is guaranteed with harmony insured. But what price must be paid for this comfort?

The implications of Descartes' "solution" are enormous. A first consequence of the infusion of substantiality into the ego is that it completely destroys the unity of body and self. A pure self-sufficient ego does not require a body (nor a history) for its existence, but it simply "possesses" that body with which it interacts. But even a dualist must account for some means of interaction between matter and spirit which Descartes proposes via the "pineal gland" located between the hemispheres of the brain.[12]

The far-fetched nature of this "solution" underscores the extent to which the matter/spirit relation remained a problem which Descartes could not resolve with his two-substance model. When the ego as mind is completely separate and independent the laws of the physical universe are not applicable to it, just as the human body becomes reduced to physical matter subject only to the laws of motion, thereby rendering it a machine.[13] Body and spirit remain permanently separated.

A second consequence of Cartesianism concerns the nature of "truth". Since truth or certainty is visible only via thinking, only the activity of thinking uncovers reality. "Experiential" paths to truth including the pathways of feeling and inclination become suspect. Mathematical models alone can uncover what is true. Since mathematical models come closest to certainty, that which is measurable and quantifiable is most certain.[14] We find here the seeds of a one-sided empiricism which equates truth only with the numerically quantifiable.

What is more troublesome than mere methodology, however, concerns the primary ontological status given to the thinking ego. As noted, Descartes places essence (self-contained Being) in the hands of the knowing ego. Since the ego is its own subject and object, objects in the universe (including other human beings) are perceived as being separate from the knowing subject "as something placed there by and for the subject."[15] To gain reality everything becomes an **object** for the ego which is its own **subject** and **object**. The human ego becomes its own reference point leaving the rest of reality separate from this ego and therefore subject to the ego's inquiry, control, and manipulation.

It would be grossly unfair to blame Descartes for all the ills of human egoism. What can be safely said is that Descartes' matter/spirit split accelerated the ego's separation from the wider reality of the world and the "living" connections within which an ego moves. Furthermore, in granting the ego a static, frozen existence at the right hand of a timeless God, Descartes eliminated developmental considerations from the ego while also cutting God off from this changing universe.

However, the development of human self-understanding may have needed a Descartes to shatter the medieval "fused" identity between God and transcendent, human self. What Descartes began was completed by Feuerbach, Nietzsche and Freud. In the end, Descartes' attempted reconciliation of science and faith failed. Nevertheless, often magnificent efforts were made to modify his Cartesian dualism, perhaps the most notable of which occurred in the person of Immanuel Kant. But before we discuss Kant's revolutionary attempt at reconciling these two worlds we must face the skepticism of David Hume who relentlessly attacked Descartes' imposition of eternal ego onto the world.

The Challenge of David Hume (1711 - 1776)

Hume was not the first scholar to attack notions of a split universe. Thomas Hobbes (1588-1679) and John Locke (1632-1704) had both challenged the idea that innate self-contained ideas are found in a separate spiritual realm cut off from matter. Locke, as the first great British empiricist, particularly challenged rationalism by proposing the possibility that mind is a "tabula rosa", a blank slate at birth having its contents constructed only by sense experience and subsequent reflection.

With these Enlightenment presuppositions in hand, Hume was well equipped to challenge the notion of a split-universe and the God-like transcendent ego which hovered over the "real" world of sensation and reflection. Descartes' great question "Of what can I be certain?", and its "I think therefore I am" answer, had seemingly settled once and for all the issue of what was real in the universe. But rather than challenge the reality of this Absolute directly, Hume redirected the inquiry by looking into the construct of the ego, this "I", which provided so-called certainty.

The Nature of Experience

Hume begins his challenge of Cartesian rationalism by asserting that perceptions of the mind are the only legitimate source of knowledge. These he divides into two classes (1) thoughts or ideas, and (2) sense impressions.[16] These two ways of obtaining data he distinguishes as either more or less "lively" referring to what we could call their immediacy, the directness of our experience of them. Hume suggests that sense impressions such as sight, touch, smell, and hearing, are more "lively", more direct, than the thoughts generated subsequent to data provided by the senses. For Hume our thoughts or ideas are "fainter" or once-removed from the immediacy of experience, yet nevertheless determined only by experience. Every awareness, concludes Hume, whether a sensation or a thought arising from sensation is necessarily distinct and isolated, a singular unit of experience.[17] How did he arrive at this conclusion?

Hume's particular argument hinges on the nature of the association between experiences and ideas. Descartes had argued (on the basis of causal convictions), that the mind uncovers the inherent unities which are built into the structure of reality. The glue which allows all of this to hang together is of course the permanently stable substance of the timeless ego.

For Hume such a law of inseparable connection simply does not fit with experience. What we experience as somehow "connected" is rather the result of our empirical generalizations. The human mind, he claims, has the capacity to simply associate its raw data of sensation or its ideas into patterns determined by the experience. As we look at Hume's specific attack upon the notion of self as substance we see more clearly how his argument unfolds.

Is There a Self?

Hume insists that there can be no talk of the "substance" of any object in the universe that is not simply a product of the qualities we attach to it. This is particularly true when it comes to this entity called "self". The following extended passage explains:

> There are some philosophers who imagine we are every moment intimately conscious of what we call our self; that we feel its existence and its continuance in existence; and are certain, beyond the evidence of a demonstration, both of its perfect identity and simplicity... Unluckily all those positive assertions are contrary to that very experience which is pleaded for them; nor have we any idea of **self**, after the manner it is here explained. For from what impression could this idea be derived ... But self or person is not any one impression, but that to which our several impressions and ideas are supposed to have a reference. If any impression gives rise to the idea of self, that impression must continue invariably the

same, through the whole course of our lives; since self is supposed
to exist after that manner ... For my part when I enter most
intimately into what I call **myself,** I always stumble on some
particular perception or other, of heat or cold, light or shade, love or
hatred, pain or pleasure. I can never catch **myself** at any time
without a perception, and can never observe anything but the
perception.[18]

Having cut through the notion of detached thought-processes, Hume arrives at his
famous "nothing but" pronouncement:

... they (selves) are nothing but a bundle or collection of different
perceptions, which succeed each other with an inconceivable
rapidity, and are in a perpetual flux and movement.[19]

There is no such thing as a stable, abiding self or ego insists Hume; any
continuity to consciousness or self-consciousness is simply an accumulation of
sensate perceptions. But if there is no subjective or objective thread tying
personhood together what becomes of human identity? How is it we have a sense
of personal identity with no "self" to maintain continuity?

The Dilemma of Personal Identity

If human consciousness consists only of the flow of successive
perceptions, what happens to our identity as persons? Hume answers this question
by analyzing the nature of identity which creates the dilemma in the first place. For
Hume it is important to distinguish between the identity of a singular object which
remains the same over time and the identity of several objects existing in
succession, yet seen as connected or related. In the first instance, suggests Hume,
a singular object alone cannot convey the idea of identity. Because one object is the
same as itself it carries the idea of **unity,** not **identity.**[20] For something to be
identical it must be the same as something else which implies at least two, in some
sort of relation. On the other hand, a multiplicity of objects cannot convey the idea
of identity since some distinction between objects is always found.[21] Therefore,
says Hume, since identity is not to be found in the one or the many it must lie in
something which is neither. To resolve this ambiguity Hume introduces the idea of
time or duration.

For Hume, time is the medium which causes us to distinguish between the one and the many. Since time means succession or duration, when a succession of the same object is perceived by us, **we** give it the idea of identity. Writes Hume:

> This fiction of the imagination almost universally takes place; and it is by means of it that a single object placed before us, and surveyed for any time without our discovering in it any interruption or variation, is able to give us a notion of identity.[22]

The key word here is **imagination**. Hume sees the human organism **projecting** the idea of identity or sameness-over-time onto objects including the so-called self. In other words, the resemblance with which I give myself the label "I" is but a trick of my mind as it works with the data presented to it. What prompts the error is a sloppiness on my part, a mistaking of identity for what is really resemblance. Hume's explanation reads as follows:

> The relation [of objects] facilitates the transition of the mind from one object to another, and renders its passage as smooth as if it contemplated one continued object. This resemblance is the cause of the confusion and mistake, and makes us substitute the notion of identity instead of that of related objects.[23]

Hume concludes with a final salvo which intends to strike down once and for all this idea of substantiality:

> In order to justify to ourselves this absurdity we often feign some new and unintelligible principle, that connects the objects together and prevents their interruption or variation. Thus we feign the continued existence of the perceptions of our senses to remove the interruption, and run into the notion of a **soul**, and **self**, and **substance,** to disguise the variation.[24]

The intensity of these words even today lets us appreciate their scandalous impact in his era. This radical skepticism not only broke apart the inert substantial unity of the soul which had persisted for 1500 years, it dislodged this "self" from the Divine support which had propped it up.

If Not a Self, What is There?

If human subjectivity is "nothing but" a bundle of different perceptions what meaning is there, if any, to the construct "I"? The ego for Hume is strictly the capacity for individual conscious experiences, with the perceived unity of the ego through time simply a product of the imagination. The ego in Hume is thus a moment-to-moment consciousness of experience with no abiding unity, coherence, or permanence. But Hume acknowledges that we **do** attribute permanence and identity to ourselves even though we do so erroneously. How does Hume explain this phenomenon?

Hume's answer is that identity is strictly a function of memory: "As memory alone acquaints us with the continuance and extent of this succession of perceptions, it is to be considered upon that count chiefly, as the source of personal identity."[25] Memory facilitates personal identity by creating a relation of resemblance among my perceptions. In other words, memory ties together units of experience by highlighting their association. Without memory, there is no identity. Most importantly, identity is not a property of any object including the ego; it is the unity of associations **we** place upon ourselves and upon our world.

The brilliance of Hume's challenge must be acknowledged even as we face its limits. To be sure, Descartes' ego as static, cosmic "object" had to be pulled off its pedestal. It should not come as too great a surprise to any reader that since the self is not a "thing" there is no way Hume could have found it.

The gift of Hume is that he brought a much needed empiricism to bear upon the question of human identity. Regrettably, much contemporary psychological reflection upon identity has remained stuck in reductionistic forms of empirical inquiry in which the operations of personal identity become broken into ever smaller and more fragmented bits and pieces. While modern behaviorism represents the outer limits of such reductive empiricism, empirical inquiry need not be divorced from the realities of unified human existence. In short, while Hume appropriately dismantled the eternal intellectual edifice called soul, mind, ego, and so forth, he could not satisfactorily account for the capacity for cohesion of "a self" which not only "puts together" the succession of associations allowing for a knowledge of a changing physical universe, but also the "holding together" of a subjective sense of personal identity. Hume seemed to negate the possibility of any unity or structural integrity to selfhood which would account for the maintenance of awareness of the continuity **and** diversity of objects over time, even objects as complex and varied as other selves. If the self were only a loose collection of associations it would surely be unable to grasp its own multifaceted unity within its wide-ranging fluctuations.

This critique notwithstanding, the skepticism of Hume found its most formidable opponent in the person of Immanuel Kant. Kant directly acknowledges the vital role Hume played in awakening him "from his dogmatic slumbers."[26] In being roused from his own Pietistic assumptions of artificial or "given" unities, Kant not only needed to overcome the skepticism of Hume, but the lingering dualisms left in the wake of Descartes. By confronting these increasingly polarized positions of the day another significant step forward was won.

Immanuel Kant (1742 - 1804):   Answer to Hume and Descartes

Immanuel Kant enters the scene at a critical point in the story. The dualism of Descartes which helped break open the medieval unity of reason and faith, God and Universe, had reached the skeptical dead end of Locke and Hume, resulting in the death of the artificially unified self. Kant was deeply affected by the split between science and faith which had arisen since the Renaissance. Hume had of course not only been attacking religious and moral claims upon truth, but also the Newtonian universe with its insistence that discernible underlying principles govern the workings of the universe, i.e. that the universe is ordered according to reason. Hume's skepticism had declared that there is no "necessary connection" between facts, that reason is simply the instrument we use for detecting relationships in the universe, with no basis for asserting that it is meaningfully ordered.[27]

In short, the challenge facing Kant was not simply to justify faith or reaffirm the unity of the physical universe, but to reconcile these two worlds to one another. Kant thus had to campaign against both **Empiricism** and **Rationalism**, the former because it reduced knowledge to one's perceptions in the tangible world, the latter assuming that the universe is completely rational with an orderly pattern readily visible in the world. We will discover that in responding to this challenge Kant remained very much a Cartesian - at least as far as method is concerned. By examining personal experience from a new vantage point, Kant hoped to discover a legitimate foundation for subjectivity thereby establishing a new basis for human identity. But behind this hope rested his main concern, namely, "the mutual defense and reconciliation of scientific knowledge and the practical values of morality and religion in a single 'systematic' view of the universe."28 By changing the way we understand experience, Kant replaced the Cartesian dualism of **mind vs. matter** with a Cartesianism of **kinds of experience** thereby profoundly affecting the way we understand the self.

Knowledge and the Kantian Self

Kant's *Critique of Pure Reason* contains in its introduction the phrase: "That all our knowledge begins **with** experience there can be no doubt."29 In tipping his hat to Hume, Kant acknowledges that the critical starting point is the fact of experience. Although knowledge begins with experience it does not follow for him that all that one knows arises **out of** experience.

Kant suggests that human beings bring certain "a priori" patterns or "capacities" to the experiencing event. This "a priori" process he distinguishes from "a posterior" knowledge which draws from prior empirical experience. To say it another way, Kant concludes that all knowledge contains an **experiential** component (primary data such as sense perceptions), and an **integrating** component (the conceptual organizing of primary data).30 Knowledge must contain these dual elements of **perception** and **conception**.

The capacity to conceptualize, i.e. judge or organize one's experience requires that the human organism be able to "put together" its experience into some meaningful pattern. This synthesizing capacity takes certain discernible forms which Kant calls categories (taken from Aristotle).31 These categories or types of judgment consist of (1) quantity, (2) quality, (3) relation and (4) modality.32 They represent the synthesizing operations by which an ego comes to know the objects of the world. This synthesizing capacity, the capacity to put things together, brings a unity to experience which implies for Kant a unity to that which has the experience i.e. a self. This unity of self can be experienced as can any object: it can become an object to itself.33

What is so profound about Kant's conclusion is that self, whatever else it may be, is no longer separate from the experience of objects. Human subjectivity can no longer be envisioned as an autonomous process **creating** the objects it encounters. Nevertheless, selfhood does something with its objects in the sense that it unifies them (for itself) in a certain way. It presents them to itself as a "unified representation" which in some way impacts the self.

As will be restated many times from this point forth in our study, self and object are not separate entities but "reciprocal elements in experience."[34] As one commentator has declared:

> If we start from object, we are led to self; if we begin with self, we are led to object. The experience of either one involves the experience of the other, and the experience of both depends on the prior occurrence of certain synthetical acts.[35]

Subject and object have been brilliantly interwoven in this Kantian vision of dynamic operations. But what are we to make of the self's a priori synthetic acts?

The Transcendental and Empirical Egos

In attempting to answer the question how one both **has** an experience and a **knowledge** of that experience, Kant proposes that we bring "something" to every experience. This something is the a priori synthetic act(s) which Kant calls "transcendental apperception" or the **transcendental ego**. It is transcendental because it is never directly experienced and simply serves as the basis for all experience, namely, the capacity to organize the subject and object components of experience according to the judgments identified above.

The **empirical ego** on the other hand is made up of the raw data of our experience, the foundation for which is the transcendental ego. It is the transcendental ego, however, which provides the unity, the categories, which makes the experience of the empirical ego and the world of objects possible. We should take note of Kant's extended description:

> The consciousness of oneself... is, with all our internal perceptions, empirical only, and always transient. There can be no fixed or permanent self in that stream of internal phenomena. It is generally called the internal sense, or the **empirical apperception** ...
>
> No knowledge can take place in us, no conjunction or unity of one kind of knowledge with another, without that unity of consciousness which precedes all data of intuition, and without reference to which no representation of objects is possible. This

pure, original and unchangeable consciousness I shall call **transcendental apperception** ...

The mind could never conceive the identity of itself in the manifoldness of its representations (and this a priori) if it did not clearly perceive the identity of its action, by which it subjects all synthesis of apprehension (which is empirical) to a transcendental unity and thus renders its regular coherence a priori possible.[36]

These difficult words represent a critical turning point in the Western understanding of the self. By dividing the self Kant is the first scholar to formally suggest an objective and subjective dimension to selfhood. On the one hand, there is the empirical ego - it is an empirical object like any other. Its thought and behavior can be studied like any other object in the world and it can provide us with usable, sensate data. All products of this ego such as feelings, moods, thoughts and behaviors, can be examined, observed, objectified, and classified just as one would classify any other object in the universe.

On the other hand, claims Kant, there are transcendent functions, the organizers of experience, which undergird and make possible all empirical experiences, namely the experiences of the empirical ego. For Kant this synthesizing capacity is the prerequisite for **any** recognition of the world of objects - even of the empirical self or ego. This transcendental ego provides the unity (makes the connections) which coalesces experience into meaningful patterns although it cannot be directly experienced.

It is worth noting that this synthesizing ego is a total departure from the Cartesian idea of ego as self-contained substance. For Kant the transcendental ego is **not** a given or a **static** thing, but a **process** or unifying function which gives selfhood its subjective cohesion. As helpful as this revolutionary shift might seem, however, one is left with the gnawing suspicion that all is not well in the land of the self. Its fatal flaws are soon to surface.

The Ego - Self Relation

To set the stage for this central problem which will reappear throughout the quest for selfhood, I must offer the reminder that Descartes' "thinking ego" unified consciousness (ego) in the form of a substantial, static, and immortal soul. This became no solution at all after Hume finished with it. His devastating critique finally reasserted once and for all the necessity of experience. But because experience is fragmented, transitory, and separated by time and space, no unity to personhood remained.

As Kant faced this dilemma, he had to explain how human consciousness, is unified, never mind the deeper question of self-conscious unity. His novel approach was to divide the ego into two separate (albeit unified) components. One portion (the empirical ego) is the data-collector facing a real world of objects, and the other portion (the transcendental ego) provides the unity which synthesizes or orders the experiences of the empirical ego.[37] In short, the **empirical ego** (objective ego) and **transcendental ego** (subjective self) are one. Ego and self in Kant are in **automatic** unity.

The problem this creates is that the "a priori" unity of the transcendental ego which "ties together" the experiences of the empirical ego remains independent of the experiences it in fact has. But how can the transcendental ego serve as the unifying ground of all experience without using experience to do so?

Kant suggests that the transcendental ego produces self-awareness by reflecting upon itself, but if this is so then this self-aware ego cannot also be identical with itself. It cannot be both fully known to itself and in some process of discovering itself.[38] How can it be both fully developed and bringing about its own development at the same time? Kant, when faced with this very dilemma can only conclude the following:

> I have no knowledge of myself as I am, but only as I appear to myself. The consequences of oneself is thus very far from being a knowledge of oneself.[39]

Kant's hasty retreat into a revised dualism which holds that the ego which knows, cannot know itself, does not eliminate the question. If an experiential foundation is essential for self-knowledge then the attainment of such knowledge should not be divorced from experiential criteria!

Several thorny questions emerge at this point: (1) Is self-awareness an automatic function of an ego, a built-in given in which an ego knows itself fully as self (Descartes)? (2) Does self-awareness emerge out of the subsequent reflection of the ego upon itself (Kant)? If so, ego and self cannot be the same, with Kant being unable to call upon the one to unify the other. (3) Is the self of self-awareness a product of the ego at all or is it perhaps given through a Universal self (J.G.Fichte and C.G. Jung)? (4) Do ego and self come into unity through some other as yet unknown process?

I have consistently challenged the first option, the "solution" of the substantialists who would have us believe that self-consciousness is somehow automatically given. But this still leaves unanswered the Kantian question whether self-awareness is born out of the ego's own activity, or by some other process. Before I proceed to consider the third option as represented by J.G.Fichte, it would be helpful to put Kant's revised dualism to rest.

Kantian Consequences

There are numerous consequences which grow out of Kant's revolutionary perspective. The first is that it challenges the Empiricists who conclude that there is no such thing as a self. Since the self is not a static substance, an object, one can never find such an objectified self. Not only does this step disarm the Empiricists, it undercuts the Rationalists who impose preset metaphysical concepts onto the workings of self and world. In one bold move, both positions are undermined. In this manner Kant is able both to free empirical inquiry from a metaphysical bias, and at the same time counter the reductionistic skepticism of Hume. Kant thus lays the foundation for a genuine empirical psychology - a study of the empirical ego - although Kant pays a high price for this contribution.

We have before us then, the new Cartesianism of Kant, not one of **thought** vs. **matter**, of **"eternal"** mind vs. a **transient** decaying world as in Descartes, but a dualism of **experience**, essentially two worlds each with their own guiding principles. The one world is the world of science knowable through **understanding**, which relies only upon the data of experience and comprehends the particular and finite objects of the universe, including the empirical ego. Such understanding provides knowledge of things in space and time but **not** of their underlying unities.

The second world is the world of absolutes such as God, morality, freedom, the transcendent ego, and so forth. This is the world of universal realities supposedly outside our sphere of experience. Our access to this world is not direct, but through **reason** we apply the categories which arise out of experience to this larger universe, including of course the transcendent ego and its God. Tragically, however, we cannot know this other world **in our experience**, but can only intuit its reality through the data arising from the tangible world of phenomena. This radical separation of the world of **particular knowledge** from the **knowledge of ultimates** creates much alienation for the life of self. Science and faith, knowledge and reason, objective self (ego) and subjective self all have their legitimate realm but have little to do with one another.

Thus, the Kantian legacy concerning selfhood is a mixed blessing. On the one hand a great service was provided by placing selfhood fully within experience. A self is a self **only** because of its encounter with the objects which enter its life. Regrettably, however, this Kantian self (or ego) is but a collection of all the data which defines its existence. Its true nature is an unknowable substrate fully self-contained.

As I will restate numerous times in this study, a self that is only an accumulation of its self-images is still a dead self. It has no life, direction, energy, or characteristics of its own, but lives on "borrowed" impulses, in Kant's case the accumulated representations of the empirical ego.

Without a doubt, the most problematic feature of Kant's self is its empirical/transcendental split. We are left with no direct experience whatsoever of our own inwardness or subjectivity, claims Kant; what we do experience of ourselves and others is always mediated by the unknowable forms (categories of the transcendental ego).[40] In short, the Kantian self is only a **by-product** of the encounter between subject and object. What Kant could not answer is how such a self comes to self-consciousness and how it comes to the unity of purpose seemingly inherent to selfhood. To answer this unavoidable question we must turn to the work of J.G. Fichte, who not only paved the way for Hegel's brilliant efforts thirty years later, but whose insights and limitations are most relevant to our contemporary scene.

J.G. Fichte (1762 - 1814) and the Ego-Self Relation

To place Fichte in perspective I would draw our attention to comments made by C.G. Jung in the forward of a book by Mehlich entitled *Fichte's Psychology and Its Relation to the Present* (1935). In his comments Jung marvels at the conclusions of a figure such as Fichte, who, working from the perspective of philosophical idealism arrived at conclusions remarkably similar to Jung's psychological observations. Jung correctly identifies Fichte as belonging to the Romanticist stream of German Idealism which was not as interested in the object of experience as much as the subject of experience, what Jung calls "a knowing of the knower."[41]

As I have just noted, Hume's dethroning of Reason (intellect) as an autonomous and inherent structure of reality became replaced by Kant's view that the laws of rationality are the means by which persons order the world thereby gaining an understanding of it. But in reopening the possibility that there is legitimacy to human subjectivity, Kant maintains a dualism which allows the ego to know the objects of the universe but not itself. This leaves open the question of how the knowing ego comes to its own self-knowledge, a question which haunts human self-inquiry to this day.

We would be sadly mistaken if we concluded that the issue of the ego-self relation is only relevant for vague historical reasons. What makes Fichte so noteworthy as one who intensively wrestled with this relationship is that so much contemporary psychological thinking either ignores the question, or assumes an ego-self unity without bothering to understand its dynamics or exploring the path by which such unity becomes actualized.

Fichte, although a thoroughgoing Kantian, was very aware of the problems created by Kant's dualist, two-self perspective: the empirical ego tied to the world, and the transcendent ego reflecting the unity of the transcendent order. While Fichte was not necessarily able to overcome these difficulties, he nevertheless serves as a key transition figure between the dualistic self of Kant and the more dynamically integrated self of Hegel.

The Fichtean Proposal: The Ego as Absolute

Kant, as had Hume before him, asserted the centrality of experience, but in such a way that the knower of experience cannot be known. Thought and being stand apart in Kant and this became completely unacceptable to Fichte for whom the search for unity overrode all other concerns.

Fichte's "solution" presents itself in his best known work *The Science of Knowledge* (1794) in which he maintains the centrality of experience, but shifts his gaze to the "I" which, he claims, in some way unifies thought and experience and thereby itself. The question Fichte sets for himself is how consciousness comes to a sufficient unity to allow it to make knowledge-claims, and more importantly, what basis there might be for proclaiming a unity to self-awareness.

Fichte begins his inquiry by claiming that all experience contains particular contents of awareness which he calls representations (Vorstellungen).[42] Of these representations some have the quality of **freedom**, others the quality of **necessity**. The first type involves those products of the imagination which Fichte considers the spontaneous products of mental activity not directly determined by events occurring outside of oneself. The free flow of fantasy would illustrate such "representations".

The remaining representations carry a quality of "necessity" and include those awarenesses which impose themselves upon me directly through the engagement with a particular situation. Both patterns of awareness, insists Fichte, are based upon experience: "A finite rational being has nothing beyond experience."[43] But what is Fichtean "experience" and how does human awareness become unified in it?

Every act of consciousness contains at least two components: something experienced, and something experiencing, an **object** and a **subject**, claims Fichte. Through abstraction or what Fichte calls the "freedom of thought" we are able to separate out these two inseparable components to experience. As we raise ourselves "above" experience by reflecting upon it two options present themselves. Either we explain experience by highlighting the role of the **object**, or we do so by highlighting the role of the **subject**. The first option Fichte calls the path of **dogmatism**, the second, **idealism**.[44]

If emphasis is placed upon the **object** as determining reality, then materialism and determinism results.[45] This option philosophical thought calls the "thing-in-itself", a strictly object-determined explanation of consciousness which requires that the object be absolute. Such an ego is completely dependent upon and determined by objects making passive dependence the essence of human subjectivity.[46]

118

In rejecting this option Fichte proposes the "self-in-itself", an affirmation of the **subject as absolute** in the sense that the ego in some fashion shapes itself as it enters into experience. Fichte's hope is to provide selfhood with a legitimate basis for its freedom thereby avoiding the complete passivity and determinism of the dogmatic position. While Fichte (to his great detriment) cannot allow the self to be determined by its objects, he also realizes that this self cannot do without objects since that would violate its basic experiential foundation.

All that seems left for Fichte to conclude is that the **subject** determines reality. In technical language this option has been called "subjective idealism" and in its extreme form the subjective principle is completely determinative with the objective world simply a shadowy mirage of subjective processes. Some of Fichte's contemporaries, most notably Shelling and Hegel, accused Fichte of just such subjectivism.[47] Such charges no doubt prompted Fichte's "clarifications" and it remains to be seen whether Fichte was able to overcome the difficulties which came with his idealist position. But before we examine the inevitable limits of a purely idealist framework, we must be clear about the Fichtean contributions. These include (1) an understanding of selfhood as both active **and** passive; (2) an insistence upon a subject-object interaction within selfhood, and (3) a vision of self as finite **and** infinite.

The Self as Active and Passive

Philosophical thinking prior to Fichte had rendered human subjectivity largely passive, whether in the form of empiricism which absolutized the object (Hume), or in the form of a theocentrism which allowed the human soul to share in the eternal unchangeableness of God (Augustine, Aquinas, Descartes). Between these extreme positions jumped Fichte who declared that the human subject is above all - active.

> The (ego) is absolutely active, and merely active - that is our absolute presupposition. From this we have inferred in the first place a passivity of the (not-ego), insofar as the latter is to determine the (ego) ...[48]

Because a subject-object interaction is crucial for Fichte two forms of action are envisioned by him, these being (1) **positing** (setzen) i.e. to set in place, and (2) **striving**, to seek or struggle for.[49]

Positing refers to that action of the ego which does something to the objects of its phenomenal world. It not only engages them but uses them to determine itself - it sets them in place for itself even as it is impacted or "shaped" in some way by these objects. Fichte's proposition reads:

> Both (ego) and (not-ego) are posited, in and through the (ego), as capable of **mutually** limiting **one another**, in such a fashion, that the reality of the one destroys that of the other, and **vice versa**.[50]

Two conclusions emerge out of this proposition for Fichte: (1) **The (ego) "engages" the (not-ego) as limited by the (ego), and (2) The (ego) "engages"itself as limited by the (not-ego)**.[51] At first glance these conclusions seem contradictory with the ego supposedly active in both instances, but somehow limited or "driven into itself" both by itself and by the object.

Rather than canceling each other out, these principles represent the action of the ego in engaging the world as governed by the mutual limitation one places upon the other. If the emphasis is placed upon the ego **"creating itself"** as limited by the not-ego (i.e. by what is other or object) we affirm the ego's **activity**; if the emphasis is placed upon the **limitation** imposed by what is not-ego, we affirm the ego's **passivity**.

The question nevertheless remains, is the ego **active**, shaping itself, or is it **passive**, being shaped by the objects of the world? To resolve this dilemma Fichte relies upon the now famous dialectic, more fully developed by Hegel, which defines the movements of human subjectivity using the formula: thesis, antithesis, and synthesis. How might this formula resolve the ambiguity?

Fichte considers the ego to be active in the sense that it infinitely seeks to move beyond itself (referring to the activity of **striving** to be discussed below), but in so doing it bumps into what is not-ego thereby being driven back into itself in the form of **reflection**. This two-way process; (1) a seeking what is outside of itself, and (2) being confronted by an inevitable barrier (Anstoss) which drives the ego back into itself through reflection, allows the ego to come to its own self-discovery (posit itself) as shaped (determined) by what is not itself. In other words, the synthesizing capacity of selfhood refers to the active **engagement with** and **internalization of** those limiting objects which allow the ego to define itself as self. This proposal stands as the most noble of Fichte's contributions which I will trace through 200 years of further development to our own day and age.

The Self as Subject and Object

That selfhood concerns the engagement of ego with not-ego emerges consistently in Fichte and will become central for subsequent understandings of the operations of selfhood. In short, the very subjectivity of self cannot be understood in isolation from the otherness which impacts its existence. But, Fichte wonders, if otherness is so central to selfhood, how does one arrive at a sense of "self-ness" without it being completely determined by something outside of oneself thereby undercutting the nature of self as subject?

Fichte's answer is to suggest that the self is an "absolute subject." How is this to be understood? Fichte writes:

> **That whose being or essence consists simply in the fact that it posits itself as existing,** is the self as absolute subject. As it **posits** itself so it **is**; and as it **is** so it posits itself; and hence the self is absolute and necessary for the self. What does not exist for itself is not a self.[52]

To translate, Fichte claims that what is not conscious of itself is not a self. Selfhood, as self-consciousness, is fully and immediately mine, without mediation by some other agent. "Was I a self before I came to self-consciousness?" Fichte is asked, to which he replies "No," for the self exists "only as it is conscious of itself." The very question, he suggests, is based upon an artificial separation between the self as subject (me) and the self as object (ego) to itself (I).[53]

This unity of the self within itself, he claims, exists **absolutely**:

> **To posit oneself** and **to be** are, as applied to the self, perfectly identical ... Furthermore, the self-positing (ego) and the existing self are perfectly identical, one and the same. The (ego) is that **which** it posits itself to be; and it posits itself as that which it is. Hence **I am absolutely what I am**.

In a strong summary added in 1802 Fichte writes:

the self is a necessary identity of subject and object: a subject-object; and is so absolutely, without further mediation.[54]

A thorny problem presents itself for Fichte at this point. If the self (as self-conscious ego) "sets" or "creates" itself into self-awareness through some sort of interaction with not-self, would this not make self a product of the interaction? If this were the case would not the images or representations generated out of this interaction be the mediating agent which ties subject and object together? Or, correspondingly, would this not appropriately allow for the possibility that self in some form **requires** non-self in order to come to its identity? In both instances a surprising answer is given.

Writing in 1800 *(The Vocation of Man)* Fichte first of all rejects the notion that the mental images with which I present myself to myself constitute the essence of selfhood. If the self were constructed of mere mental representations I would be deceived into concluding that only my thoughts are real, retorts Fichte.[55] Is there then a legitimacy to the object? Not really, replies Fichte! The object necessarily provides the "content" of consciousness, the "this and that," but not the **form** of selfhood, he insists.[56] That there even is consciousness and self-consciousness, and that its life takes particular forms lies in the **subject** and **not** in the object as far as he is concerned. Fichte thus declares:

> The reason why the subjective **mirrors** lies in it itself. The reason why just this and nothing else is **mirrored** lies in the objective.[57]

But this still leaves unanswered the question of what ties together subject and object within me.

Fichte asks himself this same question as follows: "How does the thing (my ego) get inside me? What is the connection between the subject, myself, and the object of my knowledge, (my ego)?" His surprising reply is that the question is simply irrelevant:

> This question does not arise about **me**. I have knowledge in myself for I am intelligence. What I am, thereof I **know**, because I am it. And that which I know immediately simply by existing that is **me**, because I immediately know about it. Here no connection between subject and object is required; my own being is this connection, I am

subject and object: and this subject-objectivity, this return of knowledge into itself is what I designate with the concept "I".[58]

Fichte's "answer" to the question of what ties together subject and object is that there is no tie - it is intrinsic to the nature of "I".

For Fichte, then, the unity of subject and object, of self and ego, is the product of the "I" by virtue of the "return of knowledge into itself."[59] Indeed, the ego is made into the automatic agent of unity through its own reflective action thereby undermining the experiential foundation which seemed so central for him. Fichte acknowledges that coming-to-consciousness requires an inevitable separation of subject and object - there must be a consciousness of something. But Fichte insists upon a unity which is **prior** to their separation and this unity is given with the Absolute Ego or Self (here capitalized to represent its primordial oneness). The reason I know myself as me is that I automatically attain this unity through the ego's immediate capacity for knowing.

Again, the lingering question first directed at Kant reappears: Can an ego unify itself independent of its experiences? The answer would seem to be no, which is where Fichte runs into his unresolvable contradiction. An ego which acts as a unifying agent cannot be identical with what it unifies. Such a conclusion would not only violate the subject-object distinction, it would eliminate space/time and developmental criteria from selfhood.

Fichte was not oblivious to these problems, but before we elaborate upon his proposed "solutions" a final polarity to Fichtean selfhood deserves attention.

The Self as Finite and Infinite

Fichte's preoccupation with the self's ability to posit itself (create itself) makes him a champion of the self's autonomous freedom (even as it is eventually collapsed). This is a freedom not only to be actualized in thought, but more importantly, in **action**. But if self is in fact determined by the limits and constraints of its environment, a built-in limitation inherent in its subject-object structure, how can it still be regarded as free, never mind infinite?

Self as active agent is understood by Fichte in the two forms we have come to know as (1)**positing** (to set in place) and (2)**striving**. The former refers to the ego's engagement of the objects (otherness) of the world, including becoming object to itself; the latter to its efforts at transcending these objects: Fichte writes:

> The (ego) is infinite, but merely in respect to its striving; it strives to be infinite. But the very concept of striving already involves finitude, for that to which there is no **counterstriving** is not striving at all. If the (ego) did more than strive, if it had an infinite causality, it would not be a (self): it would not posit itself, and would therefore be nothing.[60]

Fichte's ego is infinite, not with regard to what it **is**, but with regard to what it infinitely seeks **to be**. The limitations of the external world check this striving of the ego through the imposition of the world's boundaries which drives the ego back into itself. But the very nature of "ego-hood", its reflecting upon itself, depends upon objects in what Fichte calls "**a drive towards the object**."[61] This seeking of the object is an infinite (endless) seeking resulting in **feeling** as the subjective manifestation of the satisfaction (or non-satisfaction) of having found (or not found) the object, including its very own self. Furthermore, the ego experiences a yearning for a new fulfillment or self-realization as new self-defining objects are sought. The full range of human feelings thus reveals the subjective condition of the ego in its seeking of the objects through which it shapes itself.

This **striving** and **mirroring** represents the dual life of the Fichtean self: its infinite seeking and the constant limitations by which it becomes a self. The tension between infinite striving and ever-present limitation is the ground of human subjectivity (feelings) and action in the world, and again reveals Fichte's efforts at maintaining a unity for the self.[62] Feeling and action, thinking and being are not separate functions but manifestations of the unity of purpose he calls a self.

Fichte's insistence upon selfhood as eternally or infinitely active has a two-fold purpose, on the one hand intending to insure the self's freedom, on the other hand tying it to a larger purpose or universal activity he calls God. This eternal impulse within self is beyond all mental products or representations as far as he is concerned and speaks of the essence of selfhood, which is the capacity to act.[63] Fichtean personhood is no longer grounded in Descartes' "**I think**, therefore I **am**," but through self-validating activity: "**I act**, therefore I **am**."

While modern psychological scholarship will resurrect the notion of self as a center of initiative, Fichte sees selfhood as much more than simply goal-directed, but a quality of activity which expresses unbridled **freedom** and self-sufficiency. He writes:

> There is in me a drive to absolute independent self-activity. I find nothing more intolerable than only to be in another, for another, and through another. I want to be and to become something for and through myself. I feel this drive just as soon as ever I become aware of myself; it is indivisibly united with the consciousness of myself.[64]

The harshness of these words is jolting. It reveals a self which must devour otherness to maintain itself. Its very identity is maintained through annihilation and detachment, a result painfully noted by contemporary feminist scholarship. Tragically, the centrality of object-engagement for self-maintenance has evolved in Fichte into a model of self which must posit another as opponent in order to find and maintain itself. As Catherine Keller, for one, has noted, this is a self in oppositional transcendence.[65] But this is not the only fatal flaw of Fichtean selfhood.

Fichtean Consequences

By 1802 Fichte had become increasingly aware that the self cannot be the sole agent of its own unity. Rather than attribute the unity of self-consciousness to the role of the object toward the ego, which would have left the ego object-dependent, Fichte retreats even further into his subjective Idealism for a solution. This "solution" is to move further away from the reality of finite objects toward the Absolute Ego or Self.

Fichte's final answer takes the form of an arrogant religious mysticism in which self-consciousness becomes a manifestation of God.[66] Since the ego cannot be the agent of its own unity, nor can this unity be attributed to its experience of finite objects, selfhood is "inserted" into unity with itself by virtue of its reflection of the unity of God.

In true Romantic fashion, Fichte bases his new unity upon a spiritualized view of reality which holds that the Absolute permeates all that is, with nature, life, and human self-consciousness simply reflecting or manifesting Absolute Self. Not only is the Absolute knowable in the human self because of this manifestation, but more importantly, Absolute Self realizes itself through human consciousness which it permeates. All that is, is but a means of the Absolute's self-realization.[67] What we are left with in Fichte is a grand monistic vision of a universal Absolute Self actualizing itself through finite human selves. It is no wonder that Jung was so pleasantly surprised to see the affinity between his own archtypal Self and Fichte's Absolute Self.

All but the staunchest Idealist would be hard pressed to find this solution an improvement. The end result of Fichte's model is again the imposition of an a priori, non-historical unity onto human identity which needs time, history, and relatedness to develop. In the end both human autonomy and inter-dependence becomes sacrificed by Fichte as self is swallowed up by the Absolute.

It is not surprising that Fichte's idealist conclusions ran aground. Even the great Idealist Hegel had serious difficulty with Fichte's collapse of personal identity into this abstract Absolute Self. Thus, rather than overcoming the **dualism** of Kant, Fichte could only replace it with a **monism** which in the end sacrifices the centrality of experience which he had pledged himself to uphold. To know the knower (transcendent Ego) which Kant had declared is impossible, and which Fichte had determined to find, ends in failure even for him. The subjective life of the Fichtean self is made up exclusively of its self-contained thoughts and self-representations. In attempting to grasp itself all it can see are its images, not its self. The Fichtean self can never be known, leaving him no option but to resort to affirming a primordial Absolute unity of the self - revealed of course only to him.[68]

These are legitimately devastating critiques which threaten to undercut any possible contribution he might have made to the quest. However, one or two contributions remain noteworthy. He was among the first to grapple with the ego-self distinction as a consequence of his attempt at finding a unity for self-consciousness. He was among the first to affirm the activity of selfhood organized around its drives. He was able to identify the drive to reach out to objects, even as he identified the drive to turn inward (through reflecting upon oneself) as a form of self-engagement. Although Fichte's mystic monism eventually destroyed this insight, he initially reaffirmed the centrality of subject-object operations as essential to the life of self.

Nevertheless, Fichte's hostility toward the role of otherness pushed him increasingly toward a self-contained Ego - one which does not really need objects

126

other than as a barrier through which the ego is driven back into itself. The object in Fichte is at best **faceless** and **powerless**, a problem which will come to haunt both Jung and to a lesser extent Freud in this century. At the same time, however, Fichte did name the factor of longing as the doorway to self-consciousness thereby becoming a forerunner to drive and libido theory.

While Fichte remains one link in the chain of the discovery of dynamic selfhood, his efforts also mark the collapse of the various attempts at resolving the problems of a dualistic self. With this collapse we have reached the end of what I have called the transition to the modern era. We are now in a position to grapple with the richness and complexity of the two giants who stand at the threshold of the modern struggle to understand self: Hegel and Kierkegaard. Whether either of them were able to resolve the contradictions of self can now be determined.

1.   Runes, 1980, p. 45

2.   Rene Descartes, *Discourse on Method and the Mediations*, Trans. by F.E. Sutcliffe (New York: Penguin Books, 1968), p. 53

3.   Ibid., p. 53, 54

4.   Ibid., p. 54

5.   Michael E. Zimmermann, *Eclipse of the Self*, (Athens, Ohio: Ohio University Press, 1981), p. 209

6.   Descartes, *Meditations*, 1968, p. 124, 130-131

7.   Wolfhart Pannenberg, *Anthropology in Theological Perspective*, Trans. by Matthew J. O'Connell (Philadelphia: The Westminster Press, 1985), p. 216

8.   H.D. Lewis, *The Elusive Self*, (London: The MacMillan Press, 1982), p. 45. *Italics mine.

9.   Rene Descartes, *Principles of Philosophy*, trans. by Haldane and Ross, 1931, vol. 1, p. 239; Principle LI.

10.   Peter A. Angeles, *Dictionary of Philosophy*, (New York: Barnes & Noble Books, 1981), p. 279

11.   Ibid.

12. Descartes, *The Passions of the Soul*, translated by: E.S. Haldane and G.R.T. Ross in The Philosophical Works of Descartes, (Cambridge: Cambridge University Press, 1931), Vol. 1, p. 345

13. W.T. Jones, *A History of Western Philosophy: Hobbes to Hume*, Vol. III (San Diego: Harcourt Brace Jovanovich, Publishers, 1969), p. 188

14. Descartes, *Meditations*, 1968, p. 98

15. Zimmerman, 1981, p. 210

16. David Hume, *"An Inquiry Concerning Human Understanding"*, Ten Great Works of Philosophy, Robert Paul Wolff, Ed. (New York: New American Library, Inc. 1969), p. 186

17. W.T. Jones, Vol. III, 1969, p. 301

18. David Hume, *A Treatise of Human Nature*, Vol. I, (London, J.M. Dent and Sons Ltd., 1961), p. 238-239

19. Ibid., p. 239

20. Ibid., p.193-194

21. Ibid., p. 194

22. Ibid., p. 94

23. Ibid., p. 240

24. Ibid., p. 241

25. Ibid., p. 247

26. W.T. Jones, Vol. III, 1969, p. 349

27. W.T. Jones, *A History of Western Philosophy: Kant and the Nineteenth Century*, Vol. IV (New York: Harcourt Brace Jovanovich, Inc. 1975), p. 12

28. Robert C. Solomon, *In the Spirit of Hegel*, (New York: Oxford University Press, 1983), p. 70

29. Immanuel Kant, *Critique of Pure Reason*, Trans. by F. Max Muller (Garden City, New York: Anchor Books, 1966), p. 2

128

30. W.T. Jones, 1975, p. 34

31. Kant, *Critique of Pure Reason*, 1966, p. 62

32. W.T. Jones, 1975, p. 35

33. Ibid., p. 37

34. Ibid., p. 38

35. Ibid., p, 38

36. Kant, *Critique of Pure Reason*, 1966, p. 105

37. Ibid., p. 77 - See also p. 248-249

38. Pannenberg, 1985, p. 202

39. Kant, *Critique of Pure Reason*, 1966, p. 92

40. W.T. Jones, 1975, p. 53

41. C.G. Jung, *The Symbolic Life*, C.W. Vol. 18, Trans. by R.F.C. Hull (Princeton: Princeton University Press, 1976), p. 770

42. J.G. Fichte, *Science of Knowledge*, Edited and Translated by Peter Heath and John Lacks, (Cambridge: Cambridge University Press, 1982), p. 6

43. Ibid., p. 8

44. Ibid., p. 9

45. Frederick Copleston, *A History of Philosophy*, Vol. 7 Westminster, Maryland: The Newman Press, 1963), p. 38

46. Alan White, *Shelling: An Introduction to the System of Freedom* (New Haven: Yale University Press, 1983) p. 15

47. G.W.F. Hegel, *The History of Philosophy*, Vol. 3 Translated by   E.S. Haldane and Frances H. Simpson (London: Routledge and Regan Paul Ltd., 1955), p.486

48. Fichte, *Science*, 1982 I, 250, p. 221-222. It should be noted that the term used by the translators in this instance to designate *das Ich* as (the self) is inappropriate particularly when used by Fichte as the centre of consciousness, i.e. the ego. I will use the term ego in my discussion of Fichte to represent consciousness, and reserve use of the term self for self-consciousness or the ego's reflection upon itself. For a more

extended discussion of this problem note Wolfhart Pannenberg, 1985, p. 201-204. See also Alan White, 1983, p. 15-24, as well as Copleston, 1963, Vol. 7 p. 44

49.   Ibid., See pages 155 ff. and pages 233 ff.

50.   Ibid., I, 125, p. 122

51.   Ibid., I, 126, p. 122

52.   Ibid., I, 97, p. 98

53.   Ibid.

54.   Ibid., I, 98, p. 99

55.   Johann Fichte, *The Vocation of Man*, translated by Peter Preuss, (Indianapolis: Hackett Publishing Co., 1987), p. 67

56.   Ibid., p. 49

57.   Ibid. The notion of mirroring here picks up a theme present in the Genesis account of the Hebrew Scriptures and developed particularly in Augustine and Meister Eckhart; it is again picked up and developed by contemporary Psychoanalytic Object Relations Theory (Italics mine)

58.   Ibid., p. 48

59.   Ibid.

60.   Fichte, 1796, I 270, p. 238

61.   Ibid., I 291, p. 256

62.   Ibid., I 294, p. 258

63.   Fichte, *Vocation*, 1987, p. 67

64.   Ibid., p. 68

65.   Catherine Keller, *From a Broken Web: Separation, Sexism, and Self*, (Boston: Beacon Press, 1986), p. 20, 79

66.   Pannenberg, 1985, p. 203

67.   Robert C. Solomon, *In the Spirit of Hegel*, (New York: Oxford University Press, 1983), p. 92

130

---

68.   Fichte, *Science of Knowledge*, I 295-296; p. 259-260. See also
       Copleston, 1963, Vol. 7, p. 84

Chapter V

G.W.F. HEGEL (1770 - 1831) AND THE UNIFIED SELF

The towering figure of G.W.F. Hegel, presents itself at a critical juncture in our search. The split between nature and spirit, human subjectivity and objective world, God and the universe, which had been so firmly established by Descartes and refined by Kant had not been overcome. Neither the path of the full autonomy of the object (Hume) nor the path of the complete self-sufficiency of the subject (Fichte) could resolve the question of how selfhood could be both spiritual **and** tied to the realm of nature, how it could be free yet bound to matter.

The separation between subject and object made the realization of unified selfhood impossible. Cut off from the objects through which it is constituted, selfhood was either forced into the artificiality of its own self-contained internal process, or it was robbed of the possibility of becoming a centre of initiative with any meaning to its striving.

This bleak situation confronted Hegel and in his efforts to overcome the stalemate a genuine breakthrough may well have been accomplished, which, when placed alongside the devastating challenge of Kierkegaard, may provide us with solutions which have thus far eluded human inquiry.

In drawing upon Hegel and Kierkegaard as essential contributors toward a comprehensive model of "living" selfhood I am not making an arbitrary choice based upon their chronological emergence after Kant and Fichte, and clearly not a choice based upon ease of understanding. Rather, Hegel and Kierkegaard provide a range and scope to selfhood against which all ancient and modern notions of self must be measured.[1] Paul Ricoeur underscores this declaration in his insistence that together Hegel and Kierkegaard form a composite picture of the meaning of selfhood, furthermore suggesting that each completes what is unfinished in the other.[2]

Given Hegel and Kierkegaard's importance for defining selfhood I will offer an extended discussion of both, beginning with Hegel, with Kierkegaard to follow. In the process surprising similarities will emerge even as we encounter major differences. Nevertheless, their respective insights must first be allowed to stand on their own. It would be simplistic to assume that the distinctiveness of great scholars is primarily the result of their attempt to separate themselves from the errors of their predecessors. To only think of Hegel as a critic of Kant or Fichte, or to define Kierkegaard simply as over-against Hegel does violence to the complexity and depth of their thought. For these reasons I am presenting their proposals relatively independently, reserving the necessary interaction between them to the conclusion of chapter six.

SURVEY OF THE HEGELIAN PARADIGM

Hegel's Purpose

The decade of the 1790's was one of intense ferment and upheaval. Not only had the French Revolution swept away the prevailing social order, it unleashed an intoxicating vision of freedom which sought legitimization within individual human existence. But with the rampant march of empiricism the possibility of a free and creative subjectivity seemed evermore remote and unrealizable, with natural forces alone supposedly determining human life. The more nature became objectified the more remote seemed the possibility that human beings are agents able to choose the shape of their personal and corporate life in ways other than determined by the raw demands of nature.

Like Kant, Fichte had sought to re-establish human freedom by reasserting the inherent spirituality of nature which seeks to actualize itself in the material realm. For Fichte this spiritual principle took the form of the Absolute Ego which not only guides the process of nature but which serves as the reference point toward which the human ego must orient itself. But while granting the human ego a limited freedom to shape itself, Fichte robbed nature of its autonomy. The real world became devalued, serving simply as a testing-ground for the self-realization of the Absolute Ego with human consciousness the tool through which the Absolute could work its intentions. This basis for freedom and subjectivity became completely unacceptable for Hegel.

Hegel's first publication entitled *The Difference between Fichte's and Schelling's systems of Philosophy,* (1801) quietly but effectively undercut the Fichtean thesis. To provide a genuine basis for human freedom the claims of **both** nature **and** human subjectivity must be honored, insisted Hegel. Freedom for Hegel cannot be won if the realization of spiritual aims swallows up **either** individual subjectivity **or** nature, but only if there is a full autonomy one from the other, with spirit nevertheless "informing" nature or seeking to complete itself in it. If subjectivity is indeed a higher-order achievement of goals and purposes, then matter must somehow be embodied with so-called spirit, just as spirit cannot be divorced from the material universe it supposedly guides. But how is it possible to envision a relation between a subjective presence in the universe, however construed, and individual human subjects, i.e. persons?[3] How can one envision a relation between universal spirit and human subjectivity?

If Fichte were correct, then universal spirit would be the sum total of the capacities of the human ego. Nature simply serves as the arena where this universal subjectivity (Spirit) realizes its purposes. Nature has lost its autonomy.

If, however, one wishes to preserve the autonomy of nature while nevertheless allowing for a spiritual force to be present in it, then Pantheism becomes attractive. Pantheism's appeal lies in the possibility that all of nature is a material manifestation of a spiritual force. This, however, is also Pantheism's great weakness. For Pantheism spirit becomes **fully** contained within nature thereby denying spirit's capacity to transcend matter. The autonomy of both is again sacrificed.

The German Romantics of the late Eighteenth Century were not oblivious to these problems. Novalis, Schlegel, Schelling and Schleiermacher all rejected Pantheism for the reasons just indicated, even as they rejected the Fichtean option. In its place they presented an intruiging possibility.

Rather than see persons as cumulative parts of the whole, the Romantics took the novel approach of seeing human personhood as a microcosm of universal spirit.[4] Persons, declared the Romantics, are not simply part of the whole, they **reflect** the whole within themselves. Because persons "contain" the whole, the spirit which infuses matter is not only able to interact with the human subject, but more importantly, this universal spirit comes to conscious expression in human consciousness.[5] This possibility would become the cornerstone of Hegel's great intellectual edifice.

But a burning question remains. If such unity exists, how is it compatible with human freedom? What meaning is there to human autonomy if persons simply reflect the underlying spiritual cohesion of nature? This is the dilemma the Romantics could not resolve and which Hegel took upon himself as his great challenge.

The path by which Hegel attempts to maintain freedom **and** autonomy **without sacrificing unity** is to see human personhood not only **reflecting** the spiritual unity of the universe but **completing and fulfilling** it. As one Hegelian commentator has summarized, "the cosmic spirit which unfolds in nature is striving to complete itself in conscious self-knowledge, and the locus of this self-consciousness is the mind of man.[6] Personhood is more than simply a mirror of the wholeness of nature for Hegel, **but the very means whereby universal spirit gains its own identity as spirit.** This became Hegel's overriding vision and grand task: to demonstrate the process whereby "nature" comes to realize itself as spirit, that is, as self-conscious, even as persons come to an awareness of themselves as interwoven with this spirit.

This marks a revolutionary shift for understanding selfhood. The "decaying" material substance of the universe need not be separated from spiritual possibilities (Plato, Augustine), nor does spirit need to retreat into a non-material transcendent realm (Descartes). Most shocking of all, Hegel grants human beings the status of agents of the self-realization of cosmic spirit! In so doing he attempts to maintain **both** human continuity with nature **and** personal autonomy and self-directedness. Human identity is to become the vehicle of the self-realization of universal spirit and thereby itself. Whether this grand model, or **Notion** as Hegel came to call it, can carry all that is claimed for it remains to be seen. And of course Kierkegaard will have a thing or two to say about its legitimacy. But before discussing the details of this process two important terms require elaboration.

Spirit and Self in Hegel

Spirit

It is essential to understand certain key Hegelian terms in order not to become hopelessly lost in the grand model he develops. Among the most important is the concept Spirit (Geist). Hegel's Spirit not only refers to individual human spirit(s) but to universal spirit as "subject".[7] What might this mean? A "subject" contains the capacity for self-knowledge, self-realization, and the accomplishment of particular purposes. We should not only understand such self-realization in the Aristotelian sense, as the ability to realize a certain functional form, but as the achievement of a **unity of purpose**, the capacity to be the agent of its own intentional activity. In short, being a subject has something to do with a knowledgeable self-directedness. Hegel's own words may be helpful here:

> Spirit is the knowledge of oneself in the externalization of oneself; the being that is the movement of retaining its self-identity in its otherness.[8]

Spirit, Hegel suggests, is a coming to self-consciousness through a process of engaging what is outside of itself. Spirit involves becoming aware of **continuity** in the midst of **change**, becoming aware of a **unity** in the midst of **otherness**. Spirit means becoming self-aware as a unified self-consciousness, this not being automatically or eternally given but accomplished within space and time. Hegel elaborates:

> But Spirit becomes object because it is just this movement of becoming an **other to itself**, i.e. becoming an **object to itself**, and of suspending this otherness. And experience is the name we give to just this movement...[9]

Experience is what allows Spirit to become a subject or self. Spirit, as subject aware of itself, is not to be equated with sameness (Descartes) or changeability (Hume) but with the engagement of continuity with change.

Because the knowledge of oneself as subject (i.e. spirit) occurs only through the **encounter** with otherness, the chasm between subject and object has been overcome claims Hegel. The attainment of "spirit" is thus not the autonomous property of a timeless God, nor automatically given with human consciousness, but a grand mutual engagement, a process which requires "fleshing-out" in time and space. What, then, is the Hegelian self?

Self

Hegel's grand purpose is to finally do away with the idea that selfhood is an inert substance. Rather, he develops the notion of self as a living, full-integrated unity of subject with object. The various dualisms against which Hegel was reacting had understood self as a thing, a soul somehow sufficient unto itself. Indeed, this self as soul became an autonomous center of knowledge able to operate quite nicely in isolation from its bodily home. The static soul no longer needed anything outside of itself just as God needed nothing to be complete in himself. Human subjectivity, including thoughts, feelings, perceptions, etc. were self-sufficient products of this Cartesian "mind" even as matter, the body, and history became ever further removed from the life of soul. This state of affairs was completely unacceptable to Hegel.

In challenging such rampant dualisms and the various attempts at correction, Hegel believed he needed to reconcile what he saw to be a basic bi-polarity to selfhood. To be a self, namely a subject in an intentional living-out of a particular purpose, requires an integration or **"holding-together"** of certain opposites which constitute selfhood.

Selfhood, it seems to Hegel, contains certain contradictions, none of which can be dismissed without violating the nature of self. There seems to be an ever-present clash within selfhood between the factor of **stability** and the factor of **change**, between so-called **permanence** and **variation**. Correspondingly, there seems to be a complete vulnerability or contingency to selfhood even as certain of its capacities such as the insights of reason "live" in a timeless, eternal realm (For instance, two plus two always seems to be four).

For Hegel, these timeless laws of reason are incompatible with the fluidity of life, with the natural conditions of life, and the bodily givens within which life moves. So, observes Hegel, this self is both fully immersed in the contingencies of life, yet able to transcend them through various capacities which maintain a certain stability through inevitable decay. This self, it seems to Hegel, is an entity of utter contradiction and conflict.

How, then, does Hegel overcome this opposition between sameness and change, identity and difference, which is intrinsic to selfhood? As obscure as Hegel's language may be it is vital that we hear his first description of the self.

> The realized purpose, or the existent actuality, is movement (Bewegung) and unfolded becoming (entfaltendes Werden); but it is just this unrest (Unruhe) that is the self; and the self is like that immediacy and simplicity of the beginning because it is the result, that which has returned into itself (Das in sich zurueckgekehrte), the latter being similarly just the self. And the self is the sameness and simplicity that relates itself to itself.[10]

As it stands, this definition is far too convoluted for us to grasp its full meaning, forcing us to unpackage it with greater care.

In true Aristotelian fashion, Hegel describes the self as "purposive activity," the movement or restlessness whereby what is uniform (pure or undivided) becomes differentiated and thereby object to itself. In its pre-developed form the self is an "unconscious" relation, what Hegel calls an immediacy, which must nevertheless proceed out from its primordial unity and become divided from itself. This movement or "unfolded becoming" is the self. At the same time this self is the movement of returning to itself which completes its process of gaining an **identity** - its dynamic (**changing and abiding**) - shape. The self, then, is the result of a "mediation" (Vermittlung) in which that which is experienced as separate (or object), becomes re-engaged and internalized as self. This mediation or integration within selfhood is what Hegel calls "becoming."[11]

To be a self, then, means to be a self-aware spirit which undergoes a process of becoming aware. This process is of necessity historically bound, as a matter of fact, it **is** history. I have already hinted that this process is not to be construed as either an individual **or** a universal process. For Hegel this developmental journey must occur at both universal **and** individual levels, or more precisely, they are two sides of one process.

This engagement of encompassing universality (cosmic spirit) in dialectic encounter with individual particularity (human persons) takes infinitely varied form for Hegel. Literally everything in the universe from individual thought process, to family and social life, to the history of nations, is contained within this process he calls "self". The very development and history of the universe is the story of this cosmic self Hegel calls God. Said another way (in a manner highly reminiscent of Meister Eckhart), God is the self of everything.

The identification of self with the totality of Absolute Spirit brought with it the charge that Hegel simply collapses all individuality into God. This is the critique which undermined Fichte's Absolute Ego and will be inherent in Kierkegaard's relentless attack against Hegel, namely, that all uniqueness and autonomy is inevitably smothered in the crush of unity. While there may well be merit in the accusation that Hegel squeezes all development into the perfect unity of his all-consuming synthesis, it would be premature to dismiss Hegel at this point before allowing his model to stand on its own **and** before presenting the case of his nemesis: Kierkegaard.[12]

The Process of Hegelian Development

As a final task before embarking on the developmental journey of self as mapped out in Hegel's *Phenomenology of Spirit* (1806) we would do well to understand the outlines of the Hegelian methodology. How does Hegel envision this developmental process and is it legitimately transferable to the disciplines of anthropology, theology, psychology and history?

The "standard" dialectic of thesis, antithesis, and synthesis has been so popularized and over-used that it should be temporarily suspended from the reader's mind, at least until its true intent becomes visible. In its current usage, dialectic has become so mechanical, so impersonal, that Hegel would likely consider it anathema. Anything that automatic has nothing to do with spirit or self.

As a reminder, we should recall that Hegel's overriding purpose is to offer the "itinerary" of self as it "rises to spirit" through the process of becoming conscious.[13] He intends to map out the processes within consciousness and self-consciousness whereby self comes to its identity as spirit.

Hegel insists that a developmental model of selfhood must incorporate the reality of increasing differentiation even as a relationship is maintained to what went before. Hegel suggests for example, that a human embryo is already **"in itself"**, a human being, although hardly a human being **"for itself"**, that is, it has not yet won consciousness for itself even though it potentially contains consciousness within itself.[14] Hegel's point is that there is a "wholeness" or internal unity present within every level of development with its further development, its potentiality, "hidden" within it, so to speak. Hegel is not only making a developmental claim but an ontological one, namely, that the "being" of any substance "carries" the whole within it. This amounts to a declaration of the radical immanence of spirit, along the lines of the Romantics spoken of earlier.

Be that as it may, any state of blissful oneness would be static if left in its unitive "unconscious" state. Any movement or development out of such a condition suggests a process which goes beyond itself which furthermore implies a teleology, a direction, even if that direction is governed by randomness. A process still goes somewhere. In going somewhere it must leave something behind - this being the first dialectic step which Hegel calls **Negation**. The second dialectic step called **Aufhebung**, which I will translate as **"transforming integration"**, completes the growth cycle to be discussed shortly.

Negation

Negation for Hegel is the ever-present antithesis or cancelling-out of "what-is" into a "what-has-been". It is the death which accompanies the movement of the universe. While Hegel's abstract philosophical language is obtuse, his declaration of the inevitability of negation is hard to miss:

> But the life of Spirit is not the life that shrinks from death and keeps itself untouched by devastation, but rather the life that endures it and maintains itself in it. It wins its truth only when, in utter dismemberment, it finds itself .. Spirit is this power only by looking the negative in the face and tarrying with it. This tarrying with the negative is the magical power that converts it (Spirit) into being. This power is identical with what we earlier called the Subject.[15]

To be a subject, then, in some fashion requires that a negation, a separation, be accomplished. While it is obvious that Hegel is referring to cosmic or universal spirit, this same necessity applies to individual human spirit. How, then, is negation to be understood as an essential factor within human subjectivity?

Fichte and Kant had both declared that an ego comes to its awareness only by setting a non-ego (object) in place for itself. Hegel qualifies this conclusion by insisting that awareness requires otherness in the sense that every subject requires an object, something to become aware of. This bi-polarity of awareness means that a subject inevitably becomes confronted by its distinction from the object, a separation which is the very condition for consciousness.

This built-in duality at the heart of human consciousness is a simultaneous discovery of the object and an act of knowing subsumed under the term "experience".[16] Experience for Hegel is the process within time and space through which the object and the knower of the object come to life. Without "experience" there is no object and therefore no self. Experience, then, is a process of verification, of coming to know not only the object but also itself i.e. that which does the knowing. Experience is the process whereby consciousness comes to know itself as spirit or self.[17]

Jean Hyppolite, a well-known Hegelian interpreter, suggests that there is a reciprocal relation between knowing an object and knowing one's self. He writes: "In its object it (consciousness) experiences itself, and in its knowledge it experiences its object."[18] An example may serve useful. Let us assume that I am walking briskly through a familiar room and suddenly and unexpectedly I stub my toe and double over in pain. My familiarity with my surroundings had rendered certain physical objects largely unconscious for me (at least until that moment). The literal collision with an object reminds me (again) where I end and the object begins. I simultaneously become aware of the object and myself. Selecting an object which impacts me at the level of physical sensation only does not invalidate the point, that awareness requires separation and that I **need** separate objects to come to myself. One could therefore claim that human consciousness requires separate emotional objects, relational objects, cultural objects, and so forth. But upon what basis can this be called negation?

Negation for Hegel speaks of the fluid transition from one object to another. Negation facilitates the letting-go of one object and the discovery of a new. Hegel is not suggesting that conscious experience is disjointed, but that selfhood of necessity experiences itself and its object as separate.[19] Hegel thereby challenges the disjointed self of empiricism (Hume) which reduces human subjectivity to memory (as the association of past objects). A selfhood built only upon associated units of memory has no structural cohesion and can therefore hardly be called a self. Negation, then refers to the inevitable separation of subject from object and the "letting-go" which accompanies the infinite movement between a subject and its objects. A second vital step now presents itself in the movement called self, a step which Hegel calls **"aufhebung"**.

Aufhebung (Transforming Integration)

Aufhebung is the word Hegel uses to describe the second phase of the dialectic process of selfhood in which a new unity is attained. This word has regrettably often been mis-translated as sublating, transcending, preserving, and so on, thereby missing the richness of term. Hegel's intent in using the term is to describe how the separation of the prior negation is overcome. If "Aufhebung" amounted to a simple "leaving behind", then the term "transcending" may well have sufficed. But Hegel insists that **both** prior phases of the dialectic, (1) the **initial unity** and (2) its **negation** or annulment be "taken-up" or (3) **integrated** into what follows. This inclusion of what has gone before does not eliminate or smooth over the negation or separation, but gathers both prior elements into the life of the new.

Because the new unity does not simply eliminate the tension, Hegel refers to the resolution accomplished as a "reconciliation" implying that what came before remains, only now brought into the service of a new unity.[20] The following elements therefore constitute Aufhebung: (1) a **separation** from what has been, (2) an **integration** which preserves what went before, and (3) a **transformation** which allows for the new. How is this movement accomplished? Is it a jump, or a smooth, inevitable transition? And by what means is it actualized?

To begin with, the negation spoken of a moment ago is the first step toward the transformation which follows. An encounter with an object of any sort creates a "barrier", which drives human awareness back into itself. All raw experiential data, whether arriving in sensate form, as emotional content, or as a "new" idea, challenges a prevailing state of awareness which is forced to come to terms with the new reality now presenting itself. The unfamiliarity of the "new" reality, the "new" object, forces the ego to make a revised connection between its accumulated history of objects and its current self-representation; i.e. its current knowledge of the world and its knowledge of itself. Such a new connection does not undergo a quantum leap as much as a double realignment.

Aufhebung (transforming integration) first of all requires a **reminder** or **recollection** (Erinnerung) of what has gone before, and secondly, a **conversion** (Umkehrung) into something new. Spirit, as subject aware of itself, must recollect [(re)member] aspects of its past status in order to be able to move through the state of negation toward a new form of itself.[21] Correspondingly, **Aufhebung** requires conversion, the critical moment in which an ego puts together a new connection, a new image of itself in relation to its phenomenal world.[22] This transformation takes the form of images or metaphors which reflect the new arrangement, a new self-representation. Hegel's heavy reliance upon thought betrays his dependence upon the power of rationality to generate new structures and patterns, but in so doing he is not using rationality in a narrow, cognitive sense, but as the full range of representational processes including imagery, language, art, religious ritual, etc.

Again, we must pause in order to concretize the obscurity of Hegel's **Aufhebung.** Contemporary psychoanalytic scholarship describes a process called "transmuting internalization" which bears a striking resemblance to Hegel's term.[23] This process speaks of the internalization of psychological material, i.e. the taking-in of feeling-laden images (self-objects) of one's experiential world, which one incorporates into one's self system. According to Heinz Kohut these images (self-objects) do not just sit as lifeless statues within us but are themselves **transformed (converted)** or "transmuted" into the structures of the self. This metabolizing of the self's experiences builds selfhood.

What a care-giver does with her/his child at age four contributes to that child's identity, but not in isolation from the child's larger life context. Prior experiences of the care-giver (among others), already provides a structured rubric, a gestalt which in part determines how the experience at age four is "absorbed". Furthermore, the subsequent experiences of this child will cluster within her developing psyche to create the patterns of awareness which constitute her self. The experience at age four will thus come to mean different things to the individual as the developmental process continues. Every step thus potentially undergoes a "transmuting internalization", a transforming integration, allowing selfhood to be constructed.

The Meaning of Hegelian Development

I have sought to portray Hegel's purpose as an attempt to validate human identity and subjectivity and to ground this identity both within history and within the eternal or universal. In so doing, however, we must be absolutely clear as to the **meaning** Hegel seeks to uncover thereby.

Hegel's brilliant volume, *The Phenomenology of Spirit*, which serves as our guide, has as its overriding purpose an analysis of the path along which Absolute Spirit moves. As Hans Kung has noted, Hegel's *Phenomenology* describes the development or "career" of God.[24] This dynamic God who is spirit externalizes her(him) self and leads the universe toward its fulfillment as nature **and** spirit. This divine spirit **is** history and actualizes itself **in** history. Only what is spirit has a history as far as Hegel is concerned because only spirit has the capacity to maintain a relationship to what has already passed (which it has internalized), and only spirit has a future which it projects ahead of itself because it must become what it is.[25]

Profound implications leap out of this vision both for God and for humans. God no longer has the luxury of remoteness, in fact, God can only be understood to be God through full participation in the processes of time and decay. All duality, all negation, is now inherent in the life of God, is a form of the manifestation of God. In this fashion, Hegel sees himself resolving the dualisms of previous centuries by drawing these polarities together and reconciling them within the very life of God. Human life and God's life are two sides of one process with each coming to itself through the other.

Human life is given a completely altered meaning through this vision. The goal of human life becomes directed toward becoming self-conscious spirit. The developmental journey of the individual ego is no longer proceeding in isolation but gains a partnership with universal ego understood as Spirit (that which knows itself fully as self). The goal of human life becomes making this spirit self-conscious within my self.

The particular intent of Hegel's *Phenomenology* is therefore to trace the multiple and vast forms of human awareness and demonstrate that they are all contained within the development of self-conscious spirit. The history and evolution of consciousness "is thus the history of its experience, the progressive revelation of spiritual substance to the self."[26] It is the story of the One (God) becoming actualized in the life of the many (individual), and the story of the many expressing the life of the One.

The stages (phases) or "forms of spirit" are all implicitly contained within human personhood for Hegel. As immanent structures of consciousness they only become realized through experience, however. While numerous forms thereof are "unconscious" and are what Hegel calls "slumbering spirit", the goal of human identity is to attain a full knowledge of all of who one is, thereby revealing that one's essence truly is that of absolute spirit.[27] When human consciousness comes to grasp this, its own essence, it will complete the circle so inevitably broken.

HEGEL'S PATH TO SELFHOOD

Having prepared ourselves through the survey just concluded we must embark with Hegel on the lengthy journey which traces the evolution of spirit as self. As Hegel writes in the Introduction to the *Phenomenology,* this path is

> the way of the Soul which journeys through the series of its own configurations as though they were the stations appointed for it by its own nature, so that it may purify itself for the life of the Spirit, and achieve finally, through a completed experience of itself, the awareness of what it really is in itself.[28]

This is a mystic path in continuity with the mystic paradigm of Meister Eckhart, and easily traceable to the Biblical vision of Genesis 2:26 and John 1:1. As if weaving a tapestry, Hegel will attempt to hold in creative tension the ever-increasing differentiation within selfhood even as it remains linked to a larger unity called spirit, namely itself.

The outline below offers a sketch of the Hegelian forms through which selfhood moves. Great debate has raged over the years concerning the appropriateness of interpreting this model on an individual scale (as plotting a path for personal selfhood), or whether it uncovers a universal process indifferent to or at least irrelevant for personal existence? This very question, however, reveals an ignorance of the comprehensiveness of Hegel's vision and I will allow his own words to settle the issue.

The single individual must also pass through the formative stages of universal Spirit so far as their content is concerned, but as shapes which Spirit has already left behind, as stages on a way that has been made level with toil.[29]

Hegel's Forms of Selfhood

A. **Personal Selfhood** - as expressed through:

   1. Consciousness
      a. sense-knowing
      b. perception
      c. understanding

   2. Self-consciousness
      a. desire
      b. work and play
      c. stoicism and skepticism

   3. Reason
      a. theoretical or observing reason
      b. active reason
      c. realized individuality

B. **Social/Ethical Selfhood** - as expressed through:

   1. Substantial spirit (The imitating Self)

   2. Self-alienated spirit (Conforming or Rebelling Self)
      a. Saint and the Rebel
      b. Faith vs. Pure Insight

   3. Self-certain spirit (Moral Self)
      a. morality

b. conscience

c. the beautiful soul

C. **Religious Selfhood** - as expressed through:

1. Nature Religion (undifferentiated religion)

2. Artistic Religion

3. Revealed Religion

4. Absolute Knowing

The above outline serves as a rough map of the terrain through which selfhood passes as it seeks its fulfillment or completion. As a universal process it cannot be divorced from its actualization in individual existence just as individual selfhood comes to its own nature, its essence, through its participation in these processes and structures which have evolved in the history of the human race.

Hegel's organization of the *Phenomenology* leaves something to be desired if one is looking for neat linear progressions. Hegel's rush to finish the book on the eve of Napoleon's battle at Jena in 1806 no doubt contributed to its structural flaws. Be that as it may, Hegel highlights three broad movements which I am calling (1) Natural Selfhood (2) Social/Ethical Selfhood, and (3) Religious Selfhood. These three "movements" suggest a shift in focus from (1) **personal identity concerns** i.e. the path of emergence as an autonomous, self-knowing individual; to (2) **social/cultural engagement**; i.e. the process of coming to terms with the nuances of one's life as a social being and (3) the **seeking of a universal identity** via the various forms of **religious awareness** which have emerged throughout human history.

In each of the above components Hegel develops the dialectic process through which the structures of identity are formed. Thus in each case there is a three-way process developed including (1) an initial state of consciousness i.e. an awakening to some object, whether sensate, inter-personal, or religious; (2) **self-consciousness**, (negation), the process whereby selfhood comes to see itself through the otherness now established and (3) the transforming integration (Aufhebung) by which the constituting elements are tied together.

Finally, it should be noted that Hegel is not simply mapping chronological or age-related factors to human development. He is not concerned with describing a personal psychological path as much as describing the internal structures and patterns which govern subjective life. His contribution to the search for the self is to give us a grasp of the **structures of consciousness and self-consciousness** which are the parameters of selfhood and the developmental process.

Personal Selfhood

This first component of Hegel's model of selfhood is marked by three dialectically connected subphases called **consciousness, self-consciousness,** and **reason**. The first subphase concerns how we come to know the objects of the world, the second how a knowing subject discovers itself **in** the known object, and the third, Reason (Vernunft), attempts to unify both through a higher-order integration.

Consciousness

Consciousness comes in three forms for Hegel: (1) sense-knowing, (2) perception, and (3) understanding. Through these processes we come to know the world and its objects which is foundational for knowing ourselves.

Sense-knowing. Hegel's first question is: "How do I come to know the objects of the world?" i.e. "How do I come to consciousness?" His answer is that at its most rudimentary level selfhood is governed by pure **sensation** as the primary means by which I come into contact with the world. At a superficial glance it would seem that raw sensory data would give me the most direct access to the world because of its so-called "immediate" or pure form i.e. through direct sensory input.[30] Although such an immediate and concrete experience of the world may give me the most complete data or information, it gives the poorest truth as far as Hegel is concerned.

The knowledge obtainable through the senses is infinite, insists Hegel, "either when we **reach out** into space and time in which it is dispersed or when we take a bit of this wealth - and by division **enter into** it."[31] The limitation of sense - knowing is that we have access only to the simple concrete presence of objects with no awareness of their larger context, never mind their meaning for us. Such knowledge is empty for Hegel and all we can describe about such an object is its "thingness". What might this mean?

Because sense-knowing can only relate to an object as isolated or "pure", it turns all objects into "unique particulars" cut off from wider reality.[32] In seeing what it has found in the here and now as unique, this first-level awareness turns the object into what Hegel calls a "universal", which becomes its "truth". When experiencing an object only in the here and now (within sense-knowing) the human ego remains unrecognized and serves simply as a passive filter which receives the data, leaving the object primary or essential, with the ego itself non-important.[33] For pure sense-knowing, the immediate moment and the immediate place remains separate and unique.[34]

Sense-knowing, as the first step within personal consciousness, seeks to move beyond this fragmented condition. What nudges the process forward is the capacity for representation such as language. Sense-knowing may well provide data in the "here and now" but as soon as one attempts to capture this moment it disappears. In other words, when I attempt to grasp a here and now moment through representation, as soon as I begin to describe it, it is gone and replaced by another.[35] Hegel's point is that knowledge is not "out-there" somewhere in the object, but that my ego brings a connecting capacity to my experience of objects which allows me to "comprehend" rather than simply "apprehend" them.[36]

Perception. Sense-knowing is unable to provide a detailed knowledge of objects since it only acquaints us with objects "in general", with what Hegel calls their universality and not their distinctiveness. As an ego experiences a consistent flow of sensations it begins to discover that a particular object has multiple properties and that these properties distinguish it from other objects. Whereas with sense-knowing objects are experienced as one "thing" after another, in perception they become identified as "particular things", as a unity, yet in distinction from other "things".[37] When capable of perception an ego is not a passive filter as it was with sense-knowing, but can **grasp** an object through the objects' similarity and/or distinction from other objects. The object is no longer experienced as isolated but is "apprehended" as an object with multiple properties.

Let us take an infant's "recognition" of its primary caregiver as an example. In the early stages of an infant's life sensory input seems primarily present as unrelated "islands of experience." With continued experience of a primary care-giver the properties of touch, sound, sight, and smell take on a unity based both upon the objects' resemblance to itself over time **and** the unifying capacity which an ego brings to the data. Thus even though a care-giver will **not** be the same from day to day, with variations in dress, voice, touch, mood, etc., there will emerge a growing **recognition** of the constantly changing object. Through perception, an ego begins to bring a unifying and recognizing capacity to the objects it encounters, in this case the maternal object.

Perception, therefore, represents a dialectic movement for Hegel in which the ego returns to itself after encountering the object world. Sense-knowing does not allow the ego to return to itself since it remains in an unconscious unity with its objects. By being able to "withdraw" from the object, an ego is able to discover what belongs to it and what belongs to the object.[38] In this fashion an ego begins to gain its own unity within itself in engagement with the object world. In perception, an ego has separated from objects **and** can see them in their "unity-in-diversity" i.e. their distinctiveness and their cohesion.

Support for this conclusion may be found in the process Ego Psychology calls separation-individuation.[39] The symbiotic merger of an infant with its environment is lessened both as the infant's perceptual capacity grows, and as the otherness of the environment keeps imposing itself. The infant's very helplessness reinforces its separation from the world it so absolutely needs for its survival, thereby beginning to drive a wedge between the ego-in-formation and the world with which it is blended. This wedge takes the form of the rhythm of comfort and discomfort, soothing and distress, which separates the ego from its original unity. Perception in the Hegelian sense thus acts as the first step in the recognition of the otherness of the world in which an ego begins to "put together" its world and thereby itself as shaped by its experience.

Understanding. We move beyond perception, claims Hegel, when we try to understand our world and our place in it. Understanding tries to get at the "why's" and "wherefor's" of the world and how the world "out there" works. Whereas **sense-knowing** could only draw upon sensation for its data, and **perception** could only put such data together in order to recognize objects, understanding tries to get beyond outer recognition to grasp the "inner workings" of the object world.

Understanding attempts to comprehend the connection between the outer form of an object (its existence) and its internal dynamics (its essence) by uncovering the so-called laws by which the object operates. In looking to understand why an object moves and behaves as it does we attempt to move beyond seeing reality as simply an accidental process, hoping to find instead predictable or meaningful patterns.[40]

At the level of understanding, declares Hegel, we begin to grasp or infer the rules by which objects operate, which we attribute to the objects themselves using the category of "laws."[41] We seek predictability which **understanding** provides by offering explanations for the seeming stability behind the changeable flow of appearances. Scientific laws are one example of such an effort. For instance, the law of gravity attempts to look behind the simple existence of objects in the universe to explain their motion in relation to each other. But, insists Hegel, such laws do not **explain** what happens in the universe, they simply describe what is observed in more sophisticated ways. Furthermore, any "law" whether material or psychological which attempts to penetrate into the inner connection of events inevitably breaks down because what we think is stable and unified is not. Upon what basis does Hegel make this claim?

Understanding is overwhelmed through the experience of contradiction.[42] Through contradiction, paradox enters the "simple" equations through which the world "makes sense". Hegel again makes the familiar epistemological point that both **Empiricism** and **Rationalism** are limited. The first is limited because the objects of the world are more than the equations we impose upon them; the second is limited because it splits apart what changes from what does not. Understanding the world through laws erodes because of the continual flux between the law and the event it seeks to understand.

A well-known contemporary example is Heisenberg's Uncertainty Principle. Heisenberg has shown that in attempting to measure subatomic particles the law of causality breaks down because of the inevitable shift caused by the action of the observer. Not only are there no such things as independent laws running their course in space and time, declares Heisenberg, but what we observe is not nature itself, but nature exposed to our method of questioning."[43] This is exactly Hegel's point, that our so-called laws are the product of our interaction with the world.

The same limitation surfaces when we encounter so-called psychological laws. The law of stimulus-response adhered to by the behaviorist breaks down when it meets the individual agent, limiting behaviorism to a science of the measurement of probabilities. Even so-called subjective psychologies such as the Freudian or the Jungian stumble over Hegel's point. In Freud for instance, the action of human individuality is reduced to the patterns of psychological energy Freud called Eros and Thanatos. While few would deny that forces of attraction and repulsion are active in psychic life, Freud's attempt to classify these into universal patterns called the Oedipal phenomenon or the death instinct, runs aground when it attempts to predict their action within the individual human subject. The same limitation can be found in theories of psychological type which cannot account for the meaning of a particular inclination to personality but can only offer a more descriptive summary of one's orientation to the subject and object parameters of existence.

The inevitability of paradox begins to drive home the point that the laws by which we attempt to describe reality are secondary to the interaction of changing structures, in this case between our ego and the world as it appears to us. What we originally see through **Understanding** as a static world described by law, is shaken and turned up-side down by the discovery of paradox and flux. In the end nothing can be completely nailed down.

Self-Consciousness

The stations named thus far have mapped out our coming to awareness of objects which prepares the way for a discovery of our subjectivity. Hegel's concern now shifts from our knowing the object world to knowing ourselves.

There are three sub-phases to this process which Hegel calls (1) Desire, (2) Work (3) Stoicism and Skepticism.

    Self-Consciousness as Desire. In attempting to answer the question "What causes awareness to turn in on itself?", Hegel suggests that cognitive processes alone cannot awaken a knowledge of oneself. He insists that **appetite** or **desire** is essential for self-consciousness to be born.[44] Desire is at the heart of what it means to be and become a self. But what is this desire?

    Desire is a seeking after objects through which a subject can define itself. Desire involves a taking-in of the object and making it part of oneself. Such desire is insatiable - it constantly seeks objects through which it tries to find itself. This too is an essential phase because only through the hunger for otherness can selfhood recognize that it is its own self it is seeking.

    Objects exist strictly for the subject within desire.[45] The desiring subject absorbs or takes-in the objects which give it its rudimentary self-awareness. This first relationship to the objects of desire is not only in the Freudian sense of the libidinal seeking of pleasure but the narcissism in which selfhood seeks union with itself through its objects. Such desire involves the libidinal seeking of objects through which selfhood is realized (as reaffirmed by Object Relations Theory in this Century).

    Within this first phase of self-consciousness the otherness of the object is overcome i.e. negated. Because of this pervasive hunger, frustration is the inevitable outcome since the desire is insatiable. Frustration results because the subjects' total reliance upon the object only highlights the radical incompletion of the subject within itself. This frustration prompts a shift from the original negating of the object to a negating of itself because of the discovery of its radical dependence. This marks a most critical juncture in the evolution of selfhood for Hegel since self-consciousness can never be fully formed by simply taking-in objects. **Recognition** by another self-conscious agent is an essential element in the process of coming to selfhood. Hegel declares: "self-consciousness achieves its satisfaction only in another self-consciousness."[46] To become a self-conscious self, a subject must engage another self-conscious subject **and be recognized** as an authentic self. This is by no means an automatic event and the nuances of a self's engagement with otherness beyond simple desire constitutes perhaps the most brilliant of Hegel's insights.

Self-consciousness as Lord and Slave. Hegel recognizes that the process of coming to self-consciousness is not a linear progression but involves conflict and opposition. His famous analogy of Lord and Slave depicts the ingredients of this struggle to come to self-awareness through another. The Lord-Slave analogy is a picture of the forces which are present within one's emerging self-system. The analogy suggests that the struggle to come to self-consciousness involves the attempt to win recognition from another thereby finding one's identity and hoped-for worth. Ironically, however, the very act of seeking recognition from another reveals one's dependence upon the other for defining oneself. Any attempt at defining oneself, i.e. finding one's subjectivity by gaining recognition from another sets in motion the Lord-Slave dialectic.

Hegel suggests that the universal struggle to find oneself begins when a self attempts to define itself by seeking acknowledgment from another.[47] Self-consciousness as **bondage** or **slavery** is activated when recognition from the other is not forthcoming which makes the unrecognized subject the **Slave**, and the seemingly self-sufficient entity the **Lord**. In Hegel's imagery, the Lord is an ego which exists only for itself, but which has to define itself **through another ego** in such a way that the other remains a thing or an object for it. The Lord's nature is to exist only **for** himself, a state which is maintained by the "thingness" or devaluation of the slave. Conversely, the slave is a radically dependent entity whose being is defined only by the approval of the other. The primary themes within this struggle for recognition are the factors of dependence-independence and submission-dominance. Selfhood (and the relationships which reveal its structures) lives out a tension between these poles at all points in the human life cycle. The following examples from childhood and adulthood illustrate Hegel's point.

A child even in its earliest expressions of autonomy can take on the pattern of Lordship. The first no, the regular temper tantrum, all reveal an initial claiming of independence by a negating of the parent. A child must define itself, even if only momentarily, as over-against the parent - in this fashion it for an instant takes on a self-consciousness of mastery and control and comes to a first awareness of its own power. In extreme forms of parental indulgence a child can literally become Lord and the parent, Slave.

Conversely, a parent who demands constant rigid compliance on the part of a child uses the negation of the child to define himself as Lord. Here the child must remain Slave in order for the parent to find a certainty for his identity. Such selves can become locked into a self-consciousness of bondage which reflects both the state of their relationships and the shape of their selfhood. These patterns do not end with the passing of childhood. Any human relationship, whether wife-husband, employer-employee, teacher-student, friend-friend, can contain residual layers of Lordship - Slavery.

Allow me to offer the student-teacher relationship as another example. To the extent that both parties carry within them a self-dynamic of bondage (Slave) they **require** the other to be a certain way in order to know who they are. A teacher for instance, may be anxious about his worth as knowledge-provider and therefore be dependent upon the student for affirmation of his teaching powers. Although at one level the teacher may be Lord and the student Slave, at another level the reverse is true. The more the teacher needs the student to lap up the wisdom pouring forth, the more the teacher is dependently related in an inverse way to the student. Similarly, this heightened subservience of the student to her teacher also locks in the Slave-Lord dynamic for the student who is Slave at one level but Lord at another. Thus both persons live out a dual Slave-Lord polarization within the self. Their identity is only shaped through a negative relationship to the other leaving them with a negation of a portion of their own self-system.

Hegel has concluded that self-definition is always determined by the degrees of dependence - independence and power - powerlessness which are played out within and around the self. The closer the dependence-independence polarity moves toward the extremes of dominance-submission, the more pronounced the Lord-Slave clash of opposites becomes. In brilliant fashion Hegel has intuited the polarization within self-consciousness which later Object-Relations Theory came to call splitting and fragmentation when this opposition is present in extreme forms.[48] What Hegel has determined is that there is no selfhood without recognition by another, with this recognition (or lack thereof) playing itself out in one's own identity. What does Hegel see as a way out of this thicket?

Work and Play. The first attempted step out of the Slave-Lord split for Hegel is what he calls **work** (and I would also suggest - play).[49] Work and play does not **negate the object** as was the case with desire, but **transforms the subject** as a subject **externalizes itself** through work and play. In other words, as a self gives expression to itself through its own creative efforts it comes to experience a relative independence through its own creativity. However, this so-called independence is not just a positive step but also brings fear and dread with it claims Hegel.[50] The reason for this fear is that even as slave self-awareness gains a so-called "mind of its own," this rudimentary form of self-will realizes it is still subservient to forces far greater than it. Hegel's point is that anxiety is an inevitable by-product of any emerging self-consciousness as one recognizes the contingency and vulnerability of one's being. But work and play are not the only attempts at finding freedom and so-called autonomy for selfhood. Hegel describes two other attempts at resolving the Lord-Slave tension which he calls **Stoicism** and **Skepticism**. While these entities are both challenged as dead-end philosophical systems, they also reflect types of self-consciousness.

The Search for Freedom: Stoicism and Skepticism. Whereas work and play attempt to find autonomy through external "products", **stoicism** is a seeking after freedom by retreating into thought. Hegel explains:

> In thinking I am free, because I am not in an **other** but remain simply and solely in communion with myself, and the object, which is for me the **essential** being, is in undivided unity my being-for-myself; and my activity in conceptual thinking is a movement within myself.[51]

And yet the freedom of thought is not fulfilling because it is removed from life and remains abstract. This "solution" is withdrawal from the world, a freedom which requires a dualistic denial of anything which is not pure thought. Hegel dismisses this supposed pathway to freedom for the same reason that desire alone could not bring about authentic selfhood. Namely, the stoic has only a negative relation to what is "other" which only leaves one with a **negative dependence,** not freedom.

The inevitable outcome of stoic withdrawal for Hegel is the dead-end of skepticism. While stoicism simply withdraws from the world, skepticism denies that one can know the world at all.[52] Skepticism turns against the world because such a self is "already complete in its own self".[53] This is a self stuck in singularity and separateness, living out a contradictory identity. Seemingly independent and self-sufficient it is rather negatively dependent by denying or running from the very forces that have driven such a self into itself.

Hegel is of course directing a stinging critique at the skepticism of his day (Hume included) which attempted to base its world-view upon experience alone, while at the same time denying the larger unities which experience actualizes. Hegel is also making a psychodynamic point, however, that there are negative paths to personal freedom and autonomy which involve a withdrawal from a painful world into one's own subjective processes of thought or fantasy. Stoicism and skepticism can thus represent schizoid withdrawal or even more massive forms of dissociation. Thus whether understood as ways of knowing or as shapes of selfhood these paths toward freedom are negative and demand separation from the world and ultimately one's self.

Such a self Hegel calls an "**unhappy consciousness**" i.e. a self living out a dualistic and internally divided being.[54] Unable to find its unity, an unhappy consciousness takes its internal tensions and lives out only one side of itself and projects away the remainder. Caught between conflicting opposites such a divided self is inclined to project its more stable side toward a transcendent "absolute other" far beyond the self, making this other into an "essential Being". The remaining portion, the changeable, it identifies with itself as unworthy, i.e. completely transient and fragmented. Although Hegel does not say so explicitly, he is attacking world-denying dualistic Christianity which rejects the world for the sake of finding this eternal, unchangeable reality in heaven and its remotely transcendent God.

This unhappy self is torn between its "natural" existence in the world and the other-worldly "heavenly" existence for which it yearns. As far as Hegel is concerned this split found its most traumatic expression within Medieval Christianity where heaven and earth were fully separated. The Twentieth Century is of course not beyond such dualisms.

It is noteworthy that Hegel attributes the first appearance of God-consciousness to this negative retreat inward. As we begin to look inside ourselves we see forces at work within us which we have difficulty attributing to our own selfhood so we split what we discover into two separate worlds, the heavenly and the earthly, the one containing all goodness, the other badness. While Hegel will develop this point more fully within Religious Selfhood, unhappy consciousness already leaves us with the hint that any world-view which divides us either from nature **or** the Absolute cuts a self off from the vast wholeness within which it moves.

Reason

The dialectic of Personal selfhood reaches completion in the synthesis Hegel calls **Reason** (Vernunft). The stations described thus far have attained a limited unity both within (1) **consciousness** (an ego's knowledge of external objects) and (2) **self-consciousness** (an ego being born to itself), but have failed to synthesize these components within selfhood to one another. **Reason** is Hegel's term for defining this higher-order synthesis between subject and object.

Within consciousness as we recall, only external objects were held to be real, while for self-consciousness the subject came to life but only by relating to objects as something to be either desired or negated. The problem inherent in the birthing of self-consciousness is that the individual is only aware of herself through a relationship of **opposition** (over-againstness) or **subservience** to external objects. In Reason however, a higher degree of unity is attained in which the negative relationship to otherness is transformed into a positive relationship in which reality becomes claimed as **mine**. Reason "pulls together" consciousness and self-consciousness in the sense that the world and its objects are mine - mine to know, experience, experiment with, etc. as I try to find myself in them. Reason, concludes Hegel, "is the certainty of consciousness that it is all reality."[55]

Reason represents the effort to make the universe mine by declaring that my mind contains **all** truth and reality for me.[56] Reason can be understood as containing all those human efforts at discovering the rationality and order of the universe and the place of the human therein. It is a means of intuiting the coherence of reality by attributing it to nothing else but my own rationality.

Hegel describes three forms taken by Reason as it seeks this ordered world which he calls (1) observing reason, (2) active reason, and (3) realized individuality. These phases or movements within Reason represent forms of human effort at **rationally** explaining the interface between human subjectivity and "objective" world, between human finiteness and infinity, between the particular and the universal. Reason, as the highest achievement of human consciousness, will in the end however turn out to be an inadequate vehicle for spirit, again prompting Hegel's shift toward more comprehensive modes of Spirit's activity.[57]

Observing Reason: Observing Reason points to our attempts at describing and explaining our world, ourselves, and the relation between them. The operations of **Observing Reason** are closely related to the process described earlier within consciousness under the term **understanding**. In both instances Hegel is highlighting the limits of science as a means of finding a meaning behind what is observed and classified. The primary difference which has surfaced within Reason is the human desire to find "self-maintaining form," in other words, the attempt to find a rationale, a why, for the order discovered in the universe in a way which will allow the subject to find itself therein.[58] In short, efforts at classifying our world and discovering the "laws" by which it might operate are attempts at finding a coherence to our universe and a "reason" for our place in the world.

Through Reason we attempt to prove **objectively** what we hunch **subjectively**, which is why Reason turns to observation to find evidence of meaningful patterns.[59] In looking for evidence of meaningful linkage, human Reason searches for laws which explain why matter and organisms do what they do, whether in inorganic nature, organic nature, or with regard to the physical and psychological aspects of the human organism. In the end, however, science as a form of observing reason is unable to find such an underlying rationality. Upon what basis does Hegel make this judgment?

To begin with, Hegel is not challenging the legitimacy of empirical investigation, but is reminding us of its limits in firmly determining the why's and wherefor's of the world.[60] As useful as empirical inquiry may be, the "laws" it proposes to explain human functioning inevitably lose their predictive value the more one looks for verification through **individual** persons. What observation sees as a universal law is undercut by the possibility that each individual will respond to life in a unique and distinctly personal way. Thus the "nature" vs. "nurture" polarization would be an artificial issue for Hegel for whom the impact of the environment upon the individual is assumed. But as important as this environmental impact may be, Hegel insists that its effect upon the individual **is**

determined by the individual. The claim that universal "laws" determine human personhood (whether understood behavioristically or biologically) is rejected by Hegel because of personal freedom. Human freedom undermines all strictly "objective" approaches to determining human personhood and behavior. The very nature of observation which relies upon objectification cannot accommodate the human capacity to give shape to oneself.

Hegel understands that the effort to see a link between subjective and objective reality has taken some truly absurd forms. In Hegel's day these included popular "sciences" such as phrenology, for example. In this grotesque "science", the factor of spirit was reduced to what Hegel calls a "thing", to the bumps and shapes on one's head.[61] Modern thought is not immune from such pseudo-sciences and in our day and age it finds expression, for example, in somatotyping in which personality is related to one's bodily shape. As the effort to link subjective intentionality with inert matter reaches its inevitable dead end, Hegel sees Reason undergoing a shift in which it no longer looks to **prove** the presence of subjectivity within matter, but looks to its own **activity** to demonstrate this link.

Active Reason. If spirit cannot be reduced to a physical thing, then perhaps spirit can be realized through reasons' own activity. In Active reason, selfhood turns itself into a thing i.e. an object like other objects in the world.

Hegel sees this form of selfhood living itself out in what he calls "pleasure and necessity".[62] Hegel understands this phenomenon to be different from simple desire since desire attempts to take-in or devour the other. Hegel elaborates:

> Its action is only in one respect an action of desire. It does not aim at the destruction of objective being in its entirety, but only at the form of its otherness or independence, which is a show devoid of essence; for it holds this objectivity to be **in principle** the same essence as itself, or its selfhood.[63]

The primary impulse within desire is orality, the ingesting of the object, in what has been called object-hunger. Within pleasure, however, the seeking is for the satisfaction of overcoming the **otherness** of the object. In its raw form it is **hedonism** in which an individual seeks himself in the pleasure available **through the other**. This style of overcoming "otherness" maintains the self along the lines of Freud's pleasure principle. Such a self finds itself through the pursuit of personal wants and needs thereby finding its own nature externalized "in the moment."[64] This becomes its "reason-for-being."

As Hegel insists, however, such a realization of one's individuality is "the poorest form of self-realizing Spirit", because it is not one's own unique or complete individuality which is being lived out but only the momentary impulse of one's current neediness. What realizes itself in the moment only is the lowest form of self-realizing Spirit.[65]

Realized Individuality. Selfhood realized only in immediate fulfillment soon collapses into non-fulfillment since selfhood constantly dissolves with the completion of every pleasure, which prompts its seeking another fulfillment, and so on. A dialectic reversal is therefore activated in which fulfillment is not sought in the **particular** but in the **universal**. Instead of seeking its own pleasure it seeks the attainment of the universal good, which, such a self believes, is an extrapolation of its own good desires.

Hegel's need to challenge the Enlightenment's belief in the innate goodness of persons no doubt gives this transition its forced quality.[66] Nevertheless, Hegel rejects the belief that persons are universally "reasonable," with all claims regarding universal goodness running aground in the clash of individual interpretations thereof. Such a unity is not a unity at all for Hegel because it is not mediated, not arrived at through the rigors of conflict and reconciliation.

In this last form of reason, then, Hegel sees persons affirming their individuality through an uncritical belief in the reasonableness of rational laws which seem universal **for them**, or, through a blind trust in their own spontaneous feelings, which they assume, are shared by all. Such a "law of the heart" as Hegel calls it, can never contain the diversity of the world but will always collapse in contradiction and conflict.[67]

In the end, all forms of Reason, whether the "laws" of physical science, the seeking of universal psychological laws, or the hoped-for universality of my own beliefs cannot provide a viable linkage between purposive activity (Spirit) and world. Through Reason we seek a **universal pattern** or **norm** for the universe (as was also true for unhappy consciousness), but in both instances the effort collapses. It does so because the universal cannot be found simply by extrapolating my own singularity or individuality but only by discovering the presence of immanent spirit in all that is. To see the movement of spirit as self in a subject-object dialectic which goes beyond singular individuality, the **social world** must be included. The social order is the next visible manifestation of Spirit, what can be called the communal soil governing the emergence of self.

Social/Ethical Selfhood

Whereas the movement through personal selfhood focused primarily upon the personal subject-object differentiation which forms individual identity, social selfhood describes the relationship between the individual (ego) and the larger social or cultural network. This is also a subject-object problem for Hegel in that an individual subject is enmeshed in an object Hegel calls "social substance." Social or ethical substance refers to the spiritual inclinations of a social group as embodied in cultural, moral, and religious norms and "objectified" in public institutions.[68] Selfhood cannot be envisioned in isolation from the communal life with which an individual subject is in dialectic encounter. To describe this three-step process of engagement Hegel uses the terms (1) substantial spirit or the imitating self, (2) self-alienated spirit or the conforming/rebelling self, and (3) self-certain spirit or the moral self.

Debate has raged over the years regarding Hegel's intent as he discusses social/ethical selfhood with many commentators interpreting Hegel strictly on the level of the grand sweep of human history. It is no doubt true that Hegel is offering social and political commentary, particularly since so many of his analogies are drawn from historical epochs such as the ancient societies of Greece and Rome, or from dramatic events such as the French Revolution. Nevertheless, we cannot forget that for Hegel the personal and the communal are interwoven, with the life of universal spirit recognizable in social and political structures. These structures are, however, not independent of the persons who constitute them; furthermore, personal selfhood flourishes or is suffocated within the soil of corporate life. I will therefore continue to see the individual and the social in dialectic engagement which seems much more consistent with Hegel's vision.

One further clarification is needed. The entire process of Social selfhood does **not** chronologically follow the completion of Personal selfhood. Rather, Social selfhood **accompanies** Personal selfhood at another level. As was true for

Personal selfhood, Social selfhood involves a dialectic expansion of awareness. It is the story of how an ego comes to terms with its social world or with what could be called the **spirit of its world**.

Substantial Spirit (The Imitating Self)

The process of social selfhood begins with an ego in a state of blissful union with the norms of its social world. Selfhood at this level assumes that the rules which govern its particular life are universal. It lives in an uncritical, totally accepting way toward the norms of its social environment. Such a self is called "substantial" because it is stuck in an undifferentiated oneness with its world, in an acquiescence which Hegel calls "Sittlichkeit" (properness) or "ethical order."[69] At this level, personhood is totally enmeshed in the customs and norms of the social group.

The foremost context within which this unreflective ethical ego lives is the family, which lives out the ethical norm in an immediate or "unconscious" way. The family, for better or for worse, carries the ethical norms for selfhood in the direct way the family shapes individual attitudes and behavior. This ethical shaping goes beyond simple do's and don'ts to the deepest structures of sexual and relational life such as the incest taboo, for example.

Because of the unconscious and uncritical nature of selfhood at this level, imitation and acquiescence is the extent of its ethical life. Such a self is ignorant of the complexity of the social world, being unaware of competing and conflicting laws, customs, authorities, and institutions. This simple harmony cannot be called mature or authentic selfhood which requires that such naivete be lost and ultimately replaced with a new **differentiated unity** in which one is aware of the complexity of the social fabric and one's place therein. However, its very naivete becomes its downfall.

Since an undifferentiated self is blind to individuality, it inevitably comes into conflict with other selves who operate out of a different set of rules. This drives a wedge between persons who see themselves more and more as separate individuals. At the same time, the social fabric itself, whether represented by family or community rules begins to seem at odds with the interests and purposes of the individual. This friction between an emerging self and its social world is a very necessary step since it allows for (1) a division between the self and the ethical substance within which it is immersed, and (2) a new level of division to emerge **within** the self as a prerequisite for the development of **conscience**. In this fashion selfhood slowly loses its ethical uniformity, but the price it pays is that it sees itself as more and more isolated and impotent (what Hegel calls "Wesenlos") in the face of this all-encompassing social order.[70]

To the undifferentiated self its growing alienation from its ethical womb is quite a shock. It's unconscious immersion in its social **spirit** has now been dissolved into alienation from that spirit. The social world has jumped into awareness in the sense of a vast, immovable "given" toward which the individual must now develop some sort of relationship.

Self-Alienated Spirit (The Conforming or Rebelling Self)

With ethical immersion dissolving, the individual finds herself at odds with social norms, no longer united with them. This division or alienation selfhood finds unacceptable prompting attempts to somehow reunite with this lost world. The process whereby selfhood attempts to reclaim its lost unity Hegel calls "Bildung" or "culture", referring to the wide-ranging activities of education, self-development, and socialization.[71]

The process of socialization becomes the means whereby an individual lets go of her own isolated selfhood by identifying with that which now has objective reality for her, namely, the culture. However, in seeing the culture as real and herself as unreal, such a self has only found a negative solution similar to the process we saw within personal selfhood (in which stoicism, skepticism, and unhappy consciousness became the negative unity of self-consciousness). How does Hegel see this dialectic unfolding?

The Saint and the Rebel. Hegel uses the terms "noble" and "ignoble" consciousness (the saint and the rebel), to depict the two polarized responses on the part of selfhood to the moral, political, and economic structures of one's social world.[72]

The noble or saintly ego is found in the **compliant conformist** who finds a so-called unity by collapsing her spirit into the norms of the prevailing social order. Such a person identifies fully with social authority in its various forms and responds with full obedience and respect because of course her "essence" or "worth" is out there in the social norm. Such a person worships the status quo and believes authority can do no wrong. We can observe this state in a child (or adult) which never questions the divine wisdom of its Mother or Father, or in an adult (but ethical child) who applauds every political or economic decision an authoritarian ruler might make. The inner impulse however, is to avoid the tension which comes with facing the ambiguity of one's social world.

And yet, claims Hegel, even though such a self behaves as if it were conforming to its social power source, "the truth about it is rather that in its service it retains its own being-for-self and that in the genuine renunciation of its personality, it actually sets aside and rends in pieces the universal Substance."[73] In typically dialectic fashion, Hegel reveals the dark underbelly of this noble self. Although outwardly compliant and obedient, such a saintly self remains self-seeking or selfish since its wholeness is outside of itself. What it seeks "out-there" is really confirmation of its own self, but through an artificial harmony with the social world as a short-cut from the necessary struggle for a more mature relationship to the social matrix. Although claiming to have the larger good in mind, the saintly self is really only looking after its own vested safety interests whether economic, status, or power-related.

Rebel consciousness on the other hand reverses the above. It sees the powers that be as oppressive, and although such a self may grudgingly submit, it is always seeking to overthrow the oppressive rulers (in whatever form they come). This self also lives with a negative unity, only in this case by defining itself as **over-against** the prevailing values of the social order.

Our reaction to these insights may be to dismiss them as typically Hegelian, armchair abstractions. However, if we remember that Hegel attempts to describe universal patterns of awareness, it will protect us from taking his images too individualistically. Hegel's stations define the outer limits within which selfhood moves, in this case between the extremes of **compliance** and **rebellion**. The more a self lives out one extreme or the other, the more it ends in what he calls a "disrupted" or "**lacerated**" **consciousness**, not unlike the unhappy consciousness found within personal selfhood.[74] This step marks the outer limit of the alienation of social spirit, a retreat into either an all-good or all-bad world view with one split from the other.

The "truth" of Hegel's observations is not so narrow, however, that it applies only to the bizarre outer limits of life. Hegel's point is that every self in some ratio or other lives out the rebel vs. saint both internally **and** in one's relation to the social world (family, community, or nation etc.). Every individual attempts to come to terms with the sources of power in her world and her own will in relationship to this power. Hidden in every state of acquiescence is a desire to take power into oneself in a form of unconscious identification with the powerful one. Conversely, hidden in every state of rebellion is the desire to acquire the supposed freedom of those holding power in order to share in their sublime life.

Faith (Belief) vs. Pure Insight (The Secular World). Given this tendency to see the social world as either all-bad or all-good, the rebel and the saint as two types of alienated selfhood try to resolve their internal and external tension in two very different ways which Hegel calls **Faith** vs. **Pure Insight**.[75] These terms represent two types of experience through which selfhood attempts to resolve the ambiguity it feels toward its social and ethical world.

The so-called solution of "faith" must be distinguished from "Revealed Religion" which represents a higher level of development as we will discover shortly. Faith in this instance refers to simple **"belief"** as the attempt to overcome the negative unity of ethical/social selfhood by affirming an **Absolute Being** residing in a transcendent realm, very much like the resolution sought by Unhappy Consciousness. Belief not only projects all unity "upward" toward the realm of heaven or the remote transcendent, it sees its worth also residing there, being unable to find itself in the world.

Believing selfhood attempts to find its unity only in the spiritual realm which splits reality into a real but alien actual world, and a pure spiritual world. Because the worlds remain juxtaposed, no unity can occur. Such simplistic faith is an abortive attempt at finding unity since it imposes a transcendent union into the objects and events of the world in a rigid literalism. For instance, the insistence of the Creationists that God created the world in six days, or that Adam and Eve are the literal first parents reveal this projection of a naive spiritual unity onto the world. Hegel directs the same critique at literalistic sacramental practice which believes that the consecrated wafers **must be** the literal body and blood of Christ. In short, any form of superstition or the imposition of a spiritual unity onto a separate physical, social, or personal world, is a manifestation of dualistic "belief".

Pure insight, on the other hand, takes the opposite approach as it sees all truth residing within the self, not in some objective other-worldly realm. Whereas belief sees Spirit only in the transcendent realm, "pure insight" locates "truth" within its ego capacities. As was the case with Reason, pure insight sees the world as its own product. Pure insight claims to be able to understand the object world and measures itself only in relation to objectivity. Hegel writes:

> This insight as the self that **apprehends** itself, completes [the stage of] culture; it apprehends nothing but self and everything as self, i.e. it **comprehends** everything, wipes out the objectivity of things and converts all intrinsic being into a being for itself. In its hostility to Faith (Belief) as the alien realm of essence lying in the beyond, it is the Enlightenment.[76]

Pure insight as represented by the **Enlightenment** is a form of awareness which acknowledges only the objects of the world, now empty of sacred content. Such an "enlightened" individual sees human capacities as the essence behind culture, art, and scientific progress. The Enlightenment is the fully secularized world for Hegel, a world devoid of the sacred, finding itself only in its self-contained products.

As with anything else, Hegel sees two poles within this emergence of enlightened insight, a positive and a negative. The positive pole is represented by the phenomenon of **Utilitarianism** which says that everything is the domain of the human person with other persons deserving equal treatment. Hegel writes:

> Just as everything is useful to man, so man is useful too, and his vocation is to make himself a member of the group of use for the common good and serviceable to all. The extent to which he looks after his own interests must be matched by the extent to which he serves others, and so far as he serves others, so is he taking care of himself: one hand washes the other. But wherever he finds himself, there he is in his right place; he makes use of others and is himself made use of.[77]

Utilitarianism offers a strengthened valuing of selfhood as an object alongside others, with others treated in the same way as oneself. While this step may set aside the self-social world tension at one level, it also contains a destructive side in Hegel's estimation.

Utilitarianism in the end denies self true life because it eliminates all difference and distinction claims Hegel. This generates a new form of self-alienation, because selfhood sees itself as the norm with the social world an extension of the self's own will. Selfhood thus makes its own subjective life the basis of its truth.[78]

Hegel sees this form of being degenerate into an "absolute freedom" in which "the world is for it simply its own will."[79] A selfhood guided only by its own subjectivity is a spirit on rampage, a condition in which the human ego becomes its own absolute, its own normative criterion in willful self-assertion. This is a state of alienation which allows nothing to stand over-against it, leaving it free only to destroy. All otherness must be swallowed up. Any self which terrorizes or so violates others lives out such a radically alienated spirit. As a raging fire it attempts to consume all that is perceived as different, from which it is so estranged. Ultimately, such a totally alienated self either destroys itself or becomes transformed by coming to accept "difference" between itself and the social world. For this to happen a reconciliation is needed in a process Hegel calls morality and conscience.

Self-Certain Spirit (The Moral Self)

The emergence of morality and conscience marks the dialectical resolution of the two earlier phases within social/ethical selfhood which we came to know as (1) the imitating and (2) the alienated self. Within imitating selfhood there was no sense of oneself in relationship to the social world, with personhood absorbed in the social matrix of family and community. A dialectic reversal occured as human identity emerged from social enmeshment but in so doing it became inevitably alienated from its social foundation. In this third phase, selfhood attempts to resolve the clash between the constraints of culture and the need for personal freedom through a process Hegel calls **Morality.**

Morality. Morality develops as a component to selfhood through a clash of two elements which Hegel calls **duty** and **nature**.[80] Duty represents our

168

absorption of the "should's" and "should-not's" of our social world. These demands are not experienced so much as an external imposition, but as an internal appropriation of constraints, along the lines of Freud's superego.

Such a sense of duty is, however, inevitably challenged by our natural inclinations which determine our distinctively individual response to the social world. Any individual impulse, whether in the form of personal desire or personal self-assertion, will inevitably clash with the constraining force of social order. We could even call this the clash between Id and Superego.

Morality attempts to resolve this clash of demands by directing my individual inclinations into normative (social) ideals in the sense that my self will attempt to live out its natural inclinations in a morally ideal way. However, the inevitable conflict between natural inclination and moral obligation will again push my selfhood into contradiction.

A standard attempt at resolving this clash is to envision a God who functions as Transcendent Moral Legislator, laying down universally binding laws. The Mosaic law operative within the Jewish tradition and acknowledged as a unifying, if suffocating, force by Paul (Chapter Two) qualifies as one such effort. The fact that Hegel uses this "solution" as a platform for challenging the moral absolutism of Kant and Fichte gives it a forced quality. Nevertheless, the achilles heel of all Moral absolutism is that it allows only the transcendent God to reconcile these opposites within himself, leaving the poor instinctive self alone to fight with its natural inclinations, and most tragically of all, separated by a vast gulf from its remote law-giver.[81]

Such an external reference point acting as a criterion for selfhood is doomed to collapse. Moral awareness divorced from natural inclinations and the uniqueness of circumstance is self-contradictory and self-defeating.[82] Any absolute morality faces inevitable bankruptcy because the fulfillment of such laws is impossible due to the never-ending gap between what is and what should be. It is this very bankruptcy, however, which prompts selfhood to internalize these norms, to take more responsibility for itself, in a process Hegel calls conscience.

Conscience. Conscience is the integration of duty and moral norm as one's own internalized guide. In conscience (Gewissen), selfhood is certain (Gewiss) of its identity with the moral law but in a way which is integrated into its own life.[83] It is the highest expression of ethical life. This describes the "conscientious" self which **internally** resolves the tension between duty to oneself and to the larger world. Through conscience, selfhood maintains a link between its own inclinations and the needs of others, being able even to exist **for** others. This constitutes Hegel's **self-certain spirit**, an individual capable of honoring the viewpoint of another and recognizing oneself in the other. Again, however, Hegel is not content with this development as he claims it carries a fatal flaw.

Hegel is reacting to the "conscience" of the Romantics who were challenging the austere moral order of Kant. Novalis, Schlegel, and Schleiermacher all saw conscience as a perfect unity of "divine law" and "internalized" norms, i.e. a matching of absolute norms with individual inclinations.[84] This Hegel cannot accept. Not only does he dispute the automatic and "natural" presence of universal inclinations, he believes that the supposed "universal" action of one person will sooner or later clash with the "universal" impulse in another.

The "beautiful" soul. Since any automatic harmony within conscience is not a harmony that can be realized in actual life, it is at best an abstract harmony. This is the artificiality of the so-called "beautiful soul" of the Romantics whose heroes of literature, music, and religion could attain their sublime unity only on the stage of the imagination. Only words and images could maintain the "purity" of the universal soul, at least on paper.

Hegel, on the contrary, insists that spiritual reality must be embodied, must be made flesh, which means that it must realize itself in concrete life situations, must find expression in **particular** situations and in **actual** persons. To protect the spiritual from the particular or concrete situation is to condemn it to abstraction and non-existence.[85] However, since all that is particular and finite is transient and passes away, when the spiritual is exposed to transience it too must sacrifice itself and die, as Hegel insists it must.

Hegel declares that Spirit must die to its pure oneness, its universality, and become present to itself in the particular. The life-process of Spirit must externalize or embody itself thereby coming to itself. This process only finds completion for Hegel within the history of religion. Religion as it has evolved through the ages contains the story of Spirit in its process of embodiment and self-externalization.

Just as earlier phases of Hegel's model plotted the development of selfhood within its physical world, its personal and social world, the journey is not complete until this final integration of human and divine spirit is accomplished and understood.

This final step will reveal Hegel's great ontological declaration: **individual human subjects are fully autonomous centers of being whose life-process and the real, tangible living thereof is the vehicle of the separation and differentiation of Universal Spirit (God) and thereby their very own selves.**[86]

Religious Selfhood

The full mutuality of individual spirit(s) and absolute Spirit occurs under the rubric of religious selfhood. Again, Religious selfhood is **not** a process undertaken upon the completion of prior phases, but a process which **parallels** all prior patterns of development. The Hegelian history of religious awareness reflects two poles: (1) the human search for absolute Spirit from the vantage point of human history **and** (2) the story of absolute Spirit as it seeks itself in human history.

Whereas prior developments tended to focus upon "horizontal" themes, namely selfhood's seeking a certain unity with itself and with other selves, religious selfhood describes the seeking of unity on the "vertical" plane where the object is Spirit itself.[87] This process therefore plots the forms by which the human self comes to discover and relate to that reality within which its selfhood is grounded.

Religious awareness, as Hegel sees it, can manifest itself along a vast continuum from total unconsciousness of Spirit to full consciousness of Spirit. In using developmental motifs to name these forms, Hegel is not suggesting that they simply succeed one another chronologically, but that they represent the full range of manifestations of Spirits' self-revelation as appropriated by human consciousness.

Religious themes have been present throughout the Hegelian model depicted thus far. In all cases, however, Absolute Spirit has either been completely unconscious (within natural consciousness, for example) or seen strictly as a transcendent other (as in unhappy consciousness). Within religious selfhood, however, human awareness begins to relate to the Absolute **as its own self,** or said another way, selfhood comes to its deepest self in dialectic encounter with the Absolute.

Just as earlier dialectic processes moved from (1) a discovery of the object (consciousness), to (2) a discovery of the subject (self-consciousness), and finally, (3) a harmony between subject and object, so too does religious selfhood manifest this same pattern. These three steps Hegel calls (1) Nature Religion (2) Artistic Religion, and (3) Revealed Religion. This three-step movement describes the progressive manifestation of Spirit as Self.

One final caution deserves mention. Hegel is not painting an **individual** historical picture as if one person moves through all these phases. His intent is to highlight the grand sweep of religious awareness from the most primitive to the most sophisticated with the entire range representing the many forms through which the human self has experienced its union with the Divine.

Nature Religion

Nature religion is religion in its inert form where "spirit knows itself as its object in a natural or immediate shape."[88] Spirit becomes known through the direct encounter with nature, with Spirit identified simply with manifestations of the natural world. In its simplist form it is represented by God as **light** as found in ancient Sun-worship or in the religion of early Zoroastrianism. At this basic level Spirit is present simply as inert substance or "pure being."[89] There is a rudimentary awareness of Spirit but only as a "formless" form. Religious awareness at this elementary level is analogous to sense-knowing, in which awareness of objects occurs but without recognition of the complex patterns and relationships occurring between subjects and objects.

As religious awareness moves beyond formlessness it arrives at a pantheism which attributes divine qualities to objects in nature such as plants or animals."[90] Pantheism is the religious equivalent to "perception" as discussed earlier. Spiritual "perception" as we might call it, establishes a linkage between the Absolute and the world by "housing" the divine in the beings of nature. The worship of plants or animals invests them with a "quasi-self" with the particular plant or animal deity "carrying" selfhood so to speak. Totemism and Animism represent such a rudimentary connection between objects and a universal subjectivity.

As spiritual inclinations move beyond the simple identification of natural objects as divine, there emerges the tendency to create "artificial" objects which are intended to reveal a deeper spiritual presence. At this point spiritual reality begins to be represented by shapes (images) and material entities such as the pyramids of Egypt or the Black Stone of Mecca. What makes this transition so critical for Hegel is that the sacred object becomes not simply something "found" by us but "created" by us, thereby moving human awareness closer to the possibility that it is itself sacred.[91] No longer content to passively observe the sacred moving about in animal form, spiritual awareness has begun to produce itself as an object.

Nevertheless, this noteworthy step is severely limited because spirit remains an alien force residing in lifeless objects which cannot speak. The "self" or subjectivity of the statue has not yet emerged leaving inner and outer split and unrelated. There is as yet no **internal recognition** so necessary for the fullness of identity, but only an **external**, but unconscious identification.

This marks the highest level reachable for nature religion. Such religion has gained an awareness of the Absolute, although it is restricted to seeing the Absolute in "objective" or external form only. To move further, religious awareness must discover itself as self (subject) which Hegel claims occurs within the process he calls Religion as Art.

Artistic Religion

Why would Hegel attempt to tie art into a model of unfolding spiritual self-awareness? In Hegel's estimation, artistic activity brings subjective processes to the light of day via the objectification of the artistic product. Such activity therefore allows the human spirit to become more fully known to itself bringing it closer to its full subjectivity as self.

Just as Nature Religion finds its highest expression in Egyptian religious consciousness according to Hegel, Greek religion represents the highest achievement of the anthropomorphic embodiment of the Absolute. The divine is no longer "other" for the Greeks, but finds expression in human physical form (statue), human ritualistic practice (cultic manifestations), and human language (literature and drama etc.). These manifestations require brief elaboration.

The so-called "lowest" form of art Hegel calls abstract, referring to an artistic product that is static or lifeless and therefore a poor reflection of self or spirit.[92] Although an artist might create a "beautiful" marble statue in human form, it is not a self. While the use of human form is a major advance from the infusion of spirit into plants or animals, it cannot reflect the movement vital for spirit as self. Selfhood has gained an objectification, but only in its **form** and not in its **content**, not in its full subjectivity. This Hegel calls "an individuality that is at rest."[93]

To move beyond a strictly object-focused spirituality, a higher medium becomes necessary which Hegel finds in **language**. Language allows for the dynamic qualities of self to emerge, providing an immediate link between inner and outer. Just as language became an important vehicle for the establishment of personal self-awareness as discussed earlier, so too does language facilitate a higher expression of union between the human and the divine.

The most elementary forms of language used to depict spirit Hegel calls **Devotion** and **Oracle**.[94] The former represents the simple utterance of a believer toward her undifferentiated deity, the latter the pronouncements of the God received by the devotees as universally-binding truth. In both instances human identity has found a connection between its own life and its God, with this linkage expressed in very simplistic and naive terms.

The simplicity of the language which the self directs towards its deity reveals the shape of a self's self-perceptions. When a self has not differentiated its existence it

> utters equally simple and universal statements about the divine Being, the substantial content of which is sublime in its simple truth, but on account of this universality at the same time appears trivial to the progressively developing self-consciousness.[95]

This too is an unsatisfactory expression of religious selfhood because just as the static statue was only an objectification of spiritual form, simplistic religious language is locked into simple or uniform subjectivity.

The human effort to bring divine reality closer to a wider range of subjective experience occurs for Hegel through the various manifestations of cultic and ecstatic experience, including even the worship of athletic skill. These developments mark the beginning of a **living** or **animated** unity of human and divine life. This relationship may still be unconscious and dualistically divided, but it is nevertheless alive and active.

Cultic life represents the first formal attempt to bring a transcendent deity together with human self-consciousness. Cultic experience becomes a primary means through which persons attempt to find a more complete unity with their perceived God. In cult, the remote object of belief is made more real, more direct, with the core of personhood identified with this pure divine element.

Cultic activity includes rituals such as cleansing, sacrifice, and feasting, which in Hegel's mind suggests a "surrender" of what is unique or particular and an absorption of divine essence.[96] In surrendering one's uniqueness, selfhood symbolically lets go of its finiteness in order to become unified with the Absolute. The self is therefore split into a holy or cleansed portion, with the remainder rejected, with its cleansed core nevertheless guaranteeing the self's entry into heaven or the divine kingdom.

At the same time, the divine has entered into finite human form which makes the God more directly available to selfhood. In Hegel's estimation any cultic experience of undisciplined revelry or any experience of ecstatic self-transcendence illustrates such a taking-over of selfhood by the God.[97] Modern charismatic religion with its manifestations of "slaying in the spirit" and glossolalia, would serve as contemporary examples of the divine "showing up" in sudden, but brief form.

Although an important breakthrough, the emergence of feasting, ritual, or ecstasis is also inadequate since "the mystery of bread and wine is not yet the mystery of flesh and blood."[98] Its insufficiency, as we might guess, stems from the fact that self is only beginning to become aware of itself as spirit with its spiritual essence still very much in the hands of the remote, generally unavailable Deity.

Briefly restated, the formal presence of Spirit within Religious selfhood is first identified with the statue which incarnates only the outer shape of selfhood. With the emergence of simple devotion and accompanying cultic acts a further step is taken in which the God is now internally appropriated. This "taking-in" of one's God occurs through the parallel process of sacrificing one's distinctiveness, one's separation, while at the same time experiencing "oral" union with the divine through food or drink and ecstatic excitement. Thus, claims Hegel, in the statue we have the self in "perfectly free repose" while in ecstasy we have the self in "perfectly free movement."[99] Ecstatic feeling and movement is therefore a first level awareness of the animating presence of Spirit.

Hegel also suggests that the athlete represents another form of honoring an animating spiritual force, only in this case devoid of formal spiritual content. Hegel declares that the athlete provides a replacement for persons of the "god in stone" thereby carrying "the highest bodily representation among his people of their essence."[100] In both ecstatic experience and athletic excellence, then, there is reflected the animating potential of spirit. In the case of cultic enthusiasm the self is simply "beside itself" and lost in its inwardness, while in athletic prowess selfhood is "outside" of itself through the accomplishment it must maintain.

To move beyond the limits of either a **momentary** or **externalized** spirituality, a more articulate path must be taken which Hegel finds represented in Greek classical literature. Within the genres of Greek **epic, tragedy**, and **comedy**, he finds examples of spiritual life at a higher level of development. While not yet reflecting the full life of selfhood, such representations are a useful form of "picture-thinking" which "synthetically" link inner life with external reality.[101]

Legends and myths are the form of this picture-language. In the struggles and dilemmas of the gods, heroes, and villains, internal spiritual reality comes into focus. Hegel's allegiance to Greek examples reflects his conclusion that they represent the highest forms of divine-human interaction. Each of the three forms he names represent a higher gradation of the interweaving of human and divine life.

In **Epic** (such as Homer's **Iliad** or the **Odyssey**) the narrator or singer is the only "real" person in the story even though this individual does not personally participate in the drama. All other characters, whether gods or heroes, represent spiritual forces in general without human ownership of them. These still alien forces are the factors which define the human-divine relationship. Within epic, for example, Hegel identifies what he calls the "irrational void of necessity."[102] The power of necessity (fate) controls both gods and persons suggesting that selfhood is becoming aware of the power of destiny or contingency for its life. While fate is seen as autonomous or detached within Epic, it is taken more fully into selfhood within the more advanced genre of **Tragedy**.

In **Tragedy**, fate is no longer active as external force but is becoming a consequence of one's own actions. In Tragedy the actress participates in the role, takes it into herself, although still behind the mask or Persona.[103] Here the actress is not simply hopeless in the face of fate but fights against it and through the narrative reveals the inner workings of her selfhood. In the trials and tribulations of Oedipus, for example, we see a particular internal pattern of selfhood beginning to be revealed. In Tragedy, "archetypal" truth makes itself known, but still in the form of something which "happens" to its victims. What the self ascribes to fate or circumstance is at this point still unrecognized truth about itself.

The final development of artistic religion Hegel calls **comedy**. In comedy, the attributes of selfhood which were projected onto the Gods are now appropriated. In comedy the mask falls away and the weaknesses and foolish foibles of the Gods are exposed. The unconscious unity between the human and the divine represented by fate is overcome, and a fuller ownership of oneself becomes possible. In short, the Gods and heroes of mythology, of epic, tragedy and comedy, are "moments" or snapshots of internal life played out on a universal stage. But because they are products of the "imagination", they are "universal moments" and therefore not a self.[104] For a self to be a self it must actualize itself in concrete, specific terms, in a real, here-and-now existence.

Through the creative process, then, human subjectivity becomes objective for itself. When it does so fully, it reverses the process which occurred within Nature Religion. Within Nature Religion as we recall, there was no autonomous human subjectivity to speak of, with all processes of human life attributable to the nature Gods who manipulated the substance of the universe including of course, human life. For Artistic Religion, however, this process has reversed itself. The artistic process slowly revokes the autonomy of the Gods bringing their power more and more into the service of the human self within which these forces operate. The culmination of this path is reached by the comic who uncovers the powerlessness of the gods, revealing them to be mere "clouds", a mist of "imaginary representations."[105]

Hegel's summary of this final outcome is quite instructive:

This incarnation of the divine Being starts from the statue which wears only the outer shape of the Self [with] the **inwardness**, the

> Self's activity, falling outside of it. But in the Cult, the two sides have become one; and in the outcome of the religion of Art, this unity, in its consummation, has even gone right over at the same time to the extreme of the Self. In spirit that is completely certain of itself in the individuality of consciousness, all essentiality is submerged. The proposition that expresses this levity runs: "The Self is absolute Being".[106]

Hegel's point is that when selfhood is stripped of its divine linkage it becomes its own God which in his mind is a bad joke.

Hegel is of course attacking the declarations of the secular spirit of his day which declared selfhood to be completely self-sufficient. The essence of such a self resides strictly within itself, a selfhood in communion only with itself. This "self-certain spirit" sees itself as Absolute, and is drunk with the wine of its own individuality. This supposedly blissful state of affairs is most tragic for Hegel since the essence of selfhood becomes lost. When selfhood reaches such an arrogant self-sufficiency it can only declare that "God is dead!" claims Hegel.[107] This harsh phrase is the password of a self which has reduced the Absolute to itself. In so doing it loses the capacity to transcend itself thereby losing its very self. As inevitable as this step may be it is of course not Hegel's final word.

Revealed Religion

Revealed religion names the Hegelian path by which the above negation begins to be overcome and the self and the divine become united. In order for this union to occur the Absolute must become flesh, with Spirit taking on bodily form, and body taking on spiritual form. In the crucible of authentic religious experience the infinite and the finite become united, with the identity called **"child of God"** when viewed from the human perspective, and **"child of a Human"** when viewed from the vantage point of the divine. This fully integrated relationship is one in which the human and divine come to themselves through the other. Hegel does not suggest thereby that the human and divine are identical, but that they find their true nature through the other. We would not be in error to sense a strong echo of Meister Eckhart in this declaration, nor of the Biblical motifs which first gave hint of this vision.

178

For Hegel this process finds its clearest expression in the incarnate God. Only spirit's radical kenosis or emptying of its transcendent otherness allows Spirit to fully actualize itself as self. Conversely, human selfhood is now able to appropriate Spirit as its very own self. Because of the eternal gap between the finite and the infinite, this final reconciliation requires a mediator - one who in his/her own being perfectly ties together the universal and the finite. It is not enough, however, to envision this mediator as an object of devotion since this would leave the devotee seeking the other in a remote beyond as has undermined so many prior efforts at unification.

This divine being must become fully **actualized** in the life of the self, not simply as a form of correct thinking, feeling, or believing. The truth of the God-person, the mediator, must be both the object **and** subject of self-awareness - it must itself become a subject. **This moment-to-moment incarnation of Spirit is the Self.** In perhaps the most noteworthy words in the entire *Phenomenology of Spirit*, Hegel offers us his final vision:

> This incarnation of the divine Being, or the fact it essentially and directly has the shape of self-consciousness is the simple content of the absolute religion. In this religion, the divine Being is known as Spirit, or this religion is the consciousness of the divine Being that it is Spirit. For Spirit is the knowledge of oneself in the externalization of oneself; the being that is the movement of retaining its self-identity in its otherness. This, however, is Substance, insofar as Substance is, in its accidents at the same time reflected into itself, not indifferent to them as to something unessential or present in them as an alien element, but in them, it is within itself i.e. insofar as it is subject or self.[108]

What makes these words so significant is their vision of integration which has eluded all prior reconciliations. For every prior step along the way, there was always something which was labeled as alien, something other, thereby excluding it from selfhood. However, in the unity of Revealed Religion, all negation dissolves because infinite and finite become one.

In Revealed Religion the divine Being becomes fully known. Because this divine Being is self-conscious, it reveals itself as self-conscious. For this reason human self-consciousness can recognize its identity with the divine. Hegel elaborates:

> Spirit is known as self-consciousness and to this self-consciousness, it is immediately revealed, for Spirit is this self-consciousness itself. The divine nature is the same as the human, and it is this unity that is beheld.[109]

In the life of particular beings, God reveals God's self. God reveals God's life in the form of self in unity with itself.

This vision is not merely a nice idea for Hegel, but one which is made real in a concrete, living process. Absolute being is not static - it did not create the world once for all - but it eternally reveals itself in opening itself up in and for the world. This activity of pouring itself out finds itself actualized in the human self. In coming down from its eternal purity, Absolute Being gains its "highest essence".[110] It must be this way, insists Hegel, because Universal Being is only complete when it actualizes itself through the individuality of selfhood.

In Revealed Religion, then, God becomes known as universal selfhood **and** as its particular manifestation. This does not mean that completion is achieved only by the God, but that human self-consciousness recognizes itself in God. This "self-discovery" is the source of the world's hope and joy asserts Hegel:

> The hopes and expectations of the world up till now has pressed forward solely to this revelation, to behold what absolute Being is and in it to find itself. The joy of beholding itself in absolute Being enters self-consciousness and seizes the whole world; for it is Spirit, it is the simple movement of those pure moments, which expresses just this: that only when absolute Being is beheld as an **immediate** self-consciousness it is known as Spirit.[111]

Absolute Knowing

The great limitation of revealed religion however, which leaves it handicapped is its on-going propensity to appropriate this truth in "picture" form only. When the truth of revealed religion is kept at arms length so to speak, then a full identification of human subject with divine object cannot occur.

Hegel's concern is that the process of discovering one's universal self (without losing one's individuality) can run aground in one of two ways. It can deteriorate to a form of "sense-knowing" where the Universal is sought only in sensate, historical form. For such an individual, the Absolute is then known only as a particular being who, although fully God, was present only in a historical past

(Jesus). Such a perspective can only look backwards in the hope of finding its truth in an ever-receeding past, thereby revealing that it has not overcome the separation of otherness. Such an individual knows the historically objective God, but not itself, as Spirit.[112]

Revealed Religion also runs aground when it can only imagine itself unified with its object of devotion at some undetermined future date.[113] The remoteness of this hope again reveals the inability of such a self to come to a full and immediate identity of itself as Spirit. Religious awareness must move beyond such picture-thinking to become a self, a step which is only accomplished through Absolute knowing.

Absolute knowing sheds all otherness and becomes aware that all the stations encountered thus far are its very own self. Absolute knowing takes absolute ownership of all that is and reconciles itself to it.

This brings us to the Hegelian conclusion that human self-awareness must come to fully reflect divine life as an incarnation of universal Spirit, even though this union has already been accomplished in the unique God-person. As vital as it is that this truth have occurred as a single, historical event (for the reason that the eternal must be fully finite), it must also be an eternal event, that is, made real in the wider flow of life. For as long as the form of universal selfhood resides only in another (even if the other is the God-person) it remains remote and unreachable leaving personhood stuck in self-depreciation.

The great vision of Hegelian selfhood is that the truth of the God-person is the truth of universal selfhood and is the essence of all persons. The individual human subject can now recognize herself as a finite and temporal manifestation of the eternal life of the Divine, grounding human identity in the full life of God. The fullness of this subjectivity is realized only in the eternal drama of Incarnation, Crucifixion, and Resurrection which finds actualization in every moment. All of the many tensions of life are "taken-in" by such a self as it maintains a loving stance toward all the otherness it encounters, knowing that through this very otherness it is born and for this otherness it must die.

Preliminary Responses

A great deal was promised by Hegel as we ventured onto the grand path of unity toward which he beckoned us. You have no doubt experienced your own reactions to Hegel and formed your own impressions of the adequacy of his model for carrying all that is claimed for it. As you will recall from my introduction to this chapter, I suggested that Hegel should not be seen in isolation, but that he and Kierkegaard together represent a composite picture of the process and purpose of selfhood.

In order to remain true to this thesis we must wait for Kierkegaard's response to Hegel before our own final verdict can be issued. Nevertheless, this does not mean we can say nothing further about Hegel. Surely he can be evaluated on his own terms and what better way to do so than to see if Hegel delivered what he promised? What was Hegel's overriding purpose?

The matter/spirit split which had frustrated so many efforts at resolution forced itself upon Hegel after the failure of Kant, Fichte, and the Romantics to resolve the contradictions inherent in their attempts to provide nature with a meaning and direction. Increasingly, scholars had looked to human subjectivity as the highest form of meaningful activity in the universe, implying that within human persons this strange mixture of nature and spirit must find harmonization. While the Enlightenment skeptics scoffed at this possibility, their repulsion seemed directed largely at the autonomous Cartesian "mind" which supposedly harmonized all human thoughts, feelings, and perceptions, independent of the body and the material universe.

As I described, the attempted correctives of Kant and Fichte were only marginally successful in that the movement of Spirit in the universe remained more or less self-contained within itself, thereby not only robbing nature of any subjectivity, but also undercutting the possibility of freedom for the self. Into this dilemma plunged Hegel, who offered us **the** definitive effort at describing the spiritual cohesion of nature as it becomes focused within human subjectivity.

Hegel's revolutionary approach was to take the **practical functionalism** of an Aristotle and wed it to the **mysticism** of a St. Paul and Meister Eckhart thereby infusing everything that is with a meaningful role in the unfolding of Absolute Spirit. A limited unity had already emerged in Plato and Augustine but for them the link between God and persons was a one-way street with human subjective life simply reflecting the eternal self-contained unity of God. Now, in Hegel, human personhood not only reflects the unity of God, but completes, or better said, actualizes it. By allowing for movement and development within the Absolute -- **even as it fully is what it is** -- Hegel is able to bring together **being** and **becoming** while furthermore giving human selfhood an indispensable role in this process. God and persons become partners in a grand drama of **separation - individuation - reconciliation.**

How is Hegel able to accomplish this partnership while maintaining a sense of self as living, self-conscious organism? What is the factor which allows Hegel to weave human subjectivity into the subjectivity of God without sacrificing the freedom of God or persons **and** without violating (or abandoning) nature?

The key ingredient which allows Hegel to accomplish this feat is the **bi-polarity of selfhood**. To be a self, claims Hegel, involves divisions, or better said, differentiations, so that what is once uniform becomes nuanced and present to itself. This process of **separation, individuation**, and **integrating transformation** is determinative for Hegel, not only for the human life cycle, but for the life of God. But as brilliant as this mechanism of enmeshment - separation-individuation - reunification may be, are there any flaws we can detect without robbing Kierkegaard of his critique?

While we may grant Hegel a legitimacy to his quest, his means of arriving at his all-encompassing destination leaves much to be desired. As we moved through the Hegelian model it took on an increasingly forced quality because of his need to fit its stages into the formal categories of **logic** and **cognition.** In order to distance himself from the Romantics, Hegel was forced to abandon **affectivity** and **interior process,** and in so doing he purified the process of its passion, consistently forcing it into the thin air of abstraction. Its artificiality and rigidity emerges because of this heavy reliance upon thinking and logic through which everything must pass.

Hegel, we may conclude, grounds human identity in its **immanent** union with the Absolute. God and self are locked into an eternal dance with one determined by the other. While this Absolute union may be noble, is it not an artificial and a forced union? It is legitimate to ask whether **Absolute knowing** as Hegel understands it, can truly "carry" or justify a possibility as absurd as a divine-human identity. Furthermore, can individual or corporate human subjectivity legitimately fulfill or complete the universe, however "Universal" one might envision such subjectivity? Hegel's need for total comprehensiveness (as mediated by himself, the philosopher) hints at an Hegelian arrogance which may yet find a massive deflation. To determine whether this is so we must proceed with the one whose wrath was aroused by this grand scheme: Soren Kierkegaard.

1. Mark C. Taylor, *Journeys to Selfhood: Hegel and Kierkegaard* (Berkley: University of California Press, 1980), p. 10

2. Paul Ricoeur, "Two Encounters with Kierkegaard", *Kierkegaard's Truth: The Disclosure of the Self*, Joseph H. Smith, Ed. (New Haven: Yale University Press, 1981), p. 341

3. Charles Taylor, *Hegel*, (Cambridge: Cambridge University Press, 1975), p. 43ff. I am largely indebted to Taylor for my response to this question.

4. Ibid., p. 43

5. Ibid., p. 43

6. Ibid., p. 44

7. G.W.F. Hegel, *Phenomenology of Spirit*, translated by A.V. Miller, (Oxford: Clarendon Press, 1977), p. 12

8. Ibid., p. 459

9. Ibid., p. 21

10. Ibid., p. 12

11. Ibid., p. 11

12. George Connell, *To Be One Thing*, (Macon, Georgia: Mercer University Press, 1985), p. 102, 190

13. Jean Hyppolite, *Genesis and Structure of Hegel's Phenomenology of Spirit*, translated by Samuel Chermak and John Heckman, (Evanston: Northwestern University Press, 1974), p. 11

14. Hegel, *Phenomenology*, 1977, p. 12

15. Ibid., p. 19

184

16.   Ibid., p. 55

17.   Martin Heidegger, *Hegel's Phenomenology of Spirit*, translated by Parvis Emad and Kenneth Maly, (Bloomington and Indianapolis: Indiana University Press, 1988), p. 25

18.   Hyppolite, 1974, p. 23

19.   Hegel, Phenomenology, 1977, p. 55

20.   Taylor, 1975, p. 119

21.   Donald Phillip Verene, *Hegel's Recollections: A Study of Images in the Phenomenology of Spirit* (Albany: State University of New York Press, 1985), p. 22

22.   Hegel, *Phenomenology*, 1977, p. 17

23.   Heinz Kohut, *The Restoration of the Self*, (New York: International Universities Press, Inc. 1977), p. 220

24.   Hans Kung, *The Incarnation of God*, translated by J.R. Stephenson (New York: Crossroad Publishing Company, 1987), p. 220

25.   Hyppolite, 1974, p. 33

26.   Ibid., p. 579

27.   Hegel, 1977, p. 57

28.   Ibid., p. 49

29.   Ibid., p. 16. See also Clark Butler, "Hegel and Freud: A Comparison", *Philosophy and Phenomenological Research, Journeys to Selfhood*, Hegel and Kierkegaard (Berkley: University of California Press, 1980), p. 80

30.   Hegel, 1977, p. 58

31.   Ibid., p. 58

32.   Richard Norman, *Hegel's Phenomenology: A Philosophical Introduction* (London: Sussex University Press, 1976), p. 34

33.   Howard P. Kainz, *Hegel's Phenomenology, Part I: Analysis and Commentary*, (The University of Alabama Press, 1976), p. 63

34.   At another level, however, Hegel may also be describing an observable process within human development. Sense-knowing as an initial form of consciousness seems supported by the experiments of Rene Spitz and Margaret Mahler among others. In their observations of very young infants these researchers concluded that early ego capacities of seeing and hearing seem to "absorb" the stimulation emerging from the environment without the capacity to digest or fully process the data coming at the undeveloped ego. In this initial phase of development which psychoanalytic theory calls **autism** and early **symbiosis**, the impact of the object seems absolute.
Rene Spitz, *The First Year of Life*, (New York: International Universities Press, 1965). Margaret Mahler, Fred Pine, Anni Bergman, *The Psychological Birth of the Human Infant*, (New York: Basic Books, Inc., 1975)

35.   Hegel, 1977, p. 61

36.   Solomon, 1983, p. 322

37.   Ibid., p. 339

38.   Kainz, 1976, p. 68

39.   Mahler, Pine, and Bergman, 1975

40.   Norman, 1976, p. 40

41.   Hegel, 1977, p. 90

42.   Ibid., p. 95, 96

43.   Werner Heisenberg, *Physics and Philosophy*, (New York: Harper and Row, 1958), p. 58

44.   Hegel, 1977, p. 103, 105. Throughout our study, from Plato, through Augustine, Eckhart, Fichte, and now Hegel and Kierkegaard we will find the subject-object linkage activated through desire. Contemporary psychoanalytic theory will develop this notion in the 20th Century through the concept of libido.

45.   Ibid., p.109

46.   Ibid., p. 110

47.   Ibid., p. 113

48.   Ibid., p. 115

49.   Ibid., p. 118

50.   Ibid., p. 119

51.   Ibid., p. 120

52.   Solomon, 1983, p. 461

53.   Hegel, 1977, p. 123

54.   Ibid., p. 126

55.   Ibid., p. 140

56.   J.N. Findlay, *Hegel: A Re-examination*, (New York: The Macmillan Company, 1958), p. 103

57.   Taylor, 1975, p. 161

58.   Ibid., p. 162

59.   Kainz, 1977, p. 99

60.   Hegel, 1977, p. 193-195

61.   Ibid., p. 186ff

62.   Ibid., p. 217

63.   Ibid., p. 218

64.   Findlay, 1958, p. 110

65.   Hegel, 1977, p. 219

66.   Taylor, 1985, p. 164

67.   Hegel, 1977, p. 221

68.   Mark C. Taylor, 1980, p. 202

69.   Hegel, 1977, p. 266ff

70.   Hegel, 1977, p. 292

71.   Ibid., p. 297ff. Note also Hyppolite, 1974, p. 384

72. Hegel, 1977, p. 305

73. Ibid., p. 312

74. Ibid., p. 316

75. Ibid., p. 321

76. Ibid., p. 296

77. Ibid., p. 342

78. Kainz, 1983, p. 84

79. Hegel, 1977, p. 356-357

80. Ibid., p. 365

81. Charles Taylor, 1975, p. 192

82. Findlay, 1958, p. 128

83. Hegel, 1977, p. 390

84. Charles Taylor, 1975, p. 193

85. Ibid., p. 194

86. Hegel, 1977, p. 409

87. Kainz, 1983, p. 126

88. Hegel, 1977, p. 416

89. Ibid., p. 419

90. Ibid., p. 420

91. Solomon, 1983, p. 602

92. Hegel, 1977, p. 427

93. Ibid., p. 428

94. Ibid., p. 430

95. Ibid., p. 431

96.   Ibid., p. 433

97.   Ibid., p. 439

98.   Ibid., p. 439

99.   Ibid., p. 439 .

100. Ibid., p. 438

101. Ibid., p. 440

102. Ibid., p. 443

103. Ibid., p. 443

104. Ibid., p. 443

105. Ibid., p. 451-452

106. Ibid., p. 453

107. Ibid., p. 455

108. Ibid., p. 459

109. Ibid., p. 460

110. Hegel, G.W.F. Hegel, *Lectures on the Philosophy of Religion.* edited by
      Peter C. Hodgson, Translated by R.F. Brown, P.C. Hodgson, and J.M.
      Stewart (Berkley: University of California Press, 1988), p. 469

111. Ibid., p. 469

112. Hegel, 1977, p. 463

113. Ibid., p. 589

CHAPTER VI

SOREN KIERKEGAARD (1813 - 1855) AND THE SYNTHESIZING
SELF

THE KIERKEGAARDIAN SELF

If Hegel is the great champion of universal selfhood, then Kierkegaard stands as the guardian of the self's radical isolation. Hegel's overriding purpose was to plot the path by which "the Absolute" becomes aware of itself. It accomplishes this feat by overcoming all objectivity in an ever-expanding circle of self-awareness. This possibility repelled Kierkegaard.

The winter of 1841-1842 found Kierkegaard attending the University of Berlin and being particularly captivated by the lectures of Schelling who strongly critiqued the analytic perfection of Hegel's system. An anti-Hegelian mood was sweeping intellectual circles at the time and Kierkegaard found much useful material at his disposal for attacking the rationally-based unity of Hegel which was so offensive to him.

However, we should not allow the obvious tensions between Hegel and Kierkegaard to obscure our recognition of a common concern which motivated them both. Kierkegaard stands closely aligned with Hegel in challenging all static and dualistic understandings of self. Both insist upon the subject-object interaction as central to the process of self, and both describe self as a relational synthesis, a dynamic and living interaction between its constituted elements. It is in their divergent understandings of the **make-up** of these elements and how these relations are **lived out** that the great gulf between them will emerge. What, then, is the Kierkegaardian self?

The Self as Synthesizing Process

"The self is a relation" - so begins Kierkegaard's description of selfhood.[1] But a relation of what? In its most elemental form selfhood is constituted by the seemingly dichotomous entities of "matter" and "mind" commonly called body and psyche. These entities-in-relation must attain a union, a synthesis, in order for one to even speak of selfhood. This synthesis is unthinkable for Kierkegaard without the two being united in a third factor which he calls spirit.

> A human being is spirit. But what is spirit? Spirit is the self. But what is the self? The self is a relation that relates itself to itself.[2]

For Hegel, Spirit is also the integrating or uniting factor, an **outgrowth** of the encounter between a subject and its objects. For Kierkegaard, however, this third factor is not the **outcome** of the unity gained by subjects and objects, but the process which **relates the factors to each other** and brings them into harmony. This third factor is the self.

Hegel, as we recall, also defined the self as a relation which relates itself to itself, which can only leave us wondering what all the fuss is about. What makes Kierkegaard's position so different?

In Kierkegaard's estimation, Hegel's notion of self as spirit is simply a relation between two polarized elements, this being a negative unity.

> A synthesis is a relation between two. Considered in this way a human being is still not a self. In the relation between two, the relation is the third as a negative unity...[3]

As far as Kierkegaard is concerned, it is insufficient to simply bind together in a relation two radical opposites such as body and psyche. To be truly related requires a synthesis in which the polarities of selfhood are united in a third element **which itself synthesizes.**

This Kierkegaardian use of synthesis is very different from the Hegelian. For Hegel, synthesis represents the resolution of the dialectic process through which self is unified. In Hegel all opposites are eventually reconciled and overcome. Kierkegaard finds this completely unacceptable - a negative unity only.[4]

The self for Kierkegaard is **not** a harmonious synthesis in which opposition is overcome, but the capacity to hold the polarized elements in a creative tension. But if this synthesis is a positive "third" element how is it discernible? Kierkegaard answers:

> This synthesis is a relation and a relation that even though it is derived, relates itself to itself, which is freedom. The self is freedom.[5]

The predominant manifestation of this positive "third" element is the **freedom** which allows selfhood to steer between its polarities. In equating selfhood with freedom, Kierkegaard is highlighting the self's capacity to choose itself, to give itself shape. It is this capacity which is the source of the self's anxiety. But what are these polarities which constitute selfhood?

There are three polarities which make up the structural framework of the Kierkegaardian self: (1) **possibility-necessity** (2) **finitude-infinitude** and (3) **temporal-eternal**. The self is the living process which not only **mediates** between these polarities (Hegel) but is the relation which actively relates itself to these elements which are its building blocks, i.e. its self. The self does not simply mediate between these opposites (negative unity) but becomes a new entity (positive third). This self synthesizes itself within the confines of its history and its structural givens and in so doing gives shape to itself for better or worse.

The Possibility-Necessity Polarity

This first polarity defines the boundary of the self with regard to its existence in the world. We must again declare that the Kierkegaardian self does not simply steer a course **between** necessity and possibility, but must **embrace** both possibility and necessity within itself. But what does this polarity really represent?

Possibility/necessity stakes out the structure of the self in its historical existence i.e. in the trenches of its existential realities. A self must deal with the fact that it is dependent upon and determined by the limits of its body, its history, and its time, just as it is open to the possibilities which are available to it. We might say that a self establishes a relationship towards its **limits** and its **possibilities** and in so doing becomes a self. To relate itself to these elements is what makes a self free. A self which relates itself only to its necessities is not free, just as a self which only chases its possibilities is in bondage. The freedom which makes it possible to be a self is never an absolute freedom but a dual freedom embracing both possibility and necessity.

The possibility/necessity tension suspends a self between what is and what can be. The questions "who have I been?" "Who can I be?" "Who can I not be?" capture the tension of the ever-present need to define oneself against the possibilities which present themselves throughout life, even as these possibilities are hemmed in by the limits and givens of my body, abilities, social and familial histories, and so forth. Even as the final limit, death, imposes itself possibilities remain, unless of course sudden death presents itself which only underscores the very contingency and finiteness of my being as the next polarity illustrates.

The Finite-Infinite Polarity

If the above polarity highlights the existential or historical boundaries of selfhood, then this second polarity highlights the self in its basic nature (its essence). Kierkegaard says the following of this second polarity:

> The self is the conscious synthesis of infinitude and finitude that relates itself to itself, whose task is to become itself which can be done only through the relationship to God. To become oneself is to become concrete. But to become concrete is neither to become finite nor to become infinite, for that which is to become concrete is indeed a synthesis. Consequently, the progress of becoming must be an infinite moving-away from itself in the infinitizing of the self, and an infinite coming-back to itself in the finitizing process.[6]

A key word used in this summary is the word "becoming". The self's development is governed by finitude and infinitude, by the embracing of the finite, immediate self one is, while infinitely moving toward a re-constellation of selfhood in the not-yet. To be finite and infinite at the same time is to be real - to be one's self. To be finite means to accept the reality of one's body, the realities of one's cultural/social/familial environments into which one is born, and to accept the particular history which makes up one's self. To be infinite is to be infinitely confronted by the possibilities through which a self must actualize itself - must make itself real.

What, then makes finitude-infinitude different from the necessity - possibility polarity? First of all, possibility - necessity defines the **actual** life experience of a self through which it becomes the self it is. The finite-infinite polarity on the other hand represents the limits and limitlessness which constitute selfhood. In other words, selfhood is governed by the endless process of moving away from itself through the various possibilities which present themselves to a self, and by an endless returning to itself by the actual realization of a particular possibility. This is what makes a self "concrete" or real and this re-constellating of selfhood is infinite even as a self becomes finite.

Secondly, we as selves are not only infinitely called upon to choose ourselves but this choosing of ourselves has the ideal of infinite possibility before it, claims Kierkegaard. Infinite possibility refers to the self's capacity to transcend its limits through its projecting of an image of itself. Kierkegaard elaborates:

> Inasmuch as the self as a synthesis of finitude and infinitude is established [as dynamic], in order to become itself, it reflects itself in the medium of imagination, and thereby the infinite possibility becomes manifest.[7]

Imagination is the mechanism through which we reflect the various images of ourselves. It is the means by which we relate ourselves to ourselves as we engage the polarities of our being. This capacity of imagination is foundational for Kierkegaard to all other capacities, such as feeling, knowing, or willing. Kierkegaard explains:

> When all is said and done, whatever of feeling, knowing, and willing a person has depends upon what imagination he has, upon how that person **reflects himself*** - that is, upon imagination.[8]

It is through imagination that we contemplate ourselves and actualize or shrink from the possibilities before us. Imagination or **self-reflection** is the spring-board which launches us toward our possibilities and limits, the encounter with which gives rise to our joy and despair. The images which the self holds before itself become its guiding light, the reality against which it measures itself.

The self, therefore, relates itself to itself by virtue of its projected images of itself.[9] These images can reflect a wide range of selfhood, from the highest unity to the grossest disarray.

To have grounded the self's relation to itself in its relationship to its projected images of itself is the genius of Hegel's and now Kierkegaard's insight. Together, they affirm that these images grow out of the self's relationship to otherness. As will be confirmed with the advent of 20th Century psychoanalytic thought, such images can range from the earliest internalization of parental mirroring, to the "imprinting" of all interpersonal life, to include even the relation to an ultimate "other". Every encounter with an object becomes a building block for the self, an "introject" through which it defines itself.

The Temporal-Eternal Polarity

The self as eternal is by no means a static, unchangeable soul cut off from time. For substantialists such as Descartes the self as soul was an abiding, permanent, and stable structure which stayed the same amidst the flow of its experiences. For Kierkegaard the self is a living process with "temporal" and "eternal" describing the stability of the self even as it changes.

As temporal, a self is changeable, developing through time in its on-going formation. As eternal, a self is not unchangeable but stable or abiding even over time. There is a continuity to selfhood, a self-identity even through its changes.[10] The unchanging "given" of the self-system is its ever-present capacity to relate itself to itself. A self is eternally in relationship with itself making choices based on this relationship which gives it its specific shape. Even though the particular shape of the self is in constant change, the fact that it does such changing never changes. It is this eternal factor which allows the self to be free.[11]

As eternal I have the capacity not only to live in continuity with my past and toward my own future, but I am able to be "real" or congruent with myself as I change. To be eternal allows my real self to emerge even as I undergo the changes which life requires of me.

All polarities which make up the self system come together for Kierkegaard in **the moment**, the instant when the self makes those choices which bring together its historical givens with its ever-present possibilities. The story of this "choosing" is the story of the self's development. This is the source of the tension within us, as we attempt to discover and accept who we are in the midst of who we **have been**, who we think we **should** be, who we legitimately **could** be, and the lingering guilt over who we **might have been**. The following diagram illustrates the coalescing of self in the moment of choice.

Thus, choosing oneself is not some simple one-dimensional mental act but a complex process in which a self attempts to accomplish the realization of its eternal possibilities as they collide with the givens of its necessities - historical, bodily, social, etc. Every phase of the human life cycle brings different necessities with it which define the outer limits of a self's possibilities. Each attainment of a possibility further defines the necessities (givens) which one brings to the next moment of self-formation, and so on. The moment, then, becomes the crucible of self-constellation, the balancing between what has been and what can be. It is this inevitable choosing which gives rise to the self's anxiety and despair.

The Self in Despair

Despair is Kierkegaard's term for the various forms of disorder which can occur as a self synthesizes its components. These forms of despair are directly related to the degree to which a self has or has not attained its selfhood.

Natural (Unconscious) Despair

The first type of despair is the despair of not having a self.[12] To be a self involves becoming a conscious synthesis of the dynamic elements which make up one's being. An individual who only lives out of one side of the self's polarities is in despair precisely because she is not a self.

Kierkegaard suggests that despair results when one side of any polarity swallows up the other. For instance, when a becoming self is caught in its infinitude to the neglect of its finitude then the individual becomes grandiose or carried away by his infinity.[13] Any function of selfhood, whether feeling, knowing, or willing, can become grandiose. If I become "carried away" with myself, I only lose myself more and more - resulting in despair. To lack finitude, then, is to lose oneself in thoughts, feelings, or actions in ways which are divorced from one's larger life context. To lose a sense of proportion, to value something in excess of its "real importance" is to become swallowed up by infinitude.

Conversely, despair also occurs when a self lacks infinitude, when it is stuck in its own narrowness or encapsulated existence. This is the despair of depersonalization, of becoming a number in the faceless crowd, of being totally hemmed in by one's own narrowness of thought, feeling, or action. This is for Kierkegaard the despair of secularism - of giving "infinite worth to the indifferent," thereby completely finitizing the self.[14] Kierkegaard writes of this despair:

> So it is with finitude's despair. Because a man is in this kind of despair he can very well live on in temporality, indeed, actually all the better, can appear to be a man, be publicly acclaimed, honored, esteemed, be absorbed by all the temporal goals. In fact, what is called the secular mentality consists simply of such men who, so to speak, mortgage themselves to the world.[15]

Despair, then, arises out of a lopsidedness of any of the polarities making up the self-system.

Just as is true with finitude/infinitude, a self without necessity becomes lost in its possibilities whether in the form of desire and craving, or in the form of the unlimited potential which it never actualizes, since that would concretize the self and force an end to the dreaming which offers such allure.

Conversely, a self without possibility becomes lost in necessity. A **fatalist** lives out a self where everything has become determined and therefore necessary. To be a self means to live with both necessity **and** possibility which Kierkegaard compares to inhaling and exhaling.[16] The determinist suffocates because he is without the oxygen of possibility. At the same time, possibility can be destroyed through trivialization, which Kierkegaard calls the despair of spiritlessness.[17] A self which trivializes collapses possibilities into **probabilities**, in a shallow comprehension of experience. To trivialize means to run from the possibilities which activate fear and hope, both of which grow out of an openness to what can be.

These forms of despair emerge out of the self's "natural" existence and refer only to the structural components which make up selfhood. Such despair is the inevitable by-product of a self unable to synthesize the parameters of its being. I have called these forms of despair "natural" in order to contrast them with the despair which comes with self-awareness.

The Despair of Self-Awareness

Kierkegaard suggests that despair increases its intensity in direct proportion to the degree of self-awareness attained.[18] The more aware or better said, "self-conscious" one is, the greater the potential for despair. It would be appropriate to ask what makes this despair so different from natural or unconscious despair? Natural despair is distinguished from self-conscious despair in that the former simply lives out the natural imbalances of selfhood as they arise out of the self's openness or closedness to its world of experience. Self-conscious despair on the other hand refers to the lack of awareness that one is spirit or self.

To fully become a self in Kierkegaard's estimation requires a dependence upon one's transcendent criterion, upon God, as the power which constitutes the self.

> Such a relation that relates itself to itself, a self, must either have established itself or have been established by another. If the relation that relates itself to itself has been established by another, then the relation is indeed the third, but this relation, the third, is yet again a relation and relates itself to that which established the entire relation.[19]

Kierkegaard's claim is that the ontological foundation of the self is the relation between the synthesizing self one is, and the transcendent author of the relation. It is this relation which gives the self its status as spirit. The form of despair which denies this relation is most visible from the vantage point of the temporal-eternal polarity of the self.

According to Kierkegaard, an individual with no relation to the eternal is governed only by the temporal, by what is immediately at hand, such as the temporal objects which make up one's life. Such an individual Kierkegaard calls an "immediate self", with despair inevitable because one is determined only by immediate needs, desires, interests, etc.[20] This first form of self-conscious despair involves "ignorance of the Eternal" which Kierkegaard compares to an individual who owns a mansion but is content to live in the basement.[21] The pleasure/displeasure engine alone runs such a life with no ownership of self as spirit.

A second level of self-conscious despair is the despair which has an awareness of the eternal demand placed upon it, in response to which it either (1) shrinks back in **weakness**, or (2) **defiantly** rejects this awareness as it **wills itself into existence**.[22]

Despair as Weakness. This first instance represents a self-aware individual who in attempts to take responsibility for the self while bumping up against some problem within this self. This confrontation with the limits or "flaws" of my selfhood can be so frightening that I am tempted to shrink back from claiming the self I vaguely see. I therefore choose not to be myself.

When despairing over its weakness a self has stopped identifying itself only with "externals" and has found a dim awareness of the eternal within itself, but it cannot sustain the rigorous effort required to become fully responsible for the self one actually is. This shrinking back from authentic ownership of oneself lives itself out in the most common form of despair as far as Kierkegaard is concerned - "the despair over something earthly."[23] This concern over finite things becomes the distraction or diversion so necessary to be able to avoid the real issue of ownership of oneself as spirit. The most tricky time of all for such a person is when he begins to turn inward to search for who he really is, with the impulse all to often deflected by focusing on some side issue such as "financial security," for example.

Another turn which can accompany the rudimentary awakening to selfhood is to clobber the self for being so weak. Kierkegaard calls this "in despair not to will to be oneself."[24] Such a self tries to run from the self it is but in rejecting a portion of one's selfhood one simply enters into a negative relationship to it, just as a lover who curses his beloved becomes negatively tied to and even consumed by the now hated other.

Despair as Defiance. The final form of self-conscious despair for Kierkegaard is the path of defiance in which one wills to be oneself through one's own power. In this instance the self resorts to "the despairing misuse of the eternal within the self to will in despair to be oneself."[25] This type of despair tries to acknowledge the eternal within as does the response of faith (to be discussed below), the difference being that the defiant self does not wish to lose itself in order to gain itself, but rather **wills** to be itself by its own efforts.

In order to despair with defiance there must be an awareness of an infinite self. But this awareness is only present in abstract form thinks Kierkegaard, in that the self has been severed from any relation to the power which established it.[26] Such a despairing self "wants to be master of itself or to create itself, to make his self into the self he wants to be, to determine what he will have or not have in his concrete self."[27] Such a self is aware of its strengths and limitations but at the same time it has taken the job of fashioning its self completely upon itself. This is the self-made man or woman.

Kierkegaard further distinguishes two forms of this defiant despair: (1) the acting self, and (2) the self acted upon.[28] The first form is the self actively shaping its world in order to find itself in it. This active defiance gives infinite worth and significance to its own products thereby creating its own kingdom which it can rule. What creates the despair, however, is that such a self rules over nothing. Such a self is a "hypothetical self", subordinate to the completion of whatever product, success, or validation it has set before itself. Consequently, such a self infinitely cancels itself out only to place a new "reason-de-etre" before itself, which **it** of course will master.

The other form of defiantly despairing selfhood is the self **acted upon** - which wills to be itself - but in **passive** form. This self also defiantly asserts itself, only here through its defects. This is the self which glories in its sufferings, holding onto them dearly because they so nicely define its self. This gives the person the means to be both related to the eternal, by defiantly asserting oneself against "fate" or the "gods", while at the same time being able to glory in carrying such a great burden. To have the burden lifted, to find a hope which might require a dissolving of the idolatrous load is unthinkable.

This pattern becomes a fixation, the self's justification for being what it is. Such a self has become so "concrete" that to have the eternal with its openness break into such a locked-in identity is abhorrent. It feels far better for such a self to

> keep rebelling against all existence, [because] it feels that it has obtained evidence against it, against its goodness. The person in despair believes that he himself is the evidence, and that this is what he wants to be, and therefore he wants to be himself, himself in his torment, in order to protect against all existence with this torment.[29]

Such a self becomes more and more "spiritual" in an inverted or twisted way by creating its own special spiritual kingdom with itself on the throne of its despair. To tear itself loose in defiance from the power which established it is not the point, but to denounce this power using the only weapon available to it - the misery of its very own self.

The Dialectic. of Sin and Faith.

In moving toward the specialized language of sin and faith Kierkegaard lifts the structure of selfhood to another level. The critical factor which pushes forward this next step is the criterion by which selfhood is measured or the **goal** toward which it moves. Up to this point Kierkegaard has hinted at various gradations of self-awareness (using the language of despair). Until now, the human self "in-itself" was the norm - living out a synthesis of the components of its being such as the temporal/eternal. Now, however, the criterion becomes God which gives the self an infinite criterion far beyond the criterion of humanity in general. Kierkegaard elaborates:

> The child who previously has had only his parents as a criterion, becomes a self as an adult by getting the state as a criterion, but what an infinite accent falls on the self by having God as the criterion! The criterion for the self is always: that directly before which it is a self...[30]

As suggested earlier, a self is made up of the objects which it internalizes and through which it defines itself. These objects become the self's criterion, its mirror, its norm. Kierkegaard insists that the self is "shaped" in relation to its criterion, and infinitely so when God is the criterion. In fact, says Kierkegaard, "the greater the conception of God, the more self there is; the more self, the greater the conception of God."[31] It is only when the self is consciously aware of existing before God is it the infinite self and it is this self which sins before God. But what is sin and faith for Kierkegaard and how do they reveal a higher increment of selfhood?

> **Sin:** "before God in despair not to will to be oneself, or before God in despair to will to be oneself."[32]

Faith: a state in which the self "in relating itself to itself and in willing to be itself, rests transparently in the power that established it".[33]

Sin and faith are two modes of being which describe selfhood in its presence before God. Sin is not some petty list of violations of an idealized code of conduct, nor is faith the holding of a set of dogmas which somehow give access to the Divine. Sin and faith are two ways of structuring selfhood in relationship to the God who defines its parameters.

The reality of sin stamps our individuality because it leaves us standing naked in solitary responsibility for the shape of our being. Sin defines my ontological status before my maker. Precisely this point distinguishes Kierkegaard so sharply from Hegel. The gulf between the human and the divine is not bridged by the natural unfolding of selfhood, but is made even sharper as the self becomes more and more itself - before God. Kierkegaard concludes that:

> The teaching about sin ... confirms the qualitative difference between God and man more radically than ever before ... In no way is man so different from God as in this, that he, and that means every man, is a sinner, and is that "before God," whereby the opposites are kept together in a double sense ...[34]

Only the leap of faith resolves this dilemma for Kierkegaard, not that it removes the great gulf between the human and divine, but it allows the self to constitute itself along the lines of the one who fully unifies the temporal and eternal in his own being: Jesus Christ.

Christ is the true paradigm of selfhood for Kierkegaard since in him all opposites are reconciled. The claim which Christ makes upon the self is a claim like no other.

> A self directly before Christ is a self intensified by the inordinate concession from God, intensified by the inordinate accent that falls upon it because God allowed himself to be born, become man, suffer, and die also for the sake of this self. As stated previously, the greater the conception of God, the more self; so it holds true here: the greater the conception of Christ, the more self. Qualitatively a self is what its criterion is. That Christ is the criterion is the expression, attested by God, for the staggering reality that a self has, for only in Christ is it true that God is man's goal and criterion.[35]

To have Christ as the criterion for selfhood is to exist in his mode of being - to actualize one's self in the fullness of Christ-likeness. The formula by which this can occur is that "in relating itself to itself and in willing to be itself, the self rests transparently in the power that established it."[36] This, Kierkegaard reminds us, is precisely the definition of faith.

KIERKEGAARD'S PATH TO SELFHOOD

Having explored the structure of selfhood in its dynamic polarities, and identified the norms against which selfhood is measured, we are free to proceed with an overview of the Kierkegaardian path by which the self develops. For Kierkegaard, as with Hegel, the movement is one from spiritlessness to that of self as spirit. The similarities between their respective pathways are striking even as they end in very different places due to their divergent assumptions about the nature of the divine-human relation. The Hegelian path sees the self attain an **ever greater identity with the Absolute** via a **mediation** of internally reconciled opposites.[37] For Kierkegaard, the opposites are maintained, but are **transcended** as the self **synthesizes** itself by choosing itself before God. For Kierkegaard the self does not **evolve** into Spirit but becomes Spirit only as it **chooses** its self before God.

Kierkegaard identifies three major stages in the emergence of selfhood which he calls (1) the aesthetic (2) the ethical, and (3) the religious. The following outline highlights these stations along the way to full selfhood.

Aesthetic Selfhood (Natural Selfhood)

    A. Immediacy (Three Phases of the Erotic)

        1. Dreaming Desire
        2. Searching Desire
        3. Desiring Desire

    B. Reflection

Ethical Selfhood

    A. The Choosing Self

1. Attainment of Self-consciousness
   (Choosing oneself)

B. The Deciding Self

1. Actualization of Selfhood
   (Reaching for the Universal)

Religious Selfhood

A. Religion A (Infinite Resignation)

B. Religion B (Authentic Selfhood)

Natural or Aesthetic Selfhood

Kierkegaard uses the terms **immediacy and reflection** to describe the shape taken by selfhood within natural or aesthetic existence. Strictly speaking, there is no self at this level since by definition selfhood requires the capacity for authentic choice which is missing in both these modes of existence. In any case, they represent types of immersion, unconsciousness if you will, whether in the form of enmeshment or non-differentiation, or in the form of cognitive abstraction cut off from concrete existence.

Immediacy (Three Phases of the Erotic)

You may recall from our preceding discussion that immediacy refers to the self "in immediate connection with 'the other,'... in desiring, craving, enjoying, etc... Its dialectic is: the pleasant and the unpleasant."[38] This is a self totally immersed in its environment and/or natural neediness. Such a self is buried within its current reality, living out only its immediate natural inclinations. In short, one has attained no separation from one's internal or external world.

The clearest overview of natural existence is found in Kierkegaard's Mozart essay in Volume 1 of **Either/Or**. In this essay three operatic figures reveal the types of "desire" which mark the non-mediated life. These three states of the "erotic" and their representative characters are:

a. dreaming desire (The Page in *Figaro*)

b. searching desire (Papageno in *The Magic Flute*)

c. desiring desire (Don Juan in *Don Juan*)[39]

Dreaming Desire is a completely non-mediated state within Aesthetic existence. It represents total unconsciousness or non-differentiation, with no distinction between subject and object, self and other. The self is immersed in an unconscious sea, carried along by the currents of its immediate experience. Because desire and its object are still "joined" at this point it is premature to even speak of desire since the object has not been born. Inner and outer, self and world are united in undifferentiated oneness. This unawakened state is prepersonal in the sense that selfhood is only potentially present.

Searching Desire. Desire's awakening goes hand in hand with the birth of otherness, of the object. Kierkegaard explains:

> only when the object exists does the desire exist, only when the desire exists does the object exist; desire and its object are twins, neither of which is born a fraction of an instant before the other ... but this movement of the sensuous, this earthquake, splits the desire and its object infinitely asunder for the moment; but as the moving principle appears a moment separating, so it again reveals itself as wishing to unite the separated.[40]

In a manner strikingly parallel to modern theories of psychological development, Kierkegaard recognizes that identity formation begins with the birth of otherness as generated by the experience of separation. This creates the urge for reunion with the object, but since the object is not clearly defined the seeking remains scattered, the object diffuse. The Kierkegaardian self has nevertheless been born, a desiring but unconscious seeker for a lost paradise.

Desiring Desire. With fully awakened desire, the scattered or poorly defined object has become a specific object. What was unconscious in the first phase became a vaguely defined object in the second, and a particular, real object which is now desired, in the third. None of these stages are truly "conscious" for Kierkegaard since they are all governed by **immediacy**, by a selfhood which does not yet "mediate" or harmonize itself.[41] This self which synthesizes itself must do so through reflection and decision, two vital capacities to be discussed shortly.

When immersed in immediacy selfhood is simply driven by the desire which governs it. Although such a self increasingly separates from its objects within these phases, it has not yet faced **the desire** which runs its life. A self may well have come to a point where it has "separated" from the objects of its world, but not yet differentiated itself from the restless seeking which propels it toward its determining objects. Immediacy, therefore, does not just refer to an unconsciousness with regard to a self's objects, but to the "spirit" which governs its seeking. Spirit, then, identifies the energy by which a self seeks its defining objects.

The critical point to remember is that a non-mediated condition offers no unity for the self because (1) its building blocks are not consciously integrated by such a self, and (2) the self remains unaware of the energy/power behind its seeking. A self may even have attained a certain "object constancy" (stable relationships with objects) in its phenomenal world, but have no ownership of the force (desire) which causes it to seek these objects in the particular way it does.

Any non-mediated condition is "spiritless" for Kierkegaard when it does not move toward the syntheses which constitute authentic selfhood. Whenever a subject is relating only to her necessity/finitude/ and temporalness, to the neglect of her possibility/infinitude/and eternity, then she lives in the bondage of unconsciousness, of not being a self, since to be a self requires an integration of its polarities.

To summarize, immediacy is a state of unconscious union with the objects of one's world, whether parental, erotic, social, material or religious. Even as self and object differentiate through the awakening of desire, non-mediation remains in that the individual is controlled by the urge to satisfy the desire for the object without conscious choosing. To move out of immediacy requires another step which Kierkegaard calls reflection.

Reflection

Reflection for Kierkegaard is the process by which full self-awareness is born. Strictly speaking, there is no awareness in immediacy since consciousness requires duality which is not present within non-differentiated states. What then triggers the movement from unconsciousness to consciousness and self-consciousness?

Kierkegaard insists that movement out of enmeshment is brought about by language (as was true for Hegel). Language is the vehicle of reflection because in "re-flecting" reality, what was immediate is separated thereby allowing the separated elements to come into relation. However, the use of language and its companion reflection does not automatically generate awareness for Kierkegaard, never mind self-awareness. Reflection is the **presupposition** for awareness.[42]

Kierkegaard argues that while reflection is a dichotomous process, it simply registers a possible relation between two entities. Such an activity is not yet a self. For as long as experiences or objects simply "register" without engagement as to their "value", their place in the experiential grid, no self-consciousness can emerge. Nevertheless, in reflection, the realities of experience "touch each other" and do so in a way that a relation becomes possible. Through reflection, reality is re-presented which makes possible the operations of consciousness or what we could call our ego capacities. Kierkegaard elaborates:

> Reflection's categories are always dichotomous ... In reflection they [categories] touch each other in a way that a relation becomes possible. The categories of consciousness, however, are **trichotomous**, as language also demonstrates, for when I say: I am conscious of **this sensory impression**, I am expressing a triad. Consciousness is mind [spirit] and it is remarkable that when one is divided in the world of mind [spirit] there are three, never two. Consciousness, therefore, presupposes reflection.[43]

How, then, is self-consciousness born?

What begins as undifferentiated oneness within immediacy is shattered by all experiences of separation and their affective currents which Kierkegaard identifies through the various forms of desire. Once the object world jumps into awareness, language and reflection facilitate the transition from unconsciousness to consciousness, not only because they bring the object world into view, but because they allow the self to begin to see itself. The differentiation made possible by language and reflection is first the **conscious distinction** between **self** and **world**, and secondly **self** from **itself**.[44] The capacity of human consciousness to look at itself awakens self-consciousness.

In looking at itself human consciousness relates to itself and in so doing identifies with what it sees. We could say that consciousness becomes "invested" in itself. Therefore, as the world of objects opens before me, my ego (consciousness) becomes aware of itself as the agent of this discovery. This is why the ego "takes interest in" or becomes invested in itself as the agent of the discovery of its world.[45] To be self-conscious is to be interested in oneself.

What Kierkegaard has brilliantly intuited is the developmental thread of **narcissism** as a primary form of self-relatedness. Contemporary psychodynamic theory has validated Kierkegaard's point with its empirical confirmation of the narcissistic pattern as the pathway by which self comes into relationship with itself.

Any preoccupation with oneself, any self-concern or self-interest is evidence for Kierkegaard of our inevitable tendency to compare ourselves with ourselves. We do this as the automatic activity of the ego-self relation. In other words, through language and the ability to conceptualize, my ego (consciousness) projects its possibilities before itself. This becomes the way in which my ego moves into its future and in doing so it differentiates itself from itself - I become subject and object to myself - I become a self-conscious agent who has discovered himself and has the potential to relate to himself for better or for worse.

While it is one thing to become self-conscious, it is still another to become a self, insists Kierkegaard. It is true that self-consciousness has been reached within the reflection phase of Aesthetic existence, but this simply means that one has become aware of the possibilities of selfhood, not that they have been actualized. This is the great trauma of reflective-aesthetic existence, that it is stuck in possibility. Kierkegaard elaborates:

> The mirror of possibility is no ordinary mirror; it must be used with extreme caution, for, in the highest sense this mirror does not tell the truth. That a self appears to be such and such in the possibility of itself is only a half-truth, for in the possibility of itself the self is still far from or is only half of itself.[46]

To become a self requires that one not just become conscious - even of all the options open to selfhood - but that one **actualize** this potential self. For a self to truly become itself it must bring into a unity its real past and anticipated future in the here and now decisions of its actual existence. Simple aesthetic reflection cannot accomplish this. To become a self requires actualization which only comes with the next step on the journey, namely, Ethical existence.

Ethical Selfhood

There are two important passages in **Either/Or** which help us distinguish aesthetic from ethical selfhood. Kierkegaard asks:

> But what does it mean to live aesthetically, and what does it mean to live ethically? What is the aesthetical in man and what is the ethical? To this I would answer: the aesthetical in a man is that by which he is immediately what he is; the ethical is that by which he becomes what he becomes.[47]

To be aesthetic is to be governed by immediacy, by whatever presents itself, by that which temporarily fills the space left open by the absence of self. To be ethical, however, means to **choose oneself**. Kierkegaard continues:

> He on the other hand who chooses himself ethically chooses himself concretely as this definite individual, and he attains this concretion by the fact that this act of choice is identical with this act of repentance which sanctions the choice. The individual thus becomes conscious of himself as this definite individual, with these talents, these dispositions, these instincts, these passions, influenced by these definite surroundings, as the definite product of a definite environment. But being conscious of himself in this way, he assumes responsibility for all this.[48]

The Choosing Self

What does Kierkegaard mean when he places the choice of oneself at the heart of becoming a self? He writes:

> The ethical individual knows himself but this knowledge is not a mere contemplation... it is a reflection upon himself which itself is an action, therefore, I have deliberately preferred to use the expression "choose oneself instead of "know oneself."[49]

Kierkegaard deliberately moves the norm of selfhood beyond the Socratic "know thyself" toward the individuation-enhancing "choose thyself." To choose oneself is not simply the choice for various options as if the emergence of selfhood were a psychological flipping of a coin. To choose oneself means to first claim one's capacity as a choosing being.

This capacity for choosing is a direct outgrowth of the self's structure. In examining the Kierkegaardian structure we discovered that the fulcrum which balanced the various polarities making up the self-system was freedom. This freedom is the moment-to-moment actualization of the concrete particular being that I am. Kierkegaard calls this the self's "eternal validity" or its "internal infinity," that is, its absolute or eternal capacity to constellate itself. Kierkegaard elaborates further:

> He chooses himself, not in a finite sense for then this "self" would become a finite thing along with other finite things, but in an absolute sense; and yet he chooses himself and not another. The self he chooses is infinitely concrete, for it is himself, and yet it is absolutely distinct from his earlier self, for he has chosen the absolute. This self has not existed before, for it came to be through the choice, and yet it did exist, for it was indeed "himself."[50]

In insisting that choosing myself is not a choosing of a finite 'this' or 'that' Kierkegaard is challenging the assumption that my self is made once-for-all, as if I can find myself in some external act, accomplishment, or role.

The truly ethical individual, says Kierkegaard, has an internal tranquillity and security because her "duty" is inside not outside herself.[51] There is nothing more miserable in Kierkegaard's estimation than to have the norm of selfhood outside of oneself while at the same time constantly trying to meet this external expectation.

In defining the self through its capacity to choose it would be easy for us to conclude that the self is disconnected from what preceded it - that it remakes itself into something new with this newness its eternal validity. To reach such a conclusion, however, would miss the whole point of the polarity of selfhood. We must remember that to be a self is to become a synthesis of the actual and the potential. Every self is the product of a particular environment, contains certain gifts and limitations, and carries a certain history. Much of this history is completely "given" in the sense that the self has no say in the matter. I do not choose my family of origin, my national identity or social context, nor do I choose many of the joys and traumas which come my way. How then do I choose myself?

The choosing of myself is the process by which I consolidate myself, or better said, **collect myself** and thereby become a concrete self. I must embrace my history as my very own and in embracing it I am choosing to tie together the threads which make me a self. Only in so doing do I become free and able to move into the **now** which brings together who I have been and who I am becoming.

As my self develops, the so-called higher does not discard the so-called lower. My self does not simply leave behind earlier modes of being, but the choosing of myself brings them into a unity with the self I now am. Thus, says Kierkegaard, even the entire aesthetic self is now chosen:

> This self contains within itself a rich concretion, a multitude of determinants, of properties, in short, it is the entire aesthetic self which has been chosen ethically. Therefore, the deeper you penetrate into yourself the more you will feel the significance even of the insignificant, not in a finite but in an infinite sense, because it is posited by you ...

To choose myself means to take full ownership of the self I have been and now am even though I did not fully create this self.

This is what drives many a self to despair. I may not want this responsibility of relating myself to myself i.e. of synthesizing my limits with my potentials and so I try to find myself in one or the other, to no avail. When I reject myself I look for myself only in my finiteness, not in my openness, and hence I am not free. Similarly, when I seek myself by identifying only with my possibilities, I am not choosing myself but am simply locking myself out of my true self.

On the other hand I may in fact have freely chosen myself as a synthesis of my life's givens and its possibilities, but conclude that I have now "arrived", that I now "possess" the self I have.[52] This too is bondage, since I have then lost sight of my dynamic openness which requires that only as my self is consistently chosen can it remain free.

The only authentic step which leads to ethical selfhood is to take radical responsibility for the self I am which means taking ownership of the darkness or evil within me. This cannot simply be a pleasant ownership of my actual life decisions, but a **repentance** for all of who I am, including those dimensions of myself attributable to the darkness or evil of others. While this demand may seem absurd Kierkegaard is quite insistent:

> Only when in his choice a man has assumed himself is clad in himself, has so totally penetrated himself that every movement is attended by a consciousness of a responsibility for himself, only then has he chosen himself ethically, only then has he repented himself. Only then is he concrete, only then is he in his total isolation in absolute continuity with the reality to which he belongs.[53]

Only when my self acknowledges my full continuity with my racial, national, and familial environments do I come to embrace the self I am. The attitude of repentance for the sins of others with whom I am in continuity is not for the sake of **their** "salvation" but **my own**. The darkness within the other with whom I am in continuity is also my darkness in that I too as self am free to live it out. I must claim it as the potential of which I am capable.

However, to repent of the darkness or brokenness around me is not simply to stay stuck in some remorseful rumination about it but to transform it by virtue of the new awareness/action of which I am now capable. This is the expression of the eternal within humanness insists Kierkegaard:

> For man's eternal dignity consists in the fact that he can have a history, the divine element in him consists in the fact that he himself, if he will, can impart to his history continuity, for this it acquires only when it is not the sum of all that has happened to me or befallen me but is my own work, in such a way that even what has befallen me is by me transformed and translated from necessity to freedom.[54]

This radical ownership of oneself is the true meaning of self-consciousness for Kierkegaard. Only of such total acceptance comes the capacity to give authentic shape to oneself.

The Deciding Self

You may be asking what makes this current development "ethical"? The ethical phase as we have come to understand it thus far involves the choosing of oneself in radical self-awareness and self-acceptance. However, it also involves ethical decisions which "reveal" the self one is becoming. These ethical decisions are attempts on the part of the self to approximate "universal" norms, namely, the highest and most widely-applicable norms developed by human morality.[55]

However, this striving after the universal is always an ambivalent experience for selfhood since it remains suspended between the paradox of the real and the ideal.

> This self which the individual knows is at once the actual self and the ideal self which the individual has outside himself as the picture in likeness to which he has to form himself and which on the other hand, he nevertheless has in him since it is the self. Only within him has the individual the goal after which he has to strive, and yet he has this goal outside him, inasmuch as he strives after it. For if the individual believes that the universal man is situated outside him, that from without it will come to him, then he is disoriented, then he has an abstract conception and his method is always an abstract annihilation of the original self. Only within him can the individual acquire information about himself. Hence, the ethical life has a duplex character, that the individual has his self outside himself and in himself.[56]

It is this ambivalence which leaves the self restless and searching - that in relating to itself through the norm of universal duty and morality, it has only partially found itself, and above all, is not yet resting within the power that created it.

To summarize, we can say that ethical selfhood marks the arrival of self at full individual personhood. It is a process of individuation whereby one attains a unity for one's self, not by eliminating the elements of prior stages, but by taking them up within oneself. Such a self is able to bring past, present, and future into a unity as it harnesses the desires of aesthetic existence through the capacity for authentic choice. The self has found a continuity for itself even though its center resides outside itself. Whereas aesthetic selfhood is guided by the pleasure principle, ethical selfhood is built through the act of choosing. In neither case, however, does one find a direct relationship to the ultimate impulse of selfhood.

In the case of aesthetic selfhood such a relationship is impossible since the self has not yet distinguished itself sufficiently from its immediate environment. The ethical self may well have found itself, but without recognizing its dependence upon God. The ethical norm serves as its God with duty or morality its guiding light. But morality does not bring the self into relationship with God - it only serves to define the upper limits of human ethical striving. The goal of such a self is simply its ethical norm which cannot allow the self to come to rest. When ethical norms alone guide a self they take on the role of the "condemning law" as the **unifying third element** as was noted in our survey of the New Testament. Still separate from God, the ethical self is left to rotate in orbit only around its own idealized norms, unaware of the larger source of its power and striving.

In the end, an ethical self becomes bankrupt either because it collapses under the weight of its idealized norms, or because life calls it to take a stand against its very ideals.[57] In the first instance the self must face its own intrinsic "weakness" in that it is unable to reconcile or unify itself in any final way. In the second instance, life confronts the individual with dilemmas which do not "fit" with the universal norm. This occurs because as a self seeks to find its uniqueness, its individuality, it inevitably clashes with the universal norm. This clash is the wedge which drives a breach between the self and the universal moral order. However, experiences of alienation and separation from universal norms are a critical step in the awakening of the self to its radical dependence upon God, the author of selfhood. We are now in a position to examine the shape of the most authentic forms of self for Kierkegaard.

Religious Selfhood

The journey toward selfhood which began with aesthetic existence finds its completion in the dual forms of experience Kierkegaard calls **Religion A** and **Religion B**. Before discussing the shape of selfhood represented by these terms it would be useful to identify the critical feature of this phase which so sharply distinguishes Kierkegaard from Hegel. This key factor is the **God-self relationship**.

For Hegel, God and self become **one** even as they become distinct. In Hegelian development the self slowly awakens to its identity with the unfolding life of God. This Kierkegaard vehemently rejects. He pushes the identity between God and self to its opposite extreme, seeing them as absolutely different.[58] This absolute difference highlights not only the Divine's absolute transcendence, but the self's contingency, its nothingness. **How** this great Kierkegaardian gulf is resolved is what sets **Religion A** apart from **Religion B**.

Religion A

Religion A is a type of religiosity in which the radical distinction between God and self breaks into awareness. There are two essential features which set this phase apart from the ethical stage which preceded it and which serve as a bridge to Religion B which follows. These two features are (1) the separation of God and world, and (2) the self's yearning for salvation.

The God-Self Schism. Religious selfhood is born for Kierkegaard by any experience which drives home the point of my nothingness before God. During ethical selfhood my self is sailing along quite nicely since I am aligning my self with my God, the universal ethical norm. Such a self rests "immanently" in itself, and makes itself its own project.[59] For as long as I blend my identity with this self-referent I am "safe" in that I am in step with the norm.

However, my individual inclinations inevitably fall short of universal norms which breaks my continuity with these norms and ruptures the protective moral/ethical bubble which safeguards my worth and identity. The bursting of the ethical bubble is what awakens my self to the God reality, through the recognition of my weakness and inability to bring myself into equilibrium by myself. As a consequence of the discovery of my insufficiency I may try to renounce my self and/or the world in the process. This **renunciation** is the hallmark of **Religion A**.

The graphic example Kierkegaard uses to illustrate this first awakening to God and the shape selfhood takes therein, is the story of **Abraham's sacrifice of Isaac**.[60] Abraham is an individual who is confronted by God and asked to sacrifice his only son Isaac. This demand is absurd, it is murderous, and goes against every possible ethical obligation. This absolute God demands the absolute acknowledgment of God's supremacy and the corresponding contingency of Abraham's own being. This point is driven home by the demand to sacrifice that which is closest to one's heart - in this case the only son who is the sole carrier of Abraham's identity - the very flesh and blood which is to ensure the future of the tribe and nation. This "awe-ful" demand evokes fear and trembling before the Almighty.

This encounter with the highest ultimate, God, forces what Kierkegaard calls a "teleological suspension of the ethical".[61] But why must the ethical be suspended? Kierkegaard's answer is that the retreat back to the ethical is simply a way out of the dilemma, a temptation or seduction which attempts to hold us back from what we must acknowledge, namely that all of life - including one's very self - is not one's own property but is constituted by God and God alone.

The demanded sacrifice pushes the encounter with the divine to a new level. Prior forms of self-discovery could perhaps find certain ethical rationales for such an act, such as when a tragic hero must sacrifice his child to save a nation and in doing so be able to attain a larger good.[62] What makes this demand so agonizing is that there is nowhere to turn, no rationale, no justification, simply oneself before God. What is thereby forced into awareness is that a **personal** relation to God is now required.

To discover the absoluteness of God brings with it the response Kierkegaard calls "infinite resignation."[63] Infinite resignation is **Religion A's** way of recognizing human contingency before God. In acknowledging one's absolute dependence upon the Absolute there is an inevitable devaluing and negating of self and the world. This negation of oneself is the death of self-reliance and self-sufficiency and as such is a necessary, if incomplete, transition toward faith. The importance of infinite resignation is that it expresses the existential principle that the individual can do absolutely nothing of himself, is as nothing before God.[64] In maintaining the nothingness of the self, ontological dependence upon God is declared.

Self-Consciousness as Guilt. There is a further manifestation of **Religion A** which is of vital importance to Kierkegaard's developmental scheme, this being the phenomenon of guilt. Guilt is an indicator of a higher increment of self-awareness because it reveals the presence of the eternal within the self (although in a negative way). It is true that self-awareness was awakened during aesthetic and ethical existence through the gradations of desire and duty which opened the self to the polarities of possibility/necessity and finitude/infinitude.

However, the appearance of guilt suggests that an awareness of the temporal/eternal polarity has emerged in a new way.

Kierkegaard clarifies that this "guilt" is not an ordinary feeling - he is not simply talking about feeling sorry for something, but a state of being which defines my essential relation to my existence. To be able to feel guilty for my being is a massive jump forward, yet paradoxically also a jump backward - deeper into my pathos.[65] Guilt-capacity, is the ability to apprehend my existence in a deeper way. What might this imply? Kierkegaard suggests that the meaning of existence is "**to put things together.**"[66] To be guilty means to be able **to put things together** in such a way that I take radical responsibility for my life **from the perspective of the eternal.**

Guilt is a paradoxical state which allows me to attain a (negative) unity with myself. It reflects an attempt to find a resolution of the subject-object tension of my being. Strictly speaking, guilt is a form of self-awareness in which the self seeks a relationship toward its eternal validation, but it does so **within itself**. Two types of guilt surface at this point. On the one hand guilt can take the form of a self-negating self which has violated some standard outside of itself. This is a "low" form of guilt, with guilt the affective evidence that the self has violated the norm of an object with which the self identifies. The guilt simply expresses one's negative self-identity with this source of power.

In the "higher" form of guilt to which Kierkegaard appeals, the self begins to measure itself against the "higher" object of "eternal happiness."[67] In this instance guilt is generated not only by my awareness of my inability to stay in harmony with myself, but also by my failure to stay in a true relationship to the eternal. The guilt highlights the impossibility of remaining fully conscious of what is absolute and what is relative in my life. This is the inevitable result, claims Kierkegaard, when a self seeks God within the self - sees God as immanent within the self. It is hard to miss the indictment of Hegel in this point.

The Search for Eternal Life. While "infinite resignation" and "guilt" may destroy any immanent linkage of God and self, it also locks in a negative relationship to the Divine. The principle concern of a self in **Religion A** is "salvation" or "eternal blessedness". This means that a self residing in **Religion A** becomes invested in finding "eternal life" or immortality as a way of resolving its separation and gaining salvation. Eternal life is ensured by extending immortality to the divinely touched portion of selfhood - the immortal soul. Religion A attempts to resolve the paradox between the finite, transient self and the eternal God through the construct of the **immortal soul.** This "solution" Kierkegaard cannot accept.

As can be recalled from my discussion of the self's structure, Kierkegaard had insisted that the self is a **synthesis** of the temporal and eternal. For him the self's eternal or unchanging reality is its **freedom** by which it chooses itself from the possibilities before it. The eternal is **not** some static inner core within the self but the eternal openness by which a self defines itself. **Religion A,** therefore, is a grossly inadequate "solution" for Kierkegaard (even within Christianity).

The practical consequence of **Religion A** is a self ultimately unconcerned with daily experience and governed by an other-worldliness which renounces all that is temporal. Such a self may now know it is radically dependent upon God, but this God remains remote, trapped in the eternal, and unrelated to the vicissitudes of life. Such relationship to God is dead and no better than paganism, claims Kierkegaard. Its error lies in the fact that it only sees a **limited paradox** between God and the self (between the temporal and the eternal) which is overcome by the common element, the eternal. Kierkegaard must reject this paradox because it does not go far enough. The paradox must be **Absolute,** complete, not partial. This **Absolute Paradox** is only lived out for Kierkegaard in the God-self relation represented in his understanding of Christianity as **Religion B.**

Religion B (Christianity)

If the primary indicator of self-awareness for **Religion A** is the self as **guilty,** then the corresponding factor for **Religion B** is the self as **sinful.** The state of sinful selfhood finds resolution, however, in the Absolute paradox of the Incarnation. **Religion B** brings selfhood to its final destination through the confrontation with sin and the appropriation of forgiveness which comes through encounter with the God-man.

Self-consciousness as Sin. Sin is an ontological category for Kierkegaard which describes a higher level of self-awareness. The highest level of self-awareness reached thus far is identified by the capacity for **guilt** which points to degrees of dis-equilibrium of the self within itself and its estrangement from eternal law. Sin-consciousness, however, raises self-awareness to an infinitely higher level because the object of awareness is the highest manifestation of selfhood - the God-man.

Sin serves a new level of self-awareness in that the self now exists fully "before God."[68] True, even the self of **Religion A** has a God but this God is still "immediate" in the sense that the self has internalized the eternal "static" God while it rejects the finite, changeable side of its own life. It is this rejection or resignation of a side of its life which leaves the self of **Religion A** so guilty - it is always being dragged down by its inability to stay in harmony with the objects of the world, and its inability to find harmony with the eternal which it is unable to please. Sin as a category of selfhood radically breaks with all prior levels which are stuck in varying degrees of "immanence", and drives home the point of the total separation of God and persons. Kierkegaard declares:

> The teaching about sin ... confirms the qualitative difference between God and man more radically than ever before...[69]

To elaborate:

> The paradoxical religiousness (Religion B) breaks with immanence and makes the fact of existing the absolute contradiction, not within immanence, but against immanence. There is no longer any immanent fundamental kinship between the temporal and the eternal because the eternal itself has entered time and would constitute there the kinship.[70]

In our earlier discussion it was noted that sin took two basic forms: (1) before God in despair **not** to be oneself and (2) **in despair** to be oneself.[71] These forms refer to (1) the failure of the self to be itself **(weakness)**, and (2) the despairing attempt to be a self **(defiance)**. However, sin is not only defined by the self's inability to relate to itself, but through its unwillingness to do this **before God**. Because a self does not create itself but is constituted by otherness - it must eventually acknowledge its dependence upon the power which undergirds its total being in order for it to be truly at home with itself. When a self is unable to find its equilibrium, is unable to accept itself, it is living in exile, in either passive (weakness) or aggressive (defiance). By not resting in the power which unifies it the self runs from its freedom by blindly plunging into its possibilities or by becoming stuck in the quagmire of its actuality. Sin is the refusal **before God** of the self to be itself, by not accepting its actualities or possibilities, **and** by denying its ontological dependence upon God.

Sin, then, defines the shape of object-relations when God as fully transcendent is the object. With the awareness of sin, Kierkegaard understands the self to take an important step forward in its individuation because it has come to recognize itself as created and dependent upon the God-object for its very being. As we recall, the self is infinitely intensified when God is its criterion because only then is its full infinity visible (its capacity to eternally choose itself). With God as the criterion the self finally sees itself as sinful (before God), because it recognizes it can never choose itself into a state of reconciliation by its own efforts.[72]

Sin-consciousness, claims Kierkegaard, has moved the criterion for selfhood beyond the narrowly human to the Divine. Anxiety and guilt as the signposts of disequilibrium are only preliminary signals for sin. They are the evidence of a self's disordered relationship to itself and the world and hint at the self's alienation from God as Holy Object. This alienation surfaces as rebellion or the denial of dependence i.e. "un-faith".

Kierkegaard identifies three responses to sin: (1) the dread of the good or the **demonic response**, (2) the dread of evil or the **repentant response**, and (3) belief in forgiveness or the **faithful response**. Kierkegaard calls anything demonic which refuses to reveal itself. Selfhood becomes demonic when it closes in on itself and shuts out any possible contact with that which would transform it.[73] A self closing in on itself seeks a negative internal consistency with anxiety (dread) directed toward that which might release the self from entrapment (i.e. grace).

A second response is when the self recognizes its failure to find harmony within itself and with God leaving it in a state of dread and sorrow over its sin. To sorrow over one's sin is the step of repentance or remorse. The repentant self knows it is unable to pull itself into harmony by its own bootstraps and this creates anxiety (dread) for the self. Kierkegaard writes:

> Remorse cannot annul sin, it can only sorrow over it. Sin goes forward in its consequence, remorse follows step by step, but always an instant too late.[74]

Although the attitude of repentance awakens the awareness of the need for forgiveness, the repentant self can also be drawn into the whirlpool of regret. Such a self attempts to justify itself through its own self-flagellation thereby again running from the power which truly reconciles. The only solution possible for Kierkegaard remains the leap of faith.

The Leap of Faith. The only response able to overcome sin and its companion remorse, is faith: "only faith is capable of doing this, for only in faith is the synthesis eternally and every instant possible."[75] Faith is the opposite of sin, says Kierkegaard, drawing on Romans 14:23. As we noted earlier, faith is a self being itself and in so doing resting transparently in God.

The leap of faith marks the end-station of the Kierkegaardian journey to selfhood. A self living in faith recognizes its sin **before** God and accepts the acceptance and forgiveness offered by God thereby being able to rest transparently (with full openness to itself) **in** God. This leap of faith is a radical jump, not as something one **understands**, but as a **recognition** which demands a radical response.

There are two phases of faith for Kierkegaard, namely, (1) the believing recognition that Jesus is the Christ, the God-man, with the Absolute Paradox united in him; and (2) an action, an act of will through which the self re-constellates or accepts itself achieving thereby a new and fuller unity.

The incarnation as we might suspect is central to this process for Kierkegaard. The incarnation of the God-man serves not only as the ultimate mirror against which human sinfulness becomes visible, but it makes possible a new and reconciled relationship with oneself and with God. In the incarnation the eternal becomes fully historical and the historical becomes fully eternal.[76] Since the Kierkegaardian self cannot finally reconcile itself, an act of God is required, this occurring through the Absolute Paradox of the God-man. In the God-man the paradox is united with the eternal fully entering time, and time being fully taken up into the eternal. The incarnation offers the self the possibility of entering into a new relationship with itself which adds a new dimension to its freedom. The incarnation to which one responds in faith opens up the self allowing it to take a new and enhanced relationship to itself which had been closed due to sin. The contradictions which had generated its guilt and anxiety are reconciled with the polarities of possibility and necessity, finitude and infinitude, time and eternity being brought into a new unity.

The incarnation of God becomes the **object** of faith through which the self shapes itself, nurtures itself, reconciles itself. Again, the Kierkegaardian faith response is not one of rational understanding.[77] If anything, the incarnation remains absurd and offensive to the intellect. The faith response is the leap into acknowledging one's failure to become one's self before God **and** a believing receptivity to the forgiveness and reconciliation offered by God. This allows the self to embrace its duality and to choose itself with new freedom and authenticity. The self that has lost itself over the course of its journey is reborn through faith. In faith it not only finds new freedom to rebuild itself but it gains its salvation i.e. establishes a relation to that which constitutes it.

This completes the journey of selfhood as seen through the eyes of Kierkegaard. The self has found its authenticity by reconstituting itself before its maker through the moment-to-moment decisions which define its identity. This self is born anew to itself as it plunges into the paradoxes of life and in its movements (through faith) it unifies the opposites of its being.

The end station of Kierkegaardian selfhood, then, is the **singular self** standing naked before God. This self is as far as we could possibly be from Hegel's **unified self** in which God and self become one. My final task in this Chapter is to determine if any basis exists for overcoming these radically polarized positions.

HEGEL AND KIERKEGAARD REVISITED

It is a most risky proposition to suggest that a model of selfhood which honors the polarized conclusions of Hegel and Kierkegaard is possible. Nevertheless, if we hold fast the vision that together they represent a composite picture of selfhood we may yet be in a position to integrate their insights. We should not assume, however, that one is simply compensating for excesses in the other. Rather, when held **together,** a **comprehensive picture** may become visible which (itself) integrates the living movement of selfhood. In order to sharpen these distinctions and prepare the way for a possible resolution, I will highlight Hegel's and Kierkegaard's conclusions from two perspectives: (1) the process of self's development, and (2) the self's final destination.

The Self as Process

The model which allows for the clearest depiction of selfhood as process for both Hegel and Kierkegaard is that of **dialectic**. Dialectic is most often popularized through the famous **thesis - antithesis - synthesis** trilogy. Although first made explicit by Fichte, neither Hegel nor Kierkegaard made heavy use of these particular terms even though the process itself is central for both. What **is** held in common, is that **dialectic represents the process** whereby the **self** first **finds**, then attempts to **resolve** the **dualities** of its world of experience. These dualities are inclusive referring to the subject-object duality, of inner-outer, self-other, internal-external, individual-social, divine-human, life-death, thinking-feeling, masculine-feminine, and so on.

The common theme which runs like a thread throughout the deliberations of Hegel and Kierkegaard is that the experience of separation and reintegration is the fuel which runs the engine of the self. The essence of their vision of dialectic selfhood is that the reality of the self operates by moving from multiple forms of **non-differentiation** through **negation** or **contradiction**, finding **resolution** in a **union which incorporates** the former elements only to again be negated by another separation/contradiction and so on.[78] But how is this dialectic path to be understood?

The first phase of the dialectic (thesis) is often referred to in philosophical language as a state of being "in-itself" pointing to any state of immediacy or enmeshment. A self which is **"in-itself"** has not yet come into its identity, has not yet become what it is, even though it carries its uniqueness within itself. As far as selfhood is concerned, the subject and object components of experience are unified or blended in this phase with no awareness of opposition or distinction within the subject.

At so-called lower levels of development which may take the form of symbiosis, selfhood resides in a state of blissful innocence - a self turned in on itself. Even when "higher" levels of development are considered, any residue of non-differentiation, of non-identity or enmeshment, can be depicted as a self residing in-itself.

The movement out of immersion or enmeshment is a step of negation and contradiction through which otherness and consequently a self is born. For an object (or a subject) to become known in all its complexity, a prior state of unconsciousness must be overcome. The emergence of otherness is **the central feature** of this second dialectic phase. Of course, when the object is the self itself, we arrive at the birth of self-consciousness. For this reason the second phase is often called **"for-itself"**, an ego which has made itself visible to itself through its distinction from its environment.

As we have seen in the journeys mapped by Hegel and Kierkegaard this negation takes many, many forms. Any movement of independence which "separates out" from an unconscious unity is a form of differentiation. This movement is "for-itself" in that a subject becomes an active participant in the shaping of its identity. Even though a subject may negate what is outside of itself by swallowing up the object or by destroying it (as we saw in the various forms of desire), it nevertheless defines itself by those acts of negation or externalizing of itself - hence it is **"for-itself"**.

The third and final movement of the dialectic (**synthesis**) is the overcoming of the **negation,** what has been called a self **"in-and-for-itself.**[79]**"** This third phase is the resolution of the prior phases whereby they are brought into harmony. The mechanism of this unity has been described with the German word "Aufhebung" which has no English equivalent but literally means "to take up."[80] Every prior phase which has been negated must be **taken up** into a new unity. This unity must **internalize and integrate** the prior elements and this is what constitutes a self.[81] Up to this point Hegel and Kierkegaard remain in essential agreement. Where, then, comes the parting of the ways?

The Kierkegaardian dialectic can be called a **dialectic of paradox** for the reason that the contradictory poles are "held together" in a heightened tension.[82] Their distinction is not blended or overcome but **highlighted** even as they are "reconciled." The Kierkegaardian self is the "**positive third**" which relates these polarized elements to each other.

The Hegelian dialectic on the other hand is a **dialectic of mediation**. Here the opposition is unified by **integrating the elements** and **removing the**

previously polarized elements. This radical difference goes to the heart of what it means to become a self.

In Kierkegaard's definition of the self he complains that the Hegelian "unity" is a simple synthesis in which the relation is the third element and as such is a negative unity - this for him is not a self.[83] If, however, "the relation relates itself to itself," **then** we have a **positive third** and this is the self, claims Kierkegaard. The self is not simply the blended outcome of the polarized elements finding a unity but the process which keeps the tension alive and brings the elements into harmonious relationship. By way of analogy, the Hegelian self is a standing bridge upon which traffic moves freely and easily from object on one side to subject on the other. The Hegelian self contains both shores within itself.

The Kierkegaardian self on the other hand is not a **passive bridge** but an active "draw bridge" which engages the subject and object poles of experience, reconciles them to each other, even as the separation between them remains sharp, even absolute. The implications of this difference are profound, not only as far as the dynamics of the self are concerned, but extend to the ultimate question of whether God is or is not contained within the process.

To summarize, the fundamental difference between the Hegelian and Kierkegaardian dialectic is that for Kierkegaard **every unity must hold the tension of its constituted elements in even greater contrast, while for Hegel they are superseded as aspects which are taken up and absorbed by the new unity.** In order to demonstrate this difference with greater clarity I will draw on the respective Hegelian and Kierkegaardian positions concerning **identity**.

Both Hegel and Kierkegaard agree that identity emerges out of enmeshment. In order for awareness and self-awareness to emerge out of unconsciousness there must occur inevitable separation and individuation they insist. For Hegel such separation results in a fragmentation which must be overcome as selfhood develops an **internal** relation to what is now other to it. The self must **"take-in"** the object, incorporate it into its very self in order to be able to become a self.

Kierkegaard, conversely, sees the great Hegelian error to be this smothering of distinction. He insists that true selfhood only emerges as the self holds its tensions and **maintains the otherness of self and object**. The Kierkegaardian self does not "take-in" objects through an internal absorption but maintains a sense of separation from its constituting objects. Is there any way out of this seemingly irreconcilable opposition?

The radical difference between these two visions may in fact be reconciled by the possibility that each has highlighted one side of the coin of differentiation, namely, the essential elements of (1) **taking-in** and internally appropriating and engaging otherness, and (2) the corresponding **pushing-out** or maintaining of separation and autonomy also necessary for selfhood. As we examine the contemporary psychological evidence describing the development of the self in subsequent chapters I propose that we will find this possibility confirmed.

I therefore wish to restate my conclusion that Hegel and Kierkegaard **do** complete what is unfinished in the other - at least as far as the dialectic movement of self is concerned. To proclaim a wider vision which integrates their polarization within the self does not resolve a bigger question. What remains is the final and perhaps insurmountable difficulty - the relationship of God to the self. To put the question bluntly: **"Is or is God not contained within the self?"**

The Self's Final Destination

No wider gap can be found between Hegel and Kierkegaard than is evident in their understanding of the God - self relation. While for Hegel the self moves toward an ever greater unity with-difference with the Divine, in Kierkegaard the opposite is true. Each increment of Kierkegaard's **Religious Selfhood** drives home the point of the self's **lack** of identity with God. By the time full sin-consciousness is attained there remains **no** God-self identity whatsoever. It is only when this opposition is made **absolute** that the self can stand before its author and ultimately synthesize itself through the leap of faith. No, insists Kierkegaard, there is **no built-in evolutionary unfolding of the self** within God - this for him is sheer immediacy - a collapsing into undifferentiated oneness that which is absolutely different, the human and the Divine.

Kierkegaard vehemently rejects the Hegelian conclusion that the incarnation brings God and the world into harmony because for him God and the world are radically different. Because of this radical difference any such union is absurd, offensive even. The union is only attained in the **Absolute Paradox** of the God-man, the Christ. In a direct challenge to Hegel, Kierkegaard insists:

> Man is not the unity of God and mankind ... the God-man is the unity of God and an individual man. That the human race is or should be akin to God is ancient paganism; but that an individual man is God is Christianity, and this individual is the God-man.[84]

There is no immanent tie between God and the self claims Kierkegaard, but only the Transcendent God who **does not reconcile** the opposites in his own being but **expresses** the absurd coincidence of opposites which represents the God-man. Only as a self receives the forgiveness and acceptance available through faith in the God-man can the self realize its authentic selfhood.

To depict this great gulf as clearly as possible I must restate that for Hegel the self finds its identity in **immanent union** with the divine, while for Kierkegaard the self finds its identity only **by faithfully choosing itself before the Transcendent** giver of life. How then do we respond to this gulf? It seems as if we have been pushed to the edge of an either/or by the Kierkegaardian challenge - a position he would likely applaud. Before making our choice we must be clear about what each perspective forces into our awareness.

Kierkegaard reminds us that the Hegelian self can indeed be swallowed up by an encompassing unity. History and becoming can be rendered superfluous by such an eternal, a-historical process. In a system where unity is guaranteed, the ultimacy of choice, responsibility, and freedom can be eroded. This critique we must grant Kierkegaard. On the other hand, Kierkegaard's relentless splitting of the self from its objects (in this case the Divine object) means the self is forever searching for the completion of its identity. It must be ever vigilant in maintaining its moment-to-moment unity through its choices. The ever-present possibility exists that the self will lose sight of itself and its remote transcendent beacon.

It seems ironic that Kierkegaard sees the self's final destination as the place where the self "rests" transparently in the power that established it.[85] Of all the things we can say about the Kierkegaardian self, **"at rest"** is **not** one of them. Because the self is never allowed to awaken to its participation in the life of God it must remain ever vigilant in its responsibility to shape itself **before** God, not **in** God. Of course a self must unify itself to be a self, Kierkegaard would insist, but it must do so through the heightening of its polarities in the moment of choice.

This state Hegel would describe as being stuck in unhappy consciousness. This is for him simply a form of fragmentation, of spiritlessness, because such a relationship to oneself through the mediation of remote Higher Other stamps the self as a **negative reflection** of this Other. Hegel would say to Kierkegaard:

> there is on the one hand, a going out from my finitude to a Higher; on the other hand I am determined as the negative of this Higher ... What is present is only this going out on my part, this aiming to reach what is remote: I remain on this side and have a yearning after a beyond.[86]

Such a self only remains trapped in an isolation from the ultimate source and goal of its identity.

Furthermore, it must be noted that Hegel would challenge Kierkegaard's assumption that the Hegelian unity means collapse of all distinction. Hegel insists that the integration of the elements which constitute selfhood is **not** the collapse of distinction, but the development of an **internal relation** to otherness. He asserts that otherness must be maintained, **but with a new relationship toward it**. To be a self means to be separate - but now without over-againstness. Furthermore, life in the here and now does not lose its value for Hegel. True, the reconciliation of the temporal and the eternal has been actualized through the life of the God-man, but for it to be fully true insists Hegel, it must become part of the **internal fabric of every self**. The God function cannot remain remote but acts as the very essence of the self.

Does this mean that Hegel is correct and Kierkegaard wrong? That would be far too simplistic. Rather, I must again insist that they have each highlighted two sides of the God-Self relation.

For God to be living and dynamic Subjectivity this subjectivity must realize itself in its objective development. Just as personal selfhood requires object(s) in order to be born, to come to its nature as subjective agent, so too must Absolute subjectivity engage an objective otherness in order for the Absolute's nature to be actualized. The universe must serve as the arena of God's self-actualization with the human self contributing to God's mirroring, just as God acts as the absolute mirror for human selfhood.

The selfhood of God demands that the world be the separate, differentiated object through which the fullness of God can be realized. This is not to say that

God is not complete in God's self, but that this completion must be **realized**. The Word must become flesh. It is this **realizing** or actualization of God's nature in the universe which ensures the self's immanent identity with God.

But this identity is not automatically given. It is here where we need the reminder of a Kierkegaard that a self **stands before** God and only as it is separate can it be called to freedom and accountability. The selfhood of God and humans **demands** that they become object and fully subject to one another.

And yet this objectification cannot be resolved from one side only since that would violate the freedom of one by rendering the other a passive participant. Rather, each comes to its own self **through** the other. God must embrace the finite object fully in all its finiteness and otherness in order for God's nature to be revealed. Divine entry into creation, into the savage otherness of death, is essential for God's nature as love to be completed. In parallel fashion, the finite self comes to itself only as it awakens to its full participation in the life of God. Until finding itself in God, the self remains alienated whether it knows it or not. This is where Hegel serves as a vital corrective to Kierkegaard.

For the self not to become exhausted by the relentless task of relating itself to itself (harmonizing the various dimensions of its being) it must find its home immanently in God who shares its joy and its sorrow. The self's very nature is to unify or integrate itself even as it differentiates. Unless it can discover its utter relatedness, its identicalness, it remains incomplete and non-unified in any final sense. This is the source of the self's fragmentation, by becoming locked into seeking itself in counterfeit and inauthentic reflections of itself.

Only through the radical otherness of the Divine and human can the freedom necessary for selfhood be maintained. Only when that gulf is absolute does genuine identity emerge (Kierkegaard).

On the other hand, this absolute gulf is absolutely overcome through the incarnational nature of the Divine. The reconciliation and reunification of the finite and the infinite, the human and the divine, is not simply a once-for-all historical event, but to be truly living it must continue to actualize itself in the flow of time (Hegel). Thus in its very development - its separation/individuation/differentiation - the self lives out its life as a reflection and manifestation of the one who called it into being.

With this dialectic vision complete I am free to proceed to an analysis of modern versions of selfhood as found in 20th century Psychological Science. What will make this task interesting is that a framework is now available for measuring the conclusions of these modern explorers. Although they have developed a new language for describing their observations I will highlight many parallels to what has been discovered thus far. At the same time I will also be revealing gross deficiencies in modern understandings of selfhood. It is imperative that the historical overview as I have traced it thus far be placed alongside the exciting developments of modern empirical observation.

1.   Soren Kierkegaard, *The Sickness Unto Death*, Translated by Howard V. Hong and Edna H. Hong, (Princeton: Princeton University Press, 1980), p. 13

2.   Ibid., p. 13

3.   Ibid.

4.   An excellent study which charts Kierkegaard's use of dialectic is found in Stephen N. Dunning, *Kierkegaard's Dialectic of Inwardness* (Princeton: Princeton University Press, 1985). See also John Douglas Mullen, *Kierkegaard's Philosophy* (New York: New American Library, 1981), p. 45

5.   Kierkegaard, *Sickness Unto Death*, 1980, p. 29

6.   Ibid., p. 29, 30

7.   Ibid., p. 35

8.   Ibid., p. 31 (Italics mine).

9.   Taylor, 1975, p. 113

10.   George Connell, To Be One Thing: *Personal Unity in Kierkegaard's Thought*, (Macon, Georgia: Mercer University Press, 1985), p. XI

11.   Taylor, 1975, p. 116. Taylor makes the useful point (p. 94) that this allows Kierkegaard to dialectically unify being and becoming assuring continuity through change within the self.

12.   Kierkegaard, *Sickness Unto Death*, 1980, p. 30

13. Ibid., p. 31

14. Ibid., p. 33

15. Ibid., p. 35

16. Ibid., p. 40

17. Ibid., p. 41

18. Ibid., p. 42

19. Ibid., p. 13

20. Ibid., p. 51

21. Ibid., p. 43

22. Ibid., p. 47

23. Ibid., p. 56

24. Ibid., p. 62

25. Ibid., p. 67

26. Ibid., p. 68

27. Ibid.

28. Ibid., p. 68-71

29. Ibid., p. 73-74

30. Ibid., p. 79

31. Ibid., p. 80

32. Ibid., p. 81, 82

33. Ibid., p. 49

34. Ibid., p. 121

35. Ibid., p. 113-114

36. Ibid., p. 131

37. Taylor, 1980, p. 230

38. Kierkegaard, *Sickness Unto Death*, 1980, p. 51. It is worth noting the clear parallel to Freud's pleasure principle.

39. Soren Kierkegaard, *Either/Or*, Ed. by Stephen L. Ross, Translated by George L. Stengren, (New York: Harper and Row, Publisher, 1986), p. 36-39

40. Soren Kierkegaard, *Either/Or*, Volume 1, Translated by David F. Swenson and Lillian Marvin Swenson, (Garden City, N.Y.: Anchor Books, 1959), p. 78-79

41. Taylor, 1975, p. 140

42. Soren Kierkegaard, *Johannes Climacus*, Edited and Translated by Howard V. and Edna H. Hong, (Princeton: Princeton University Press, 1985), p. 169

43. Ibid.

44. Kierkegaard, *Either/Or*, 1980, p. 54

45. Kierkegaard, *Johannes Climacus*, 1985, p. 170

46. Kierkegaard, *Sickness Unto Death*, 1980, p. 37

47. Kierkegaard, *Either/Or*, 1986, p. 182

48. Soren Kierkegaard, *Either/Or*, Vol. II, Translated by Walter Lowrie, (London: Oxford University Press, 1944), p. 210

49. Ibid., p. 216

50. Kierkegaard, Either/Or, 1980, p. 203-204

51. Ibid., p. 207

53. Ibid.

54. Kierkegaard, *Either/Or*, Vol. II, 1944, p. 208-209

55. Ibid., p. 209-210

56. Kierkegaard, *Either/Or*, Vol. II, 1944, p. 214

57. Ibid., p. 217

232

58. Soren Kierkegaard, *Fear and Trembling*, Translated by Howard V. Hong and Edna H. Hong (Princeton: Princeton University Press, 1983), p. 70

59. Soren Kierkegaard, *Concluding Unscientific Postscript*, Translated by David F. Swenson and Walter Lowrie, (Princeton: Princeton University Press, 1941), p. 290

60. Kierkegaard, *Fear and Trembling*, 1983, p. 54

61. Ibid., p. 70 f

62. Ibid., p. 56

63. Ibid., p. 58 f

64. Ibid., p. 37

65. Kierkegaard, *Concluding Unscientific Postscript*, 1941, p. 412

66. Ibid., p. 470

67. Ibid., p. 473

68. Ibid., p. 472-473

69. Kierkegaard, *Sickness Unto Death*, p. 83

70. Ibid., p. 121

71. Kierkegaard, *Postscript*, 1941, p. 507-508

72. Kierkegaard, *Sickness Unto Death*, 1980, p. 96

73. Ibid., p.80

74. Kierkegaard, *Sickness Unto Death*, 1980, p. 109; see also *The Concept of Dread*, Translated by Walter Lowrie, (Princeton: Princeton University Press, 1957), p. 110

75. Kierkegaard, *The Concept of Dread*, 1941, p. 102

76. Ibid., p. 104

77. Kierkegaard, *Philosophical Fragments*, 1985, p. 61

78. Ibid., p. 49

79.   Dunning, 1985, p. 6-30. Dunning does a masterful job of comparing and contrasting the common Hegelian and Kierkegaardian use of dialectics.

80.   See also Hegel, *Phenomenology* (Translated by Baillie, 1967), p. 37-39

81.   Dunning, 1985 p. 8

82.   Twentieth Century Object Relations Theory will come to echo this conclusion through Heinz Kohut's concept of "transmuting internalization" to name but one example.

83.   Dunning, 1985, p. 8

84.   Kierkegaard, *Sickness Unto Death*, 1980, p. 13. The key statement reads: A synthesis is a relation between two. Considered in this way, "a human being is still not a self."

85.   Kierkegaard, *Training in Christianity*, p. 84 (12, 79)

86.   Kierkegaard, *Sickness Unto Death*, 1980, p. 14

87.   Hegel, *Philosophy of Religion*, Vol. I, p. 177, (16: 171)

CHAPTER VII

SIGMUND FREUD (1856 - 1939) AND THE PSYCHOANALYTIC PATH TO SELFHOOD

The individual who has impacted human self-understanding for the 20th Century more than any other figure is without a doubt Sigmund Freud. Although Freud is very much a product of the 19th Century, the 20th Century has embraced his thought in ways too numerous to mention. Many would acknowledge that Sigmund Freud is the most formidable shaper of psychological constructs in the history of human self-reflection. His presuppositions and revolutionary methodology allowed him to examine the depths of the human psyche in ways which remained blocked for the other great stream of psychological inquiry which can be traced from British Empiricism through to modern Behaviorism.

Although we might label the comment as arrogant, Freud referred to himself as performing the same function for the psyche as Copernicus and Darwin had for astronomy and biology respectively.[1] History may well agree with Freud's self-assessment even considering his "errors" and reductionisms. In any case, I intend to present the Freudian model with sufficient depth in order to allow his vital contributions regarding selfhood to emerge, while recognizing his inevitable limits. It is impossible to reflect psychologically on human subjectivity with any sophistication whatsoever without Freud. Any attempt to understand selfhood from a psychodynamic perspective requires a grappling with his genius.

Freud's Historical and Philosophical Background

The intellectual climate of the mid-to-late nineteenth century was governed by the continuing ascendancy of science and the scientific method. The Newtonian system and the evolutionary constructs of Darwin had defined the universe and the place of the human therein. The Newtonian model with its rigid determinism and closed system offered a clear and predictable unfolding of the secrets of nature. Science was now offering the certainty that the workings of the universe and its organisms could be unraveled by discovering the "laws" by which these systems worked.

The Darwinian and Newtonian influence upon Freud was no doubt intensified through Freud's familiarity with Aristotle. Freud's Aristotelian threads can be readily traced to his three year participation in Franz Brentano's courses in Philosophy at the University of Vienna.[2] This Aristotelian background gave Freud a phylogenetic perspective, which declared that the higher or more developed forms of life contain the lower. Matter and form make up what is real and the particular form taken by matter actualizes what it inherently contains as its potential. As I noted in Chapter One, these constructs allowed Aristotle to see nature as dynamic and changing, with the essence of nature its very changeableness in which the less complex is taken up and "maintained" by the higher, although in different form. These Aristotelian ideas were reintroduced into the history of inquiry via the inductive scientific methods of Darwin and found fertile ground in Freud given his own Aristotelian foundation. We see these Aristotelian ideas of continuity-in-change and the transfer of psychological "material" from lower to higher levels of development in Freud's instinct theories, models of sexual development, and the topographic approach to psychological life, to name but a few.

However, in addition to this more "naturalistic" stream represented by Newton and Darwin there was another vital (although highly ambivalent) influence upon Freud, this being the "Philosophy of Nature" as represented by Goethe and other German Romanticists such as Friedrich Schelling. Freud writes in his autobiography that it was Geothe's essay on Nature read aloud at a public lecture which prompted his entry into Medical School.[3] Romanticism finds its place on the philosophical map as the first movement of German Idealism in the transition from

Kant to Hegel. It asserts the dignity of nature and attempts to grasp nature "directly" since it is the tangible manifestation of the Absolute or Spirit. The Romanticism which ambivalently impacted Freud valued feeling, intuition, and imagination as the means whereby the underlying unity of reality could be apprehended in its raw immediacy.[4] As a form of pantheism it concluded that "God" or the Absolute **is** nature and its laws. As one great organism, the workings of the Absolute can be known through nature which is simply Absolute Spirit in visible form. Although an early colleague of Shelling, Hegel became a strong critic of this form of Idealism as had Fichte before him. In short, the centrality of nature for determining what is "real" was the intellectual climate which shaped Freud and gave direction to his work throughout his life.

The particular way in which Freud "absorbed" Romanticism's vision, while at the same time reacting strongly to it becomes clearer as we consider Freud's lengthy six-year exposure to Brucke, the great Vienese physiologist of the late 19th Century. Brucke was an adherent to what was known as the Helmholz School of Medicine. This particular school carried forward in the physiological arena the Romanticist deep appreciation of nature, while vehemently rejecting its mystic and spiritualized leanings.[5] This Helmholz School, with Brucke as its representative in Vienna pledged itself to purify the understanding of nature from these leanings toward vitalism and mysticism as had occurred within full-blown Romanticism. One of the members of this school writes in 1842:

> Brucke and I pledged a solemn oath to put into effect this truth: 'no other forces than the common physical-chemical ones are active within the organism. In those cases which cannot at the time be explained by those forces one had either to find the specific way or form of their action by means of the physical-mathematical method or to assume new forces equal in dignity to the chemical-physical forces inherent in matter, reducible to the force of attraction and repulsion'.[6]

These ideas represent the core philosophical and methodological foundation which sustained Freud throughout his scientific life.

The influence of these ideas can be found throughout the entire range of Freudian constructs. As suggested, Freudian psychoanalytic theory reflects the following perspectives:

(1) **A Gestalt perspective** - all behavior is integrated and part of a larger whole.

(2) **An Organismic perspective** - all behavior belongs to the working of the total organism.

(3) **A Genetic perspective** - there are historical antecedents to all behavior and what exists in the here and now can only be explored and understood through its genetic roots.

(4) **A Topographic perspective** - there is a "depth" to all human activity referred to as the Unconscious, which operates by its own set of laws which differ in some respects from the laws which govern other "layers" of mental life.

(5) **An Instinctual perspective** - the ultimate determiners of human activity are the instincts or drives which "push" the organism in unifying (eros) or separating (thanatos) directions.

(6) **An Economic perspective** - all human activity is regulated by psychological energy, and disposes of psychological energy (via abreaction, neutralization, reaction-formation, displacement, etc.)[7]

Each of these "perspectives" is consistent with the philosophical presuppositions Freud brought to his work. This is not to suggest that Freud simply squeezed his clinical observations into his a priori assumptions, but that these theories arose out of his particular intellectual tradition.

With this background identified I am now able to proceed with a more detailed analysis of Freud's thought with my eventual goal the uncovering of the Freudian contribution to the discovery of selfhood.

Freudian Models of the Psyche

As a pioneering figure Freud's ideas underwent numerous changes throughout his lifetime. His work has been classified into a variety of "periods" with most scholars dividing his efforts into four major epochs:

(1) 1886-1895 - The Exploration of Neurosis
(2) 1895-1899 - Self-analysis
(3) 1900-1914 - Id Psychology
(4) 1915-1939 - The Structural Theory and Ego Psychology

Of particular interest to this study are those Freudian theories which describe (1) the structure, and (2) the dynamic life of personhood. To understand the dynamics of psychic life and the "forms" through which it moves I will need to examine both Freud's structural models and drive theories in some depth.

The Freudian Structure of Personality

There are two essential Freudian models which depict the "shape" of subjective life. The first model was developed by 1900 and came to be known as the **Topographic Model** and covers roughly the period from 1895 to 1914. By 1915 the inability to resolve certain thorny contradictions forced Freud to rework the entire framework into what came to be called the **Structural Model** through which he laid the foundation for **Ego Psychology**.

The Topographic Model

The early years of exploration culminated for Freud in 1900 in the watershed book *The Interpretation of Dreams*. Here for the first time Freud constructed an explicit model of the psyche for the purpose of explaining dream processes. In examining these processes Freud discovered that dream life underwent certain "distortions" which needed explanation. These distortions or disturbances in dream activity included phenomena such as the forgetting of dreams, the seeking of the fulfillment of "wishes", and a **repressive** as well as a **regressive** function.[8]

To explain these activities Freud proposed a model of mental life consisting of three systems called the unconscious, the preconscious and the conscious.[9] In order to explain the distortions evident in dream life, two "paths" or psychic agencies were proposed by Freud.[10] The first path is the reception of perceptual stimuli which lead immediately to the motor activity sparked by the stimulus, in a form of reflex action. There remain no memory traces of this activity. This path is the most simple given its automatic nature and is known simply as the reflex arc. Freud calls this the "perceptual system" in the sense of simple perception or awareness.[11]

A second path or "psychic agency" was then proposed by Freud in which "permanent traces" were left behind by the "momentary excitations" of the first model.[12] Here, perceptions are linked with one another through memory, not simply in the sense of something "registering", but through a linkage which Freud calls "association". These associations are collected to form "memory systems." Freud writes:

> The first of these [memory] systems will naturally contain the record of association in respect to **simultaneity in time**; while the same perceptual material will be arranged in the later systems in respect to other kinds of coincidences, so that one of these later systems, for instance will record relations of similarity, and so on with the others.[13]

There is nothing particularly earth-shattering about the conclusion that memory requires the capacity for association i.e. the recognition of perceptual objects in their similarity and distinction in the flow of time and space. Hegel said much the same thing in his analysis of the transition from sense-knowing to perception. What is noteworthy is that Freud took this second path **through the Unconscious** which allowed for psychic activity to move in a backwards direction. Dream activity, says Freud, moves in a reverse direction, namely, from motor activity through sensation to eventual perception. It is this backwards direction which makes the dream **regressive**.[14]

In stumbling across the phenomenon of regression Freud was given a conceptual key which unlocked all manner of psychodynamic processes far beyond dream phenomena. The many pathological conditions present during waking states were now able to be explained and responded to with new sophistication. Freud explains:

> My explanation of hallucinations in hysteria and paranoia and of visions in mentally normal subjects is that they are in fact **regressions** - that is thoughts transformed into images but that the only thoughts which undergo this transformation are those which are intimately linked with memories that have been suppressed or have remained unconscious.[15]

Freud concludes that the contents of the unconscious are inaccessible to consciousness except as they pass through the "filter" of a preconscious censor which renders them acceptable. Furthermore, among the primary functions of this unconscious is the fulfillment of its "wishes." What does Freud mean by this term?

The Nature of Wish

It was suggested earlier that wish-fulfillment is one of the key tasks of dream life which is of course the "royal road" into the unconscious. But this does not tell us what a wish is nor what function it serves. For Freud a wish represents the entire range of psychological needs or drives, carried in a particular mental form. A wish does not only represent one's desire for a particular object of which one is consciously aware, but a process referring to all seeking of satisfaction.

Freud worked from the premise that all organisms seek pleasure or satisfaction, suggesting furthermore that they avoid unpleasure or tension, i.e. "excitation". A wish, says Freud, is the impulse "to re-establish the situation of the original satisfaction."[16] What happens in his estimation is that an organism experiences a need which demands satisfaction. The need carries with it a force (which Freud calls an emotion) which represents itself in a perception or mental image. As satisfaction occurs it too is **re-presented** as a perception or awareness. The mental link between these two states is what constitutes the wish. It might be helpful if I draw upon Freud's own example from infant life.

Let us assume that a baby experiences the distress of a bodily need (hunger). This distress has an internal movement or force associated with it which Freud calls emotion. Even with all of its crying and screaming, however, nothing changes. Change only happens as outside help arrives and an "experience of satisfaction" occurs which removes the internal stimulus. A vital by-product of this experience is that the perception of nourishment becomes associated with the memory trace of the need itself.[17] Because of this link, says Freud, the next time the need arises a "psychic impulse" surfaces which attempts to mentally re-create the image which provided the satisfaction. This impulse is a wish. The goal of this most basic of psychological activities is to produce a "perceptual identity" i.e. an image or perception which is linked with the experience of satisfaction of a need.

A wish, then, is that mechanism whereby a link is established between a state of homeostatis, through a phase of need, and back to a state of equilibrium via the satisfaction of the need. What strikes me in this declaration is that Freud seems to recognize an operational dialectic cycle - granted at a very rudimentary level - but nevertheless hinting at a mechanism by which mental life is constructed. This equilibrium - disequilibrium - satisfaction cycle bears a distinct resemblance to the dialectic cycle I noted in Fichte, Hegel, and Kierkegaard.

Freud came to call wish-fulfillment **primary process activity** - the establishment of a "perceptual identity" with the source of satisfaction.[18] The primary process is a regressive process for him in the sense that the organism is in identity with its object of satisfaction, **but at the perceptual level only.** I could even say that the primary process creates its own objects with which it seeks identity. Freud goes on to suggest that psychotic and other hallucinatory activity is a clinging to the object of a wish and is an example of the raw primary process at work. Because of its attempt to avoid unpleasure, the primary process exhibits the mechanisms of repression, condensation, and displacement as it seeks to discharge its impulses.

Secondary process activity, on the other hand, is able to "contain" the regression of the primary process, not by presenting mental objects to itself (which is only a perceptual identity), but by the establishment of what Freud calls a "thought identity."[19] Whereas the primary process functions only on the basis of the **pleasure principle** (more accurately the avoidance of unpleasure), the secondary process operates on the basis of the **reality principle**. Secondary process activity has given up the immediate seeking of relief through perception only, and now attempts to achieve satisfaction through a concrete factual relationship to the external world. It no longer seeks only internal objects but external ones which respond to its particular level of need.

Secondary process "thinking" makes a connection between itself and the source of satisfaction in the external world, in contrast to primary process activity which is in identity only with the internal image through which it attempts to satisfy itself. Secondary process activity is able to tolerate frustration and delay satisfaction by establishing a "thought-identity" between itself as active agent and the experience of satisfaction.[20] Secondary activity is able to get on with the job of doing something about the need while "holding" the tension within itself, so to speak.

In addition to the possible linkage noted between wish and the dialectics of selfhood, it is worth noting that Freud's concept of wish approximates the dynamics of desire as described by Hegel and Kierkegaard. They insisted that the tension which is generated through separation from objects activates the desire through which consciousness is born. This surprising Freudian parallel strengthens the case that the emergence of self-awareness requires an encounter with otherness, an otherness which somehow impacts a subject.

But does this topographic model and its **primary** and **secondary** processes have any further relevance for selfhood beyond the parallels I have noted between wish and desire? At first glance, the Freudian model with its emphasis on regressive phenomena seems a far cry from the recognition of a central organizing process within personhood, never mind the movement toward higher unities which would be assumed in any sophisticated understanding of self. But if I offer a preliminary definition of self as "the capacity for internally-guided synthesis in its object-determined development", might not other parallels be visible?

I would propose that even the early topographic model and its **primary** and **secondary** components exhibits in a very basic way a Freudian recognition of the subject-object polarity within the psyche. Even though the primary process is completely governed by the pleasure-unpleasure principle and is fully unconscious, it reveals patterns of engagement of subject and object in their purely "natural" or biological form. A rudimentary dialectic within selfhood seems to be reflected in the primary process and its discharge of raw biological energies. We may find that Freud is unable to see selfhood develop toward "higher" levels but this does not invalidate his recognition of a rudimentary level of subject-object encounter.

If the primary process reveals selfhood grounded in nature, then the secondary process may well reveal selfhood as it gains a history. Secondary process activity begins to describe the subject-object dynamics of the self as it encounters a more complex world. It is no accident that Freud, in calling secondary process a "purposive idea", is echoing Hegel's point that the self is that which actualizes a particular purpose.[21] These early levels of operation may not be "mediated" in the true sense of the word due to their "unconsciousness," but this does not change the impression that interactive processes are underway. It is in Freud's early notion of transference, however, that the capacity of self to engage and shape itself becomes more clearly visible.

Transference as Dynamic Construct

Early in his theory-building Freud introduced a vital concept into his theory base which continued to be developed by him throughout his life. This central concept is that of **transference**. From the topographic point of view there are two operational systems proposed: (1) the unconscious governed by the primary process and (2) the preconscious governed by the secondary process. Consciousness (the ego) is only a by-product of the battle between these two elements.[22]

The unconscious, as the container of a vast residue of needs, drives, or instincts, seeks the fulfillment of its wishes. Because these wishes are infantile, they undergo the censorship of the preconsciousness which presents them to consciousness in acceptable fashion. Freud elaborates:

> We learn from (the psychology of the neuroses) that an unconscious idea as such quite incapable of entering the preconscious and that it can only exercise any effect there by establishing a connection with an idea which already belongs to the preconscious, by **transfering** its intensity, to it and by getting itself 'covered' by it. Here we have the fact of **'transference'** which provides an explanation of so many striking phenomena in the mental life of neurotics.[23]

What Freud suggests is that psychic life can **transfer** its energy and content from one target to another. As selfhood experiences its needs and drives it can transfer its wishes from one object to another this being true with both internal or external objects.

Although transference is most commonly understood today as a therapeutic phenomenon in which infantile residue is projected onto the here and now object of the therapist, its basic meaning remains that of an intrapsychic mechanism. What we have here is a strong (if still vague) Freudian recognition of a subject-object interaction inherent in psychic life. Through transference a subject adjusts its relationship with the inner or outer objects of its world through which it forms its identity. Transference, therefore, serves as an early Freudian manifestation of the operations self i.e. that process which synthesizes itself in the course of its development.

The ideas presented thus far represent the period of Freud's theory-building which ended in approximately 1914, but which nevertheless established the general principles which remained intact throughout his life. However, major revisions to the theoretical superstructure were undertaken. For what reasons was this topographic model rejected?

The Transition from Bi-polar to Tri-partite Model

The discovery of the phenomenon of repression as it operates in hysteria had led Freud to conclude that subjective life was made up of two portions - a repressing part and a repressed part. Those components became labelled **preconscious** and **unconscious** respectively as I have noted. Contradictions soon surfaced which undermined this simple model, among them the fact that these terms were being used both **descriptively** (as adjectives identifying degrees of awareness) and **dynamically** (as operations or functions).[24]

Freud slowly realized that even though everything repressed is (by definition) unconscious, not everything unconscious is necessarily repressed.[25] But how can one explain the presence of unconscious material that is not repressed?

Repression, as we recall, was attributed to the preconscious where its job was to prevent unwelcome material from reaching awareness. But the act of repression itself was somehow beyond awareness which created the contradiction that repression was operating at a higher level (in the preconscious), but was unable to become conscious, which contradicts the definition of the preconscious.

For these reasons Freud concluded that the terms consciousness and unconsciousness could no longer be used to represent psychic structures. They could only be used as "qualities" which may or may not be present along with other characteristics of mental life. To allow the operations of subjective life to be more accurately represented an entirely "new" nomenclature was needed. This new model came to be known as **Ego Psychology** and contained the structural elements known as Id, Ego, and Superego.[26]

The Tripartite Model

The Id

Freud offers his clearest statement about the three "regions" or "realms" of mental life in *The New Introductory Lectures on Psycho-analysis* (1933). Therein he acknowledges that the Id is in large part the inheritor of what had been called the unconscious system. The term "Id" (the It) he borrowed from G. Groddeck who himself had borrowed the term from Nietzche.[27] Nietzche had used the pronoun to represent the unknown and chaotic forces which drive life. Freud simply narrowed the concept to describe the "seething cauldron" of instinctive energy which pushes psychic activity. Freud explains:

> It (Id) is the obscure inacccessible part of our personality ... We can come nearer to the id with images, and call it a chaos, a cauldron of seething excitement. We suppose that it is somewhere in direct contact with somatic processes, and takes over from them instinctual needs and gives them mental expression ... These instincts fill it with energy, but it has no organization and no unified will only an impulsion to obtain satisfaction for the instinctual needs, in accordance with the pleasure-principle.[28]

Freud also describes this id as unaffected by time, knowing no values whether good or evil, and dominated solely by the effort to discharge its instinctual energy.

The Freudian Ego

If the Id is the churning ocean of psychic energy which pushes psychic life, then the Ego is the Island which emerges as a visible entity out of this vast reservoir. The ego carves itself out of the id through the confrontation with reality. This is its great challenge and task, to balance its instinctive "inner" forces with the demands of the external world. Freud writes:

> This relation to the external world is decisive for the ego. The ego has taken over the task of representing the external world for the id, and so of saving it... In the fulfillment of this function, the ego has to observe the external world and preserve a true picture of it in the memory traces left by its perceptions, and by means of the reality

test, it has to eliminate any element in this picture of the external world which is a contribution from internal sources of excitation.[29]

What allows the ego to "lift" itself out of the id is its relationship to its experiences, its ability to "collect" itself through the flow of time or, one could say, to the ego's history in the world of objects . The capacity which brings this about is the ego's organizing and synthesizing ability which allows it to gather itself i.e. to "pull itself together." Freud elaborates:

> What, however, especially marks the ego out in contradistinction to the id, is a tendency to synthesize its contents, to bring together and unify its mental processes which is entirely absent from the id... The ego advances from the function of perceiving instincts to that of controlling them, but the latter is only achieved through the mental representative of the instinct becoming subordinated to a larger organization, and finding its place in a coherent unity.[30]

The capacity for memory allows the ego to "store-up" its residues of experience which are carried in the form of thought and image. This use of thought is a delaying action which drives a necessary wedge between the raw desire of the id (pleasure principle) and its objects. Thus the ego goes about its business of "grasping" its environment even while it begins to harness the id. But things are not quite so easy for the ego.

Freud reminds us that the ego never outgrows the id nor moves beyond it. The ego is forever weak in the sense of being dependent upon the id from which it borrows its energy. The manner in which this is done is through identification.[31] Psychic energy is directed from the id toward the objects which would satisfy its instinctual needs. These concentrations of energy toward an object are called object-cathexes. These object-cathexes instinctively emerge from the id whereupon the ego first takes note of them. Then, says Freud, the ego identifies itself with the object, becoming a substitute object which can draw the energy (libido) of the id toward itself.

In this circular fashion the ego becomes a bridge between the world of drives (instincts) and the world of reality. But in this very bridge-building it is also building itself as the organizer of its experience. Here, again, emerges a Freudian acknowledgement of a dialectic path for selfhood. A rudimentary ego places itself "between" the instinct (drive) and the world (as represented by a particular object).

By identifying itself with the external object the ego redirects the energy of the drive toward itself. By bringing drive and object into relationship **through itself**, the ego becomes a "new" third in the equation. The ego gains "substance" or structure as it is born out of this encounter.

I wish to make it very clear, however, that this Freudian ego is not the equivalent of the fullness of selfhood. The Freudian ego is limited in that it knows only a faceless object world and organizes such, and furthermore, only vaguely knows itself. What one **can** say is that Freud's tripartite model reaffirms (from a purely naturalistic point of view), that the developmental path may well have dialectic features - although for Freud it culminates simply in the formation of an ego, an identity as "I", an object in the world alongside other objects.

In any event, what can be declared with some confidence is that the Freudian id represents recognition of a rudimentary process within self, namely, the non-mediated or instinctual relation between **soma** and **psyche** so well identified by Kierkegaard with the term necessity. Ego, on the other hand, reveals a higher development within selfhood, beyond id, namely a **mediated** (conscious) **relation** which adapts our **soma** to the **world** thereby giving shape to what we call "I".

Freud describes the relationship between ego and id using the famous analogy of a rider and his horse which I first noted in Plato.[32] A rider can only move as the horse provides the energy, even as the rider channels this energy in a particular direction. However, many a rider has been thrown from a horse, just as many a horse has ridden off on its own with the rider a helpless passenger. This too has relevance for Freudian selfhood as Freud proposes the construct of the superego as the first process by which an ego enters into direct relationship with itself.

The Superego

The final construct developed by Freud is that of the superego which did not appear in his writings until 1923. Even in 1923 his pictoral model of the psyche did not include the superego but by the time of the publication of *New Introductory Lectures* in 1933 the construct had been sufficiently refined to stand alongside the other structural elements. It is in the concept of the superego that one finds the first

Freudian recognition of the human capacity to relate oneself, to oneself in the sense of an ego coming into subjective encounter with itself.

Freud begins his discussion of the superego by suggesting that the ego can become an object to itself through observing itself and entering into relationship with itself.[33] It can treat itself like any other object in its world by becoming a harsh critic or by laying ideals onto itself. When this division occurs, says Freud, one part of the ego stands over-against the other. This capacity for "splitting" is inherent in the ego and occurs in all phases of its life. In normal states the "parts" of the ego rejoin while in pathological states they do not.

After much reflection Freud eventually concluded that the development of an observing function might be a normal feature of the ego's structure.[34] To explain the formation of this capacity Freud drew upon the two ego processes he called (1) object-choice (object-cathexis) and (2) identification. The first mechanism was used by Freud to explain how an ego draws "energy" to itself by making itself available as a substitute object for the id. As an ego presents objects to the id it allows the id to "love" the ego because it is so much like the object the id was seeking.[35] This builds the ego because of the redirecting of energy (libido) from object to ego. Freud calls this the transformation from object-libido to narcissistic libido (i.e. energy turned back toward the ego).

However, Freud also notes that ego formation does not just occur through the choosing of objects. It also takes a more "regressive" form by **becoming like** its objects. This ego function Freud calls **identification** and it represents "the earliest expression of an emotional tie with another person."[36] Freud explains the difference between (1) object choice and (2) identification as follows:

> It is easy to state in a formula the distinction between an identification with the father and the choice of the father as an object. In the first case one's father is what one would like to be, and in the second he is what one would like to have. The distinction, that is, depends upon whether the tie attaches to the subject or to the object of the ego.[37]

In the earliest phases of psychological life such as the early oral period these two functions are indistinguishable. However, surmises Freud, it may well be that **identification** is the primary means whereby the id becomes willing to give up its objects to the ego. This very shift from **object-choice** to **identification** may be at the heart of ego construction.[38] Should this be true, then the shape of Freudian selfhood may well be determined by the object-choices and identifications made along the developmental path. Even at this early stage the parallel to Kierkegaard is striking: the self constructs itself via its ever-present capacity to align itself with its identifications and the images generated thereby.

Freud illustrates this phenomenon by referring to a situation in which someone has lost or has been forced to give up a love-object. The ego compensates for this loss by internalizing (introjecting) the lost object through **identifying** itself with it.[39] In this manner the chosen object is re-created inside the ego thereby changing the ego in the process.

To restate, the two sides of the coin of Freudian identity formation are (1) **object-cathexes** by which the object is chosen as a legitimate target for the investment of energy, and (2) **identifications** by which the object is taken in and made part of the ego. In the first instance the object is adapted to the ego, in the second the ego adapts itself to the object. It is this second process which describes the emergence of the **superego** for Freud.

Superego formation, then, is the product of the accumulated identifications occurring within the psyche. In its early form this function appears as the ego-ideal which is essentially the internalization of the idealized and perfect parent - here laid upon the ego as the ideal against which it should measure itself. With the onset of the Oedipal complex, however, the picture is complicated by the birth of ambivalence toward the parents, claims Freud. No longer is the internal message "you **ought to be**" (like a particular parent), but "you **may not be**" (like a particular parent).[40] This marks the beginning of the superego's **repressive** function which can take massively punitive forms.

The fully-formed superego only emerges as a final outcome of the Oedipal phase of development, claims Freud:

> The broad general outcome of the sexual phase dominated by the Oedipus complex may, therefore, be taken to be the forming of a precipitate in the ego [superego], consisting of phase two **identifications** [father and mother identification] in some way united with each other. This modification of the ego retains its special position; it confronts the other contents of the ego as ... a superego.[41]

As the oedipal phase passes, suggests Freud, the child must give up its intense investment of energy in the parents. To compensate for this loss it intensifies its identification with them. But this identification is not simply with the parents as such but includes **the parental superego**. As the child takes-in parental superego content, this superego "becomes the vehicle of tradition and of all the age-long values which have been handed down from generation to generation."[42]

Here is Freud's answer to the charge that psychoanalysis has ignored "the higher, moral, or supra-personal side of human nature."[43] Freud can therefore conclude that religion, for instance, arises simply out of an unmet longing for the father. The gap between the **real** world and **ideal** ego (as it judges itself) produces the "religious humility" and "longing" which motivates the believer. Similarly, the gap between the ego's actual behavior and its ideal demand is the source of its guilt, just as social sensitivity is but a by-product of one's identifications with other people who have the same ego ideal.

It is not my purpose to offer a critique of these Freudian conclusions other than to acknowledge what is commonly known - that Freud takes a very reductive approach to personal life and sees its unfolding strictly through the narrow lens of its phylogenetic origins. However, even if one disagrees with him, it does not obscure the point that Freud - **in his structural analysis of the psyche** - offers a first effort at describing the "natural" development of an ego as it finds its identity through the bodily and interpersonal realities of its life. In naming various psychodynamic mechanisms such as the seeking of objects (object-cathexis), identification, introjection, repression, and regression, Freud offers the world a new language for discussing the process of coming to selfhood, even if he, like a Moses, was not granted access to the land beyond the ego. But before leaving Freud I must explain his efforts at uncovering the energies which move selfhood, even if these also turn out to be limited by his one-sided archeological approach.

The Psyche and Its Energy

The Nature of Drives

If the changes described in Freud's structural approach to the psyche are troublesome, they are nowhere near as complicated as the changes one discovers in his thinking about the energies which drive the psyche. There are several so-called instinct or drive theories developed by Freud, each of which attempts to incorporate new observations about psychological process. It is unnecessary to walk through this complicated maze in great detail other than to identify the highlights and determine if these conclusions remain useful for our contemporary search.

What did Freud actually mean by the term "instinct" or "drive" and how is this concept central to his understanding of human existence?[44] Freud's answer to the question seems quite clear:

> If we now apply ourselves to considering mental life from a biological point of view, an instinct (drive) appears to us as a concept on the frontier between the mental and the somatic, as the psychial representative of the stimuli originating from within the organism and reaching the mind, as a measure of the demand made upon the mind for work in consequence of its connection with the body.[45]

One is immediately struck by Freud's use of drive as an attempt at bridge-building between body and psyche. It would be an error to immediately read a synthesizing role into this construct, but one can nevertheless declare that it represents a Freudian recognition of the Kierkegaardian truth: to be human requires a "synthesis" of the bodily and psychial.

Drives, then, are the forces which surface in the interface between body and psyche as an impetus for action within the entire expanse of human functioning. They represent the demands made upon the psyche by virtue of the "needs" residing in the body. One also notices, however, that traffic on this Freudian bridge moves largely from body to psyche. It was this limitation which eventually led Freud to add additional features to the drive theory which I will describe momentarily.

There are four characteristics of drives which Freud calls their (1) source (2) pressure (3) aim, and (4) object.[46] The source (Quelle) of a drive is its organic foundation, i.e. a "need" or hunger present in an organ or zone of the body.[47] By pressure (Drang) Freud is speaking of the **force** or **intensity** by which a drive does its work. This intensity may vary but it never disappears altogether.

The aim (Ziel) refers to the "purpose" of a drive which in all cases is to achieve "satisfaction". This "satisfaction" is the maintenance of psychic equilibrium. According to Freud's hypothesis of energy transformation, the presence of a drive creates tension which raises the level of energy in the system, much like a river whose water level rises with increased rainfall and/or the blockage of a dam. The organism invariably seeks to lower this energy to maintain its homeostasis, which is why the drive seeks the necessary "gratification" which will bring it back to its state of equilibrium.

Finally, gratification is found in the object (Object) which is the person or thing through which the drive can satisfy its need.

The Dual-Instinct Theory

Freud did not attempt to systematically classify the drives, perhaps because his own thinking on the subject was so fluid that no one schema could account for all the data. Writing in 1915, he proposes that all "instincts" should be reduceble into two essential groups which he calls the ego or "self-preservative" instincts on the one hand, and the "sexual instincts" on the other.[48]

In this early model the opposition is between the **ego** (self-preservative) and the **sexual** (libidinal) drives. These two drives correspond to the period in Freud's life when the topographic model was still in vogue. In it, as we recall, the primary and secondary processes governed psychic life with the primary process roughly equivalent to raw sexual or libidinal energy, with secondary process having the regulatory function which controls the way in which these drives are channeled and expressed.

Although this model marks the beginning of what has come to be known as the dual-instinct theory, Freud did not develop the nature of this drive for preservation (i.e. ego-function) to any great detail largely because the concept of the ego was still rather nebulous as I have noted. What was seen as primary was the sexual (libidinal) drive, which attempts to overcome the excitations produced by the "needs" of the body (perhaps chemically induced thought Freud), as these needs are localized in various erogenous zones of the body such as the oral, anal, or genital.[49]

The operation of this system is that of a hydraulic machine in which the raw sexual (libidinal) energy of the id seeks to reduce tension via the pleasure principle to a point of equilibrium (constancy principle). In this first drive theory model the clash is essentially between the libido (pleasure principle) and the environment (reality principle). While the concept of environmental constraint is fairly straightforward, the concept of libido is not, and given its importance in the Freudian system a brief elaboration is necessary.

The Freudian Libido

Perhaps no other term in the Freudian nomenclature has been as contentious or as central to his theory than that of libido. It is this item which became the source of the great rift between he and C.G. Jung, with Freud devoting numerous pages in several books attempting to discredit Jung's tampering with the concept.[50]

The term libido is the cornerstone to Freud's great ediface, **the sexual theory**. In uncovering the genetic roots of "sexual" life down to its origins in the chemical life of the body, Freud thought he had found the key to unlocking the deepest reaches of human existence. Libido refers to the force or energy which is exchanged in the processes and transformations which come with "sexual" exitation.[51] We must remember that this concept of sexuality is not simply genital but refers to the excitation or stimulation which occurs in all zones of the body. Eventually, the term "sexuality" came to include the full range of the human seeking of union.

But at this earlier stage the concept of "sexual drive" is the psychodynamic equivalent of physical hunger or the seeking of nutrition. The sexual impulse is as basic to psychic life as food is for the physical survival of any organism. The word chosen by Freud to describe this process is a familiar German word (Lust).[52] In German the word can mean both desire and pleasure (satisfaction); what becomes lost in the translation is that libido is an **activity of seeking** in which there is movement from desire to satisfaction and back again.

In identifying the parallel between libido and desire one cannot ignore the obvious similarity between the Freudian libido and the Hegelian and Kierkegaardian recognition of desire as the doorway to self-consciousness. This similarity becomes even more striking when one moves beyond the early Freud and his narrower view of sexuality to the later Freud, who saw the **seeking of the object** as the essence of human sexuality and drive dynamics. Thus, in Freud's libidinal theory I see a virtually identical process to Kierkegaard's Immediacy phase of Aesthetic selfhood identified as (1) dreaming desire, (2) searching desire, and (3) desiring desire. It is worth remembering that for Kierkegaard each of these forms of desire represent a selfhood still buried within its environmental givens and thereby only potentially present. Perhaps I need say no more as to the limits of the Freudian self.

Narcissism and the Seeking of Objects

With the shift from the topographic to the structural model the central duality shifts from a tension between organism and environment, to a tension arising out of **the internal workings of the organism itself.** What sparked this shift was the concept of narcissism.

As I have just described, Freud had concluded rather early that the human organism seeks objects through which it gratifies its impulses (what he calls object-libido). What now needed explanation was not only that this object-libido could be blocked, but that it could also be withdrawn and turned back upon one's own ego. The following extended passage from 1915 is instructive:

> We can follow the object-libido through still further vicissitudes. When it is withdrawn from objects, it is held in suspense in peculiar conditions of tension and is finally drawn back into the ego so that it becomes ego-libido once again. In contrast to object-libido, we also describe ego-libido as 'narcissistic' libido ... Narcissistic or ego-libido seems to be the great reservoir from which the object-cathexes are sent out and into which they are withdrawn once more; the narcissistic libidinal cathexis of the ego is the original state of things, realized in earliest childhood, and is merely covered by later extrusions of libido, but in essentials persists behind them. [53]

What prompted this major adjustment in theory was the discovery of a difference in use of objects between the two major classifications of disturbed individuals. In neurotic patients the transference revealed that libido was being invested in fantasized objects; in other words, real objects had been replaced with internal imaginary ones (taken from memory). In so doing the patient was either mixing up real and imaginary objects, or simply repressing her particular desires with regard to her objects.[54]

With psychotics, however, the situation was much different. They seemed to withdraw libido from people and things without replacing them with fantasy objects. When these objects were replaced it seemed to be a "secondary" process, an attempt to recover or lead the libido back to objects. It is this shift which Freud came to describe as **primary** vs. **secondary** narcissism. In describing narcissistic activity Freud writes:

> Thus we form the idea of there being an original libidinal cathexis of the ego, from which some is later given off to objects, but which fundamentally persists and is related to the object-cathexes much as the body of an amoeba is related to the pseudopodia which it puts out.[55]

The analogy of an amoeba extending its "arms" outward to enclose an object and take it in is undoubtably chosen very carefully by Freud. On the one hand it is striking to notice Freud's acknowledgement of the dynamic rhythm between subject and object as the heart of psychic life. The essence of narcissistic activity is this **embracing and taking-in** of an object which somehow changes the active agent in the process.

On the other hand, what are we to make of Freud's use of a one-celled organism to illustrate this process? An obvious answer might be that Freud, being so acquainted with biology, would draw naturally from what was familiar. However, this conclusion would miss the critical point, that Freud consistently wished to drive home the message that psychic life is at its heart nothing more than the instinctive and chemical processes which are contained therein. No matter how sophisticated psychic processes may become they are simply an organically-induced seeking of objects which one attempts to ingest. Why could Freud not move beyond this reductive position?

Because the Freudian system is closed in a Newtonian sense, energy can only be exchanged within the system i.e. between ego-libido and object-libido. The more there is of one the less there is of the other. And so, claims Freud, when the highest state of object-libido development is reached (being in love) then "the subject seems to give up his own personality in favour of an object-cathexis."[56]

As suffocating as this conclusion may be it should not obscure the vital point - that Freud **even with his materialistic and biological bias, concludes that the subject-object dynamic is in operation at even the most fundamental levels of the psyche.**

In thus describing the narcissistic process Freud was laying the foundation for a theory of object relations and an eventual self psychology. By 1914 he had already proposed three gradations of narcissistic activity which he called (1) auto-eroticism, (2) primary narcissism, and (3) secondary narcissism.

Auto-eroticism is strictly speaking not narcissistic because there is no ego structure present to direct energy toward an object nor of course toward the ego itself. Freud recognizes that:

> a unity comparable to the ego cannot exist in the individual from the start: the ego has to be developed. The auto-erotic instincts, however, are there from the very first; so there must be something added to auto-eroticism - a new psychial action - in order to bring about narcissism.[57]

That "something-added" which gives birth to narcissism is the first faint impact of the external world. The early experiences of separation generate the very rudimentary ego toward which libido can now direct itself (**primary narcissism**).

In separating libido based upon where it directs itself (either toward the ego or objects), Freud was able to discuss not only types of pathology, but lay the foundation for a more sophisticated developmental psychology which could explain the birth and development of the ego. In the state of primary narcissism the ego is indifferent to the external world in the sense that it cares little from where satisfaction comes. This rudimentary ego seeks only pleasurable feelings and is not truly awakened to the external world. While the infant in a state of primary narcissism is self-contained in the sense that it has the capacity for self-pleasure (primary narcissism), it is hardly self-sufficient.

Given its helplessness the infant cannot remain indifferent for long and soon begins to acknowledge external objects as sources of satisfaction and/or non-satisfaction. The ego thus invests energy (libido) in these objects and this energy then returns back to the ego using the mechanisms of introjection and identification. This return of energy into the ego Freud calls **secondary narcissism**. Freud summarizes:

> In so far as the ego is auto-erotic, it has no need of the external world, but, in consequence of experiences undergone by the instincts of self-preservation, it acquires objects from that world ...

Under the dominance of the pleasure principle a further development now takes place in the ego. In so far as the objects which are presented to it are sources of pleasure, it takes them into itself, 'introjects' them; and on the other hand it expels whatever within itself becomes a cause of unpleasure.[58]

Freud recognizes that the awakening to the object during primary narcissism is not a neutral process but has pleasure/unpleasure, loving/hating qualities attached to it. The particular quality attached to any object in the external world can also reproduce itself in the internal world of the ego. It is vitally important that we understand the significant shift which has now occured for Freud.

Up to this point the instincts had been divided along pleasure - unpleasure lines, basically a body-based dualism. Now, with the shift to intrapsychic process, the dualism becomes psychodynamic not simply somatic, with a growing recognition of the impact of the object upon the subject.

A Reconstructed Drive Theory

With the publication of *Beyond the Pleasure Principle* in 1920 Freud consolidated the last major shift in his theoretical thinking. The clinical phenomenon which triggered this shift is what Freud calls the **"compulsion to repeat**," or the inevitable acting-out of a repressed item of psychic life.[59] What makes repetition compulsion so problematic, however, is that it has nothing to do with the attainment of pleasure or satisfaction. A persistent seeking of new painful experiences may well bring a certain "satisfaction" with it, but certainly not of a pleasurable type. This persistent seeking of the negative and the traumatic by some individuals led Freud to conclude that such impulses have little to do with either the pleasure principle (libidinal-instincts) or the reality principle (ego-instincts).

Two historical factors were present at this time which obviously contributed to the adjustment Freud was about to make. On the one hand Europe had just been through a war of unprecedented proportions with rampant death and destruction. The tendency toward destructiveness could not be explained as a by-product of a more basic life-force, but must itself be a primary phenomenon of psychic life, thought Freud.

258

Secondly, Freud had been plagued in the years prior to 1920 with the defections of several key disciples such as Adler and Jung. Jung's departure was likely particularly traumatic for Freud given his status as heir-apparent. With Jung's sharp move toward a **monistic** view of libido as "life-force" Freud had to take a sharp turn in the opposite direction toward reaffirming the full **dualism** of instincts.[60] The old dualism of ego-instincts and sexual instincts gives both self-preservative and pleasure-seeking qualities. Hence to leave things as they were would amount to capitulation to Jung. For these reasons Freud concludes that "the original opposition between the ego-instincts and sexual instincts proved to be inadequate."[61]

If the original dichotomy between ego and sexual instincts was now inadequate from where might a new solution come? To solve his dilemma Freud turns again to **Biology**. He writes:

> If we take it as a truth that knows no exception that everything living dies for **internal** reasons - becomes inorganic once again - then we shall be compelled to say that **'the aim of all life is death'** and looking backwards, that **'inanimate things existed before living ones.'**[62]

Freud bases this conclusion on the assumption that there is an inherent "inertia" or conservatism in all living substance which causes it to seek an earlier state of being.

> **It seems, then, that an instinct is an urge inherent in organic life to restore an earlier state of things** which the living entity has been obliged to abandon under the pressure of external disturbing forces; that is, it is a kind of organic elasticity, or, to put it another way, the expression of the inertia inherent in organic life.[63]

In attempting to sharpen the dichotomy along these more radical lines Freud proposes the dual instincts of **Eros** (life instinct) and **Thanatos** (death instinct).[64] Perhaps the clearest statement Freud makes in describing this "new" polarity is found in *An Outline of Psychoanalysis,* the last book written by him. We find him concluding:

> After long doubts and vacillations we have decided to assume the existence of only two basic instincts, **Eros** and **the destructive instinct**. (The contrast between the instincts of self-preservation

and of the preservation of the species, as well as the contrast between ego-love and object-love, fall within the bounds of Eros.) The aim of the first of these basic instincts is to establish even greater unities and to preserve them thus - in short, to bind together; the aim of the second on the contrary, is to undo connections and so to destroy things.[65]

Freud's reason for calling the destructive instinct the death instinct is his assumption that its aim is to reduce every living thing to an inorganic condition. Since all living things appeared out of non-living ones (Darwin), the death instinct serves the function of reducing what has become living back to that state which preceded it.

It was suggested earlier that Freud's intellectual foundation was the mechanistic-materialistic scientific model he had obtained from his teacher von Brucke and the larger Helmholz school. Freud's first instinct theory which affirmed (1) the centrality of chemical processes as they govern the human psyche, and (2) the view that the basic function of the psyche is to reduce "tension" to a constant low level (the constancy principle) is without a doubt the child of his earliest scientific presuppositions. The changes brought about with the second model did not tamper with the **mechanism** (there is still the seeking of equilibrium) but the **goal**. The objective has now become an inorganic state i.e. a zero level which is called the **Nirvana principle** (upon which the death instinct is based). This new model is no longer chemically driven but has been given a **biological foundation** based upon the life and death forces operating within cellular organisms.

It becomes immediately obvious that Freud's second drive theory sharpens even further the polarization between the drives. There was already an element of tension in the earlier clash between the pleasure-principle and the reality principle, but more along the lines of a "modification" of one by the other. Now, however, the clash is sharp, even absolute, as one cancels out the other.[66] If one can legitimately conclude that the polarity becomes unresolvable for the later Freud, then one must also recognize that its sharpness is attributable to the narrow biological reductionism upon which it is based. From the vantage point of a 19th century mechanistic biology, life is inevitably cancelled out by death which brings every unity back to its original condition.

While one could affirm Freud for reminding us of possible polarities within human development, I must also declare that he is stuck in what Hegel and Kierkegaard call **Natural selfhood**. Natural selfhood, as we recall, involves the attempt to analyze our "inner world" by proposing certain absolute "laws" which try to explain why we do what we do. Freud's second drive theory is one such attempt at finding a closed, but absolute rationale for human behavior, thinking, and feeling. For Freud unity is simply inherent, built-into the biological cell, and by extrapolation, into the human psyche. But as Hegel so decisively insisted, the unity necessary for personal identity is **not inherent in the psyche**, but is only achieved through the **relationship** between my ego and the world. Kierkegaard would also cringe at Freud's biological determinism, a robbing of selfhood of the capacity for choice and intentional action which in Kierkegaard's estimation defines us as human.

While I acknowledge Freud's help in reminding us of the place of negation and division within psychological process, I am painfully aware that he remains stuck in a one-sided negation. His forces of life and death never seek a higher-order unity, which would amount to a tacit acknowledgement of Jung. This cannot be allowed to happen. And so the Freudian Eros and Death instincts cancel each other out. There is no possibility for Freud that one serves the other in the seeking of a higher order unity. This would give primacy to Eros and victory to Jung. Just as there is only attraction and repulsion in the inorganic world so can there only be attraction and repulsion in the psychic world.

Before expanding my critique, however, I must nevertheless be clear in my acknowledgement of the tremendous contribution Freud has made to the study of personhood. In tying the human story so firmly into its biological and chemical roots, Freud allows us to claim a new ownership of the raw forces which operate within us. I could even say that Freud helps us uncover the nature of the self in its **necessity** or biological givens. Freud allows selfhood to be firmly grounded in its history, its body, and in the dual forces of unification and separation. That this process **never leads anywhere** other than to its destruction due to its own built-in inertia is what makes Freud's system so pessimistic. But simply to call something pessimistic is not an adequate critique. Upon what additional grounds might I critique the Freudian system?

The Limits of Freud

I have plotted several changes to Freud's theory base, particularly the changes noted with regard to instinct or drive theory. Even with the change from chemically-driven to physiologically-determined organism, however, Freud remained wedded to an **exclusively** mechanistic/materialistic model of the human psyche.

Freud's revised model made cell life the paradigm for the operations of personhood, with the objective now not the tendency to reduce tension to a constant low level (constancy principle), but to the zero level as expressed through the Nirvana principle. As suggested, this squeezed Freud into a dualistic "half" dialectic which invariably ends in dead-end negation or antithesis. Because a resolution of the polarization is always missing Freud is unable to offer a picture of the self as synthesizing process. His "self" sits on two, never on three "legs".

The best Freud is able to do is establish a limited unity between the ego and its body-based drives, but **never** in a prospective or proactive way. Because there is no teleology for Freud, there can never be a Freudian self, since to be a self requires the capacity to synthesize or generate oneself in a dialectic encounter between the givens of the past and the possibilities of the future as Kierkegaard so clearly demonstrated. Since the Freudian ego is completely bound by historical and instinctive forces alone it can only shape itself in regressive or adaptive ways. It can never transcend itself and can never be free.

The most I can claim for Freud, then, is that he is a transition figure in the search for self as synthesizing and self-creative process. This does not diminish the great step forward he has facilitated. Through the concept of libido he has helped give concrete shape to the phenomenon of desire as the doorway to our self-awareness. He has moved us beyond the abstraction of Hegel or Kierkegaard and empirically demonstrated how we are impacted throughout life by the "otherness" of internal forces and the "otherness" of objects in the world. He moves us beyond our unconsciousness about ourselves by sharpening the distinction between ego and the depth factors which stir within us. And yet Freud is unable to recognize the larger unity of selfhood simply because it could not fit with his philosophical and scientific presuppositions.

A final point of critique deserves mention, however, because it reveals a particular Freudian bias with serious implications for theory formation. The particular point in question concerns Freud's insistence on the "conservative" nature of the drives, referring to their tendency to re-establish an earlier state of existence. In the case of the so-called death or destructive instinct the goal becomes that of reducing life to its inorganic foundation. But how can Eros as the life instinct also be "conservative" since its aim is to preserve life, the opposite of the seeking of death or inorganic unity?

The only way Eros as the unifying urge could be seen as trying to restore an earlier state is if there first existed a unity which Eros was now seeking to re-establish. At one point Freud flirted with this possibility by drawing on the Platonic myth found in the **Symposium** in which humanity was originally unified but subsequently split in half by Zeus. After this split into male and female these two parts are forever on a search for the other - each desiring their missing half and seeking to grow into one.[67] In his 1920 declarations Freud is open to the possibility of a primordial union which seeks to re-create itself, but by 1936 and his final thoughts on the matter the answer is a resounding No![68] Why this adamant rejection?

One possibility is that it reflects Freud's rampant sexism which could not allow for an equal male-female polarity. While Freud is without a doubt guilty of massive sexism (as evidenced in his theories of sexual identity formation), I do not believe that this identifies the only reason for Freud's retreat from a proactive Eros.

As I have suggested earlier, there was a great battle raging between Freud and his dissidents, particularly Jung. For Freud to have agreed that Eros involves a seeking of prior unities would have amounted to a capitulation to Jung's monism. In other words, **both** the **seeking of union** and **the urge to separate** would have turned out to be in the service of a larger unity. Had Freud agreed that separation finds completion in a higher-order unity, it would have amounted to a recognition of a larger meaning to reality. This possibility could not be tolerated. Regrettably, Freud's well-documented insistence upon orthodoxy undercut the emergence of any such possibility with most of his heirs.

Although somewhat oversimplified, I would conclude that Freud could only reach the culmination of the first phase of natural selfhood which Hegel called **Natural Consciousness**, or **Aesthetic Selfhood** for Kierkegaard. Freud allows us to understand ego development from the point of view of instinctive impulses and encounters with the world of objects, but cannot bring us to full selfhood. While Freud did come to recognize the importance of the object for ego formation he was not in a position to acknowledge the fullness of subject-object interactions which come with self-awareness, never mind the full range of dynamics within self. This next step was left to the followers of Freud who began to explore the intricacies of the birth of self-identity. These descendants of Freud have come to be known as Object-Relations Theorists and it is to their contribution toward a fully developed Self Psychology that I now direct our attention.

1. Nigel D. Walker *"A New Copernicus?" The Freudian Paradigm: Psychoanalysis and Scientific Thought*, md. Mujeeb-ur-Rahman, Ed., (Chicago: Nelson-Hall Inc., 1977), p. 35

2. Ishak Ramzy, *"From Aristotle to Freud"*, Ibid., p. 28

3. Sigmund Freud, *An Autobiographical Study*, Translated by James Strachey (New York: W.W. Norton and Co., Inc. 1963), p. 14

4. Runes, *Dictionary of Philosophy*, 1962, p. 273

5. Ramzy, 1977, p. 27

6. Ernest Jones, *Sigmund Freud, Life and Work*, Vol. I (London: Hogarth, 1953), p. 40-41

7. This summary of key Freudian perspectives is an adaptation of David Rapaport's, *The Structure of Psychoanalytic Theory*, (New York: International Universities Press, Inc., 1960), pp. 40-62

8. These phenomena are described in detail in Chapter VII of *The Interpretation of Dreams*, translated by James Strachey, (New York: Avon Books, 1965)

9. Freud, Ibid., 1900, p. 580

10. Ibid., p. 577. See also p. 179

11. Freud used the word Consciousness to describe this activity although this usage gave rise to serious contradictions as will be noted later.

12. Ibid., p. 577

13. Rubin Fine, *The Development of Freud's Thought* (New York: Jason Aronson, Inc., 1973), p. 50

14. Freud, 1900, p. 583

15. Ibid., p. 604

16. Ibid., p. 605

17. Ibid., p. 604

18. Ibid., p. 641

19. Ibid.

20. Ibid.

21. Ibid.

22. Ibid., p. 579

23. Ibid., p. 601

24. Sigmund Freud, *"The Ego and the Id"*, *On Metapsychology: The Theory of Psychoanalysis*, The Pelican Freud Library, Vol. II, Translated by James Strachey; Edited by Angela Richards, (Penguin Books, 1985) p. 352. See also Editor's Introduction, p. 341-349

25. Ibid., p. 351

26. It is unfortunate that these terms have a technical and obscure quality about them in English in contrast to their common usage in German as ICH (I); ES (It); UBER-ICH (Above -I).

27 Sigmund Freud, *New Introductory Lectures on Psychoanalysis*, Translated by W.J.H. Sprott, (New York: W.W. Norton and Company, INC., 1933), p. 102

28. Ibid., p. 103-104

29. Ibid., p. 106

30. Ibid., p. 107

31. Ibid., p. 106

32. Ibid., p. 108

33. Ibid., p. 84

34. Ibid., p. 85

35. Freud, *The Ego and the Id.*, 1985, p. 369

36. Sigmund Freud, *Group Psychology and the Analysis of the Ego*, Translated by James Strachey, (London: The Hogarth Press, 1949), p. 60

37. Ibid., p. 62

38. Freud, 1985, p. 368

39. Freud, 1933, p. 91

40. Freud, 1985, p. 374

41. Ibid., p. 373

42. Freud, 1933, p. 95

43. Freud, 1985, p. 375

44. These words are a translation of the German word "Trieb" which has commonly been translated as "instinct" such as by James Strachey in the Standard Edition. However, commentators are increasingly using the word "drive" to describe the undifferentiated forces acting within the psyche. See Jay R. Greenberg and Stephen A. Mitchell *Object Relations in Psychoanalytic Theory*, (Cambridge Mass., Harvard University Press, 1983), p. 22 A. Mitchell, *Object Relations in Psychoanalytic Theory* (Cambridge, Mass. Harvard University Press, 1983), p. 22

45. Sigmund Freud, *Instincts and Their Vicissitudes, On Metapsychology*, Translated by James Strachey, (New York: Penguin Books, 1985), p. 118

46. Ibid., p. 118-119

47. An example would be the mouth and the sucking need.

48. Ibid., p. 120

49. Freud, *New Introductory Lectures*, 1933, p. 134 ff

50. As an example please note Sigmund Freud, *On Narcissism: An Introduction*, 1985, p. 72 ff

51. Sigmund Freud, *"Three Essays on the Theory of Sexuality" On Sexuality* , Vol. 7, Pelikan Books, 1986, p. 138. This particular portion of the third essay was added in 1914 and is based upon his paper on Narcissism.

52. The English version of the word (Libido) is taken directly from the Latin. The German word "Lust" is not to be confused with the much narrower meaning of its exact English equivalent.

53. Ibid., p. 139-140

54. Freud, *On Narcissism: An Introduction*, 1985, p. 66

55. Ibid., p. 67-68

56. Ibid., p. 68

57. Ibid., p. 69

58. Freud, *Instincts and Their Vicissitudes*, 1985, p. 133

59. Freud, *Beyond the Pleasure Principle*, 1985, p. 288-289. It should be noted that the German title of this book is called *Jenseits des Lustprinzips*. Hinting at the movement beyond a monistic view of libido, as Jung was suggesting.

60. Ibid., p. 325-326

61. Ibid., p. 325

62. Ibid., p. 311

63. Ibid., p. 308, 309

64. Freud himself did not use the word Thantos to describe the death instincts.

65. Sigmund Freud, *An Outline of Psychoanalysis*, translated by James Strachey (New York: W.W. Norton & Company, Inc. 1949) p. 20

66. Freud, *New Introductory Lectures*, 1933, p. 146-147

67. Freud, *Beyond the Pleasure Principle*, 1984, p. 332

68. Freud, *An Outline of Psychoanalysis*, 1949, p. 20, 21

CHAPTER VIII

CONTEMPORARY PSYCHOANALYTIC PERSPECTIVES:
THE BRITISH SCHOOL

As difficult as it may have been to grasp the variations in Freud's thought over the course of his scientific lifetime, the task of following the threads he uncovered will become more complex now that we are on the threshold of psychoanalytic divergence. Psychoanalytic purity of doctrine was crumbling long before Freud left the scene as is well known through the defections and expulsions of Adler, Jung, and Ferenczi, to name but a few. Even if we restrict our attention to those post-Freudians who function under the Psychoanalytic label, the conflicts, rifts, and schisms among them are enormous.

Although slightly oversimplified, it is clear that the scattering of the psychoanalytic community brought about by the Second World War transplanted Freudian ideas into two distinct "camps" found in Great Britain and the United States. Known today as the British and American Object-Relations Schools respectively, it was not the separation by a body of water which brought about their divergence, but two very different ways of approaching the psyche. Even within each of these "schools" divergence has occurred, with some in the British camp often ideologically closer to their American counterparts than to those within their own stream and vice versa.

In any event, the beginnings of the split within the mainline psychoanalytic community have been widely attributed to Melanie Klein. Although she saw herself remaining true to the basic principles of Freudian theory and practice, she without a doubt moved far beyond standard Freudian formulations and became a key transitional figure in the evolution from a physiologically-governed psyche to an object-relational orientation.

The first crack in the "pure" Freudian edifice (after the purges of the dissidents) occurred in the late 1920's in a disagreement between Melanie Klein and Anna Freud over technique in child analysis.[1] Freud tended to align himself with his daughter and largely ignored the contributions of Klein. After Freud's death the rift between Id and Ego perspectives widened, with Anna Freud in London and Heinz Hartmann in New York developing the stream commonly known as Freudian Ego Psychology. With the eventual contributions of Edith Jacobson and Margaret Mahler a full-fledged Ego Psychology was subsequently developed. These American Ego Psychologists adjusted Freudian theory in such a way that an opening was created for the American psychoanalytic Self Psychologies of Otto Kernberg and Heinz Kohut. Although recent developments in contemporary American Self-psychology have created great controversy because of their supposed departure from Freudian orthodoxy, it is also clear that psychoanalytic thinking on both sides of the Atlantic was increasingly evolving in these object-relational directions.

In Great Britain, the path to object-relations perspectives took a different direction by proceeding largely through the Id-Psychology of Melanie Klein. Her "followers" including R.W.A. Fairbairn, H. Guntrip, and D.W. Winnicott further developed object-relational models of the psyche which also strayed from the orthodoxy of Freud, but which eventually even discarded the drive-foundation they had inherited from Melanie Klein. What is particularly striking, however, is that these separate **Id** and **Ego** paths in Great Britain and America respectively, gained surprising convergence through the developments of contemporary psychoanalytic Self psychology. Heinz Kohut will emerge as the foremost spokesperson of this most recent development. But first I must trace the psychoanalytic path in Great Britain as represented by the work of Melanie Klein.

Melanie Klein

It is in the work of Melanie Klein that the great breakthrough from **physio**dynamic to **psycho**dynamic models comes to the foreground. The fact that she was unable to complete this transition left her in the unfavorable position of being unacceptable to either the orthodox Freudians or the reformers. Her attempt to stay true to Freud while moving beyond him in significant ways forced a stretching of theoretical concepts beyond their breaking point, eventually rendering her unacceptable to both camps.

Melanie Klein fully accepted Freud's dual-drive theory of Eros and Thanatos, with inborn aggression the hallmark of the most basic instinct: the death instinct. What Klein attempted to demonstrate is that these drives clash in an inner drama, with the outer world the stage upon which this battle plays itself out. This overarching vision was the perspective which shaped her entire clinical and theoretical activity.

Because of her primary adherance to drives, Melanie Klein's work has been labeled an **Id Psychology** by her critics. To a large extent this assessment is valid in that Klein remained fully committed to the "biological mysticism" which she inherited from Freud.[2] Her special contribution which moved her significantly beyond Freud is that she saw these forces operating within and through the **internal and external object-relationships** of the ego. To use her own words:

> The analysis of very young children has taught me that there is no instinctual urge, no anxiety situation, no mental process which does not involve objects external or internal; in other words, object-relations are at the **center** of emotional life. Furthermore, love and hatred, fantasies, anxieties, and defenses are also operative from the beginning and are **ab initio** indivisibly linked with object-relations.[3]

The die had now been cast: internal and external object-relations had become the center of psychic life.

The Nature of Drives and Objects

It has been well documented that Klein's understanding of drives is somewhere between a classical Freudian position and the fully relational model of a Fairbairn or Guntrip.[4] She sees herself as remaining faithful to the Freudian conclusions, while simply supplementing certain less-developed portions thereof. In reality, however, she marks a radical shift away from biology toward psychodynamics, and for all intents and purposes she must be considered a primary founder of the Object-Relations School.

One of the clearest distinctions one can make between Klein and Freud is that Freud saw the Id-based drives as largely objectless by assuming they have no intrinsic connection to the external world. The ego attempts to "present" objects to the id, but there is no meaningful connection between the "seething-cauldron" of instinctual energy (the Id) and the objects which might satisfy the impulse. The entire Freudian system is driven by physiological pressures residing within the body, with the task of the ego to "contain" or "manage" the autonomous drives as they bump into the objects of the external world.

For Klein, however, the drives are not object-less, but have the object inherent in them. The drives seek objects, with the object already "built-into" the drive as an a priori image which the drive seeks. The Kleinian psyche contains "images" of the objects which it seeks, this being true from the first moments of life onward.

At first glance it seems absurd to assume that an infant automatically "knows" the external world, is able to "image" the breast for instance, before having encountered it via experience. But might there not be another more defensible meaning to Klein's pronouncement?

To begin with, there are certain elements in Hegel's and Kierkegaard's reflections on desire which are recognizable in Klein. Both Hegel and Kierkegaard insist that there can be no desire without an object. Desire and its objects are born simultaneously, they claim. If we understand this to mean a propensity to seek a particular class of objects in the sense of a general attraction, one might find Klein's conclusion quite plausible. However, Klein is not content with such diffuse attraction but goes so far as to identify the precise content of these earliest images.

As far as Klein is concerned, earliest object images take the form of various body parts such as breasts and penises, including even fantasized experiences of intercourse etc., fully formed and filled with emotive content. This Hegel and Kierkegaard would no doubt reject. They would counter Klein by suggesting that object-seeking (via desire) takes many forms with varying degrees of comprehension of, and engagement with, the object. Klein's first great flaw therefore, is that she is able to operate with fully-formed and historically ungrounded images only.

Nevertheless, we should not allow this exaggeration on Klein's part to obscure her main point: **the images of objects of desire are the building-blocks around which an infant will organize its experience.** This is the first psychological confirmation we can find of Hegel's conclusion that a subject is created only in relation to its objects. For Klein also, a subject can only be understood in relation to its constituting objects.

Klein furthermore suggests that inherent in the drives themselves are the good and bad objects which the child will attempt to mirror for itself. It will accomplish this mirroring through **projection**, while at the same time taking these objects back into itself (via **introjection**). Klein elaborates:

> Fantasy activity underlies the mechanisms of introjection and projection, which enable the ego to perform one of the basic functions mentioned above, namely to establish object-relations. By projection, by turning outward libido and aggression and imbuing the object with them, the infant's first object relation comes about ... owing to the process of introjection, this first object is simultaneously taken into the self. From the outset the relations to external and internal objects interact ... A world of good and bad objects is thus built up within, and here is the source of internal persecution as well as internal riches and stability.[5]

What we find in Klein is a first psychological recognition of an interactive process in which inner and outer, subject and object are in dialectic encounter.

The Kleinian drives, called libido and aggression, have objects "built-into" them in the form of specific images toward which the child develops particular feelings. Through the processes of **introjection** and **projection** there is established a collection of "loved" and "hated" objects who are both good and bad, "and who are interrelated with each other and with the self: in other words, they constitute an inner world."[6] This inner world, says Klein, consists of:

> objects taken into the ego, corresponding partly to the multitude of varying aspects, good and bad, in which the parents (and other people) appeared to the child's unconscious mind throughout various stages of his development. Further, they also represent all the real people who are continually becoming internalized in a variety of situations provided by the multitude of ever-changing external experiences as well as fantasized ones. In addition, all these objects are in the inner world in an infinitely complex relation both with each other and with the self.[7]

It is important to recognize the truly revolutionary breakthrough accomplished by this theoretical leap. No longer is the ego simply driven by a mysterious biological engine, but it is made up of a highly individual inner world of ego-object relationships. The ego is now the product of interactions among internal and external objects which it has incorporated.

Kleinian Object-Relations: Strengths and Limits

What are we to make of the Kleinian contribution? Above all, Klein needs to be affirmed for her inclusion of a process of engagement into the life of self. She is the first psychoanalytic scholar to identify a subject-object dialectic as the foundation for the birth of ego-capacities. The awakening of the subject **through the object** via desire (the seeking of the object) is the heart of Klein's contribution. In highlighting of the mechanisms of **introjection** and **projection** she has identified for us the steps whereby a subject "takes-in" objects and thereby reaches a new and higher level of organization.

In spite of this significant accomplishment, however, the great Kleinian weakness is her inability to give true legitimacy to the object. All objects in Klein's world are faceless actors. To use Hegelian language, she sees the object as a "uniform universal," an indistinguishable entity fully contained within the operations of self. Every object is simply a blank screen upon which a child projects its own fully-formed images. The **actual** nature of an object is meaningless.

Furthermore, bad objects are predominant, and as one might suspect, strictly internally-generated for Klein. A child does not have a bad experience which it internalizes, but its innate badness is automatically projected outward through fantasy. Her insistence upon the death instinct, upon the relentless nature of aggressive fantasies etc., all skew her theoretical constructs in the direction of a closed dialectic. To use Kierkegaard's language, Klein remains limited by an **unmediated (non-synthesizing) relation** between internal objects only. A simple connection between two entities is not a self. As Kierkegaard so strongly insisted, a self must synthesize its constituting elements to be a self.

Just as Freud's ego is severely limited by being an **unmediated relation** between the body-based drives and the environment, so too is Klein's ego an **unmediated relation** between the dual forces of love and hate and their corresponding images which are directed outward. While the object has been given a place of importance in Klein it has arrived on the scene in a generic sense only, as an abstract, hollow entity.

I believe that sufficient justification has been provided for declaring that a non-synthesizing relation is not a self. The instinctive demands of the body cannot in and of themselves be in an automatic unity with environmental objects. Otherness must be real in order to give birth to self-awareness. Klein does not adequately allow for the difference between external or internal objects, nor does she allow for a difference between identifications with real or fantasized objects. In Klein we have at best found (1) a rudimentary awakening to real objects, and (2) the beginnings of a dialectic mechanism within the self called internalization and projection. It remained the task of her students and colleagues such as Fairbairn and Winnicott to move beyond these beginnings.

Ronald Fairbairn

It has been said that Fairbairn was the first psychoanalyst to develop a fully object-relational understanding of the psyche.[8] This does not make him a system-builder, but simply the first who accomplished a complete break from Freud's and Klein's physicalist and biological entanglements. One should not draw the conclusion, however, that Fairbairn completely disconnected himself from Freud. As far as Fairbairn was concerned he was simply following the natural course of

274

Freud's own development toward the personal-relational dimension, - a process continued by Klein and enhanced by Fairbairn.

Fairbairn himself offers the best introduction to his position:

> My point of view may however, be stated in a word. In my opinion it is high time that psychopathological inquiry, which in the past has been successively focused, first upon impulse, and later upon the ego, should now be focused upon **the object** towards which impulse is directed. To put the matter more accurately if less pointedly, the time is now ripe for a psychology of **object-relationships**. The ground has already been prepared for such a development of thought by the work of Melanie Klein: and indeed it is only in the light of her conception of **internalized objects** that the study of object-relationships can be expected to yield any significant results for psychopathology. From the point of view I have now come to adopt, psychology may be said to resolve itself into a study of the relationships of the individual to his objects, whilst, in similar terms, psychopathology may be said to be resolve itself more specifically into a study of the relationships of the ego to its internalized objects.[9]

Three distinct elements in Fairbairn's summary deserve elaboration. These are (1) the nature of drives (libido); (2) the role of the ego and its objects, and (3) the nature of psychopathology.

Fairbairn and the Meaning of Libido

None of Fairbairn's conclusions about human personhood are as radical as his insistence that libido is not pleasure, but object-seeking.[10] As far as Fairbairn is concerned, the old idea that libido operates as distinct units of energy somehow pushing the organism toward tension-discharge is simply an extrapolation of outmoded Helmholzian ideas imposed upon a dynamic relational being - a human **person**. Whereas drives were thought to seek automatic relief of libidinal tension through the various erotogenic zones of the body, the tension itself was reinterpreted by Fairbairn as the tension which arises out of the seeking of objects. The zones themselves are no longer the determiners of behaviors but the **channel** through which objects are sought and engaged. The real libidinal aim, says Fairbairn, "is the establishment of satisfactory relationships with objects; and it is accordingly, the object that constitutes the true libidinal goal."[11]

There is no such thing as "the libido" insists Fairbairn, but only a libido facilitating an encounter with objects. One can only speak of a "libido-toward" or "libido-of" from Fairbairn's point of view. Pleasure is not the goal of this process, but a by-product of the seeking of the object, namely, the encounter with another. This means that there is no longer a separate id for Fairbairn, no autonomous reservoir of energy, only a whole human being for whom the "structures" (ego, super-ego etc.) of psychic life are interwoven with the energy required to move the organism toward its goals. Therefore, the two basic "maxims" of Fairbairn's perspective are: (1) libido is inherently object-seeking, and (2) energy and structure are inseparable.[12]

The Nature of the Ego and Its Objects

The Freudian ego, even in its later versions, is essentially an adaptive entity organized "on top of" the raw id by virtue of its adjustment to external reality. It is mechanical, and develops certain functions which adapt it to the conflicting demands of the id and the world. Fairbairn's ego on the other hand, is "the primary psychic self in its original wholeness, a whole which differentiates into organized structural patterns under the impact of experience of object relationships after birth."[13] What does Fairbairn mean by an initial "whole" ego, and what is his understanding of the development which occurs along the way?

Simply put, Fairbairn's ego is intrinsically integrated or unified, in basic harmony with itself. In comparison with most developmental theories which suggest that an ego must be formed out of a state of undifferentiation, Fairbairn's insistence upon a "whole" ego being present at birth seems quite strange. Even as ardent a disciple of Fairbairn as Henry Guntrip had difficulty with the notion that the ego contains an intrinsic oneness.

On the other hand, Guntrip's defence of Fairbairn declares that Fairbairn is simply referring to "ego potential", the natural evolution of an ego which contains within it the innate directions of its own growth.[14] This ego-at-birth could perhaps be analogous with the acorn which contains within it the oak tree. If this is Fairbairn's intent, it is not unlike Hegel's notion of self as "unfolded becoming." From this point of view the end is related to the beginning in the sense that every developmental step carries within it the residue of the old as well as the anticipation

276

of the new. The claim that there is a continuity to ego development with such development maintaining a certain direction is not the main problem, however.

There is another more serious difficulty emerging out of Fairbairn's insistence upon the ego's implicit unity, namely, that the ego is completely at the mercy of environmental forces. The inevitable consequence of Fairbairn's position is that the environment is solely responsible for the brokenness/fragmentation experienced by the unitary ego, just as the environment accomplishes all reconstruction for a broken ego. This represents a radical departure from Melanie Klein. Whereas in Klein objects are largely superfluous bystanders to the inner imaginal process, in Fairbairn, **objects determine everything**! We would do well to understand the implications of this development for psychopathology.

The Nature of Psychopathology

The seeking of the object which is so central for Fairbairn makes the **dependence** of the ego upon the object the overriding concern of psychic life. The child **needs** the other, and if the contact with that other is traumatizing, inadequate, or unfulfilling, then the child will not eliminate the need but simply conform its ego to the twisted nature of the experience with the other. Being unable to avoid the need for objects, the child splits the painful aspects from reality and internalizes them where they are subject to greater control. In this fashion, the painful, traumatic elements of the other become internalized and repressed with the ego identifying itself with these bad, internalized objects. Fairbairn explains:

> ...this defensive attempt to establish outer security is purchased at the price of inner insecurity, and since it leaves the ego at the mercy of internal persecutors; and it is as a defense against such inner insecurity that the repression of internalized bad objects arises.[15]

While the repression of internalized objects has consequences for ego operations, Fairbairn sees a further complicating event occuring. The ambivalent other becomes both (1) **an exciting object** having a desirous quality about it in that the child still longs for recognition from the unavailable other, and (2) the on-going nature of the trauma confirms the declaration of the **rejecting object** which cannot or does not provide the security and acknowledgement needed. These two dialectic elements of (1) exciting object, and (2) rejecting object become part of the developing ego which splits itself along those lines. These object-types generate the following elements within ego structures from Fairbairn's point of view:

(1) **libidinal ego** - the portion of the ego which identifies with and continues to seek, the repressed exciting object; this part-ego can be recognized in personal relationships marked by chronic dependency and the seeking of confirmations of worth etc.

(2) **anti-libidinal ego** - (internal saboteur) this ego-component reveals the internal identification with the rejecting object as evidenced by persecutory and hostile states.

(3) **central ego** - this portion of the ego identifies with the idealized objects, in other words those positive residues left over after the negative elements have been split off and repressed; this element is the conscious aspect of the ego and is recognizable in the idealized overevaluations of others and the hostile/aggressive attitude taken toward remaining repressed portions of the ego.[16]

The degree of psychopathology depends upon the extent to which the ego is "tied-up" by its entanglement with its negative internal identifications. The more the central ego is consumed by its interactions with its **internal repressed objects**, the less it will be able to enter into fulfilling encounters with contemporary others. In seeing the ego split into these elements Fairbairn attempts to describe psychopathology as an enactment of a split within the ego itself - an ego diseased by virtue of its disordered relationship to itself.

For Melanie Klein the role of objects within psychopathology ends in the **depressive position**, as the "depressed" ego mourns the loss of its needed objects. Fairbairn, on the other hand, suggests that it is far more destructive when an ego turns in upon itself, a state he calls the **schizoid position**.

The schizoid position is more disturbed for Fairbairn since it describes a splitting in the ego itself, in which it turns toward its bad internalized objects while renouncing external objects in the process. This state is the most broken of all insists Fairbairn because it involves the flight from object-relations themselves, while in the depressive state there remains a relationship to objects through guilt and remorse.

In depressive states there remains a connection to objects because the internalized bad objects are only experienced as "conditionally" bad.[17] There remains a way out through the possibility of achieving goodness or reconciliation. An internalized sense of unconditional badness is more serious because an ego which identifies itself with this badness is forced to retreat from **any** object relatedness which might have provided a means of self-reconciliation. The main point worth noting, however, is that through Fairbairn the ego has come into direct relationship with itself as mediated by the objects it has internalized.

Fairbairn: Strengths and Limits

Perhaps the most reasonable perspective from which to assess Fairbairn's contribution to the evolving theory of the self is in relation to Melanie Klein. In Klein one finds a vision of selfhood as a **non-synthesized relation** between subject and object by virtue of the integrating power of the instincts themselves. Klein's instincts are primary and self-contained, needing objects only as the arena within which they play out their energy. For Fairbairn, the opposite is true. For him primacy belongs to the real world of **external others**. From this real world come the **impingements** or **gratifications** which become internalized in all their positive and negative dimensions resulting either in health or the disturbed object relations we see in psychopathology.

In short, Fairbairn offers us a **"partially-synthesizing self"** in which the self is begun to be seen as an active agent as it builds an identity for itself for better or for worse. The important step taken by Fairbairn is the recognition that selfhood "takes-in" **real** objects. The self has become an active agent building a bridge between real objects and its own self-representations. Upon what basis, then, do I judge him as offering us only a partially-synthesizing self? Why do I consider his view limited and incomplete?

Fairbairn's insistence on the intrinsic "wholeness" of the ego places the emergence of "badness" squarely on the doorstep of primary objects, i.e. a child's parents. More importantly, this "badness" has strictly to do with parental failure to adequately provide for infantile gratification, particularly dependency needs. Fairbairn's internal objects are established only as negative **reactions** to failures of gratification. This makes "bad" internal objects primary, with "good" internal objects only emerging as a secondary process.[18] Fairbairn does not allow the residues of good experiences to operate within the psyche in the form of healthy identifications which shape authentic values or positive self-images. Unfortunately, Fairbairn only leaves room for good internal objects as they serve to defend against bad internal object relations.

Fairbairn's ego may well be seeking and taking-in objects, but it is not fully relating itself (as object) to itself (as subject). Fairbairn's ego knows only internal compensations for the "badness" brought on by external non-gratification. Such a subject does not engage the environment and has no stake in the striving for autonomy. In denying the self the capacity to negate, to seek its genuine selfhood, Fairbairn's self can only limp along looking for gratifications for its need to belong.

While Fairbairn has helpfully declared the importance of the object, the subject is allowed only a compensatory response to the object, and only to certain dimensions of the object at that. No positive internal tension is allowed by Fairbairn, nor is a self allowed to initiate the negation of its current object-identifications for the purpose of seeking a higher-order cohesion. Fairbairn's self, to put it simply, is only a **reactive** not a **proactive** self, and finds itself only able to react to a frustrating environment.

These strong critiques should not obscure my acknowledgment of the great contribution made by Fairbairn. He was the first psychoanalyst to move toward a fully object-relational model of selfhood by giving a legitimate place to the object in the formation of identity. He confirmed from a psychodynamic perspective the brilliant Hegelian conclusion that selfhood is born only through recognition by another self.

D.W. Winnicott

In the person of D.W. Winnicott one finds perhaps the most creative culmination of psychoanalytic thought as it evolved in Great Britain through the work of Klein, Fairbairn, and Guntrip, among others. Although Winnicott attempted to distance himself from Fairbairn's revisions of Freud by insisting that he was in primary theoretical harmony with Freud and Klein, the truth of the matter is that he so thoroughly reworked the entire Freudian system that no simple continuity to either Freud or Klein can be found. It has been accurately said that

Winnicott took the elements from Freud and Klein which he needed and completely revised them to suit his own purposes.[19] What are these purposes and how do they enhance our understanding of selfhood?

In a nutshell, Winnicott's burning interest is to describe the dialectic relationship between **intimacy** and **separation** as the two foci which make up the life of the self. It has been said of Winnicott that "almost all his contributions center around ... the continually hazardous struggle of the self for an individuated existence which at the same time allows for intimate contact with others."[20] With Winnicott we finally arrive at a place in psychoanalytic theory development in which the concept "self" is used in a systematic and dynamic way. In order to better appreciate this step I will present Winnicott's theory from two perspectives: (1) the development of the self, and (2) the subject-object dichotomy and the search for God.

The Development of the Self

In spite of Winnicott's protests to the contrary, his conclusions consistently place him in the camp of those who take a fully object-relational approach to psychic life. Whether it be in his assessment that there is a drive which "could be called object-seeking," or in his insistence that selfhood develops solely through the interaction between the child and significant others, he comes down on the side of a firm acknowledgment of a subject-object dialectic as the warp and woof of the self.[21] Winnicott claims that emerging selfhood needs certain essential elements and experiences in order to proceed along the "prescribed" path. As I examine these phases of the self's life as seen through the eyes of Winnicott a distinct dialectic process will emerge consisting of: (1) forms of nondifferentiation, (2) emergence of otherness, and finally, (3) a synthesizing self. I will examine each of these phases in turn.

The Self in Undifferentiated Unity

The starting point for the development of selfhood for Winnicott is a state of absolute dependence in which an infant and its mother form a dynamic unit. He finds it absurd to talk about an infant in the abstract apart from the functioning of the mother and the processes which occur between them. "There is no such thing as a baby," insists Winnicott, only a "nursing couple."[22] This is a state of unintegration, of non-differentiation, which requires an essential ingredient he calls "primary maternal preoccupation", referring to a mother in a state of fine-tuned devotion to her child. She provides a "holding environment" which **contains** the experiences of the child in the sense that the mother "buffers" the vulnerability of the child and "gathers-together" the bits of experience for the child which it cannot fully integrate for itself.[23]

What Winnicott claims is that a certain consistency is needed in the critical early phases of life, a rhythm of care which need not be "perfect", but which must be "good enough."[24] The "good enough" mother allows the "true self" of the infant to begin to emerge by virtue of her ability to echo the infant's state of being. To elaborate:

> The good-enough mother meets the omnipotence of the infant ... she does this repeatedly. A true self begins to have life, through the strength given to the infant's weak ego by the mother's implementation of the infant's omnipotent expressions ... It is an essential part of my theory that the true self does not become a living reality except as a result of the mother's repeated success in meeting the infant's spontaneous gesture or sensory hallucination.[25]

A not-good-enough mother is not able to be in step with an infant's omnipotence nor weakness and she repeatedly fails to respond appropriately to her infant's gestures. This over or under reaction on her part amounts to impingement or abandonment, whichever the case may be.

A mother who is ill with regard to her primary maternal preoccupation is unable to **identify with** her baby and its needs and gestures and if this failure occurs in the earliest phases of development it results in a complete annihilation of the infant's self. Winnicott operates from the premise that each person is a unique individual with this uniqueness constitutionally grounded. An inadequate environment will overwhelm this innate potential causing the self to organize itself around a false premise, namely in conformity with the withholding or intruding environment. Such a false self can only respond to life in reactive, artificial ways.

What is so critical in this early phase of absolute dependence is not so much the nature of the gratifying or non-gratifying experiences as such, but their impact upon the capacity for what Winnicott calls "symbol-formation." The responsive care-giver accomplishes two very critical functions according to Winnicott. On the one hand, **she makes real** the infant's gesture or hallucination, and on the other hand allows the infant to **create an image of satisfaction** which becomes an inner equivalent to the outer reality. Winnicott writes:

> In between the infant and the object is some thing, or some activity or sensation. In so far as this joins the infant to the object (viz. maternal part-object) so far is this the basis of symbol-formation. On the other hand, in so far as this something separates instead of joins, so is its function of leading on to symbol-formation blocked.[26]

This statement is so significant that I must linger here momentarily.

The importance of this conclusion is that it marks the strongest psychoanalytic recognition thus far of the self as a synthesizing or integrating process. Here, even in the most rudimentary kernel of selfhood, there is an active process at work which attempts to "join together" the emerging subject with its objects. This activity of integration attempts to tie together what is inside with what is outside through the capacity for symbolization or image creation. (This notion will find its clearest development in Winnicott's construct of the **"transitional object"** as discussed below). As Kierkegaard has already insisted, an identity as self resides in that which is **in-between** a subject and object, as represented by the **projected images** of itself. This function of reconciling the subject to its object is what gives a self **identity** whether as true self, false self, or annihilated self. By **"bringing the world to the child"** as Winnicott calls it, the mother is the first individual to **bring the child to its self** by virtue of the images she allows the child to create. Let us look at Winnicott's specific example of the breast.

An infant in some state of need is an excited, seeking infant. Such an infant is in a state of readiness to receive the object and when the object is presented an image is generated which corresponds with that particular object. This is not simply a visual image but a fully sensual image which "takes in" data about the object through all senses. Winnicott explains:

> the infant comes to the breast when excited, and ready to hallucinate something fit to be attacked. At that moment the actual nipple appears and he is able to feel that it was that nipple that he hallucinated. So his ideas are enriched by actual details of sight, feel, smell, and next time this material is used in the hallucination.

In this way he starts to build up a capacity to conjure up what is actually available. The mother has to go on giving the infant this type of experience.[27]

Winnicott's conclusion serves as a psychoanalytic restatement of the point first made by Hegel regarding the birth of consciousness. Even in the phase of absolute dependence there is already an attempt to absorb or "grasp" the object through the internal images used as a substitute for it. Because of its complete enmeshment with the object, however, such a state is one of total grandiosity, very much in keeping with Hegel's point that such an ego makes the object essential i.e. a universal object with which it fully identifies. As far as the ego is concerned, it creates the object, and this object is its very own self.

What has been described thus far is a self immersed **"in-itself"** to use the Hegelian phrase. Even with such complete "immersion-in" the object, there is a dialectic process at work in the sense of a rudimentary symbolization process which accompanies the seeking and finding of the object.

The Self and Otherness

No state of bliss lasts forever and even the most "perfect" environment develops flaws in it sooner or later. For some the flaws will occur far too soon while for others they may come too late. Winnicott is not simply concerned about an over-or-under indulgent environment, although a "flaw" might take either form; rather, he is referring to the inevitable shifting of the maternal instinct away from primary maternal preoccupation. We should not assume, however, that it is simply the mother who is the agent of increased separation. The infant also experiences an inevitable urge toward independence.

Whereas during absolute dependence the infant's grandiosity is consistently reinforced, this soon becomes more difficult to maintain. Even fully devoted care-givers will find other commitments creeping into the symbiotic bond. In healthy development these normally coincide with the infant's growing capacity to interact with the environment, even as the child slowly recognizes the environment's autonomous reality. When things proceed smoothly, the infant-mother dyad transforms as the mother provides a non-impinging presence, with the infant experiencing a corresponding growth in ego capacity. This requires a mother able to allow the child the necessary space and freedom to come to a realization of its separation from her, and a child able to allow the world to take on a separate form not controllable by the child. Critical to this process for Winnicott are the factors of (1) **impingement tendencies** of the environment, and (2) **the capacity to be alone** for the child.

Winnicott describes impingement quite simply as those events in an infant's life which **force the infant to react**.[28] If forced to react at a very early stage of development then severe twisting of selfhood occurs. There is then no room left for authentic experience but the emerging ego must adapt itself to the quirks of the environment. This results in an individual who develops an identity around a shell, not their "core", i.e. the person develops an identity which is an extension of the impinging environment. This is the pathology-producing form of negation which overwhelms the fragile ego causing it to grow like a twisted tree constantly battered by the wind.

Within normal development, however, negation simply means **optimum frustration**. There must be a bumping into external reality or grandiosity would never be transformed. There must be a "gradual failing of adaptation" in the sense that a child's growing cognitive and symbolizing capacity allows it to build its own inner connections between its needs and the environmental response.[29] As the mothering one consistently "goes-on-being", the child's ability to "wait" is enhanced because it can "hold" its tension around maternal response within itself. For example, consistently cared-for infants are gradually able to wait for a feeding as they hear the noises of food preparation etc. through the subliminal awareness that the need will soon be met. Through the experience of optimum frustration the infant's emerging self is able to step into the breach and offer self-soothing even as it waits.

Winnicott finds that the capacity for waiting brought about through experiences of optimum frustration or negation is closely related to what he calls "the capacity to be alone."[30] For this development to occur a mother must not just be responsive to infant needs, nor be demanding infant reaction to her stimulation, but must be able to allow the infant to simply "be". The infant is then able to be "unintegrated" and is able "to exist for a time without being either a reactor to an external impingement or an active person with a direction of interest or movement."[31] This allows the infant to develop its own spontaneity and personal impulses independent from those of the environment. This awakening to its own world of sensation generates a different but essential boundary-awareness in contrast to that created by the environment. The ownership of sensations which are its very own also requires an experience of negation i.e. a departure from absolute dependence.

The Self as Synthesizing Capacity

If **absolute dependence** and **optimum frustration** are the thesis and antithesis respectively of Winnicott's dialectic of the self, what constitutes its synthesis? The construct of "**transitional object**" and "**transitional phenomena**" serves this function.[32] Transitional object is the name Winnicott gives to the "intermediate realm" which bridges subject and object. A transitional object relates itself to itself, i.e. it synthesizes the two worlds of **subjective inner reality** with the **objective external world** and in so doing generates itself. In his introduction to the term Winnicott writes:

> I have introduced the terms 'transitional object' and 'transitional phenomena' for designation of the intermediate area of experience, between the thumb and the teddy bear, between oral eroticism and true object relationship, between primary creative activity and projection of what has already been introjected, between primary unawareness of indebtedness and the acknowledgment of indebtedness.[33]

This talk of thumbs and teddy bears may seem so trivial that we might be tempted to dismiss the concept as sheer foolishness. However, the breakthrough nature of this notion will soon become evident. The following citation elaborates:

> My claim is that if there is a need for this double statement, there is a need for a **triple** one; there is the **third part** of the life of a human being, a part that we cannot ignore, an intermediate area of **experiencing** to which inner reality and external life both contribute. It is an area which is not challenged, because no claim is made on its behalf except that it shall exist as a resting-place for the individual engaged in the perpetual human task of keeping inner and outer reality separate yet inter-related.[34]

What has emerged in Winnicott's statement is a close approximation of Kierkegaard's conclusion that a self is a "positive third," not simply a relation between two, but the "relation's relating itself to itself." While Winnicott's insight is not fully a self a huge step has been taken!

Transitional objects constitute a bridge between illusory subjective objects under omnipotent control, and external objects which have a reality and substance all their own. They provide a realm of experience which is not fully under magical control, nor fully under the control of the environment. Their paradoxical nature and presence in both worlds makes them the place where subject and object meet and enter into relationship. Winnicott calls this "the substance of illusion."[35]

Winnicott suggests that transitional experience begins with the illusion that the breast is fully a part of the infant. The virtually complete adaptation of mother to child keeps this magical situation intact until gradual disillusionment sets in. The illusion is born out of the magical sense that the subject has created the object which corresponds so perfectly to the felt need. When disillusionment sets in as it inevitably does, the transitional object allows the infant to preserve an indirect relationship to its magical omnipotence while giving a certain legitimacy to external objects.

Such experience is not restricted to the early building-blocks of life, claims Winnicott, but persists in our life-long capacity for symbolization by which we bridge the gap between the subjective and objective. In his own words:

> This intermediate area of experience, unchallenged in respect of its belonging to inner or external (shared) reality, constitutes the greater part of the infant's experience and throughout life is retained in the intense experiencing that belongs to arts and to religion and to imaginative living, and to creative scientific work.[36]

While we might shudder at the reductive and "nothing-but" quality with which Winnicott treats the arts, religion, and imaginative process, we should not forget how far psychoanalytic theory has moved in the transition from Freud, through Klein and Fairbairn, to Winnicott. Winnicott can acknowledge that the creative task of interfacing subject and object is never complete and that we experience relief from this task only in this "intermediate" realm of experience.

Winnicott's Self and the Search for God

Having pulled together Winnicott's understanding of "self" I am now in a position to assess its capacity for containing the full interwovenness of subject-object. For supplementary help in this task I intend to examine Winnicott's understanding of the nature of self as it relates to what he calls the psyche-soma.

In a 1949 paper entitled *"Mind and its Relation to the Psyche-Soma,"* Winnicott makes it very clear that self does **not** exist as an **entity** or a **thing**. A superficial glance at his conclusion might lead one to believe that Winnicott simply echoes William Hume who could also find no self as thing. In reality, Winnicott has moved far beyond the Enlightenment's critique of "substantial" selfhood by redefining the self as a "continuity of being" dependent upon healthy psycho-somatic growth.[37] Even as he rejects the self as static thing, Winnicott fully affirms the dynamic "being-quality" of self as a process which synthesizes itself in the psyche-soma relation. This puts Winnicott in direct agreement with Kierkegaard's dialectic understanding of the psycho-soma relation. Winnicott writes:

> It is logical to oppose psyche and soma and therefore to oppose the emotional development and the bodily development of an individual. It is not logical, however, to oppose the mental and the physical as these are not of the same stuff. Mental phenomena are complications of variable importance in psyche-soma continuity of being, in that, which adds up to the individual's self.[38]

Through Winnicott we find a confirmation of Hegel's and Kierkegaard's "natural" life of the self, namely, the processes which give birth to consciousness and self-consciousness. I am now able to claim psychoanalytic conformation of the early stations of a self's life including: (1) the necessity for recognition by another as essential for the birth of self-consciousness, (2) the necessity of a synthesizing agent between subject and object, as well as (3) the dialectic steps of enmeshment, separation, and integration as somehow central to the life of self. With these strong parallels emerging, where is the deficiency to be found?

The first clue to the limits of Winnicott in grasping the fullness of selfhood is found in his question "What is life about?"[39] As Winnicott wrestles with the question of the meaning of life Guntrip praises him for "the most revolutionary bit of writing yet produced within psychoanalysis."[40] In virtually the same breath, however, Guntrip expresses his dissatisfaction by admitting that it is perhaps in the unexplored area of genuine religious experience that the true answer is to be found. Winnicott did not seem able to take this next step.

Even as I move to critique Winnicott, it must be acknowledged that a significant milestone within psychoanalytic theory been reached; namely, **the fullness of personal existence in an interpersonal dialectic.** We should not minimize this great accomplishment. Nevertheless, the reductive tug of Freud is regrettably still too great to overcome. This point is made quite clear by Winnicott when he reduces the religious and artistic function to the necessary illusions provided by transitional objects.

> We allow the infant this madness [transitional object] and only gradually ask for a clear distinguishing between the subjective and that which is capable of objective or scientific proof. We adults use the arts and religion for the off-moments which we all need in the course of reality-testing and reality-acceptance.[41]

On the one hand Winnicott is able to give religious and artistic expression a certain value as a synthesizing bridge between fantasy and reality. It allows us to "hold" our inner impulses while we try to come to terms with the real world. On the other hand, in restricting this function to the "off-moments", and in putting it completely in the service of adaptation, Winnicott is reducing the meaning of all God-representations to that of a cosmic Teddy Bear, which, one must assume, is eventually discarded as we outgrow the need to protect ourselves from the real world.

Winnicott, it seems, cannot allow for a transcending otherness which of course robs him of the opportunity to discover the fullness of subjectivity. We find this limitation confirmed as Winnicott reduces the meaning of all imaginal process to the effort to accommodate oneself to one's world, without seeing its power in transforming one's world and one's self.

Unfortunately, this critique constitutes the great limitation of most psychoanalytic approaches to the study of the religious impulse, namely, the reduction of all transcending subjectivity to the transitional space in which **infantile** fantasy and reality meet.[42] To be sure, psychoanalytic theory presented thus far allows for synthesizing action between real historical objects and their subjective internalization within selfhood. What it cannot envision is a synthesis between the self and its own dialectic process, never mind a grounding of the process in an encompassing selfhood. One could say that psychoanalytic methods have uncovered the bricks, mortar, scaffolding, and perhaps even the conveyer belts used in the building of selfhood, but are not able to recognize the builder.

Winnicott quite correctly put his finger on one aspect of the problem in his 1963 paper entitled "Morals and Education" in which he challenges Theology to let go of its otherworldliness whereby God is separated from individual existence. Winnicott writes:

> Religions have made much of original sin but have not all come round to the idea of original goodness, that which by being gathered together in the idea of God is at the same time separated off from the individuals who collectively create and re-create this God concept ... Theology by denying to the developing individual the creating of whatever is bound up in the concept of God and of goodness and of moral values, depletes the individual of an important aspect of creativeness.[43]

Winnicott appropriately reminds us that we cannot separate our God-concept from the images we have of ourselves. When we deny our goodness we are likely to split it off, leaving it in the safe-keeping of our God to avoid it being contaminated by the badness we also discover inside ourselves. Dualistic religion as Winnicott so appropriately notes leaves us with just such a one-sided objectification of ourselves. This critique is of course the same concern identified by Hegel in his description of unhappy consciousness.

Winnicott's critique notwithstanding, the highest level his selfhood can attain is Hegel's *Realized Individuality* in which selfhood has stumbled across its "universality" but only as something residing within the confines of its natural existence. This, as we saw in Hegel, is a self-consciousness which becomes a "thing" i.e. the limited awareness that my self-contained "natural" self contains all truth and reality. **Realized individuality** alone is a tragic form of self-identity for Hegel because the fullness of selfhood has not been discovered, only a momentary glimpse in which our subjectivity is affirmed in relation to otherness. This subjectivity mirrors only interpersonal otherness, not the fullness of our Universal subjectivity as born out of transcending immanence.

290

With the overview of the British psychoanalytic path now complete one can appreciate the significant movement beyond the pioneering efforts of Freud. The evolution of psychoanalysis in Great Britain did not simply involve cosmetic adjustments to the Freudian inheritance but brought with it a much more encompassing view of human identity, now in dialectic encounter with the otherness of the world. As I move to analyze the developments of the American psychoanalytic community, there will emerge a much stronger affinity with the Ego Psychology of Freud even as adaptations are made to it. This will bring the American School into sharp conflict with British perspectives, but after all is said and done, surprising and unexpected convergence will again occur.

1. Greenberg and Mitchell, 1983, p. 120

2. Harry J.S. Guntrip, *Psychoanalytic Theory, Therapy, and the Self*, (New York: Basic Books, Inc., 1971), p. 58

3. Melanie Klein, *Envy and Gratitude and Other Works* 1946-1963, (London: The Hogarth Press, 1975), p. 53

4. Greenberg and Mitchell, 1983, p. 136

5. Klein, 1975, p. 58

6. Melanie Klein, *Contributions to Psycho-Analysis* 1921-1945, (London: The Hogarth Press, 1948), p. 330

7. Ibid., p. 330-331

8. Harry Guntrip, *"Psychoanalytic Object Relations Theory: The Fairbairn - Guntrip Approach"*, *American Handbook of Psychiatry*, Vol. I, 2nd edition, Silvano Arieti, Ed., (New York: Basic Books, Inc., 1974), p. 828

9. W. Ronald D. Fairbairn, *An Object-Relations Theory of the Personality*, (New York: Basic Books, Inc., 1954), p. 60

10. Ibid., p. 137

11. Ibid., p. 138

12. Greenberg and Mitchell, 1983, p. 154

13. Harry Guntrip, *Personality Structure and Human Interaction: The Developing Synthesis of Psychodynamic Theory*, (New York: International Universities Press, 1961), p. 279

14. Guntrip, 1971, p. 93

15. Fairbairn, 1954, p. 164-165

16. Ibid., p. 147, 170-171. See also Guntrip, 1971, p. 98

17. Fairbairn, 1954, p. 165

18. Greenberg and Mitchell, 1983, p. 179

19. Ibid., p. 189

20. Ibid., p. 190

21. D.W. Winnicott, *Collected Papers*, (New York: Basic Books, Inc., 1958), p. 311, 314. See also p. 245

22. Ibid., p. 99

23. Ibid., p. 150

24. D.W. Winnicott, *The Maturational Processes and the Facilitating Environment*, (London: The Hogarth Press, 1965), p. 145

25. Ibid.

26. Ibid., p. 146

27. Winnicott, 1958, p. 152-153

28. Winnicott, 1958, p. 183

29. Winnicott, 1965, p. 87

30. Ibid., p. 29

31. Ibid., p. 34

32. Winnicott, 1958, p. 229-242

33. Ibid., p. 230

34.   Ibid., Italics mine

35.   Ibid., p. 242

36.   Ibid., p. 242

37.   Ibid., p. 254

38.   Ibid.

39.   D.W. Winnicott, *"The Location of Cultural Experience,"* International *Journal of Psychoanalysis*, Vol. 48, 1967.

40.   Guntrip, 1971, p. 122-124

41.   Winnicott, 1958, p. 224

42.   This limitation is best seen in Ana-Maria Rizzuto, *The Birth of the Living God*, (Chicago: The University of Chicago Press, 1979).

43.   Winnicott, 1965, p. 94, 95

Chapter IX

THE PSYCHOANALYTIC MODEL CONTINUED:

AMERICAN OBJECT RELATIONS THEORY

Since the development of psychoanalytic theory in Great Britain took the path from the instinct-driven system of Freud and Klein, to the fully object-relational dialectic of Fairbairn and Winnicott, it would be natural to wonder whether a similar pattern evolved in the United States. Did the growing recognition of the role of the object in America undermine the instinct-only approach as had occurred in Great Britain?

While in Great Britain the path toward object relations and a self psychology moved **through** the **Id Psychology** of Melanie Klein (Anna Freud's emphases notwithstanding), in America the starting point was the **Ego Psychology** of the later Freud and the work of Heinz Hartmann. Just as Klein was a transition figure from Freud to Fairbairn and Winnicott, so too is Hartmann a bridge from Freud to the emerging self psychologies of Jacobson, Mahler, and Kernberg.

Each of these individuals, although becoming increasingly relationally minded, attempted to maintain a connection to the biological substrate of Freud and Hartmann. With none of these theorists is the tension between drives and objects satisfactorily resolved. By the time we arrive at the theoretical pronouncements of Kernberg, the attempt to juggle both drives and objects as primary building-blocks of selfhood will collapse. Finally, in Heinz Kohut another attempt to integrate these polarities emerges. Whether he succeeded in this effort remains to be seen, but what can be declared at the outset is that his efforts bring together both the British and American streams as no other theorist has done. In Kohut, then, we encounter the most fully developed psychoanalytic self psychology available to us. It too will need to be measured against our emerging vision of selfhood.

HEINZ HARTMANN

The last years of Freud's life were marked by a distinct shift toward what has come to be known as Ego Psychology. With this shift Freud began to acknowledge the place of the environment in shaping the structures and operations of the psyche. Previously, the human organism had been an exclusively id-driven machine with the outer world of no consequence other than the arena within which the discharge of energy took place. Despite this emerging openness to the outer world, the particulars of that world remained largely inconsequential for Freud - in essence faceless targets for exclusively internally-driven forces.

Nevertheless, Freud also created an opening for the possibility that relations with an outer world could be determinative for a developing psyche. Into this opening stepped Heinz Hartmann, the individual who has been called the father of Ego Psychology.[1] By no means should one expect his efforts to be a radical departure from Freud. If anything, Hartmann remained completely loyal to Freud, particularly in his adherence to the drive model of the psyche. What can be said of Hartmann is that he is a transition figure toward a fully object-relational model, not unlike the role played by Melanie Klein in Great Britain. What then are the features of this emerging Ego Psychology?

The Ego as "Organ" of Adaptation

Even a superficial reading of Hartmann reveals that his approach to the psyche is fully biological. The key term which captures this intent is **"adaptation"**, this concept becoming the focus of his first major work *Ego Psychology and the Problem of Adaptation* (1939). In this book Hartmann describes adaptation largely as the ability of an organism to adjust to its environment.

> We call a man well adapted if his productivity, his ability to enjoy life, and his mental equilibrium are undisturbed...The observation

underlying the concept "adaptation" is that living organisms patently "fit" into their environment. Thus, adaptation is primarily a reciprocal relationship between the organism and its environment.[2]

While the Darwinian influence is obvious, Hartmann tries to clarify that he does not simply mean a "narrow" type of adaptation along the lines of natural selection. Rather, he is trying to highlight the processes which bring about a **relationship** between the organism and the environment.

Hartmann suggests that there are three possible ways of adapting to one's environment these being (1) **autoplastic** - adjusting oneself to the environment, (2) **alloplastic** - adjusting the environment to fit oneself and (3) the **choosing** of a new environment.[3] At first glance these capacities sound rather dynamic and process-oriented but a closer look reveals that they are process-sensitive in form only, not with regard to their content. For instance, in using the concept "average expectable environment" Hartmann suggests that an organism and environment must come to "fit" one another.[4] However, this mutality is at the most basic levels of need only, such as physical survival. For Hartmann the particular emotional and interpersonal features of the environment remain largely ignored. His "environment" is a passive participant, at best a generic other.

The great constraining factor which holds Hartmann back from a full appreciation of the role of the object is his faithful commitment to Freud's drive theory. Because Freud's narrow view of drives predominates, the pleasure principle remains the sole determiner of behavior. This is not to say that objects are unimportant for Hartmann, simply that the organism will adapt itself to objects or objects to itself (via fantasy etc.), only in the service of maintaining its "pleasure-equation." While reality is important, it is important only in the sense that it enhances the ego's capacity to adapt along pleasure - unpleasure lines. Although severely limited by the pleasure-unpleasure model, by what mechanisms does this ego operate and how does it achieve the "stability" for which it strives?

The Ego as "Organ" of Equilibrium

If the ego is the organ of adaptation between world and psyche what are its functions and how does it go about its particular business? To begin with,

Hartmann gives the ego three essential functions which he calls **thinking, perception,**and **action.**[5] In his elaboration he suggests that these

> **Functions of the ego** center around the relation to reality. In this sense, we speak of the ego as a specific organ of adjustment. It controls the apparatuses of motility and perception; it tests the properties of the present situation at hand, i.e. of "present reality," and anticipates properties of future situations. The ego **mediates*** between these properties and requirements, and the demands of other psychic organizations.*[6]

What immediately strikes one in this description is the mediating capacity of this ego, not only as it absorbs the nature of a particular situation and mobilizes the organism for action, but in its synthesis of past, present, and future. This ego is not simply a static bridge between the organism and environment. It engages past, present, and future within itself, just as it mediates between itself and other psychic structures.

I find these hints regarding the ego's mediating function confirmed in Hartmann's description of the equilibrium sought by the total system. Hartmann identifies four areas in which the mediating function operates: (1) between the individual and environment, (2) between the drives themselves, (3) between the structural elements of psyche (id, ego, superego), and (4) between the mediating function itself and the remainder of the ego. He suggests that the harmony obtained by the second and third elements is dependent upon the first, in other words, internal balance is dependent upon the balance obtained between the individual and the environment, again indicating the growing object-relational influence. However, it is in Hartmann's fourth equilibrium that one makes an amazing discovery. Hartmann says the following of this fourth equilibrium:

> Since the ego is not merely a resultant of other forces, **its synthetic function is, so to speak, a specific organ of equilibrium** at the disposal of the person. **The fourth equilibrium is between the synthetic function and the rest of the ego.***[7]

This citation is so significant that one must linger momentarily to absorb its full implications. At one level Hartmann is simply claiming that an ego synthesizes or creates balance and harmony for an individual among the three dimensions I have described. There is nothing particularly new about this conclusion since all we have really said is that the ego relates to itself, i.e. mediates itself, and, as Kierkegaard reminds us, this is not yet a self.

However, in insisting that an equilibrium must be found between the **synthetic function** itself and the **remainder of the ego**, Hartmann has given us a psychoanalytic paraphrase to Kierkegaard's claim that the self **"is a relation that relates itself to itself or is the relations relating itself to itself."** A simple connection between two elements is not yet a self, just as a self is not simply a relation between various elements. The self is the relation taken toward the very act of relating. In making his claim for a fourth equilibrium Hartmann has perhaps unwittingly underscored Kierkegaard's point, although from a purely mechanistic point of view. But is this synthetic function of Hartmann's ego a manifestation of self?

It may be recalled that in Freud's topographic model the term ego referred to a rudimentary sense of "self", a whole person determined by drives alone. With the onset of the structural model, the ego became one of three "systems" which further fragmented the wholeness of personhood. With Hartmann this fragmentation has begun to be reversed. In Hartmann's response to Freud he suggests that

> We replace the word "ego" in Freud's text by the word "self". We do so since the ego is defined as part of the personality, and since Freud's use of the word is ambiguous. He uses "ego" in reference to a psychic organization and to the whole person.[8]

To help correct this ambiguity Hartmann attempts to describe the ego as more than its "functions" such as perception and reality testing, to now include its "functioning," that is, its **integrating, synthesizing** capacity.

Hartmann says of this "system-ego":

> The integrative function of the ego also added a new aspect to earlier ideas of Freud on the problem of equilibrium in the mental apparatus. The recognition of the synthetic function ... made the ego, which had always been considered **an organization**, now also **an organizer** of the three systems of personality ... There is no longer only "compromise" as result of opposing forces, but **intended harmonization** by the ego.[9]

In giving this synthesizing ego the capacity for **intentional harmonization** Hartmann has imbued personality with direction, an intentional seeking of balance and greater wholeness. This development is a major step in our 20th Century understanding of selfhood. How did Hartmann arrive at this remarkable adjustment to the psychoanalytic framework?

The transition brought about by Hartmann came about through his redefinition of narcissism. For Freud narcissism had consisted of energy invested in the ego, but the more the ego became understood as a particular structure among others, it became problematic to talk about an investment of energy in only a portion of the psyche as compared with the investment of energy one might make in objects. To state the problem another way, if libido moves toward whole objects, why would it only move toward portions or fragments of the subject? Hartmann writes:

> However, the opposite of object cathexes is not ego cathexes, but cathexes of one's own person, that is, self-cathexes; in speaking of self-cathexes we do not imply whether this cathexes is situated in the id, ego, or superego... It therefore will be clarifying if we define narcissism as the libidinal cathexes not of the ego but of the self.[10]

What Hartmann adjusted is the understanding of desire (libido) not only as the seeking of objects (Kierkegaard's seeking desire), but the seeking of the seeker (Kierkegaard's desiring desire). The self is now seeking itself. But how adequate a self is this?

The most Hartmann can say of this self is that it is a representation, an image, not unlike the images formed of external objects. His self takes shape as an **object** of experience, not the **subject** of experience. But what of the great synthesizing capacity of which so much clamor was just made?

We must remind ourselves that as an Ego Psychologist Hartmann attributes all functional attributes to the Ego. The self is simply a by-product of the developmental path of the ego: just as this path includes accumulated object-representations, it includes accumulated self-representations. Hartmann's "self" has no capacities nor structure, and "seems to hang in mid air, without history or function."[11]

In restricting the self to an image, Hartmann leaves all functions of the psyche, including the synthesizing capacity, in the hands of the ego. This leaves us with the same question asked of Fichte almost two centuries earlier. How can a part integrate the whole of which it is unaware? How does an ego unify itself or synthesize itself into harmony prior to its very formation? In Fichte's case he simply declared the ego to be in unity with itself and washed his hands of the problem. It turns out that Hartmann must resort to the same solution.

The only way an ego can bring itself into harmony prior to being capable of doing so is if this function is somehow automatic or intrinsic to the ego. This is the only conclusion left open to Hartmann who insists that the infant and environment "are adapted to each other from the very first moment."[12] "Unity is not achieved through any subject-object interaction, but is simply assumed within the maternal matrix, actualized by the rudimentary ego seemingly before it develops.

Nevertheless, we should not allow this major handicap obscure our awareness of the fundamental shift brought about by Hartmann. The ego has become a living entity, no longer simply a by-product of the clash between instincts and environment. His emphasis upon primary and secondary ego functions allowed for ego capacities to be seen as conflict-bound or conflict-free, which moved psychoanalytic theory toward recognition of the possibility of conflict **within** a given system (ego, superego, etc.) not just **between** systems. Thus, in spite of his abiding adherence to drive theory, Hartmann's model opens the door to an inner subjective world no longer cut off from the object relations with which it is interwoven.

EDITH JACOBSON

In turning to the theoretical formulations of Edith Jacobson one discovers a close affinity with the Ego Psychology of Freud and Hartmann, even as there emerges a more fully developed object-relational view of identity and human selfhood. What makes it impossible to place Jacobson exclusively in either the **"Ego Psychology"** or **"Self Psychology"** camps is the fact that one finds strong elements of both in her presuppositions and conclusions. Predictably, this leaves her inconsistent and even contradictory at times, thereby restricting her role to that of transition figure in the movement toward a fully developed model of self. However, being a transition figure does not make her unimportant; rather, it means that a more comprehensive and consistent picture has not yet emerged. The evolution of dynamic subject-object models within psychological science did not happen through quantum leaps. It required slow meticulous steps with occasional noteworthy "corrections" along the way. Edith Jacobson is one such vital, if partial, "correction."

The "Self" in Edith Jacobson

Heinz Hartmann was the first Ego psychologist to formally introduce the term "self" into his writings. For him the word simply refers to an ego-generated product, an internal **image** which represents the **internal world**, just as other images are formed of the object world. His self has no structure or dynamic operations of its own but owes its life to the vicissitudes of ego formation. In her early conclusions Jacobson simply echoes these assumptions:

> The term "self" which was introduced by Hartmann (1950), will, in agreement with him, be employed as referring to the whole person of an individual, including his body and body parts as well as his psychic organization and its parts. As the title of this volume indicates, the "self" is an auxiliary descriptive term, which points to the person as subject in distinction from the surrounding world of objects.[13]

If this "self" is but a restatement of Hartmann's views why bother with it any further?

It is true that Jacobson cannot give the self a status within the psychic apparatus alongside an ego, id, or superego, since that would invalidate the very essence of the Freudian system, the structural model. What Jacobson can allow, however, is for object relations to determine the shape of one's self-representations. As her thought matures, she adds to Hartmann's self (**as image**), the sense of self (**as process**) whereby ego, self, and object images interact. Even with this development, however, Jacobson's self does not become an active agent synthesizing itself or psychic life but remains, as was true for Hartmann, a by-product of ego-driven operations.

Without a doubt, the primary factors determining Jacobson's orientation toward the self are (1) her understanding of **drives**, and (2) the nature and role of the **object**. All orthodox psychoanalytic perspectives insist that psychic energy is strictly id-based and inherently divided (dual-drive theory). This generates the ambiguity that "on top" of this exclusively id-driven machine sits an ever-more sophisticated ego. With each enhancement of ego-functioning it becomes more and more difficult to explain how raw id-energy can be translated into the complex patterns operating within the ego. Unwieldy concepts such as (1) neutralization of energy (Hartmann); or (2) highly developed defense mechanisms such as introjection, sublimation, and displacement (Anna Freud) become necessary to help explain how raw aggressive and libidinal energies can evolve into the complex and highly organized possibilities of human functioning.

What makes the classic approach to drives so dogmatically rigid is that they are the only allowable bridge between body and psyche. As Freud had insisted, only raw chemical/biological forces can be called upon to explain the functioning of the human animal. This was Jacobson's inheritance and she valiantly attempted to preserve to it, unlike the British Object Relational theorists such as Fairbairn who simply threw out the drive model altogether.

In Jacobson, therefore, one finds a continuing attachment to the old dual-drive model, even as she takes seriously **personal experience**. Her work therefore adds a **second bridge** to the first (the instincts), namely, a bridge made up of **images** (i.e. self and object representations) **produced out of personal experience**.

That the earliest relations with others have a profound influence upon development and the emergence of psychopathology is demonstrated again and again by Jacobson.[14] What is critical within these early relations is not so much the gratification of drives, but the nature of the object-relationships established. Although still determined by the pleasure-unpleasure tension, **the nature of the experience with the object** now determines the self and object images formed. Jacobson suggests for instance that if the object world is optimally frustrating, it enhances separation between a self and its objects, just as an overly frustrating **or** overly gratifying environment will inhibit boundary awareness and create regressive entanglement of self and object images.[15] So far, however, we have seen nothing new. But perhaps Jacobson's understanding of development will offer further insights into the operations of these "self" and "object" images?

Identity and Identification

As suggested, Jacobson's model of human development does not assume autonomous instinct-driven processes separate from life experience, but assumes that drives themselves are "shaped" by the environment from the outset. Her developmental schema has five so-called "stages" within it, each pointing to a particular maturation of the subject-object interface. These phases include: (1) An initial state of **"undifferentiated drive energy"** which contains an unstructured "primal psychophysiological self." This is a boundary-less state with a purely physiological discharge of energy. (2) Energy divides after birth into libidinal and aggressive poles which gather together "nuclei of as yet unorganized and disconnected memory traces." The earliest sensations of an infant take on pleasurable/unpleasurable or libidinal/aggressive qualities and become attached to beginning outside perceptions. (3) Psychological structures emerge as "part images of love objects and body part images are formed and linked up with memory traces of past pleasure-unpleasure experiences." These images become invested with libidinal and aggressive energy. (4) As "neutralization" of sexual and aggressive drives sets in, "tender attachments grow and affects become attached to ego functions." This allows "awareness of self to extend to awareness of ego attitudes and ego functions. A concept of the self as an entity that has **continuity** and **direction** is formed." (5) Finally, superego formation enhances the process of drive neutralization (beginning of latency phase). At this point an abiding (self) structure has emerged with realistic representations of the object world and self representations.[16]

While Jacobson's interweaving of drive and environment is interesting, what is particularly striking about her model is the allusion to self as an entity which has **continuity** and **direction**. We have stumbled across the idea of a direction to selfhood before, yet here it strikes one as odd coming from a perspective which looks for a **biological meaning** to the relationship between ego and environment. Jacobson does not deny that relationships are meaningful, but she offers no explanation as to **why** a self should strive to enhance its relational life other than perhaps to fulfill its instinctual impulses. But there is nothing **progressively** directional about the push of libidinal or aggressive instincts, nor does the impulse toward gratification have much to say about a directionality which seeks ever more complex and intricate patterns and meanings. In spite of this inconsistency, however, Jacobson reveals an evolution within object-relational theory toward seeing meanings and purposes beyond simple one-dimensional drive gratification.

Nevertheless, it is when one looks behind Jacobson's "stages" that a surprising discovery is made. This discovery concerns Jacobson's understanding of the establishment of **identity**. Jacobson recognizes that identity involves both sameness and change, in other words, identity refers to the capacity to maintain continuity even in the midst of ever-present flux.[17] Here again, this idea is not new and has been traced in my survey from Augustine through Hume to both Hegel and Kierkegaard. What is so significant about Jacobson's conclusion is that even from her limited psychoanalytic perspective, identity has become grounded in the **identifications** arrived at through the developmental process.

This viewpoint allows Jacobson to understand identity formation as arising out of the rich interactions between an infant and its parental figures. These interactions confirm a **second dialectic bridge** - now no longer simply a one-way "instinct" bridge - but a 2-way bridge consisting of the **images** or **representations** arising out of experience. She suggests for instance, that the mechanisms of **introjection and projection** are two psychic processes through which self-images take on the characteristics of object-images and vice versa.[18] While these two mechanisms were used by both Freud and Melanie Klein, in Jacobson the characteristics of the object take on new relevance.

What begins as early, very primitive fusion and "identification" with love objects must mature to become a "selective" identification. Jacobson says of this vital step:

> In fact, the child cannot establish emotional investments in other persons as objects which are different from his own self until he is able to experience his own identity; and since active strivings to acquire likenesses to others are also motivated by discoveries of differences from them, these strivings cannot develop either until the child has become aware of such differences.[19]

Simply put, separation and the discovery of "difference" is a prerequisite for identity formation.

However, Jacobson insists that this "difference" must be moderated by an attachment to the object which is activated by a mother's love. Only through the loving intention of the object toward the emerging self, is the self truly born. A mother's "image" as accepting libidinal object, allows the emerging self to find ownership of its difference from the environment. Jacobson writes:

> In fact, the better the totality of other persons and of the self can be experienced, the more easily can the distinction, the perception of the differences between one's self and others be tolerated, and likeness not only discovered but accepted, desired and acquired.[20]

We have before us an echo of the words of Hegel, that selfhood requires the radical acceptance of otherness even as it first comes to itself through the encounter with otherness.

As one might expect, however, Jacobson's subject-object linkage is not grounded in a larger understanding of the necessity for mirroring of subject and object as presented by Hegel and Kierkegaard. Jacobson's self is only capable of regressive union, a fleeting libidinal bond which must sink again into its separation until awakened by another "fantasy of libidinal union."[21] At the same time, one cannot fault Jacobson for seeing the transcending expansion of self as a regressive and transitory fantasy of union. Given the limiting presuppositions from within which she worked, the possibility that self has an eternal openness remains an impossibility. While I have already noted other serious limitations to Jacobson's "self", most notably her restricting its reality to the images by which it sees itself, I can nevertheless declare her efforts to be a genuine contribution to our search.

Through Jacobson's efforts I am able to place the operations of selfhood upon a more solid interpersonal foundation without sacrificing the self's relationship to the body, to history, nor to interpersonal otherness. However, in order to move beyond a regressive subject-object unity, an active, not a passive self must be envisioned. With a second dialectic bridge now in place (self-images arising out of experience) I have moved a step closer to my goal of a fully dynamic and comprehensive selfhood.

MARGARET MAHLER

The work of Margaret Mahler stands as a noteworthy parallel to the advancement of theory brought about by Edith Jacobson. Both trace their theoretical lineage from the Ego Psychology of Freud, through the nuances of "adaptation" as we encountered them in Hartmann, and both end with a highly object-relational view of human development. Their sense of the developmental process and its outcomes is in obvious harmony making it a legitimate question why I even need to give Mahler special attention?

The answer lies in the fact that Mahler is perhaps the most influential Ego Psychologist to have operated in the post-war period. Although her developmental paradigm closely parallels Jacobson, Mahler's terminology (which explores the nuances of the separation-individuation process) has been more widely used. As a matter of fact, it is impossible to discuss contemporary object-relations theory or Self Psychology without a familiarity with the language and the particular developmental map constructed by her.

The work of Mahler reveals that she incorporates a more **personal** environment into her model. Her concern is to understand the process of attaining identity in an inter-personal world as one moves from a primary state of fusion and symbiosis toward becoming an individual. She calls this process "psychological birth," or separation-individuation, with distinct, recognizable stations along the way. What one finds in Mahler is a psychological paradigm remarkably similar to the nuances of Hegel's master-slave dialectic as the path governing the birth of self-consciousness. Whether her model can allow for the fullness of selfhood beyond this single interactional focus remains to be seen.

Mahler's Stages of Development

There are three phases to Mahler's developmental map which she calls (1) Autism, (2) Symbiosis, and (3) Separation-Individuation. This third and final step Mahler divides into four subphases known as (1) Differentiation, (2) Practicing, (3) Rapprochement, and (4) Consolidation of Individuality and Emotional Object Constancy. While these processes are chronologically determined, they are considered to be cumulative in the sense that each phase builds upon another and cannot be artificially separated from what preceeds it.

Autism

Perhaps the most ambiguous and seriously challenged phase of Mahler's model is the first, called "normal autism."[22] In the first weeks of life an infant is supposedly object-less with no capacity to interact with the environment other than through reflex reactions to stimuli such as pain or the automatic turning toward the breast when hungry. What makes this first classification problematic is not so much the notion of an undifferentiated phase, (which we have encountered in numerous places, most recently in Edith Jacobson); its problematic quality concerns Mahler's assumption that each infant is a closed system oblivious to the world. Numerous scholars have challenged her assumptions as Mahler acknowledges in the last article published before her death. In her rebuff to her critics she flatly rejects their juxtaposed view that there exists at birth a "separate self" with certain built-in "competencies."[23] She insists that a neonate is in no way autonomous, that even from the point of view of raw biological neediness, the child is completely enmeshed with its need-satisfying environment. Mahler became willing to adjust her timetable with regard to neonate capacity, but not her assumptions about the complete absorption of the neonate in its environmental and bodily realities.[24] This debate is not some irrelevant side issue but already reveals where Mahler's model is headed. For Mahler the grand purpose of development is separation-individuation, the attainment of autonomy. As I hope to prove, Mahler may not quite reach her goal, even though her map has become a mainstay for contemporary psychoanalytic thought.

Symbiosis

If the autistic phase is considered object-less, then the symbiotic phase is pre-objectal. As a phase prior to separation there is as yet no awareness of inner or outer, self or other. Mahler summarizes:

> The term **symbiosis** in this context is a metaphor. Unlike the biological concept of symbiosis, it does not describe what actually happens in a mutually beneficial relationship between two **separate** individuals of different species. It describes that state of undifferentiation, of fusion with mother, in which the "I" is not yet differentiated from the "not I" and in which inside and outside are only gradually coming to be sensed as different ...
> The essential feature of symbiosis is hallucinatory or delusional somatopsychic **omnipotent** fusion with representation of the

mother and, in particular the delusion of a common boundary between two physically separate individuals.[25]

As scholars have noted, there is an awkwardness inherent in the symbiotic concept as one tries to integrate it with classic drive theory.[26] The problem has its beginnings in Freud's separation of object libido from narcissistic (ego) libido. For Freud, the energy directed toward an object is **not** available to the ego, in contrast to Mahler for whom libido flows toward the "dual-unity" of mother and undifferentiated self.

Secondly, and perhaps most importantly, the question emerges how symbiosis can describe a subject-object relationship when differentiation has not yet been attained? Is symbiosis a relationship between a subject and an object, or is it an internal process occurring within an emerging self? By saying **yes** to both, Mahler takes a major step forward in the evolution of psychoanalytic theories of selfhood.

We recall that for Freud and the early Ego Psychologists such as Hartmann (as well as Melanie Klein), objects are related only to the id. Every drive (instinct) needs a target and the object is simply the point of discharge where tension reduction occurs. The **only bridge** between subject and object is the **drive** as I have demonstrated. Because the old drive model needs objects for tension reduction only, the object is simply a faceless, generic target. As a passive, static "thing" the objects' particular qualities are largely superfluous.

In a noteworthy shift, Mahler now makes the object **active**, as an active **subject** along the lines identified by Hegel. It was Hartmann's notion of the **"average expectable environment"** which created the opening for Mahler's major theoretical shift. Mahler gives this "environment" a face - the object becomes **"the ordinary devoted mother"** with the clear capacity to impact and shape the emerging self much along the lines suggested by Winnicott. Furthermore, this active object is present **from the beginning** and can even impact the organism prior to birth. From the outset the object brings a particular environment to the emerging subject. For an instant it almost looks as if the emerging self seeks the other for the purpose of its own birth into self-consciousness. But this Mahler quickly denies.

For typically biologically-based reasons, the motive for Mahler's subject-object activity is simply **survival** and **adaptation**. Symbiosis for her does not suggest an inherent seeking of relatedness as I noted for Fairbairn and Winnicott, but a **merged oneness** in which the kernel of selfhood is in reaction to environmental stimuli. There is an inherent relationship to the object in Mahler but one which is in essence forced upon the infant by virtue of its radical helplessness. The **necessity of dependence** is what creates relationship between rudimentary subject and object, with the experiences which then follow giving shape to this rudimentary self.

Separation-Individuation

Since the "merged oneness" of symbiosis is the foundation of selfhood for Mahler we should not be too surprised to discover that separation-individuation serves as its dialectic opposite. Writing in 1955 Mahler makes the following declaration:

> For we need to study the strong impetus which drives toward separation, coupled with the fear of separation, if we hope to understand the severe psycho-pathology of childhood which ever so often begins or reveals itself insidiously or actually from the second part of the second year onward...
> We know that the drive is not toward separation per se, but the innate given is the drive toward individuation, which cannot be achieved without autonomous separation.[27]

While one can appreciate the dialectic legitimacy of the drive toward individuation (not simply separation), Mahler never asks why this should be so. It surely goes without saying that the impulse toward individuation (i.e. the seeking of fullness of individual identity as subject) has infinitely greater meaningfulness and complexity than simple biological survival. Regrettably, this remains a persistent limitation in Mahler.

Be that as it may, Mahler calls the first phase of separation-individuation **"hatching"** or interestingly, "second-birth."[28] Normally occurring during the four to ten month period, early differentiation proceeds as an infant becomes aware of sensations and perceptions originating from **outside** the symbiotic orbit. Early exploration takes place at this stage allowing for a beginning distinction between inanimate objects and living, animated objects. The ability to discriminate between internal (self) sensations and external (object-generated) sensations has begun. The infant is now accumulating and storing a growing residue of "good" and "bad" experiences, with the faint sense of self and other beginning to cluster around these impressions. The arrival of stranger anxiety is the primary barometer of the completion of this sub-phase. It is worth noting the close parallel we find here to Hegel's movement of natural consciousness from sense-certainty to perception.

The second step within separation-individuation Mahler calls the **practicing** sub-phase. Its arrival is signaled by the ability to move about, to literally leave the maternal orbit and explore the world to the extent that crawling and walking will allow. However, the mothering-one is never left far behind given the need for "emotional refueling."[29] The consistent availability of the mothering-one remains vital.

Mahler claims that three criteria must be met during this subphase, the first being bodily differentiation from mother; secondly, the establishment of a specific bond with the mother depending upon the "refueling" capacity; and thirdly, the growth of the "autonomous" ego functions such as locomotion and reality testing.[30] During this 10 to 18 month period narcissism reaches its peek with corresponding libidinal investment in one's body and its growing abilities and in the expanding world of objects.

Mahler's third subphase called **"rapprochement"** completes the hatching or "psychological birth" process. At its successful completion, the toddler reaches the first level of identity, "of being a separate individual entity."[31] However, this achievement is by no means easy. Together with increased mobility and cognitive function there emerges a growing awareness in the toddler that she is not the center of the universe but is really very small and helpless even with all her growing abilities. This loss of grandiosity and of the first idealized self brings about what Mahler calls the "rapprochement crisis."[32] Needs are never automatically met and the toddler's abilities, as great as they are, are not capable of preserving the world as one's personal oyster. This crisis further enhances the internal differentiation of self and object representations. The threat at this point becomes the possible loss of the love of the object, rather than the loss of the object itself.

The quality of the relationship between infant and mother becomes even more critical in this phase. Mahler insists that

> One cannot emphasize too strongly the importance of the optimal emotional availability of the mother during this subphase. It is the mother's **love** of the toddler and the acceptance of his ambivalence that enable the toddler to cathect his self-representation with neutralized energy.[33]

This means that the mother must provide "a ready supply of object libido" by sharing in the child's discoveries, and facilitating its attempts at **imitation and identification** through playful reciprocation. This allows the child to **internalize the relationship**. Whatever shape this internalization takes will determine the shape of the emerging self-representations.

The final subphase within separation-individuation Mahler calls **Consolidation of Individuation and the Beginnings of Emotional Object Constancy**.[34] This phase begins at approximately three years of age and is open-ended since it continues throughout life. The two tasks of this sub-phase are the achievement of full individuality and the stability of self and objects. Mahler distinguishes this step from Piaget's concept of "object permanence" which concerns the stability of inanimate things. Here the task is more difficult since it involves holding together and unifying highly emotionally charged material, i.e. good and bad experiences with real people.

The stability of self and other boundaries is attained as good and bad objects become unified into "whole" representations. This allows the aggressive and libidinal drives to unify within a stable self. Mahler elaborates:

> In the state of object constancy, the love object will not be rejected or exchanged for another if it can no longer provide satisfactions; and in that state the object is still longed for, and not rejected (hated) as unsatisfactory simply because it is absent.[35]

This stability of self and other marks the arrival at a mutuality of give-and-take love-object relationships, the high point of Mahler's developmental path.

Mahler's Contributions and Constraints

Mahler's importance as a contemporary psychoanalytic thinker warrants a more thorough response with regard to her contribution and limits in the search for selfhood. Perhaps the most noteworthy contribution of Mahler is her psychological uncovering of the three-phase dialectic of **fusion - separation - individuation** as a vital process within the self. She has confirmed for us that the tension between **enmeshment** and **autonomy**, between **dependence** and **independence**, is a primary ingredient to selfhood. Mahler's meticulous observations not only have relevance for healthy or normal development, but allow us to understand a wide range of pathologies from psychotic regressions to narcissistic, borderline, or schizoid lesions. These frameworks are indispensable for any clinician and for one's understanding of the subject-object tension within selfhood.

In spite of her noteworthy contributions, however, I must also highlight several serious deficiencies. Mahler's self is quite correctly built through internalized engagement with the environment, although this occurs only along adaptive lines. Mahler's biological focus can only envision a self which **adjusts** and **accommodates**. This view is in sharp contrast to Winnicott who sees **conformity** to the environment the very thing which smothers an emerging self. A self built on adaptation alone is a false, compliant self as far as he is concerned. For Winnicott and the British School a self is "awakened" or drawn out by a nurturing, facilitating environment. Individual uniqueness is already present at the outset for Winnicott, with care givers facilitating (or blocking) this emergence of self.

I find this serious critique confirmed as I realize that for Mahler, personhood i.e. a self, is only achieved at the **end** of the developmental process. This makes selfhood a static and elusive entity. For Winnicott and Fairbairn on the other hand, the kernel of selfhood is present at the beginning. In Mahler the libidinal thrust is toward separation and individuation while for Winnicott it is toward the object (other) through whom identity is nurtured.

At one level it might seem that this theoretical rift is minor and simply highlights the two sides of the differentiation process. However, the issue runs deeper. Mahler's vision leaves the self searching for a home it can never attain. Her individuated self is stalemated in either compliance or autonomous opposition, suggesting that the highest level of selfhood attainable for her is a utilitarian "give and take" self. I need only remind the reader of Hegel's stinging rebuke of suffocating utilitarianism. Mahler's self may know how to survive and may even

312

know how to do so in healthy ways, but it does not know how to seek itself nor transcend itself for the sake of larger order unities.

To restate the challenge, Mahler's self knows only **necessity** (accommodation to an environment), and knows **possibility** (freedom to transcend an environment) only in marginal ways as limited by the biological paradigm. With adaptation to the environment the outer limit of its "possibilities" such a self can never be free, to say nothing of its eternal capacity to shape itself. I find this serious limitation confirmed in Mahler's following statement:

> Here, in the rapprochement subphase, we feel is the mainspring of man's eternal struggle against both fusion and isolation.
> One could regard the entire life cycle as constituting a more or less successful process of distancing from and introjection of the lost symbiotic mother, an eternal longing for the actual or fantasized ideal state of self with the latter standing for symbiotic fusion, with the "all good" symbiotic mother, who was at one time part of the self in a blissful state of well-being.[36]

This lost paradise of the symbiotic mother is the source and goal of all human striving, the essence of selfhood. All libidinal longing, whatever seeking of unity one may experience, any searching for a transcending pattern to selfhood has now been reduced to the enmeshment with the first object. It seems we have again reached the familiar "nothing-but" position first encountered in Hume.

Perhaps this outcome should not surprise anyone too greatly, since after all, Mahler's self, as is the case with Hartmann and Jacobson, is "nothing-but" an image, a representation which has no energy or structure of its own other than what is granted it by the ego. While Mahler has moved toward an openness to the **personal experiences** which shape self-representations, the ego is completely in the drivers seat in the sense that it brings the self to birth and generates the images which constitute its self-representations.

In summary, Mahler's dialectic bridge only reaches to the earliest historical necessities of personhood. Her model of selfhood is organized strictly around pleasure/unpleasure processes which, as Hegel and Kierkegàard made very clear, is only the first step toward self-consciousness. What Mahler has contributed to our search is to solidify the increasing emphasis upon the environment and the dialectic encounter with otherness as a primary building-block of identity. In highlighting the fusion-separation pattern she has confirmed the necessity of holding the tension of these forces within the self. This capacity to unify and reconcile separated portions of selfhood Kierkegaard called **faith**. Perhaps Mahler's work has created an opening for this possibility.

OTTO KERNBERG

Otto Kernberg enters the scene as one of the first psychoanalytic thinkers to attempt to bridge the gap between the dual-drive theories of Freud, Hartmann, and Jacobson, and the person-centered object-relational theories of Fairbairn and Winnicott. This attempt to transcend and perhaps overcome the psychoanalytic split has evoked strong and sharp reaction, particularly from the neo-Freudian camp. While some reactions to Kernberg are quite neutral (Blum, 1982; Rangell, 1982), others such as Klein and Tribish (1981) are relentless in their assault.[37] A more moderate and useful assessment is given by Greenberg and Mitchell who acknowledge that Kernberg is simply following an evolving process within psychoanalytic theory in general as it moves in increasingly object-relational directions.[38] While Kernberg overstates his claim to remain true to the basic structural and drive patterns established by Freud, Hartmann and followers, he nevertheless remains an influential if controversial figure within the psychoanalytic community. His relevance is based upon the fact that he nudges the understanding of selfhood forward in noteworthy directions.

Self as Representation and Structure

Up to this point in my discussion of psychoanalytic models, the prevailing pattern has been to see the self as a **representation** - as the imaginal by-product of **drive** or **relational** forces respectively, depending upon which psychoanalytic camp is being considered. Because the tri-partite structure of id, ego, and superego reigns supreme, no fourth structure has been envisioned and particularly not a superordinate structure which ties these sub-systems together. Within psychoanalytic thought the ego has consistently been given the task of unifying experience: whatever cohesion of personal identity is attained, it is attributable to the workings of the coordinating ego.

With the arrival of Kernberg, however, a major new development occurs, with self given the status of a distinct structure. Kernberg writes:

> I propose, instead, to reserve the term "self" for the sum total of self-representations in intimate connection with the sum total of object representations. In other words, I propose defining the self as an intrapsychic structure that originates from the ego and is clearly embedded in the ego. The libidinal investment of the self - thus defined - is related to the libidinal investment of the representations of significant others, and the libidinal investment of one's own person corresponds to the libidinal investment of others (external objects). All these investments are related and reinforce each other.[39]

While tipping his hat to the notion of self as representation, Kernberg quickly moves beyond this self as image, toward a self with its own structural integrity even as he tries to stay true to the tripartite model. But in virtually the same breath as his granting the self structural status, Kernberg seems to take away what he has just given by placing this self squarely within the ego which gives it birth. Again a familiar question presents itself. How can a structure within a structure (self as embedded in the ego) unify the whole. How can a part, or better said, a part within a part, tie together the whole before the part (the self) is even born?

Kernberg seems to recognize this difficulty as his expanding definition reveals. He subsequently makes clear that his self is not simply a "composite" self-representation but the "sum total of integrated self-representations from all developmental stages;" furthermore, this "organization or structure plays a central role in development."[40]

Two difficulties emerge immediately: first, the **integration** of images must somehow occur; secondly, the structure itself must somehow impact the developmental process. The tension Kernberg cannot resolve is the passivity vs. activity of the self he envisions. A self which is simply a representational by-product of the activity of various psychic agencies has no energy or task of its own. It is simply the visible manifestation of work occurring elsewhere. On the other hand, a self as structure cannot really be called a structure unless it does something. A structure without process is dead. But if the self-structure is to be active in any way, from where does its energy come and what function does it serve? How and when is it born?

Kernberg claims a close affinity to the work of Jacobson and Mahler, even to Klein and Fairbairn in his conclusion that the development of self requires both frustrating and nurturing components, in contrast to Kohut whom he claims ignores aggression. Be that as it may, his develomental model assumes that states of merger come under the impact of frustrating and/or gratifying experiences. Such experiences give the state of merger a particular feeling-quality which results in mental representations thereof which will be invested with either aggression or libido.[41] These accumulated representations eventually lead to multiple and perhaps contradictory self and object-representations which must be differentiated and integrated, i.e. sorted-out and accepted (taken-in). Up to this point one finds largely a restatement of Mahler's separation-individuation process and rapprochement transitions. What is new, however is that this self arises out of the **integration** of **contradictory self-representations** and the corresponding investment of the self in the **positively** and **negatively** tinged images which represent it. Kernberg's developmental vision therefore unfolds as follows:

> The self, then, is an ego structure that originates from self-representations first built up in the undifferentiated symbiotic phase in the context of infant-mother interactions under the influence of both gratifying and frustrating experiences. Simultaneously the system perception-consciousness evolves into broader ego functions as well - the developing control over perception, voluntary motility, the setting up of effective memory traces, and the system preconscious. The self as psychic structure originates from both libidinally and aggressively invested self-representations. It is, in short, an ego function and structure that evolves gradually from the integration of its component self-representations into a supraordinate structure that incorporates other ego functions - such as memory and cognitive structures - and leads to the dual characteristics implied in Freud's Ich.[42]

In a later volume Kernberg is able to say that this normal self is the supraordinate organizer of key ego functions such as reality testing, synthesizing, and integrating.[43]

What is one to make of this self? It is odd, if not confusing, to have the self begin as a sub-structure and function within the ego, and end as a supraordinate structure that has swallowed up the mighty ego and its functions. Perhaps this difficulty is inevitable since Kernberg is attempting both to remain faithful to the

Freudian ego **and** to his growing recognition that wider forces are at work shaping human identity and subjectivity.

What is noteworthy about Kernberg's evolution toward a wider subjectivity is that he sees selfhood containing a dialectic process containing: (a) states of merger, which are (b) negated through either libidinal or aggressive channels, and ending in (c) varying degrees of integration of the prior elements. These phases closely parallel the Hegelian dialectic of self which assumes a process of:

(a) Unity (b) Negation (c) Synthesis: New Unity of (a) & (b)

Correspondingly, Kernberg's dialectic of self assumes a process of:

(a) Merger/nondifferentiation (b)libidinally and aggressively-charged differentiation

(c) integration of (a) and (b) which also includes the integration of contradictory self-representations.

What is striking about these parallels is not simply their common mechanisms, but their outcomes. As I have often stated, the Hegelian dialectic aims toward the complete acceptance of otherness even as this difference becomes sharper and more complete. In using the language of **integration** and **investment**, Kernberg is moving toward the similar need to "**take-in**" and have "**concern-for**" otherness as vital manifestations of self. Given the significance of this development it would be useful to unpackage Kernberg's model more carefully.

Kernberg's work with severely disturbed individuals provided a clinical context which brought these structural and dynamic observations into sharper relief. In working with such persons Kernberg was particularly exposed to their splitting capacities and the tendency to live out wildly contradictory visions of themselves. In following Jacobson and Mahler, Kernberg notes that such individuals are pathologically fixated at early stages of psychic development with the undeveloped ego unable to organize, integrate, or synthesize its divergent "good" and "bad" experiences.

According to Kernberg, early experiences leave behind "relational configurations" which reflect the nature of an infant's interaction with its environment. These patterns of relationship are **internalized** in three steps he calls (1) introjections (2) identifications, and (3) ego identity.[44] Together they constitute the "identification systems" by which selfhood is built. In other words, Kernberg is proposing that selfhood is built as it internalizes "otherness" in three dialectically related ways.

Each of these three forms of internalization includes (1) an image of the object, (2) an image of the self and (3) an affective investment in the self and object images as influenced by the drive operating at the time. The first and most basic mechanism of internalizing called "**introjection**", involves taking-in fused and undeveloped self and object images. Introjection forms a bridge between the perception of external objects and the experience of primitive affect states. An encounter with an object and the feelings generated thereby become linked.

The second type of internalization Kernberg calls "**identification**" in which distinct images of self and object are absorbed through imitation and modeling. The growing distinction between self and object consolidates their separate reality even as the self looks to the object for continuity and cohesion.

The final step in identity formation Kernberg calls "**ego-identity**" namely "the overall organization of identifications and introjections under the guiding principle of the synthetic function of the ego."[45] Not only should there be internal consistency and continuity to one's self representations at this point, but a consistent view of the external world. Identity for Kernberg therefore involves a harmonization of introjections and identifications, i.e. the maintaining of a true balance between what is inner and outer, what is me and not-me.

Kernberg insists there must be a consistent recognition of the self images both within the person and from the environment. Again, Hegel's master/slave dialectic describing the birth of self-identity finds a contemporary confirmation. The same could be said of Kierkegaard's claim that a self relates itself to itself through its projected images of itself.

With Kernberg giving such a high degree of importance to the encounter with the environment, what happens to the drives which have been so central to classic psychoanalytic thought?

The Drives Revisited

A wide range of conclusions have been identified in my survey of psychoanalytic thinking concerning drives. These conclusions have ranged from the Freudian and neo-Freudian insistence that drives are the autonomous biologically-endowed forces which place demands upon the psyche for "work", to the relational school of Fairbairn, Guntrip, and Winnicott which sees drives as object-seeking, with both libido and aggression determined only by the nature of one's life experience. In keeping with his hope of overcoming this gap, Kernberg attempts to reconcile these juxtaposed approaches. However, after all is said and done, Kernberg ends with a much closer affinity to the relational theorists than to the drive adherents. How is it that Kernberg arrives at this result?

Kernberg attempts to resolve the dilemma by asking himself which comes first, (1) the drives? (2) the seeking of object relations? or (3) the affects?[46] In choosing **affects**, Kernberg believes he has found the means of transcending the psychoanalytic rift. He writes:

> I would suggest that affects are the primary motivational system, in the sense that they are the center of each of the infinite number of gratifying and frustrating concrete events the infant experiences with his environment. Affects link a series of undifferentiated self-object representations so that gradually a complex world of internalized object relations, some pleasurably tinged, others unpleasurably tinged, is constructed.[47]

Kernberg has now unhooked drives from their one-dimensional biological foundation by giving them a complexity which comes from particular kinds of object relationships. **Affects** (as they arise out of experience) **are the building blocks of drives**.

Drives are now reinterpreted as "the activation of a specific object relation, which includes an affect and wherein the drive is represented by a specific desire or wish".[48] They remain central for mobilizing the psyche but are now linked to encounters with specific objects. But if drives are specific wishes directed toward an object does this not make the search for the object the primary motivational factor as was true for Fairbairn? To this possibility Kernberg abruptly answers no.

His reasons for this rejection are three-fold. In the first place, Kernberg claims that the seeking of the object is not primary because there is often a contradictory relation taken toward the same object. Secondly, he suggests that aggression works against the consolidation of object relationships, and may even work toward eliminating the object. Thirdly, Kernberg believes that Fairbairn neglects the shifts in libido one finds during infantile sexuality. For these reasons Kernberg rejects the possibility that drives are object-seeking.

The difficulty with Kernberg's position is that he seems to forget that the dynamics of selfhood demand the otherness of the object. Even aggression is in the service of object-relatedness: whether aggression takes the form of wanting to destroy the object or separate from it, it is still object-linked in that it reveals a seeking of a more adequate object, or perhaps a more adequate relation to the same object. It is impossible to conceive of the urge to separate or the urge to unify in isolation from an object through which the impulse defines itself.

In spite of Kernberg's pronouncements to the contrary, his persistent affirmation of the role of object-relations in the formation of selfhood brings him dangerously close to the relational theorists such as Fairbairn and Winnicott. There is no doubt that for Kernberg affects are the building blocks of the drives, with these object-determined affects preceeding the drives. In Kernberg's vision persons are not blindly sexual or aggressive but highly responsive to interpersonal experience.[49]

A Limited Self?

It is not my task to critique Kernberg for falling away from psychoanalytic orthodoxy but to assess the adequacy of his insights as a possible framework for building a more comprehensive model of selfhood. To begin with, Kernberg's elevation of self to psychic structure allows for a more comprehensive integration of interpersonal experience beyond the simple self which only mediates instinct impulses. As I have noted, making self a distinct structure containing dynamic processes such as **introjection, identification** and **internalization,** gives self a very dynamic and dialectic flavor. This development is in contrast to the static "self-representation" models we have seen up to this point. The possibility that self is capable of dynamic operations is a major step forward.

However, one quickly notices that Kernberg's self is still organized around the **pleasure-unpleasure continuum only**. It is the only fulcrum of development allowed by him. This leaves us with at best a utilitarian self driven only by the seeking of pleasure and the avoidance of pain regardless of how organized or sophisticated it might become. Beauty, truth, and meaning remain beyond its orbit.

A second major concern centers around Kernberg's understanding of the nature of the object. His psychoanalytic critics vehemently attack him for redefining the object to that of specific human person toward whom the individual is intrinsically related. For Freud and the early object-relations theorists such as Hartmann and Jacobson the object of a drive is always a faceless target through which the drive achieves its aim. For the pure Freudian there is no inherent need to be attached to another person, only the need to release internally-based impulses.[50] In short, for most drive-model theorists the person is **inherently alone**, while for object-related theorists such as Fairbairn and now Kernberg, a self is **inherently attached**.

My own conclusion is that neither option is correct to the exclusion of the other. There is not an inherent **relation** to an object because an object is not automatically or magically differentiated. Nor can one call every state of attachment inherently self-affirming, since much attachment takes various forms of enmeshment or entanglement. What can be said is that selfhood seeks objects through which it can come to life and define itself. This is its absolute impulse and eternal requirement.

Thirdly, I must acknowledge that the **object alone** is determinative for Kernberg with the subject at best an appendage. While it is true that the Freudian subject is also severely limited, even truncated, the Freudian drive at least gives the object a meaning which corresponds to the drive being released. In other words, a subject can direct energy toward an object, can give a limited "shape" to the object. For Kernberg on the other hand, the object determines the subject. The operations of the self are at the mercy of the legacy of objects it has known. Such a self can never be free.

Finally, Kernberg's self knows only a limited range of objects. It knows not the social or cultural objects which also give shape to its identity, nor does it know a universal Object toward which particular impulses move. Accumulating evidence suggests that the Object-Relational School is unable to move beyond the role of parental objects for defining selfhood.

One further point needs restating. One should remain aware that the ego-self relation question has not disappeared, with this dilemma particularly evident in Kernberg. He cannot decide whether the self is a subordinate element within the ego, a supraordinate structure beyond the ego with its roots in ego development, or both. These difficulties remain with us and await resolution.

In Kernberg I have charted the first major psychoanalytic effort at taking seriously both the biological substrate of human identity together with the object-relational dynamics through which selfhood is built. While his efforts are by no means a "failure", many ambiguities remain. Kernberg brings us to the doorstep of the final major contributor to contemporary models of selfhood, Heinz Kohut. His efforts are another noteworthy attempt to chart a dynamic model of self.

HEINZ KOHUT

In Heinz Kohut we arrive at an explicitly-named "psychology of the self", which Kohut claims is still in complimentarity with the mainstream of psychoanalytic thought. This perception is not shared by many within the psychoanalytic movement even as Kohut's revisions have won a wide following. What I am about to demonstrate is that Kohut signals an even sharper movement toward a **dialectical subject-object self** which is on the one hand a departure from classic drive and ego models, but at the same time a natural continuation of an evolving shift toward a self psychology.

Kohut's psychology of the self did not take instant form. For much of his professional life his working definition of selfhood was only marginally different from those theorists who held selfhood to be little more than the various self-representations or images generated by the individual through the vicissitudes of either drive or relational life. In the later Kohut, however, a clear shift toward self as dynamic process has occurred. I intend to plot these changes with particular attention to Kohut's final theoretical destination.

No evolution of theoretical position can be divorced from the methodological framework which guides the collection of data. For Kohut this methodological framework took a distinct turn away from Freud's **"objective"** observations of autonomous drive operations, toward the **subjective** processes active in both patient and analyst. This more subjective approach is marked by three commitments as Kohut sees it:

> the commitment to the definition of the psychological field as the aspect of reality that is accessible via introspection and empathy; the commitment to a methodology of the observer's long-term empathic immersion in the psychological field ... and the commitment to the formulation of constructions in terms that are in harmony with the introspective - empathic approach. Stated in everyday language: I am trying to observe and explain inner experience - including the experience of objects, of the self, and of their various relationships.[51]

Kohut's methodology looks not only to the interior data which comes from personal introspection, but values the data generated through vicarious entry into the life of another via **empathy**. It is immediately obvious that this perspective assumes a dynamic link between observing subject and object, a link not found in earlier formulations. How did this methodological shift impact Kohut's evolving theories?

The departure from the classic scientific models of detached observation made Kohut less likely to rely upon mechanical and objective constructs for describing human dynamics. Freud's more "objective" observations had a natural affinity with biological and chemical metaphors leading to what we have come to know as drives and their operations. For Kohut, subject and object are interwoven which suggests that relational metaphors will predominate. The primary factor governing psychic life has become relatedness, with the **quality of relationship** between self and objects determining selfhood, not the tension arising out of body-based demands. This major methodological adjustment put Kohut at odds not only with American psychoanalytic thought and its emphasis on ego/drive dynamics, it also put him at odds with elements in the British School for whom the seeking of the object itself was primary without much regard to the quality of that seeking. With this shift in methodology toward subjective process **as it is shaped by otherness**, it becomes inevitable that a revised model of selfhood will emerge.

The Self Reframed

One of the frustrations encountered when attempting to place Kohut on the psychoanalytic map is that he discounts and even denies any direct continuity or indebtedness to prior psychoanalytic developments. In claiming to have developed a full "self psychology", Kohut tends to highlight the differences rather than the continuity with those who preceeded him. Kohut's sense of the evolution of psychoanalytic thought is that it has made major leaps from **Id Psychology** to **Ego Psychology** to **Self Psychology** with Kohut seemingly the primary spokesperson of the latter development.[52] Not only does this deny the broadly based shift toward object-relations theory and self-psychology which has evolved throughout the psychoanalytic movement, it obscures the similarities one finds between Kohut and particular elements of the American School, not to speak of the close parallels between his ideas and those of Fairbairn and Winnicott, for example.

Be that as it may, the early Kohut (prior to 1971) sounds like most American Object-Relations theorists for whom the self is simply a composite of the accumulated images which reflect the identifications occurring within the psyche. Even so, the early Kohut gives this self "structural" status:

> The self, however, emerges in the psychoanalytic situation and is conceptualized, in the mode of a comparatively low level, i.e. comparatively experience - near, psychoanalytic abstraction, as a content of the mental apparatus. While it is thus not an agency of the mind, it is a structure within the mind since (a) it is cathected with instinctual energy and (b) it has continuity in time, i.e. it is enduring.[53]

In seeing the self in structural terms Kohut is careful not to regard it as a fourth element within the psyche alongside id, ego, and superego, but as the imaginal by-product of the operations of the psyche as a whole. It is a legitimate structural entity even though it has no functional capacity of its own. It remains subordinate to id, ego, and superego processes.

By 1977, however, a shift has occurred with the self no longer a static by-product of activity occurring elsewhere, but itself having become an active, organizing agent. It has thus moved from being a subordinate representation to a supraordinate configuration with its own "center of initiative" and ability to receive impressions.[54] For as long as the self is only a by-product of interactions occurring between an individual and the object world, Kohut's self remains completely in step with the representational model of the self we have seen in Hartmann, Jacobson, and Mahler. However, once the self is given its own functional responsibilities, a completely revamped model emerges. No longer is the system driven by an energy source residing elsewhere, but the self now guides and directs its own operations. How did this shift come about?

The Operational Self

In spite of his claims to the contrary, Kohut places **relationships, not drives**, at the heart of the constellation of selfhood. Relationships, as Kohut understands them, are important not for their own sake, but for the quality of experience they provide for the emerging subject. The object is important for its unique qualities, not simply because a subject needs objects. In Fairbairn, as we recall, the object was sought simply out of the need for objects. In Kohut, we find objects used in a very precise way by the self system.

If one keeps in mind Kohut's empathic/intersubjective methodology it should not surprise anyone to discover that he assumes an empathic, sensitive environment to be essential for self-emergence. Just as a child needs oxygen and food to survive physically, so too does it need an empathic and responsive human environment if it is to survive psychologically. There is nothing particularly new in this position, having encountered it previously in Hartmann's "average expectable environment" or Winnicott's "good-enough mother." What is new is Kohut's understanding of how the emerging self works with the psychological material made available to it by the environment. These vital processes Kohut describes using the concepts (1) selfobjects, (2) transmuting internalization, and (3) the self-selfobject relationship, to which we now turn.

The Nature of Selfobjects

For Kohut every human being begins life in undifferentiated unity with the psychological environment, with what Kohut calls one's selfobjects. A selfobject is not an inherited entity but an object which is experienced as part of one's self.

Selfobjects are those others with whom an individual is merged, but in such a way that they provide cohesion of experience and are used by the self to maintain homeostatic balance. They are dynamic entities which are active within the psyche throughout life. This use of the term selfobject to describe both early developmental dynamics and life-long operations created sufficient confusion that Kohut was forced to make a distinction between he calls their **general** and **specific** characteristics.

By selfobject in a **general** sense, Kohut refers to that dimension of our experience of another person which relates to this person's functions in shoring up our self, while a **specific** selfobject refers to "an **archaic selfobject**" - which relates to the beginning stages of the development of selfobjects.[55] The tension Kohut is hoping to resolve is how selfobjects can be both rudimentary building-blocks of the self and a key dynamic phenomenon throughout the life cycle. Kohut resolves the dilemma by insisting that self-selfobject relationships are present throughout life - that a healthy self needs the nurturing response of selfobjects from the first to the last breath of life. The shape of selfobjects and their effectiveness may change, but not the fact that they are used by one's self system.

Selfobjects thus form the moment-to-moment building blocks of identity, just as they function as an overarching dynamic process. The general pattern cannot be divorced from its specific manifestations along the life cycle. These building-blocks are connected "in depth", claims Kohut, with the maturely-chosen selfobjects of adulthood unconsciously linked to all preceding selfobject experiences. Given the importance of these entities how then do they operate during the life cycle?

Kohut acknowledges that life brings inevitable frustrations and trauma with it, not simply environmentally determined, but also the product of internal givens such as the assertiveness drive, for instance. In early life a child needs selfobjects with whom to merge in order to draw upon the selfobjects' more highly developed and mature psychic organization. The child essentially uses the selfobject as a **bridge** to unite the polarities and tensions of its existence and in so doing its own self-regulating bridge is being built. The child "takes-in" the feeling states of the selfobject which are transmitted to the child via touch or vocal means and these are taken-in as if they are his or her own.[56] The selfobjects' soothing and emphatic capacity is directly related to the self's ability to do the same for itself. Defects in the self are the direct result of empathy failures in selfobjects as far as Kohut is concerned. Physical deprivation is not the primary issue here but the selfobjects' capacity to respond "with a full range of undistorted empathic responses."[57]

Even in later life the necessity for empathic response from selfobjects persists:

> In the view of self psychology, man lives in a matrix of self-objects from birth to death. He needs selfobjects for his psychological survival, just as he needs oxygen in his environment throughout his life for physical survival ... But so long as he feels that he is surrounded by selfobjects and feels reassured by their presence - either by their direct responses to him or, on the basis of past experiences, via his confidence in their lasting concern - even conflict, failure and defeat will not destroy his self, however great his suffering may be.[58]

It is all fine and good to draw upon a model of internalized otherness to represent the building blocks of selfhood, but as of yet I have not clarified **how** this process works, nor **why** selfobjects do what they do. To uncover this process more fully Kohut proposes a second dynamic central to selfhood, namely the capacity for transmuting internalization.

Transmuting Internalization

Every human being builds his/her own self structure through the process Kohut calls "transmuting internalization".[59] This critical developmental phenomenon refers to the gradual or sudden **letting-go** of the functions performed by archaic or mature selfobjects and a **taking-over** of these functions by the self-system.[60] As these functions are internalized by the individual they create the stable structures and dynamics which allow for **identity** and the **capacity for initiative**, the two hallmarks of selfhood for Kohut. Kohut uses the analogy of digestion to describe the process:

> When you swallow the molecules of albumin, of protein, you swallow foreign proteins. As you digest it, it becomes broken up into the molecular constituents, and then it becomes rearranged in terms of your own protein. Beef protein or egg protein, when chewed and digested become human protein. They don't remain beef and egg protein. Still, you need protein in order to form

protein. It gets broken down into bits and then rearranged to your
own patterns.[61]

This rearranging of bits and pieces of psychological material in the metabolizing of
one's selfhood Kohut divides into three phases.

Transmuting internalization begins with the receptivity for particular
introjects, meaning the capacity to experience merger with a variety of selfobjects.
Secondly, there must be a "breaking up" of the internalized objects through optimal
frustration which separates the object into distinct portions. The letting-go quality
of this phase Kohut compares to the work of mourning. Thirdly, as the formerly
global or undifferentiated selfobject is broken up into its particular features the
smaller "bits" of the selfobject are transformed (via transmuted or 'converted'
image) into the functions and structures which make up the self. The identifications
which occur within a self are not with uniform selfobjects but with their fragmented
portions even as their operations are transformed into the operations and structures
of the self.[62]

The actions of the two phases described thus far, (1) **selfobjects** and (2)
transmuting internalization, together constitute the third portion of Kohut's
dialectic of selfhood namely, (3) **the self-selfobject relationship**. The
empathic or non-empathic quality of selfobject experience is transformed
(transmuted) into the very structures and operations of the self. The relationship
between transmuting self and selfobjects constitutes the critical third factor. In
other words, the actions of selfobjects and their transmuting internalization make up
what Kohut calls the self-selfobject relationship.

The Self-Selfobject Relationship

In moving to the third factor of selfhood Kohut is attempting to move
beyond the position that selfhood is nothing more than the introjection of selfobjects
and the borrowing of psychodynamic patterns from another. This would have left
Kohut with simply a more sophisticated version of Freud's ego which remained an
uncertain rider on the loosely bridled horse of the id. **Kohut's model is
attempting to bring the self into dialectic encounter with itself -**

through the phenomena of selfobjects and transmuting internalization the self is coming into relationship with itself.

There are two approaches to the psyche which bring Kohut to this conclusion. On the one hand he attempts to determine the role of the other in maintaining the cohesion and harmony of the self, in other words the role of the **selfobject**. On the other hand, Kohut looks at psychic life in terms of how we **seek** the other (not just how we **use** the other), and how the other becomes a target for our rage and aggression when our path to the other is blocked.[63] In a striking comment, Kohut goes so far as to suggest that we do not just seek the object in order to construct our selfhood through it, but what we seek is the experience of a "you" as object.[64] Lo and behold, Kohut seems to be saying that our seeking is a seeking for **another conscious self through which we will be recognized** (Hegel). Or said another way, our self is that dynamic relating of itself to itself as it relates to another (Kierkegaard).

Kohut's point is that a psychoanalytic psychology of the self cannot simply be concerned with the self's desiring of **objects** but must describe the nuances of the self's desire for **selfobjects**. Within Freud's original libidinal theory, narcissism was to be replaced by object love as development moved from infantile dependence to autonomy. In a direct challenge to this psychoanalytic position which found its culmination in Mahler, Kohut insists that it is impossible to move from symbiotic merger to autonomy, just as it is erroneous to assume that selfobjects are replaced by love objects, or that narcissism shifts to object love. For Kohut development can only be fully understood from the vantage point of the changes in relationship between self and selfobjects.

The traditional understanding of psychopathology is also turned on its head with this self-selfobject frame of reference. Kohut makes the claim that all psychopathology is based upon disturbances of self-selfobject relationships arising in childhood. All conflicts, whether object or drive related, including even the great Oedipal conflict are not the primary **cause** of psychopathology for Kohut, but its **result**. No wonder controversy has swirled around Kohut. If this self-selfobject relationship is so important for Kohut how does he envision its operations?

There are two basic forms which self-selfobject relationships take, though both derive from a common narcissistic root, the heart of psychic life for Kohut. Narcissism, as we recall, is the libidinal investment in the self, or one might say

the self's seeking of itself. Kohut's developmental model assumes two interwoven paths, the path from infantile to mature narcissism, and from infantile object awareness to mature object love; the traditional psychoanalytic perspective holds to a single thread approach in which narcissism is transformed and replaced by object love. In Kohut, narcissism - as the vicissitudes of self-selfobject relationship - is not left behind, but determines the very life and health of the self.

As indicated, there are two components to the self-selfobject relationship for Kohut, each serving as a stackpole around which a self will become organized. The first type of relationship sought is of the omnipotent, grandiose type in which the emerging self seeks confirmation of its inflated and global sense of itself.[65] These sublime self images (I am wonderful) must be legitimized by mirroring selfobjects who in essence echo or reflect back the admiration needed.

The second type of self-selfobject relationship is the seeking of an idealized selfobject with which the self can merge. In order for selfhood to (e)merge it must first have merged with the idealized other (You are wonderful and I belong to you). These two poles of (1) being admired by, and (2) being in-union-with the admired other form the nodules around which self becomes organized. Kohut elaborates:

> I have in mind the specific interactions of the child and his self objects through which, in countless repetitions, the selfobjects empathically respond to certain potentialities of the child (aspects of the grandiose self he exhibits, aspects of the idealized image he admires, different innate talents he employs to mediate creatively between ambitions and ideals), but not to others. This is the most important way by which the child's innate potentialities are selectively nourished or thwarted.[66]

This double process establishes a core or **"nuclear self"** structured along bi-polar lines.

The nuclear self, says Kohut, "is the basis for our sense of being an independent center of initiative and perception, integrated with our most central ambitions and ideals".[67] It is this structure which allows our body and mind to form a "unit in space" and a "continuum in time." This nuclear self is organized as noted around the two poles of (1) nuclear or core grandiosity with corresponding mirroring by selfobjects, and (2) identification or merger with the idealized selfobjects. Through **transmuting internalization** these experiences are broken down and digested thereby forming a cohesive self with **ambitions** at one pole and **ideals** at another.

Given the bi-polarity of the self Kohut attempts to explain how these two poles come to the cohesion and singularity of purposes necessary for a nuclear self. The labels Kohut uses to address this question he calls **Guilty Man** and **Tragic Man** respectively.[68] Guilty man represents the culmination of Freudian humanity which struggles to maintain its integrity in the face of the largely uncontrollable cauldron of energy we have come to know as Id forces. Guilty Man is always falling short in his/her management of the sexual and destructive impulses giving rise to the psychoneuroses. Kohut is not suggesting that self psychology does away with Guilty Man but that other forces beyond impulse control derail the self.

The "deeper" layer of conflict represented by **Tragic Man** is manifested in what Kohut calls the fragmented self, (visible in schizophrenic to narcissistic disorders), and in the depleted self (visible in empty depression). Tragic Man is a disorder of the nuclear self in which the self's bi-polar building blocks of **ambitions** and **ideals** are thwarted. Between these two poles stretches what Kohut calls the "tension arc" which is the center of initiative of Tragic Man. This **tension arc** acts as the unifying element of Kohut's bi-polar self.

> This tension arc is the dynamic essence of the complete, nondefective self; it is a conceptualization of the structure whose establishment makes possible a creative-productive, fulfilling life.[69]

If this tension arc is so very basic to health and wholeness we would do well to pause and understand its workings with greater clarity.

Regrettably, Kohut is not much help in explaining so vital a notion as a dynamic process unifying the poles of selfhood. What can be gleaned from Kohut's indirect reflections on the tension arc is that a self must attempt to unify or bring to cohesion its two poles of **ambition** and **ideal**, in such a way that the self **becomes a center of initiative**.[70] The tension arc facilitates this coalescing of purposes; it gives the self a sense of intentionality, direction, and fulfillment by virtue of the reconciliation it maintains between ambition and ideal.

It is regrettable that Kohut's labels for the two poles of selfhood (ambition and ideal) both have a one-sidedly narcissistic and an idealistic, other-worldly quality about them. If Kohut is implying that these two poles have to do with the seeking of (1) a mirror **capable** of reflecting the self's capacities back to itself, and (2) an otherness **worthy** of being reflected through the strivings of the self then it would bring him remarkably close to the conclusions of Hegel and Kierkegaard. This would allow one to conclude that through **ambition** a self seeks a congruent target able to mirror or confirm its capacities, just as through **ideal** it attempts to unify with a worthy otherness which calls it to further development. The tension arc, then, represents the capacity of Kohut's self to steer between these possibilities.

My conclusion that Kohut has found a self which relates itself to itself and in so doing transcends itself, is seemingly confirmed by his suggestion that there is a meaningfulness to the self beyond its here and now existence.

> It may ultimately be, not in the content of the nuclear self, but the unchanging specificity of the self-expressive, creative tensions that point toward the future - which tells us that our transient individuality also possesses a significance that extends beyond the borders of our life.[71]

For a fleeting instant Kohut almost seems willing to grant the self the status of spirit i.e. the meaningful and intentional unfolding of self. Since one never hears of the possibility again one must assume that Kohut chose not to pursue the matter any further.

The Adequacy of Self Psychology

I must remind the reader that my purpose is not to evaluate Kohut from a psychoanalytic vantage point. The in-house conflicts which preoccupy the psychoanalytic movement are of no concern to me other than as windows through which I see evolving a model of self as dynamic construct. In Kohut, I would suggest, we have gained a breakthrough into a fully dialectic self along the lines envisioned by Hegel and Kierkegaard. While Kohut seems unable to appreciate the particular meaningfulness of what he has concluded, his model comes closest to naming a paradigm within which the movements of self are visible.

Through the use of the tripartite processes of (1) selfobjects; (2) transmuting internalization and (3) self-selfobject relationships, Kohut has given us a language and mechanism to describe the inner workings of the self in dialectic encounter with itself. In the empirical phenomenon of selfobjects we have available to us a framework for understanding the vicissitudes of seeking and merger. This now allows us to describe the processes whereby selfhood seeks otherness in order to provide cohesion and structure for itself. Whether the two poles of grandiosity (ambition) and idealization (ideal) are sufficiently comprehensive to describe the varieties of seeking remains an open question.

Furthermore, Kohut's process of transmuting internalization powerfully illustrates the necessity of engaging and taking-in otherness vital for the building of selfhood. This is not a simple act of coming to recognize something as different (as encountered in the separation-individuation phase of ego development), but rather a dialectic process of engaging and taking-in. A self transmutes/converts the raw materials of its selfobjects into the very essence of its life and identity. Its own uniqueness causes it to respond to the particular qualities of its selfobjects by absorbing some and expelling others. In this fashion a self aligns itself with welcome components as it expels others. However, even the discarded portions continue to impact to the larger system as any clinician knows. As a matter of fact, much of the story of a self's journey toward healing involves the recovery of split-off, non-metabolized elements of itself which it needs to embrace. These are the transformations by which selfhood is built and which form the basis of its freedom.

In the self-selfobject relationship, then, I find Kohut's version of the famous Kierkegaardian synthesizing self. This self comes to itself as it relates itself to another. Through the eternal process of merger - negation - embrace, an orchestration is accomplished. This process is not without dissonance, as a matter of fact, it requires dissonance to come to the fullness of which it is capable.

Serious questions nevertheless remain with Kohut's self. To begin with, Kohut seems to work primarily from a restrictive meaning of selfobjects. He does acknowledge via his definitions of **specific** (archaic) vs. **general** selfobjects that they have particular (early life) and universal (life-long) features. In spite of this provision, I am consistently left with the impression that Kohut can only rely upon archaic selfobjects. Kohut obviously allows for maternal selfobjects, even paternal selfobjects, but rarely if ever sibling selfobjects, social/aesthetic selfobjects, cultural selfobjects, and by no means an encompassing or ultimate selfobject. How is it that archaic selfobjects can help maintain homeostatic equilibrium for a self as they recede further and further into a hazy past? To say that the transmuting internalization has already incorporated selfobject material into the self system only explains the fact that a self has gained a certain structural consistency. However, a self which is fed only by archaeological transfusions of empathy is dead and cannot become a center of initiative. True intentionality demands a seeking of something beyond itself, namely, **its very own self**.

There is an eternal need for a self to mirror itself which Kohut clearly acknowledges. But not every selfobject is adequate for mirroring or metabolization purposes. A self requires here and now experiences of mirroring and acknowledgment, which is why the empathetic context of the therapeutic process is so vital for fragmented selfhood. However, even such corrective experiences will be limited if there is not an on-going transmutation, namely, the internalized capacity of the self to encounter itself and find self-nurture and self-engagement even as it seeks more enabling selfobjects which help move it along the developmental path.

A further problematic feature of Kohut's system is that the breakdown of the self is largely due to environmental failure. His self is **intrinsically healthy** with conflict not an inevitable feature of the developmental process. To be sure, Kohut recognizes the importance of optimum frustration as necessary to set in motion transmuting internalization, but I am left with the growing impression that self-emergence is an **inevitable occurrence** when all the conditions are correct. The distance Kohut has placed between himself and Freudian drive determinism is perhaps responsible for this inclination.

Finally, Kohut may need to be critiqued for the narrowness of the narcissistic lens through which he envisions the self's development. The validity of the critique depends upon the meaning and comprehensiveness Kohut gives to the concept of narcissism. If narcissism is used in the broad sense as the self's seeking of itself it becomes less problematic than if it refers to the need for grandiose mirroring. Kohut's insistence that narcissism itself must develop from archaic to mature forms may remove the difficulty particularly if we remember that it is the **recognition** by another self-conscious self that is the issue (Hegel). To have infantile grandiosity mirrored at early stages of development is certainly appropriate, but not necessarily in other phases. Kohut is vague in his depiction of the transformation which must occur within narcissism even when defined as self-love or the self's desire for itself. All Kohut seems able to say is that mature

334

narcissism expresses itself through healthy ambition and ideals. One is left with a haunting suspicion that this is a self turned in on itself, one which is not able to die to itself for the sake of the other. There is even the sense that Kohut's mature narcissism "chews up" otherness, in other words, it metabolizes itself through the selfobjects it of necessity absorbs, but does not in turn let-be. In denying the autonomy which must also accompany selfhood Kohut may be collapsing the freedom necessary for self and object to come to the fullness of their very own selves.

In Kohut my survey of the psychoanalytic search for the self has come to an exciting conclusion. The mechanisms of self-formation intuited almost 200 years earlier by Hegel and Kiekegaard have been recast in the 20th Century language of psychodynamics. The fact that the psychoanalytic paradigm can see the mechanism only, without grasping its larger meaning need not be of great concern to us. The psychoanalytic task has been to unravel human brokenness and entanglements in all its depth and pathos. This is its primary mandate and for this reason it will remain an indispensable tool for us.

Nevertheless, the deepest yearning of the human self cannot be reduced to its infantile roots, just as the search for the fullness of selfhood cannot be divorced from its archaic foundation. Other psychological paradigms have evolved in the 20th century to attempt to chart the movement of the self beyond its infantile beginnings, and for this further development we must direct our attention at perhaps the greatest systematizer of the seeking self: Carl Jung.

1.   Rubin and Gertrude Blank, *Beyond Ego Psychology*, (New York: Columbia University Press, 1986), p. 5

2.   Heinz Hartmann, *Ego Psychology and the Problem of Adaptation*, (New York: International Universities Press, Inc., 1958), p. 23-24

3.   Ibid., p. 27

4.   Ibid., p. 35. See also Heinz Hartmann, Ernest Kris, and Rudolf Loewenstein, *Papers on Psychoanalytic Psychology*, (New York: International Universities Press, 1964). p. 37

5.   Hartmann, 1964, p. 30

335

6. Ibid., p. 31, 32 *Italics mine

7. Hartmann, 1958, p. 39 *Italics mine

8. Hartmann, 1964, p. 33

9. Hartmann, 1964, p. 291 *(Italics mine)

10. Hartmann, 1964, p. 127

11. Greenberg and Mitchell, 1983, p. 300

12. Hartmann, 1958, p. 51

13. Edith Jacobson, *The Self and the Object World*, (New York: International Universities Press, Inc., 1964), p. 6 (footnote).

14. Edith Jacobson, *Psychotic Conflict and Reality* (New York: International Universities Press, Inc., 1967). See also Edith Jacobson, *Depression: Comparative Studies of Norman Neurotic, and Psychotic Conditions*, (New York: International University Press, Inc., 1971).

15. Jacobson, 1964, p. 56

16. These "stages" paraphrase Jacobson, 1964, p. 52-54

17. Ibid., p. 28, 29

18. Ibid., p. 45, 46

19. Ibid., p. 63

20. Ibid., p. 64

21. Jacobson, 1964, p. 69

22. Margaret Mahler, Fred Pine, Anni Bergman, *The Psychological Birth of the Human Infant*, (New York: Basic Books, Ind., Publishers, 1975), p. 41

23. Margaret Mahler and John B. McDevitt, *"Thoughts on the Emergence of the Sense of Self, with particular emphasis on the Body Self,"* Journal of the American Psychoanalytic Association, Vol. 30, 1982, No. 4. p. 827-848. This puts her in direct conflict with Fairbairn and Winnicott.

24. Rubin and Gertrud Blank, *Beyond Ego Psychology*, (New York: Columbia University Press, 1986), p. 13

25.   Mahler, Pine, and Bergman, 1975, p. 44-45

26.   Greenberg and Mitchell, 1983, p. 281

27.   Cited in Mahler, 1975, p. 9-10

28.   Ibid., p. 10

29.   Ibid., p. 69

30.   Ibid., p. 65

31.   Ibid., p. 76

32.   Ibid., p. 76

33.   Ibid., p. 77

34.   Ibid., p. 109

35.   Ibid., p. 110

36.   Margaret Mahler, *"On the First Three Subphases of the Separation-Individuation Process*, International Journal of Psychoanalysis, 1972, Vol. 53, p. 333-338

37.   Harold P.Blum *"Theories of the Self and Psychoanalytic Theory,"* Journal of the American Psychoanalytic Association, 1982, 30, p. 959-978
       Leo Rangell, *"The Self in Psychoanalytic Theory,"* Journal of the American Psychoanalytic Association, 1982, 30, p. 863-891
       Milton Klein and David Tribich, *"Kernberg's Object-Relations Theory: A Critical Evaluation",* International Journal of Psychoanalysis, 1981, 62, p. 27-43

38.   Greenberg and Mitchell, 1983, p. 328

39.   Otto Kernberg, *"Self Ego, Affects and Drives,"* Journal of the American Psychoanalytic Association, 1982, Vol. 30, p. 900

40.   Ibid., p. 911

41.   Ibid., p. 904

42.   Ibid., p. 905

43. Otto Kernberg, *Severe Personality Disorders: Psychotherapeutic Strategies*, (New Haven: Yale University Press, 1984), p. 191

44. Otto Kernberg, *Object Relations Theory and Clinical Psychoanalysis*, (New York: Jason, Aronson Inc., 1976), p. 26

45. Ibid., p. 32

46. Kernberg, 1982, p. 907

47. Ibid., p. 907

48. Ibid., p. 909

49. Greenberg and Mitchell, 1983, p. 339

50. Klein and Tribich, 1981, p. 30

51. Heinz Kohut, *The Restoration of the Self*, (New York: International Universities Press, Inc. 1977), p. xxi-xxii

52. Heinz Kohut, *The Search for the Self*, Vol, I, Edited by Paul H. Ornstein, (New York: International Universities Press, Inc., 1978), p. 91

53. Heinz Kohut, *The Analysis of the Self*, (New York: International Universities Press, Inc., 1971), p. xv

54. Heinz Kohut, *The Restoration of the Self*, (New York: International Universities Press, Inc., 1977), p. 99

55. Heinz Kohut, *How Does Analysis Cure*, Edited by Arnold Goldberg and Paul Stepansky, (Chicago: University of Chicago Press, 1984), p. 49

56. Kohut, 1977, p. 85, 86

57. Ibid., p. 87

58. Heinz Kohut, *Advances in Self Psychology*, Edited by Arnold Goldberg, (New York: International Universities Press, Inc., 1980), p. 478-479

59. Kohut, 1977, p. 86

60. Kohut, 1978, Vol. I, p. 63

61. David M. Moss, *"Narcissism, Empathy and the Fragmentation of Self: An Interview with Heinz Kohut."* Pilgrimage, Vol. 4, No. 1, 1976, p. 34

62. Kohut, 1978, Vol. I, p. 64

63. Kohut, 1984, p. 54

64. Ibid.

65. Kohut, 1977, p. 53

66. Ibid., p. 100

67. Ibid., p. 177

68. Ibid., p. 243

69. Kohut, 1984, p. 4-5

70. Ibid., See pages 4-5, 42-43, 99, and 211 for Kohut's thoughts on the matter.

71. Kohut, 1977, p. 182

CHAPTER X

C.G. JUNG (1875-1961) AND THE TRANSPERSONAL SELF

No attempt at understanding selfhood can claim completion if it ignores the contributions of the analytic school as represented by the work of C.G. Jung. In Jung I have arrived at the final paradigm to be discussed in this study, a paradigm which is often defined by its over-againstness to the Freudian school. In some ways this radical juxtaposition is artificial and maintained for reasons of psychological denominationalism which allows the adherents of one school to dismiss the other, thereby never having to bother looking for a larger unity which might transcend both.

Freud and Jung are themselves responsible for the beginnings of this feud as any student of their relationship is aware. Freud's famous fainting spells in the face of the challenge to his authority is matched only by Jung's intransigence in resisting the central role of infantile experience in the etiology of psychopathology. By all indications Jung must have stopped reading psychoanalytic literature after 1912. Be that as it may, my task at this point is not to simplistically attempt to reconcile these very divergent approaches to the psyche, but to present Jung's efforts at compensating for the archaeological one-sidedness of Freud. In so doing Jung presents us with a framework, language, and model of the psyche which is teleological, one which aims for an encompassing destination. While the content Jung finds within the psyche is unrecognizable in comparison to the Freudian legacy, I will present surprising resemblances to Freud with regard to the dynamic life processes of the self. But first I must set the stage for the Jungian paradigm.

Jung's Philosophical Inheritance

While Jung consistently attempted to distance himself from idle philosophical speculation divorced from experience, his indebtedness to certain systems of thought is readily visible. The largely Platonic thread that runs throughout the Jungian infrastructure can be traced from Heraclitus through Plato to the neo-platonism of Augustine, reemerging in the wide sweep of German Idealism, and finding its most influential form in the 19th Century philosophers of the unconscious, Edward von Hartmann and Carl Gustav Carus. It is beyond my purpose to examine these influences in great detail, although the intensity of their impact upon Jung can be easily demonstrated.

From Heraclitus, Jung appropriated the notion of enantiodromia, a vision of reality which assumes eternal change in the form of the balance of opposites. This seeking of balance permeates the entire Jungian infrastructure with all psychic processes intent upon achieving their innate harmonization. All energy exchanges within the Jungian psyche adhere to this overarching perspective.

As suggested, the primary framework which guides Jungian thought is the Platonic. In Plato Jung found a perspective which insists upon the eternal harmony of reality. This unity manifests itself in the ideal forms or "archetypes" of which all things are copies. These metaphysical models or paradigms **are** reality with all psychic processes reflections or copies of these eternal "ideas."[1] This so-called genetic perspective causes Jung to trace all psychic material to its universal form, its archetypal essence, with every psychic product a manifestation of a primordial unity. The emphasis upon an eternal (trans-historical) unity to psychic life pushes Jung sharply in an opposite direction to Freud for whom the genesis of psychic life remains biologically and historically determined.

Jung credits Augustine for first providing him with the notion of the archetypes, although he fully recognizes their Platonic foundation and further development in Irenaeus, Dionysius the Areopagite, Meister Eckhart, and the Alchemists among others.[2] Jung laments the decline of this metaphysical perspective and its reduction to the one-dimensional processes of thinking and cognition as it occurs through Descartes and the advent of Empiricism. However, Jung's spiritual kinship with German Idealism, most notably Fichte,

Schopenhauer, and Schelling, offered strong validation for his metaphysical position.

The Idealist reaffirmation of the eternal unity of reality became intensively focused for Jung in the philosophy of Edward von Hartmann. Although Leibnitz was among the first to propose the idea of the "Unconscious," it was von Hartmann who further developed the concept in an effort to unify the divergent views of the German Idealists. Von Hartmann's "Unconscious" sought to integrate feeling and reason, matter and spirit, as a neutral but hidden metaphysical "Absolute" which permeates and guides all things. This intentional Unconscious combined Shopenhauer's idea of Universal "Will" with Schelling's notion of "world soul" as living principle, allowing von Hartmann to give all natural processes the sense of purpose and direction one consistently finds in the Jungian teleological psyche.

The Bi-polar Psyche

The Jungian psyche is fundamentally dual or bi-polar and it maintains this duality throughout the structural developments one encounters along its path.[3] No matter how one examines the Jungian psyche it maintains its dual nature as it goes about its life. The divisions one consistently finds in Jung are first of all a polarity between **consciousness** and **unconsciousness**, and secondly, between **matter** and **spirit**. These poles are not dualistically opposed to one another, but are the opposite "forms" which make up a dynamic whole. Psychopathology is the result of their being split asunder in some fashion. How might this bi-polarity compare with Freud?

Although Jung tends to be labeled **monistic** in contrast to Freud who is seen to be **dualistic**, these labels refer primarily to their respective understandings of the forces at work in psychic life - in Jung's case the eternal seeking of "Self" - in Freud's case the inevitable decay of the organism as it is torn apart by its dual instincts of Eros and Thanatos. While Freud and Jung may be dualistic and monistic respectively in terms of the forces at work in psychic life, an interesting shift is visible when one looks at their respective understandings of the psyche's destination. While Jung sees the psyche in dynamic rhythm of opposites, a bi-polar dance seeking unity-with-tension, Freud sees the psyche seeking constancy

(Nirvana Principle or Death Instinct) as a by-product of the biological and chemical forces inherent in bodily life.

The Ego as Seat of Consciousness

Of the many polarities within the Jungian psyche the conscious-unconscious tension is among the most important. Jung's polarity is reminiscent of Freud's early topographic model which divided the psyche into conscious and unconscious components. As a matter of fact, the Jungian ego is also a small island carved out of the churning archtypal sea, not unlike the fragile Freudian ego sitting precariously upon the biologically-driven Id.

Jung defines the ego as the **center of consciousness**, possessing the capacity for maintaining continuity and identity.[4] These capacities are necessary for one to even speak of consciousness, claims Jung. The ego-function always carries a certain content within it which Jung calls the ego-complex. A complex is a rather nebulous Jungian concept due to its presence on the boundary between consciousness and the unconscious. Nevertheless, Jung describes a complex as an emotionally-laden collection of images, a constellation of ideas, feelings, experiences, and universal motifs, all coming together within an individual psyche. All complexes are given an autonomy by Jung which means that they can resist conscious intentions "and come and go as they please."[5]

At first glance it is very confusing to call the seat of consciousness - **the ego** - a complex, since I have just stated that the complex often goes its own way in contrast to the conscious attitude. While Jung seems to allow for a possible splitting of the ego implied by the notion of complexes, it is not the internal tension within the ego which interests him, as much as the ego's tenuous engagement with the infinite unconscious.

Because of its relative insignificance, Jung's ego is always a rather fragile, superficial entity in contrast to the universal psyche within which the ego must find itself. The real action as far as Jung is concerned is between the ego and the vast archetypal currents within which it swims. While personal historical material is not completely insignificant for Jung, if one wishes to discover **real** patterns and processes within the psyche, the ego-self relationship must be analyzed. Since the personal ego is but a small player on the stage of the universal unconscious, we would do well to understand this larger phenomenon before returning to grapple with the ego's relation to the Jungian Self.

The Unconscious and Its Archetypes

In directing my attention to the unconscious I have arrived at the heart of the Jungian paradigm. While grudgingly tipping his hat to Freud's early efforts at naming the hidden currents within human subjectivity, Jung consistently ridicules the nothing-but quality of the Freudian unconscious. Jung chastises Freud for giving the unconscious an exclusively personal quality as the gathering place of repressed and forgotten material only.[6] While the personal components to the unconscious must be acknowledged, Jung sees them as superficial in relationship to the vastness of the unconscious universe he proposes. Jung writes:

> A more or less superficial layer of the unconscious is undoubtably personal. I call it the **personal unconscious**. But this personal unconscious rests upon a deeper layer, which does not derive from personal experience and is not a personal acquisition but is inborn. This deeper layer I call the **collective unconscious**. I have chosen the term "collective" because this part of the unconscious is not individual but universal; in contrast to the personal psyche it has contents and modes of behavior that are more or less the same everywhere and in all individuals. It is in other words, identical in all men and thus constitutes a common psychic substrate of a suprapersonal nature which is present in every one of us.[7]

One is immediately struck by the Platonic flavor of these words, particularly the eternal and non-historical quality of this central core to personhood. But how does this eternal "collective" essence become visible in human existence?

To be sure, this vast unconscious reservoir can be encountered only as it becomes accessible to human consciousness. Even unconscious material must take on a particular form otherwise nothing could be said of it. Just as the content of personal unconscious material becomes visible through what Jung calls the "feeling-toned complexes," the content of the collective unconscious is manifested through the **archetypes**.

The archetypes can be described as collective universal patterns or motifs which are the transcendent source of all psychic products. Jung distinguishes between the **archetypes as-such** which are irrepresentable and numinous, and the **specific archetypal images, symbols,** and **ideas** which manifest a particular form of universal psychic substance. Archetypes are literally pre-existent forms which do **not** develop individually but are inherited.

Since archetypes are both eternal yet somehow present in individual historical existence, it raises the question of their origins and the means by which they touch historical life. Jung explains:

> Archetypes are, by definition, factors and motifs that arrange the psychic elements into certain images, characterized as archetypal, but in such a way that they can be recognized only from the affects they produce. They exist preconsciously, and presumably form the structural dominants of the psyche in general ... As a priori conditioning factors they represent a special psychological instance of the biological "pattern of behavior," which gives all living organisms their specific qualities. Just as the manifestations of this biological ground plan may change in the course of development, so also can those of the archetype. Empirically considered, however, the archetype did not come into existence as a phenomenon of organic life but entered into the picture with life itself.[8]

Jung's answer is clear: the archetypes are eternal forms, untouched by time and space, with only their particular manifestations open to historical adjustment.

Since the matter-spirit tension is the most polar opposite imaginable for Jung, the archetype must reflect the tension arising both out of the demands of **organisity** and the demands of **spirit**. The psyche is energized by its efforts at finding an equilibrium between these opposites, in other words, the very life of the psyche represents the effort of maintaining a balance between the energy flowing between spirit and matter.

Archetypes, then, as entities on the boundary between matter and spirit, mediate one to the other. As a matter of fact it is impossible to speak of archetypes without recognizing their respective "material" and "spirit" poles. But what do these two forces in fact represent?

The Archetype as Instinct

Jungian archtypes operate in the material realm in the form of instincts. We recall that Freud defined a drive or instinct as a demand placed upon an organism for work i.e. the mobilization or activation of a behavioral pattern. Jung's meaning is virtually identical to Freud in its mechanics, although radically different with regard to its intent. Writing in 1919, Jung paraphrases Kant in describing an instinct as an "inner necessity," a recurring pattern of action or reaction not necessarily connected to conscious motivation.[9]

Jung insists that every instinct is intimately linked to the image by which it is represented. Every instinct bears within it its larger contextual pattern. The instinct of an ant must contain all the ingredients of ant, food-source, transport, and interdependent function etc., with no activity occurring if any of the ingredients are missing. This "image" or contextual pattern represents the **meaning** of the instinct.[10] It is its "meaningful pattern" which links an instinct so intimately with the archetypal image by which it is represented.

Jung insists that instinct and archetypal image are of necessity fully interwoven:

> The primordial image [archetype] might suitably be described as the **instinct's perception of itself,** or as the self-portrait of the instinct, in exactly the same way as consciousness is an inward perception of the objective life-process.[11]

Just as **instinct** refers to **patterns of energy** which determine and regulate action or behavior, so does **primordial image** [archetype] refer to the **patterns of perception** through which one recognizes the meaning of the instinct. Jung continues:

> Archtypes are typical modes of apprehensions and wherever we meet with uniform and regularly recurring modes of apprehension we are dealing with an archetype, no matter whether its mythological character is recognized or not.[12]

Archetypes, then, are the gatekeepers of the boundary between instinct and spirit and as gatekeepers they make the one known to the other. However, in order to better understand the varieties of archetypal patterns we must also understand the spirit pole of the archtype.

The Archtype as Spirit

In shifting one's attention to spirit as the "other" pole of psychic reality one must heed Jung's caution not to split spirit from matter as if they are two separate substances. Rather, they must be seen as the two sides of the same coin.

While Jung's variability in usage of the term "spirit" makes it a risky proposition to nail down his "exact" meaning, it can be said with some certainty that spirit represents the factor of **direction** or **purpose**, now seen from the mental/symbolic rather than the material end of the continuum. When these two poles are in harmony the intentionality of matter is in step with the intentionality of spirit. Conversely, when psychic process shifts to one end at the expense of the other, a splitting occurs within the psyche. An individual living out of the instinctive pole of the archetype, for instance, will be unaware of the larger spiritual unities within which he moves, just as someone else might deny instinctive demands, leaving him in an ungrounded or distorted inclination toward spirit.

Jung believes that the spirit's activity follows three principles:

> firstly the principle of spontaneous movement and activity; secondly, the spontaneous capacity to produce images independently of some perception; and thirdly, the autonomous and sovereign manipulation of these images.[13]

Jung admits that the transcendent ring to his description sounds strange to our modern ears, but in the same breath he claims that the reason for this strangeness is that our modern world has incorporated the function of spirit into itself, leaving us foolishly thinking that **we** have created spirit, that it is now in our possession. In reality the opposite is true, insists Jung, with spirit having possession of us. Even as spirit appears to be at the mercy of our manipulations "it binds (our) freedom, just as the physical world does with a thousand chains and becomes an obsessive idee-force."[14] This conclusion seems highly reminiscent of Hegel's **self-certain spirit**.

Jung, along with Hegel, warns us of the dangerous inflation of such a "possession" of spirit. His prophetic rebuke to modernity is that our fantasy of spirit-ownership tempts us to either succumb to an externalization of ourselves through materialism (attachment to external objects), thereby sacrificing our relation to spirit, or that it forces us to extinguish our autonomous spirit, our individuality, by crushing it under the heel of totalitarian existence.

In short, spirit is the archetype active as spontaneous psychic motion. The demands of nature as expressed through instinct are **symbolically integrated** with the freedom of spirit through the archetypes. Spirit moves where it will, but this movement must be reconciled to the givens of matter. This reconciling function is the task of the archetype.

But how are archetypes recognizable? As symbolic patterns operating on the boundary between spirit and matter, conscious and unconscious, how is harmonization accomplished? By what mechanisms do archetypes operate and to what extent can they be classified?

The Archetypes Identified

Any attempt to "classify" the archetypes is a risky proposition since it implies that they have a predictable content by which they can be recognized. This conclusion would be inappropriate since archetypes are numinous and capable of infinite variety and differentiation. To decide therefore how many archetypes there are or in what precise form they occur is futile. What Jung does claim is that general archetypal patterns are recognizable, although individual configurations thereof will be as variable as the persons within which they are contained. "There are", writes Jung, "types of **situations** and types of **figures** that repeat themselves frequently and have a corresponding meaning."[15] These repetitive patterns Jung calls "motifs" or the prevailing archetypal patterns along which the psyche organizes itself.

Archetypes, as "a priori" forms, become visible as patterns of psychic organization universally present within the human family. Jung suggests that there are predominant archetypal clusters which are universally recognizable, the more common of which are the persona, the shadow, the ego, the hero, the Great Mother, the anima and animus, and of course, the Self. While there is a "hierarchy" to the archetypes it is not so much a matter of one being superior to another, but that each archetypal pattern is capable of its own infinite development. An archetype becomes more basic or primary the more universal it becomes i.e. the less it reflects individual variation. A more basic level of archetypal activity would include global expressions of shadow material such as Nazi Germany, for instance, in contrast to secondary or tertiary manifestations of shadow in a particular culture, family, or individual.

I must offer a reminder that particular archetypes are not necessarily "higher" or "lower" than any other, but that different archetypes mediate different dimensions of psychic life. Their hierarchical nature depends upon where on the continuum of universality - individuality the archetype becomes visible. At their ineffable core, what Jung calls the archetype-as-such, they become essentially non-representable and "universal".

Jung claims that human individuation, or the process of attaining one's unique individuality, follows a certain universal path which inevitably passes through particular archetypal forms. Just as a seed carries within it the imprint which will bring the plant to full maturity, so too does the psyche follow a prescribed archetypal path whether the destination is arrived at or not. It is to an analysis of these key archetypal patterns along the path of individuation that I now direct our attention.

The Ego

I have already introduced the "ego" as the archetype of consciousness in my overview of the Jungian paradigm. This allows me to restrict my efforts to the specific task of highlighting the ego's functions and relationship to the psyche at large. As mentioned, the ego (the sum total of consciousness) rests upon a material and spiritual foundation which is essentially unconscious and from which it must carve out its identity i.e. its stability, organization and continuity. The unconscious sea upon which the ego floats contains infinite objects of which the ego is unaware, but which are encountered on its developmental path. The Jungian ego is acquired during one's lifetime and arises "from the collision between the somatic factor and the environment, and once established as a subject, it goes on developing from further collisions with the outer world and the inner."[16] If we stopped here, Jung's position would be in loose agreement with the conclusions of **Ego Psychology** and contemporary **Object Relations Theory**. But this is not Jung's final word.

As vital as this "organ of consciousness" may be, Jung reminds us that the ego is never more than "consciousness": it offers us at most a picture of our current conscious personality with all unknown and unconscious factors missing, not unlike the perverbial iceberg. He insists that our total personality does **not** coincide with the ego, but must be distinguished **from** the ego. In a statement vital to my conclusions Jung proposes the following:

> I have suggested calling the total personality which, though present, cannot be fully known, the self. The ego is, by definition, subordinate to the self and is related to it like a part to the whole.[17]

Jung's distinguishing of ego and self reintroduces the dilemma of the Ego-self relationship we first encountered in Chapter III. In Jung the ego has been bumped from its lofty position to one of subordination to this total personality called "the Self". The Jungian ego is only the **subject** of **consciousness**, while the Self is the **subject** of the **total psyche**.[18] But where does this leave the Jungian ego?

While Jung does give the ego a mediating task on the boundary between the known (consciousness) and the unknown (**unconscious**), he adds a curious limitation to its capacities. He suggests that since the ego is the point of reference for consciousness, it is "the **subject** of all **successful** attempts at **adaptation** so far as these are achieved by the will."[19] The identification of the ego as **organ of adaptation** is familiar to us through Heinz Hartmann's contributions. But to restrict the ego to an organ of "successful" adaptation only is a strange restriction of its capacities. An ego constructed for successful adjustment is a grandiose and narcissistic ego never touched by the inevitable failures and disappointments of life. Such an ego is cut off from the full range of human experience which leaves both psychopathology and wholeness at the mercy of forces beyond the reach of the ego. Jung's ego has become a minor player in the formation and maintenance of human identity. This is the first major limitation I find in Jung.

A consequence of this position is that all "flaws" and all "healing" occurring within the Jungian psyche becomes a-historical, residing in the timeless Self, with unity and equilibrium constructed and guaranteed in non-historical terms. Individual historical existence becomes superfluous, sacrified to the eternal enantiodromic unity, in which the end is determined before its beginning. This self-contained unity of the self within itself which I first described in Fichte will continue to plague our Jungian discoveries.

Nevertheless, one must be careful not to accuse Jung of a complete denial of historicity. The world is very real for Jung even though its autonomy is denied by virtue of the primordial unity Jung imposes upon it. Perhaps the conflict with Freud provides an explanation: to have given the ego the capacity to metabolize the positive and negative aspects of its experience would have given extra weight to Freud's position regarding the integrative operations of the ego. In any event, it is Jung's negation of **personal history** which leaves his framework with limited value when attempting to understand the **historical lesions** of personhood.

The Persona

In turning to the persona or "actors mask" I am identifying another archetypal manifestation of what Jung calls "personality". The persona is "a functional complex that comes into existence for reasons of adaptation or personal convenience," but in such a way that it is often incongruent with one's genuine individuality.[20] The persona is not a thing, but a functional process which shapes personhood in a particular way. It acts as a thick, impermeable membrane between the inner and outer world, by taking an exclusive relation to **external objects**, to the neglect of **interior process**. Jung suggests that the persona is a mask of the collective psyche, one which "**feigns individuality** making others and oneself believe that one is individual, whereas one is simply acting a role through which the collective psyche speaks."[21]

Jung claims that such a form of adaptation is the twisting of individuality to fit the social norm, resulting in an individual with no relatedness to their inner life, with a corresponding inauthentic or hollow relationship to the external world, built upon pure imitation. Since the social role and its required tasks and behaviors give the psyche the "content" it needs to fill itself, it makes these roles the center of its identity. However, says Jung, inherent in the persona is a kernel of the collective psyche which is attempting to individuate, which is why a particular form of persona is chosen.[22] The collapse of a persona often releases an explosion of this collective unconscious material which can overwhelm an undeveloped psyche. The persona, then, represents an archetypal pattern of adaptation in which a psyche shows minimal relatedness to its inner world, thereby leaving it at the mercy of finding itself in the empty content of social imitation.

The persona construct is an obvious modern reformulation of Hegel's **self-alienated spirit** in which the norm of selfhood is the sacrifice of all personal uniqueness at the altar of social adaptation. This hollowness of identity is among the most tragic forms of self-negation for Jung and Hegel. What becomes evident, however, is that the psychoanalytic and Jungian perspectives only consider the opposite sides of this breakdown of personhood. The limitation of the Jungian framework becomes obvious when compared with the depth of the psychoanalytic analysis of historically-based personality disorders. Jung's neglect of the place of historical selfobjects in the evolution of schizoid or narcissistic conditions for example, is matched by the inability of Object Relations perspectives to recognize the larger unities (in this case social imitation) which fills the void left by the renunciation of personal selfobjects.

The Shadow

Jung claims that the most readily discernible archetypes are those which have the most direct and intensive influence upon the ego: these archetypes are the shadow, the anima, and the animus.[23] The shadow is the most accessible of these because its contents in part reside in the personal unconscious. On the other hand, the shadow also represents universal darkness, including those raw archetypal forces which Jung calls "absolute evil."[24]

As the dark aspect of personhood, the shadow must be faced and incorporated in order for individuation to proceed. This task of assimilation is by no means easy, with an inevitable resistance to encountering the unknown aspects of oneself. Resistance takes the form of **projection**, a key mechanism within the Jungian psychic economy. As a matter of fact, the Jungian ego seems to know few mechanisms other than projection (such as introjection, condensation, displacement, etc.), largely because this ego has little energy of its own and is only on the receiving end of action occurring elsewhere. Jung confirms my suspicions when he insists that

> it is not the conscious subject but the unconscious which does the projecting. **Hence one meets with projections, one does not make them.** This effect of projection is to isolate the subject from his environment, since instead of a real relation to it there is

now only an illusory one. Projections change the world into the replica of one's own unknown face.[25]

There is an autonomy to these projective operations of the Jungian psyche which at one level undermines personal responsibility for the dark currents which stir within us. On the other hand, Jung pushes us to recognize universal patterns of darkness which are also part of our nature: without their recognition wholeness would also be impossible.

The true encounter with shadow material is often a shattering experience since it opens one to the full interiority of personhood which has been negated. Once that door is opened the entire expanse of the universal psyche presents itself as "other" which feels overwhelming and foreboding. Jung concludes that

> The meeting with oneself is, at first, the meeting with one's shadow. The shadow is a tight passage, a narrow door, whose painful construction no one is spared who goes down to the deep well ... where ... the soul of everything living begins; where I am indivisibly this **and** that: where I experience the other in myself and the other-than-myself experiences me.[26]

Again the Hegelian and Kierkegaardian claim reverberates: the encounter with otherness becomes the doorway to self-consciousness.

Anima/Animus as Patterns of Mediation

The centrality of the dialectic collision between conscious and unconscious in the Jungian paradigm cannot be overstated. Whatever layer of psychic life is being examined, whether persona, shadow, or anima/animus, each represents an organized pattern of dialectic engagement. In turning to anima/animus operations, one cannot separate their function from those of the persona with which they are in a compensatory relationship. Just as persona represents the mediating capacity between the ego and outside world, so does anima/animus represent the mediation occurring between the ego and the inner world of the unconscious.

Jung uses the word anima in two ways: on the one hand as the psychic factor of inwardness common to both sexes; on the other hand as the contrasexual feminine component in the male psyche, with animus representing the masculine component of the female psyche. Jung says of the first usage:

> The inner personality is the way one behaves in relation to one's inner psychic processes; it is the inner attitude, the characteristic face, that is turned towards the unconscious. I call the outer attitude the outward face, the **persona**: the inner attitude the inward face, I call the **anima**.[27]

This polarity (persona-anima) is again in keeping with Jung's fundamental principle of enantiodromia or the complimentarity of opposites. An anima contains all those qualities which are missing from one's conscious orientation (persona); a conscious attitude of critical harshness for example, will be matched by an anima reflecting pliable indecisiveness.

But this complimentarity goes beyond simple polarization of attitudes to include a primary division of reality along masculine/feminine lines. Masculinity and femininity represent life principles for Jung called **Logos** and **Eros** respectively, with men finding their interior life governed by Eros or Anima, just as a woman's interiority will be determined by her Logos or Animus. Jung elaborates with regard to this second polarity:

> Woman is compensated by a masculine element and therefore her unconscious has, so to speak, a masculine imprint. This results in a considerable psychological difference between men and women, and accordingly I have called the projection-making factor in women the animus which means mind or spirit.[28]

Not only do anima/animus represent generalized feminine or masculine styles of managing interior life, they determine the very nature of being a man or woman. Jung claims that women's consciousness is primarily governed by **Eros** rather than the capacity for discrimination or cognition found in **Logos**. Conversely, in a man the function of **Eros or relatedness** will be less developed than his **rational Logos**. Jung even goes so far as to suggest that in women "Eros is an expression of their true nature, while their Logos is often only a regrettable accident."[29]

While this deterministic sexism is offensive, Jung is quite adamant in insisting that men and women carry such eternal images, not of a particular man or woman, but of the composite feminine and masculine:

> this image is fundamentally unconscious, an hereditary factor of primordial origin engraved in the living organic system of the man, an imprint or "archetype" of all the ancestral experiences of the

female, a deposit, as it were, of all the impressions ever made by woman - in short, an inherited system of psychic adaptation.[30]

A familiar critique surfaces here, not unlike a critique I directed at the Freudian edifice. What concerns me in this pronouncement is the automatic psychological unity Jung imposes into the psyche. As has Freud before him, Jung needs to find a bridge to unify the dualisms he sees within the psyche. In this instance the masculine/feminine division is resolved **genetically** through the eternal anima/animus imprint.[31] Just as is true for Freud who imposes a **biological unity** onto the psyche, Jung's psyche suffers from a **spiritually-guaranteed unity** without genuine connection to life experience. The **real** nature of male and female persons in one's life becomes inconsequential and meaningless, simply blank screens upon whom the unconscious casts its eternally-determined projections.

In reading Jung I am consistently struck by the artificial division of interior objects along pre-set gender lines: one's shadow is **always** encountered as a same-sex individual in dream and fantasy content; anima figures come **only** in feminine form, animus figures **only** in male form, and so on.[32] Jung is forced into these a priori unities by virtue of his Fichtean presuppositions which consistently force him to insert the psyche into unity with itself, regardless of the particular features of an individual's historical life. That the evolution of female interiority (subjectivity) is shaped only along animus lines simply does not square with experience. But do these difficulties invalidate the Jungian paradigm?

My critique of Jung is intended to serve as a reminder of the limits of an exclusively Jungian vantage point, without rejecting his valuable contributions. Just as it was important to resist a simplistic choosing of Hegel over Kierkegaard thereby avoiding the rigors of seeking resolution which transcends both, so too would it be premature to dismiss Jung even as his shortcomings are revealed. But if there is any value in the anima/animus construct, how might it enhance our understanding of selfhood?

The valuable contribution I find in Jung's anima/animus pronouncements centers around his analysis of the process of dialectic encounter with otherness. One must remember that Jung's vantage point is the Absolute i.e. the Unconscious, with masculine and feminine representing two dialectic life-principles contained therein. As yin and yan, light and dark, they divide the human psyche and reveal otherness within it. As contrasexual elements they represent a most primary and encompassing form of otherness, touching the very heart of psychic life.

A clue as to the central role of anima/animus operations is found in Jung's claim that archetypal processes function as "regulators" and "stimulators" of psychic life.[33] They bring about a "synthesis" of conscious and unconscious contents. This implies the rearrangement of psychic material (feelings, attitudes, identifications etc.) based upon the dialectic encounter of inner and outer, conscious and unconscious, masculine and feminine elements.

Archetypal synthesis takes the form of "images", soul-images as Jung calls them, essentially the infinite variety of anima or animus figures representing one's current state of dialectic development.[34] A psyche will make its current state of being known to itself through the anima/animus projections it encounters. These personifications are snapshots of the state of one's interior life, whether good or bad. One's inner attitude thus becomes visible through one's unconscious representations of persons with their corresponding qualities.

Through the synthesizing operations of anima/animus figures the psyche attempts to find a unity and harmony with its inwardness, just as through persona it attempts to harmonize itself toward the outer world. These harmonizing anima/animus operations bring us to the threshold of the seeking of unity with the most encompassing duality of all: The Universal psyche or Self.

The Self: Alpha and Omega of Personhood

The realms of consciousness and the unconscious are not separate entities but part of a compensatory whole Jung calls the Self. The Self is the psychic totality unifying in itself all levels of consciousness and unconsciousness. As the center and circumference of personhood it is the unifying point of all psychic fragments while at the same time transcending mere individuality to represent the fullness of all psychic phenomena. Writing in 1958, Jung says of the Self:

> As an empirical concept, the self designates the whole range of psychic phenomena in man. It expresses the unity of the personality as a whole. But in so far as the total personality, on account of its unconscious component, can be only in part conscious, the concept of the self is in part, only **potentially** empirical and is to that extent

356

> a **postulate**. In other words, it encompasses both the
> experienceable and the inexperienceable (or the not yet experienced)
> ... In so far as psychic totality, consisting of both conscious and
> unconscious contents, is a postulate, it is a **transcendental**
> concept, for it presupposes the existence of unconscious factors on
> empirical grounds and thus characterizes an entity that can be
> described only in part, but for the other part, remains at present
> unknowable and illimitable.[35]

We should not let Jung's insistence upon the Self's numinous quality lure us into thinking that nothing can be said about it. Simply because its boundaries are unknown does not mean that it is removed from experience. Jung gathered voluminous data intending to show that the Self is a concept which grows ever clearer with experience, even if the totality can only be experienced in its parts.[36] Jung is adamant in insisting that the Self is not a circular idea hypostasized into its own existence, but finds recognizable and empirically verifiable form. But how can a reality supposedly straddling the border of the known and unknown, light and dark, masculine and feminine, become visible in recognizable ways?

While the Self-as-such is irrepresentable, it reveals itself through the images of unity it projects, which, claims Jung, can be empirically known. As the supreme **archtype of wholeness** it gives off representations of itself which have become visible throughout human history. The only entity which can carry the inherent polarities of such an encompassing archtype is the symbol. It becomes the empirical window into the numinous reality of the Self.

The Self as Symbol

Jung acknowledges that a wide range of symbols can present themselves as representing the totality of personhood. He even suggests that "anything that a man postulates as being a greater totality than himself can become a symbol of the self."[37] This does not mean that every symbol will have the same adequacy for carrying the totality of the psyche, only that symbolizations of Self will be as varied and fluid as the reality they reflect.

Generally speaking, Jung claims that quaternous and circular symbols best express the wholeness of Self. Throughout human history these mandala constructs have represented the breakthrough into consciousness of the underlying unity of self. One can find countless versions of such indicators of wholeness, but none approach the clarity and power of God-symbols as the supreme archtypal vehicles representing the essence of psychic completion. As a matter of fact, Jung is so bold as to make the Augustinian claim that the essence of psychic wholeness simply cannot be distinguished from the God-images prevailing in human consciousness.

> But as one can never distinguish empirically between a symbol of the self and a God-image, the two ideas however much we try to differentiate them, always appear blended together...[38]

Whether in the form of Paul's "Christ who lives in me", or the dynamics of the Christian Trinity, or the Atman principle, or the Tao of cosmic unity, each represents variations of the symbols of wholeness which break into human consciousness.

Since symbols of the Self cannot be distinguished from God-symbols, an analysis of the operations of God-symbols becomes the primary Jungian data source for understanding Self as the totality of psychic life. Jung examined numerous archetypal reflections of Self in his scientific lifetime by drawing upon a vast and rich resevoir of myth, legend, and religious ideation. Of all the Self archtypes which drew Jung's attention, few seemed to captivate him as did the numinous content of the Christ archtype. Jung claimed that "**Christ exemplifies the archetype of the self**," making it a primary window into the life of the Jungian self.[39]

As far as Jung is concerned, what makes Christ a quintessential model for an analysis of the Self is that the drama of Jesus' life reveals in symbolic form the story of the path of consciousness as it comes to find its higher unity.[40] The Christ story is the story of the ego as it suffers through the vicissitudes of establishing a relationship to its encompassing reality, a process which theology calls incarnation and which Jungian analytic psychology calls individuation.

Again, the overarching principle which frames the entire process is the Jungian bi-polarity of reality. What makes the Christ myth so enduring in Jung's estimation is that it is able to hold psychic polarities in tension even as it brings them into a larger unity. As an archetype of wholeness, the Christ-symbol integrates or bridges all splits inherent in the psyche. Since all opposites must be contained within a living symbol if it is to fulfill its integrating function, the Christ archtype must fully accomplish this conjunction for its power to be maintained. Jung writes: "As an historical personage Christ is unitemporal and unique; as God, universal and eternal. Likewise the self: as the essence of individuality it is unitemporal and unique; as an archetypal symbol it is a God-image and therefore universal and eternal."[41]

What makes Jung's formula so striking is that his quaternity of opposites combines both the Hegelian and Kierkegaardian dialectics: the former highlighting the tension between the One and the many, the latter the tension between the time-bound and the timeless. The Christ archetype thus represents for Jung the coming together of **uniqueness** and **universality**, **chronos** and **kairos**, as the four pillars of the life of the self. Just as Christ's Individuation demanded the dialectic integration of his human individuality with his divine universality, so too must every self come to its own uniqueness even as it embraces its cosmic identity.

But to call Christ the supreme symbol representing the unity- of-opposites maintained by Self says nothing of the operations of such a Self. What is the function of the self-symbol and how does it perform its integrating task?

Jung makes it very clear that the glue which holds the psyche together must have the capacity to "hold" its tensions in a new unity even as it maintains the paradox. Christ as symbol of the Self does not collapse the opposites since that would imply their annihilation, but maintains them as a "conjunction", meaning that they are sustained even as they are reconciled.[42] For instance, Jung sees Christ's crucifixion between two thieves underscoring the inevitability of the ego's crucifixion between irreconcilable opposites, a process vital for gaining a higher increment of consciousness. This necessity is analogous to Kierkegaard's use of Abraham's sacrifice of Isaac to illustrate the same principle.

Not only does the Christ hang between the human and the Divine, his two crucified companions represent warring psychic fragments heading in opposite directions, toward which a conscious relationship must also be established. Even while being crucified, the Self-related ego of Christ is able to accept the polarizations between which it hangs, only to be plunged toward a new threshold of consciousness, namely the full abyss of otherness symbolized by radical God-abandonment. The gulf between the particularity of the ego and universality of the Self is never so agonizingly represented as in the full rupture of their implicit unity.

This rupture must be complete and absolute in order for a new unity to emerge, a unity only brought about by a fully-individuated Self.

The eternal activity of the birthing of new increments of consciousness requires not only the collision of opposites but their reconciliation as actualized by the one suspended between heaven and earth. Christ unifies and reconciles in his own being the ego-Self unity sought by the psyche. The eternal collision, reconciliation, and harmonization between the conscious and the unconscious is reflected in the mediation accomplished by the Christ.

In order to accomplish its mediating mission, a symbol must straddle both sides of the psyche and face the full opposition forced upon it by the opposites. This confrontation is often massively disorienting "to the point where thesis and antithesis negate one another, while the ego is forced to acknowledge its absolute participation in both."[43] If a symbol reflects the reality of one pole more than another or even suppresses one to the advantage of the other, then a "symptom" not a symbol will emerge, claims Jung.

Jung argues that from the unconscious "there now emerges a new content, constellated by thesis and antithesis in equal measure and standing in a **compensatory** relation to both."[44] It must remain "in the middle" and there mediate the conflict. The energy generated by this tension of opposites flows to the mediatory product i.e. reconciling symbol, with both opposites attempting to "win" the symbol function to their side. If in this tug of war one side wins out over the other, then the ego will identify with the winner and organize its conscious life accordingly. For instance, the so-called conflict between sexuality and spirituality can divide the psyche with the ego aligning itself with one over-against the other. This division contributes to the formation of the inferior function, familiar to students of Jungian typology.

However, if an ego can maintain the tension without allowing either pole to overwhelm the other, then the mediating product becomes a new organizing center drawing energy from both prior elements. One may be wondering at this point which predominates, an intact, stable ego, or the mediatory process which unifies the elements of consciousness. Jung's reply is that

> The stability of the ego and the superiority of the mediatory product
> to both thesis and antithesis are to my mind correlates each
> conditioning the other ... In reality it may be that the stability of the

360

one and the superior power of the other are two sides of the same coin.[45]

Jung's point is that an ego finds its stability, is built one might say, by the very mediation accomplished through the self-symbols. The mediatory product i.e. the living symbol, draws from the thesis and antithesis alive in the psyche and in so doing builds a new attitude which overcomes the earlier divisions. The mediating capacity thus becomes **a new third, a synthesis**, which integrates the prior elements and allows the energy of the opposites to flow in a common channel. In overcoming the stalemate of unresolved tensions new directions emerge and new energies are released. This vital mediating process Jung calls the **transcendent function**, a function at the heart of the life of the Self.

The Self As Transcendent Function

It is surprising to discover that a process so central to the life of personhood as the transcendent function is given such sparse treatment by most Jungian interpreters although Jung's uncertain development of the function is undoubtedly a factor.[46] Nevertheless, no other concept seems as vital to Jung's vision of the dynamic operations of Self as this process. While there is nothing particularly new in Jung's use of this term as far as its content is concerned, it provides the clearest Jungian understanding of Self as dynamic activity living out a recognizable dialectic pattern.

As one might expect, the collision between consciousness and the unconscious provides the impetus which drives the transcendent function.

> This function of mediation between the opposites I have termed the **transcendent function**, by which I mean nothing mysterious, but merely a combined function of conscious and unconscious elements.[47]

Simply put, the transcendent function bridges the gulf between consciousness and unconsciousness and in so doing brings about the emergence of a new perspective and direction for the psyche.

Jung's use of the term "transcendent" to describe this process is not intended to suggest some unknown metaphysical factor at work; rather, the function facilitates the transition from one "attitude" to another.[48] As a "synthetic" process it takes the thesis and antithesis opposites within the psyche and weaves them into a new third. This synthesizing activity crystalizes the personality, producing "a new attitude to the world" which allows the psyche to move in new directions.[49] It is this very reorientation of attitude toward inner and outer world which Jung attributes to the transcendent function.

The eternal clash of opposites within psychic life seeks a **unifying third** which can transcend the state of tension. Symbol-formation as discussed earlier serves as the primary means of bridging this gap. Because the Jungian psyche is a self-regulating mechanism, the unconscious already contains within itself the archtypal images which can unify the waring elements. These reconciling images must be personally appropriated, not simply in a one-dimensional, intellectual way, but within life experience. Jung claims that an individual must be "grabbed" by an archtype, acting as an autonomous force not subject to conscious control. If the reconciling symbol were the creation of the ego it would simply reinforce the prevailing conscious attitude, and no transcending of the developmental log-jam would occur. As unconscious archtypal content breaks into awareness it releases the healing power of compensation and provides the psyche with a new transpersonal control-point which centers the personality in a new way.

Jung describes the transformed attitude which holds the earlier tension of opposition as a **new birth**. This process of rebirthing contains two phases which pass into one another and in so doing synthesize the "new" third. This dialectic process is identical as far as Jung is concerned with Meister Eckhart's visions of the rebirthing of God and human self as two sides of one coin. Eckhart's "flowing out" of God, interprets Jung,

> is an act of conscious differentiation from the unconscious **dynamis**, a separation of the ego as subject from God (=**dynamis**) as object. By this act God "becomes". But when the "breakthrough" abolishes this separation by cutting the ego off from the world, and the ego again becomes identical with the unconscious **dynamis**, God disappears as an object and dwindles into a subject which is no longer distinguishable from the ego. In other words the ego, as a late product of differentiation, is reunited with the dynamic All-oneness.[50]

This re-unification of the ego with its primordial Oneness brings about the release of energy and re-direction of psychic purpose characteristic of the transcendent function. Never a once-for-all process this dialectic pattern repeats itself at all levels of psychic life.

Jung makes the claim that the healing of the human psyche requires that one develop an openness to the proactive meaning and purpose inherent in the unconscious and in so doing one paves the way for the process of the transcendent function.[51] When a therapist encounters the fractured psyche of a patient she mediates the transcendent function until it becomes operational for the individual.

Transference, then, takes on a different meaning from Jung's point of view. In Freud, transference becomes the means whereby historical lesions became reactivated in the here and now; in Jung transference acts as the metaphorical expression of the direction the psyche is seeking. For Jung the unconscious relationship taken toward the therapist offers clues as to the direction needed by a psyche in order to come to its harmony - not so much a harmony with its past but with its future direction from which it is blocked. But are there any further details as to the actual process by which the transcendent function operates?

Jung offers no definitive explanation of the workings of this transcending process, but proposes a general two-fold pattern which together forms the transcendent function. These two phases Jung calls (1)"creative formulation" or the **"aesthetic"** capacity on the one hand, and (2) the seeking of "understanding" or **meaning** on the other.[52] What might these processes represent?

First of all, Jung insists upon the necessity of listening to **all** unconscious material emerging from one's psyche, essentially a listening to one's inner dialogue. This material must be externalized in some tangible form via images, thoughts, symbols, fantasies, etc. Without access to one's inner process and its verbal or pictorial representation, the transcendent function cannot operate.

Secondly, the meaning of the unconscious or subliminal product must be determined. This meaning is not measured according to some external yardstick but must always involve a seeking of its value **for the subject**. This determination of value implies that the ego must enter into relationship with the material emerging from below thereby bringing the ego and the unconscious into a new relationship. Jung elaborates:

> This is the second and more important stage of the procedure, the
> bringing together of opposites for the production of a third: the
> transcendent function. At this stage it is no longer the unconscious

that takes the lead, but the ego... It (the ego) is confronted with a psychic product that owes it existence mainly to an unconscious process and is therefore to some degree opposed to the ego and its tendencies.[53]

Out of this tension must emerge a new third which holds the opposites together in a living unity. Jung summarizes:

> The shuttling to and fro of arguments and affects represents the transcendent function of opposites. The confrontation of the two positions generates a tension charged with energy and creates a living, third thing - not a logical stillbirth .... but a movement out of the suspension between opposites, a living birth that leads to a new level of being, a new situation. The transcendent function manifests itself as a quality of conjoined opposites.[54]

In this transcendent function we find the Jungian Self at work - **the progressive uniting of opposites** - a living organism arising out of the clash of any and every polarity.

There is no doubt that the transcendent function represents the essence of Jung's vision of **self as synthesizing process**. It names the Self as a mediating phenomenon reconciling opposites within itself, the eternal unifying of otherness in a transcendent wholeness.

This completes my survey through the maze of representations referred to under the concept "self". With Jung's naming of **self as transcendent process** one could hardly have gained more distance from the **time-and-instinct-bound self** of Freud, never mind the **static self** of a Descartes, or the **hollow self** of a Hume. But simply to have traveled a vast distance does not mean an adequate destination has been reached. Before any effort at a more comprehensive integration can be attempted I must be clear as to the strengths and limits of this Jungian model.

The Adequacy of the Jungian Self

It serves no useful purpose to critique Jung for the simple pleasure of finding "holes" in his system, as if one could then dismiss the entire structure with greater ease. Just as I did not allow myself the easy comfort of choosing Hegel over Kierkegaard, or Kierkegaard over Hegel, so too must one resist the temptation to pronounce the Analytic framework superior or inferior to Psychoanalytic or

Object Relational models. To be sure, we must hold each paradigm accountable for its own internal consistency, but a comprehensive model of the life of self is not served by a quick dismissal of any model.

Perhaps the overriding contribution Jung makes to the dynamics of selfhood is his persistent demonstration of the **intentionality of the psyche**. Not only is the self an agent of purposive psychic motion, it regulates and organizes psychic life into a complex wholeness, in stark contrast to the Freudian theme of decay which eventually annihilates every ego.

Jung has not simply hypostasized a dialectic picture of psychic life but has validated his claims regarding the polar flow to selfhood with large accumulations of experiential data. There is no other explorer of psychic life who has so consistently demonstrated the dialectic flow of the selfhood as has Jung. Whether seen through the bi-polar lens of conscious-unconscious, instinct-spirit, masculine-feminine, or ego-self, the Jungian self **is** that process which mediates these coordinates to one another. But to affirm something as rich in dialectic content does not mean that the fullness of selfhood has been declared. Simply because Jung affirms an eternal clash and reconciliation of opposites does not mean that a true synthesis has been achieved. Upon what basis, then, might the Jungian paradigm be limited?

An analogy may help frame my concern regarding the Jungian model. As I explored the struggle in the eighteenth century between a static, eternal, and reason-driven self of Rene Descartes and the dissociated "hollow" self of David Hume, I noted that the first great attempt at resolution occured through the person and work of Immanuel Kant. Freud, it seems to me, came to serve the twentieth century as a Kantian figure directing us toward a greater ownership of our inwardness and of the material bases of our being. Might it be that if Freud is the Immanuel Kant of the 20th Century, that Jung is its J.G.Fichte?

Just as Kant attempted to resolve the tension between the Rationalists and Empiricists by splitting reality into two separate realms, Freud's dualism attempted to undercut Romanticist spiritualism which imposed a spiritual unity onto the material, bodily realm. In shattering this spiritualized unity, Freud, as had Kant before him, tore spirit from matter sending them into exile one from another. Into this breach first stepped Fichte, and 200 years later, his 20th century equivalent, C.G. Jung. That Jung parallels the efforts and deficiencies we found in Fichte can be established for two reasons: first, because Jungian psychic life is ultimately a-historical, and secondly, because the ego-Self relationship is eternally guaranteed. These two elements remain as my primary challenge to the Jungian edifice.

Regarding my first point of concern, I must offer a reminder of the pervasively compensatory nature of the Jungian psyche. In and of itself the sense of a polarity within the psyche is not the problem. There has been consistent agreement from virtually all paradigms examined, that the integration of bi-polarity fuels psychic life. The problem with the Jungian model is that harmony and balance is automatically guaranteed **and** is obtainable through internally-generated collective images only. **Real** relations with **real** people become secondary to **internal** relations with **internal** contents. This was the very point which had undermined Melanie Klein's approach to the psyche, although in her case all psychic products were reduced to biological and instinct-driven forces.

My second critique suggests that the Jungian self is postulated into unity with itself thereby removing wholeness from the arena of the personal.[55] The ego-Self relationship is resolved with the ego swallowed up by Self in the Jungian psychic economy. The mighty Self imposes its will onto the ego rendering personal autonomy meaningless in the crush of unity guaranteed by the Self. This opens Jung to the charge of inflation he so carefully describes as a possible by-product of the ego-Self relationship. The ego has been taken over by the Almighty Self. I find these suspicions confirmed when as notable a Jungian scholar as Edward Edinger expresses his inflationary euphoria as he declares Jung himself to be the emergence of a new collective myth. The man Jung, writes Edinger, has become "a paradigm of the prototypical life of the new age and hence exemplary."[56]

But perhaps the most problematic critique of all concerns Jung's seeming collapse of **transcendence** into **immanence**. When this tension is lost, as Kierkegaard claimed had occured in Hegel, then self becomes elevated into the former lofty position held by deity. It becomes a legitimate question whether Jung has turned "the transcendence of God into a psychological transcendence of the self over the ego?"[57] Even as Freud removes all transcendence from the psyche, Jung reinstates it by virtue of the Self's non-historical wholeness. What becomes lost in Jung is the necessity and legitimacy of the **object** for the **subject**. If the path to full self-consciousness is awakened and maintained by the otherness of the object how can the journey toward the fullness of subjectivity be maintained without consistently honoring this otherness? Ego-Self harmony becomes meaningless if this differentiation is collapsed. Regrettably, this is Jung's great weakness.

To have critiqued Jung does not mean I wish to declare him wrong. Rather, when left to stand by himself the possibility of a comprehensive model of self becomes lost. The Jungian Self, when standing alone, becomes inflated by its very universality, just as the solitary Freudian self becomes crushed by its very historicity. Any attempt to move beyond this polarity must take both paradigms seriously without collapsing their paradox into a vague syncretism. It is this final task which still awaits us.

1.   C.G. Jung, *The Structure and Dynamics of the Psyche*, C.W.Vol. 8, Translated by R.F.C. Hull, (Princeton: Princeton University Press, 1969), par. 275

2.   C.G. Jung, *The Archtypes and the Collective Unconscious*, C.W. Vol. 9.1; Translated by R.F.C. Hull, (Princeton: Princeton University Press, 1959), par. 5

3.   The Jungian term psyche is the totality of all psychic processes, conscious as well as unconscious; it is an encompassing reality in contrast to "soul" which for Jung is the individual form taken by psyche called "personality".

4.   C.G. Jung, *Psychological Types*, C.W. Vol. 6, Translated by H.G. Baynes, Revised by R.F.C. Hull (Princeton: Princeton University Press, 1971), par. 706

5.   Ibid., par. 923

6.   C.G. Jung, C.W. Vol. 9,i., par. 2

7.   Ibid., par. 3

8.   C.G. Jung, *Psychology and Religion: West and East*, C.W. Vol. 11, Translated by R.F.C. Hull, (Princeton: University Press, 1969), par. 222

9.   C.G. Jung, C.W. Vol. 8, par. 265, 270, 273

10.   Ibid., par. 398

11.   Ibid., par. 277

12.   Ibid., par. 280

13. C.G. Jung, C.W. Vol. 9,i, par. 393

14. Ibid

15. Ibid., par. 309

16. C.G. Jung, *Aion: Researches into the Phenomenology of the Self*, C.W. Vol. 9, ii, Translated by R.F.C. Hull, (Princeton: Princeton University Press, 1959), par. 6

17. Ibid., par. 9

18. C.G. Jung, C.W., par. 706

19. C.G. Jung, C.W. 9,ii, par. 11 (Italics mine)

20. C.G. Jung, C.W. Vol. 6, par. 801

21. C.G. Jung, *Two Essays on Analytical Psychology*, C.W. Vol. 7, translated by R.F.C. Hull, (Princeton: Princeton University Press, 1966), par. 245

22. Ibid., par. 247

23. C.G. Jung, C.W. Vol. 9, ii, par. 13

24. Ibid., par. 19

25. Ibid., par. 176 (Italics mine)

26. C.G. Jung, C.W. Vol. 9, i, par. 45

27. C.G. Jung, C.W. Vol. 6, par. 803

28. C.G Jung, C.W. Vol. 9, ii, par. 29

29. Ibid.

30. C.G. Jung, *The Development of Personality*, Translated by R.F.C. Hull (Princeton: Princeton University Press, 1977), par. 338

31. Vincent Brome, Jung, (New York: Atheneum, 1981), p. 277

32. C.G. Jung, C.W. Vol, 9, ii. par. 19

33. C.G. Jung, C.W. Vol. 8, par. 403

34. C.G. Jung, C.W. Vol. 6, par. 808

35.   Ibid., par. 789

36.   C.G. Jung, *Psychology and Alchemy*, C.W. Vol. 12, Translated by
      R.F.C. Hull (Princeton University Press, 1968), par. 247. Note also
      Jung's equating of self with Kant's "Ding an sich", the thing in-itself.

37.   C.G. Jung, C.W. Vol. II, par. 232

38.   Ibid., par. 231

39.   C.G. Jung, C.W. Vol. 9, ii, par. 233

40.   C.G. Jung, C.W. Vol. 11, par. 233

41.   C.G. Jung, C.W. Vol. 9, ii, par. 115

42.   Ibid., par. 124

43.   C.G. Jung, C.W. Vol. 6, par. 824

44.   Ibid., par. 825

45.   Ibid., par. 826

46.   An obvious example is Edward Edinger's *Ego and Archtypes* (Baltimore,
      Maryland; Penguin Books, Inc., 1973). The concept is given minor
      treatment by some such as Jolande Jacobi, *The Psychology of C.G. Jung*,
      (New Haven, Yale University Press, 1973), and John P. Dourley, C.G.
      Jung and Paul Tillich: *The Psyche as Sacrament*, (Toronto: Inner City
      Books, 1981). Note also Jung's comments in C.W. Vol. 6, par. 184, as
      well as Prefatory Note, C.W. Vol. 8, par. 130. For others the concept is
      seen as central to Jung's thought, most notably Peter Homans, *Jung in
      Context* (Chicago: University of Chicago Press, 1979), pp. 86, 92, 96

47.   C.G. Jung, C.W. Vol. 6, par. 184

48.   Ibid., par. 828

49.   Ibid., par. 427

50.   Ibid., par. 430

51.   C.G. Jung, C.W. Vol. 8, par. 147

52.   Ibid., par. 172-174

53.   Ibid.,par. 181, 183

54.   Ibid., par. 189

55.   C.G. Jung, C.W. Vol. 9, ii, par. 57

56.   Edward F. Edinger, *The Creation of Consciousness*, (Toronto: Inner City Books, 1984), p. 12

57.   Pannenberg, 1985, p. 264

Chapter XI

THE FULFILLED SELF

A vast terrain has been traversed in this survey of self-modalities. With a range so diverse, and a complexity so rich, it is a daunting task to formulate a model of selfhood which takes seriously the manifold efforts we have encountered.

It will have become obvious by this point that certain paths which were chosen in eras past as hopeful efforts toward self-definition, failed, as their dead-end nature revealed itself. All static options which have denied self the possibility of movement, development, and full aliveness, have been discarded. This is particularly true of the allure of otherworldliness in which self, as soul, is placed in the domain of an utterly transcendent Diety. Any option which cuts self off from life, experience, and relatedness, has emerged as bankrupt and unable to offer self anything beyond an artificial stability imposed from above.

Other paths presented themselves with promising possibilities, among them the Mystical, Romanticist, and Idealist streams. Without obscuring their obvious differences, they represent a flowering of subjectivity in which selfhood is linked to an abiding, eternal organicity, a self in permanent unity with itself. Although the ahistorical tendencies of these subjectivist paradigms are a serious limitation, they reaffirmed the factor of intentionality within psychic life in ways impossible to deny.

That there is a depth and dynamic complexity to human interiority and human identity is beyond dispute. But to declare that selfhood reveals fluidity, intentionality, bi-polarity, and so forth, is insufficient. An unbroken bond must be demonstrated between the self's structure and its movement, or better said, its structural integrity can only be made visible in its movement. The task which remains is to consolidate the trustworthy elements of this construct called self into a framework which reveals its living vibrancy. And finally, these self-propositions require a viable grounding, an ontology, which gives self its sustaining energy and persistent validation.

To facilitate this final task I will offer a working definition of self, not exhaustive, but one which contains its determining elements. While maintaining a commitment to its abiding fluidity, I nevertheless intend to demonstrate self's structural integrity. This structural analysis is not separable from the energies which drive the life of self, an aspect which also requires elaboration. Finally, the phases of the life of self reveal its yearning for connectedness, the linkages without which self cannot exist, the fulfillment without which it cannot live.

The Self Defined

No simple definition can claim to capture a reality as encompassing as self. The very demand for definition implies that it might be possible to tease out its "objective" qualities, to discover a residue of its noun-like characteristics. Such an effort is futile. Since self is not an object or thing no static descriptions will do. However, this does not mean one must remain mute. Since it is essential to name the patterns of movement of self I offer the following definition:

The self is the eternal desire to be known. As a center of initiative self engages its world and verifies itself therein. In coming to itself through otherness it seeks itself as self, the source and goal of its becoming.

Immediately, thorny questions come to mind. Is this self one or is it many? Is it momentary or abiding in time? Is self marked by energies of possession or by letting go? Is this self ever at rest and can it ever hope to find itself? While these questions will find answers in due course, a brief unpacking of this definition is in order.

Selfhood cannot be understood apart from the hunger which drives its life.[1] This appetite is not simply a devouring of otherness for the sake of self-maintenance, although it may come in this form, but an engagement which brings self to itself. Since self is never constructed once-for-all, its moment-to-moment reconstellation demands that its seeking be ever-present.

But a seeking of what? Any talk of self's seeking its essential core is futile and misguided. There is no eternal core to selfhood since this would violate the fundamental principle of the self's abiding fluidity. Rather, the self seeks itself not because it is outside of itself, but because its inwardness seeks to manifest itself, to become known. This is no reified substantiality in which its nature is simply assumed, externalized and objectified. To be sure, aspects of self can be so observed and "captured" much like a still photograph can be said to capture a moment of dramatic action. But to equate such a snap-shot with the lived experience of self is unthinkable. A realized subjectivity must do just that, realize itself in its moment-to-moment gathering-up of itself.

Self, then, is a process of becoming which requires otherness to come to itself. In going out of itself it finds what is other to it. In being found it finds itself thereby gaining its constituent nature.

If self is constructed through otherness, how can it be said that self finds itself? Is its nature inherent to it and only confirmed by otherness, or is its nature realized as it encounters otherness?

Again, if the essential principles of (1) eternal movement and (2) inherent relatedness, are trustworthy, then our answer must lean toward the latter. While there is an intactness to self, this so-called stability is only realized in the moment. As self moves from moment to moment it takes-in (ingests) otherness and in so doing shapes itself into being, only to reconstitute itself anew - even as it carries its prior moments within it. Being unable to maintain itself by itself it must release itself from its current attachments (even as they are incorporated within) so as to consolidate itself in the emerging now.

But how can it be said that self seeks itself as source and goal of its becoming if its constituent nature is shaped by otherness? My preliminary answer centers upon the factors of process and content.

The self seeks itself as living movement, to know itself in its sheer vibrancy. These patterns of movement called self have a particular content which are determined by the objects of its life. The "river" of self is filled with its object history which both binds it to its past and opens it to its future. I find my self when

I embrace **both** the internal seeker and the otherness which has been found, or more accurately said, that which has found me.

The Structure of Self

Throughout the historical path we have travelled it has been persistently asserted that self is structured along so-called bi-polar lines. Whether understood as a simple subject-object dichotomy or in various forms of ego-environment polarization, self has been presented as a duality. Agreement, however, abruptly ends here.

As Catherine Keller so ably reveals, the subject-object structuring of selfhood has generally been envisioned in dualistic terms, a subject in oppositional polarity with object.[2] I am convinced that a self structured along polar lines only is condemned to fragmentation and truncated selfhood. The principle of relatedness and engagement becomes diminished the more polarized the constituting elements become.

Another possibility with a far more enduring potential to "carry" the movements of self is to envision its structural elements as dyads. As dyads the organizing centers of self are in a continuing relationship in which they interact with each other. Only a structure which allows for reciprocal influence can hope to carry the multifarious nature of self.

Of the many structural possibilities encountered thus far several demand inclusion in any comprehensive model of self. Although limited by dualist presuppositions, the ancient matter - spirit dichotomy may require incorporation into any self-structure. The Biblical reformulation of these themes into the flesh-spirit dynamism representing factors of constriction and expansiveness, deserve recognition in any structure of self. Kierkegaard's polarities called (1) possibility-necessity; (2) finitude-infinitude; and (3) temporal-eternal represent another effort at naming the dual themes of openness and restriction which frame the life of self. Other structural requirements include the dyadic relationship between intimacy and separation as presented by 20th century Ego Psychology, as well as the bi-polar elements Self psychology calls ambition and ideal. Other possibilities include the wide range of archtypal dyads found in Jungian thought.

I therefore propose the following dyads as vital structural units within which the life of self moves: (1) singular and multiple; (2) validated and validating; (3) open and closed; (4) intimate and separate.[3]

The tone of these dyads reveals a departure from static structural terms implying solidity and firmness toward fluidity. This is intentional. The verb-like quality of self cannot be approximated if one seeks fixed barriers upon which the characteristics of self can be hung. The dynamism of self demands that its structural integrity not contradict its inherent principle of freedom.

Self as Singular and Multiple

To have structure has traditionally meant a fixed and abiding essence, an unchangeable core to personhood which guarantees the self's identity. This option has (hopefully) been permanently discarded. In its place I am proposing a structural meaning which allows us to acknowledge the self's stability over time, its consistency, while in the midst of its ever-present changeableness. Structure, then, has to do with a self's particular organization as it goes about its life. By naming four dyads as the structural framework of self, I am suggesting that these elements constitute the primary themes defining the life of self.

Theories of abiding/static selfhood rely upon the solitary oneness of self as the means of maintaining the self's identity over time. Such a self needs nothing to sustain it since its stability is guaranteed. Early challenges to stasis (such as Mysticism and Romanticism) which insist upon movement for self, fall short because self remains closed within its self-contained operations. As experience-near paradigms emerged with the onset of subjective Idealism (Hegel), selfhood was released from its solitary confinement. A subject-object linkage from henceforth became the sine qua non of self.

If self can no longer be affirmed through solitary oneness is it only at the mercy of its object-determiners? As recent developments in psychoanalytic theory have demonstrated, selfhood is first "carried" within states of merged oneness. The selfobject construct has emerged as the most helpful vehicle for naming the infusion of object material as self metabolizes itself into being. The particular developmental station where self happens to find itself will significantly determine the ratio of differentiation - fusion lived-out by self. However, even states of the highest autonomy or so-called singularity cannot be confused with solipstic self-sufficiency. No self is an island as the well-known phrase declares! The selfobject matrix is operative throughout the life of any self. The more differentiated a self becomes, i.e. the more it owns its singularity, the greater will be its honoring of all the actual entities which are part of its life.

All moments of a self's life carry within them the inheritance of prior attachments. These accumulated "states of merger" have wrought their influence upon the self even if they have been long negated and superceded. It is for this reason that Hume's "empirical self" wields no attraction. Such a self dissolves at every moment only to be re-constellated in the next moment according to its current functional potential. But personhood is not only governed by linear, chronological events but by its structural unity, the evolving themes which reveal one's current attachments and hungers. These themes cover the full range of desires, repulsions, conflicts, and transformations which fill every self.

There is no objective yardstick which dictates the particular ratio of separation-individuation arrangements for self. Within certain cultures fullest selfhood is seen in those who live out the highest communal values, while in others so-called autonomy is given highest approval. The various labels of diseased selfhood are laid upon those who violate the norm in either instance.

My insistence upon a dyad of reciprocal relation intends to maximize the range of movement for self as it arranges itself along this continuum of singularity-multiplicity. This allows self to find an authentic "spot" for itself along this continuum. A self whose history has reinforced patterns of enmeshment with its determining objects will need to come to terms with this its reality, even as it takes a stance toward the new possibilities which forever present themselves. Conversely, a self shaped around residues of isolation, even abandonment, will find itself drawn toward a different range of possibilities for self-realization. This could take the form of either object-hunger or various forms of object-annihilation, i.e. efforts at correcting object-deficiency. These object-devouring efforts are attempts at correcting imbalances in object-presence for itself. The developmental requirements of various stations of selfhood will of course determine the amount of object-supply needed by any self. Furthermore, a self's capacities for integrating object elements also determines the manner in which selfobject material is used and absorbed.

In short, **every self is both singular and multiple**. It is its very own self, even as it is nourished or starved through the manifold infusions of selfobject content. This first organizational pillar of self is in a reciprocal relation with the second, a dyad I am calling the self as validated and validating.

Self as Validated and Validating

Throughout this study it has been consistently affirmed that selfhood is guided by libidinal interests. That desire is the "engine" of the self has been affirmed by virtually every explorer of selfhood who has been willing to grant any legitimacy to the construct. Desire and its objects are birthed simultaneously we have been reminded, and this indelible link is at the heart of the life of self.

If desire is the organ of object-engagement, it remains to be demonstrated how this hunger becomes translated into structural patterns. While Aristotle and Augustine were among the first to insist upon defining self according to its style of moving toward objects, its object attachments, it took Freud and his followers to provide a more experience-near map for this process. The key which unlocked this possibility is the concept of narcissism.

Augustine had already noted the pervasive nature of self-investment, but unfortunately linked the phenomenon with inordinate self-exaltation by identifying narcissism with pride as our primary form of self-relatedness. Even Freud could not grant narcissism any permanent legitimacy by insisting that narcissistic investment in self was incompatible with mature object-love.[4] Nevertheless, Freud drove home the point that selfhood is inevitably constructed along narcissistic lines even if these inclinations are to be superceded.

It took the efforts of Heinz Kohut to fully reverse this negativity toward narcissism. For Kohut the self-selfobject relationship determines the health and vitality of the self. The selfobject, as we recall, is not a person or an interpersonal construct, but the internal, **subjective function** of **self-harmonization** and **self-sustenance**. Selfobjects, for Kohut, provide the narcissistic validation so necessary for self-maintenance.

Kohut, unfortunately, only sees self organizing itself around bi-polar lines, these being (1) **ambition** and (2) **ideal**, two modes of engagement with needed selfobjects. The first involves the seeking of mirroring by a selfobject which affirms the goodness of one's self. While the first form thereof is grandiosity, its more mature manifestations includes all creative, externalized activity for which affirmation is sought. The second pole, idealization, represents the factor of merger in which a self desires union with selfobjects carrying those characteristics for which the self yearns.

Two factors, however, prompt me to adjust Kohut's structural scheme. On the one hand, Kohut's reliance upon polar models diminishes the reciprocal mutuality within self. This artificial distance between poles makes the necessary integration all the more difficult. On the other hand, Kohut's so-called "poles" are not differentiated enough. Ambition and idealization, or if one wishes, mirroring and merger, are both forms of validation. What is vital is for self to be affirmed. This was perhaps the central truth received from Hegel, that self can only flourish as it is **recognized** and **affirmed** by another self. The self's eternal hunger to be known is therefore inextricably linked to the validation which confirms the self.

But validation is only one piece of the dyadic partnership. Validation alone leaves the self passive, strictly at the mercy of object-determined confirmations. A self as center of initiative also engages its world and seeks to confirm its place therein. Not only is self passively acted upon, it seeks to find itself in its world, to create an image of itself in that world. This factor within the dyad I wish to call the **self as validating**.

Psychoanalytic self psychology has seemingly recognized this need in its more recent offerings. Ernest Wolf, collaborator with Kohut, acknowledges that selfobjects contain what he calls "adversarial" and "efficacy" needs.[5] The need to have an impact upon one's defining selfobjects is also vital for self-construction. Whether in the simple form of being able to elicit a response from one's environment, or through the more intense need to gain mastery over one's world, both styles are reminders that self is structured according to its capacities and potentialities which it seeks to live out. The quest for self-sufficiency implies that a self demonstrate its capacities to itself, even, as Hegel so ably noted, such a self remains reciprocally linked and dependent upon its needed validators.

This second structural requirement, then, is self's ever-present need to be confirmed even as it seeks to present itself to its world. Both aspects, the need to be validated and the need to be validating, are filled with selfobject content, the legacy of a self's confirmations and/or disappointments within this dyadic requirement.

Self as Open and Closed

A third structural requirement for self is the capacity for boundary maintenance. The developmental fluidity of self necessitates that this requirement be phase-appropriate even as a wide range of possibilities exist at all levels of development. But what does it mean for self to be structured in boundary-sensitive ways?

Catherine Keller illustrates this requirement through the framework of gender.[6] Her claim is that masculine selfhood is predominantly separate, constructed around oppositional transcendence in which the self (as male) posits another (as opponent) through which this self finds itself. Conversely, female selfhood reveals a soluble self which loses itself in immanent identification with and absorption by its world. These socio-political analyses are valuable and confirm that all self-construction crystallizes around the prevailing patterns of power-powerlessness and the subsequent validation or negation experienced by a self. Certainly, a self will align itself according to the criterion for normative selfhood placed before it whether this be in accommodating (soluble) or negating (separate) ways.

Most self-models agree that the first form of self involves states of merger. Kierkegaard's dreaming desire, for example, describes a self immersed in total non-differentiation. Such a state can hardly claim the label self, and yet this phase is the inevitable precursor to all which follows.

It is perhaps understandable that all declarations about states of oceanic oneness for self (such as mystic pronouncements), are often confused with this prepersonal kernel of selfhood. States of prepersonal merger are a given for every self, our continuity with which we never lose. If our self were only attracted to historical resides of merged states then the matter would indeed be closed. But archeological states of union alone do not seem to be an abiding source of nourishment for self which also seeks itself in the not-yet.

States of merger are not simply boundary-less, however, but represent the expansiveness within which is self "carried", so to speak. Psychoanalytic Object

Relations theory offers us rich images for naming this reality such as Winnicott's "nursing couple", or Mahler's "symbiosis". These first forms of self are fully embedded in a relational matrix and are carried within. In having no "membrane" around itself, such a self is fully open to its world, ready to be impacted by it.

The rhythms of care and distress, along with self's emerging capacities, force the first boundary between a self and its world. This self-other boundary is simultaneously matched by an internal boundary in which a self arranges the satisfying and non-satisfying elements of its experience. The world, in its frustrating and gratifying moments, brings the self to itself. Stradling this internal boundary is the selfobject, the gatekeeper who directs this process of sorting out the residues of experience into their welcome and unwelcome elements.

Boundary, then, refers to the spaces "carved out" within the self for collecting its experiential legacy, even as it refers to the differentiation between subject and object accomplished by self.

Boundary intactness becomes a supreme measure for assessing the health or disarray of any self. Extreme environmental impingements, when added to limited selfobject resources for managing such distress, results in a self with destroyed, or at best, violated boundaries. A self constantly fighting intrusion will likely have a thick impermeable wall between itself and its world, matched by the wall erected around its own inner life. Or, its capacity for maintaining self-intactness will be so severely handicapped that no adequate protection will exist for warding-off unwelcome demands and threats. Thus, whether in the form of exaggerated boundaries or no boundaries, the potential of self will be thwarted.

A far healthier structure is present when the internal and external boundaries are permeable and pliable. Flexibility implies the capacity for nuanced response to environmental and internal stimuli. As with other structural dyads, optimum selfhood is obtained when self reveals both openness and closedness. What might this imply?

A self in relationship with both boundary requirements knows where it begins and the other ends, and vice versa. It does not impose itself upon the other nor does it fear being engaged. It maintains itself without devouring or negating otherness or itself, and hence lives without fear of such violation of its selfhood. Since its center is within and not external to it, it makes no demands for self-maintenance upon another.

380

Conversely, a boundary-sensitive self does not hide behind artificial self-protective barriers. It honors its indebtedness to all selfhood and strains to enhance all self-potential. It is not diminished by the fullness achieved by other selves but knows that its own subjective potential is inextricably connected to the fuller development of self wherever it is to be found. Above all, one could say that such a self maintains an empathic link toward all self-states of which it is aware.

The Self as Intimate and Separate

The boundary dyad just described identifies the dual dangers of atrophied selfhood as: (1) a self driven into itself as a retreat from object-relatedness, or (2) a self drowning in object-demands because it has not found itself. All structural arrangements named thus far: (1) singular and multiple (2) validated and validating and (3) open and closed, are linked to this final organizing center for self. Every self will find itself somewhere on this continuum of intimacy-separation.

It should be noted how far removed we are from models which suggest mature selfhood attains some arbitrary standard of separation-individuation. The journey toward so-called autonomy or separateness is only half of the developmental task. If Nancy Chodorow's thesis is correct, then men have already attained this sublime state of separation only to find that self has somehow slipped through their fingers.[7] Conversely, women's selfhood is never reached if absolute separateness is the sought-after norm.

In the final analysis, every self seems drawn toward its inherent fullness, a fullness which contains both the subject and object parameters of its life. Again, no optimum ratio of intimacy to aloneness exists. Every self needs to come to terms with its legacy of engagement and sort out the degree of entanglement versus freedom it lives out. A self tied to its determining objects whether parents, teachers, or religious authorities, will find certain forms of such attachments appropriate for particular phases of its life, but not adequate for others. What fits at one moment may not fit the next.

Similarly, a self might find a high degree of aloneness/distance from defining objects (cultural, relational, ideological etc.) as absolutely necessary for itself. It may need to clear out the clutter of suffocating intimacies in order to be able to move toward other self-potentials. Again, the historical legacy will impinge upon the next developmental demand, even as the self's skills and capacities will help define the new possibilities which present themselves.

The intimacy required of selfhood is first of all, then, an intimacy with one's very own self. The relationship with one's own emotional life is a primary barometer of the degree of comfort attained toward the self's life-process. Emotions are the breathing of the self and intimacy toward them does not mean being swallowed up by them but maintaining a full and tender dialog with them. States of external isolation are often in direct proportion to the distance one has put between oneself and the subjective (affective) aspects of one's life.

Conversely, I must be able to let go of my feelings as absolute determiners of my life. To separate from them is not to deny them but to honor them as here and now indicators of my subjective life. To identify fully with them would be to be possessed by them thereby closing the self in upon itself. The same could be said of other self-defining elements such as belief or meaning-systems. To the extent that beliefs negate the openness self needs to move into its future they deny self its freedom, hence suffocating the self.

The self's need for autonomy then, ought never to be equated with isolation. Rather, self seeks to become itself, to become differentiated, linking with all its determining elements without having to control them or be swallowed up by them. Such a self is a "layered" self, having gathered up its history, and maintaining a relationship with its manifold constituting elements. It is intimate with itself and with otherness even as it honors its singularity.

The Process of Self

If self finds its shape through the four dyadic patterns just named, it remains to be demonstrated how this movement is actualized. Not only is it imperative that the energies which drive the life of self be revealed, it must be demonstrated how these energies are linked with self's structural integrity. The following questions will need to be answered for this link to be viable.

To begin with, it must be clarified whether self is a **mediation** between its polar elements as Kierkegaard would have us believe, or whether self is a **synthesis** of its constituting factors as Hegel has declared? Or, is some other mechanism better suited to carry the reciprocal quality of dyadic relatedness? Furthermore, is self active or passive? Is its life best understood as an evolutionary unfolding, or as an intentional choosing? And what does it mean for desire to be the engine of its life?

A Triadic Formula

All dyadic links claimed for self have in common an object-relatedness. They are attempts at mapping patterns of object-seeking or object-avoidance. But self is not simply the accumulation of object-residue, but the living interaction of subject-object content. All models which avoid static unity need to find a bridge which might unify the manifold subject-object parameters of self.

The first such bridge is provided by Aristotle who uses the capacity for thinking as a primary means of both dividing subject from object, as well as synthesizing the same. This option is borrowed by Aquinas who raises rationality into the supreme vehicle of selfhood, the means by which it achieves its integration. As I have noted elsewhere, this unfortunate dependence upon rationality as the glue which holds self together locks self into exile from its full inwardness, condemning its adherents to live from the neck up.

Another attempt at connecting the dispersive self comes in the form of the instincts or drives. These body-based impulses are presented by Freud as the pathways by which an organism seeks its needed objects. Whether in the service of seeking pleasure (satisfaction), or inevitable decay (homeostasis), self completes its functional purpose. It unifies (organizes) itself in keeping with its instinctual requirements.[8]

Other bridging possibilities holding perhaps more promise emerge as early as Augustine in the form of the internal images by which self relates to itself. Even contributors as recent as the Ego Psychologists Heinz Hartmann and Edith Jacobson see the self as the accumulation of self and object representations. The fact that these images do not allow self much more than an imitative existence again diminishes their usefulness. An image where one mimics the other hardly approximates the complexity of operations of self. Nevertheless, images serve as reminders that self does present itself to itself.

After all is said and done, however, it has become clear that no subject-object link can be claimed for self if it is not accomplished through experience. Subject-object engagement is only realizable within the crucible of raw experience. This does not mean that unconscious or hidden factors are eliminated. Rather, it insists that every layer of self is born within an experiential grid.

I therefore reaffirm that the most useful device for discussing the subject-object linkages is the selfobject construct. Selfobjects, I have noted, refer to the internal function of self-harmonization and self-sustenance. This does not make them an automatic bridging-agent, however. Constructed out of both subject and object material, selfobjects draw from both, emerging as a distinct entity within the self system. As a unifying third element, they gather affect-laden aspects of experience and for better or for worse become integrated into the self-system. How, then, is this process triadic?

Mediation or Synthesis?

We have arrived again at the dilemma crystallized by Kierkegaard. Given his abhoring of Hegelian unity, Kierkegaard accuses Hegel of eliminating the polarities of selfhood through an artificial synthesis which destroys the prior elements. This Kierkegaard calls a self as negative unity. In its place he proposes a "third" element which maintains the polar components of self in a creative tension. Kierkegaard wishes to lay claim to the word synthesis to describe this triadic process but we must deny him this privilege.

It is more accurate to describe the operations of the Kierkegaardian self with the term **mediation**. In Kierkegaard the opposites are unresolveable, a permanent and fixed polarization, with the so-called third factor (reconciling agent) suspended between them. Mediation describes the process of holding these polarized factors in their abiding state of tension while attempting to navigate between them. Given my rejection of polar models as incompatible with selfobject frameworks, I believe I can safely discard the Kierkegaardian reliance upon mediation as the means of self-construction and self-maintenance. But what of synthesis? Is it any more compatible than mediation for naming self-process?

The possibility that synthesis might capture the movement of self is less easily dismissed than is true for mediation. While Hegel's ontological dialectic with its absolute synthesizing operations can perhaps be dismissed as armchair abstractions, it becomes another matter when as reputable a figure as D.W. Winnicott uses dialectic synthesis to describe a historically-grounded process of self-maintenance.

Winnicott's framework, as is true for Object Relational models generally, begins with self in undifferentiated unity. These states of absolute dependency are invariably negated by frustration which drives a wedge between the nascent self and its protective cocoon.[9] There is, however, an "intermediate" realm which ties together **both** interior and exterior components to experience even as it gathers up the rewarding and frustrating elements contained therein. These "transitional objects", the forerunners to the selfobject construct, reveal a distinct synthesizing capacity. Here the matter becomes problematic, however.

The very notion of synthesis implies on the one hand a joining of opposites, and secondly, the elimination of prior elements. These aspects of synthesis are incompatible with our evolving model. Selfhood, I would conclude, is not constructed by the mediation of oppositional elements (Kierkegaard), nor by their synthesis (Hegel), but by a hunger for selfobject content which confirms the self as itself.

There is no automatic cycle to self in which there is movement from unity, through negation, toward differentiation, but an abiding hunger which reflects the level of selfhood being sought. With Kohut, I share the view that selfobject supply is needed throughout life, this being the life-blood of the self. What, then, is the self's process and how is it triadic?

I would propose that self reveals the following flow:

(1) movement out of itself

(2) returning to itself

(3) transforming integration

Movement out of Itself. Virtually every contributor to the quest for self from Plato through Hegel, to Freud, has insisted that desire is the doorway to self. Rationality alone can never awaken self to itself. A self is activated by desire and driven by desire.[10] Desire mobilizes the self toward the objects through which a subject can define itself. Such desire is ever-present since only the encounter with otherness brings self to itself.

By its very nature this appetite is a movement out of itself toward its constituting objects. Indeed, every act of seeking is a form of object-hunger, a movement of self attempting to find itself. Not all seeking is the same, however.

Hedonistic devouring of objects is a first form of such seeking. By its very nature it is insatiable because the self can only maintain itself by consuming the object. Narcissistic neediness is another form of awakening desire which propels a subject out of itself toward its determining objects. This movement of validation and confirmation is ever-present as we have learned. While it may undergo maturation, the impulse to seek confirmation of oneself through validating objects never ceases.

Returning to Itself. The movement toward defining objects is a yearning for selfobject supply. Selfobjects are the building blocks of self. Selfobject content includes those nurturing and persecuting patterns of otherness which we have taken-in to our very own self turning them into the fabric of our being. Again, this task is never accomplished once-for-all. Archaic selfobject residues are deeply layered within us, there to nourish or destroy, even as we seek new confirming or compensating selfobject experiences.

Transforming Integration. The movement outward and its return is completed as the defining elements become incorporated into the self system. While my indebtedness to Kohut (transmuting internalization) and Jung (transcendent function) is clear, I also wish to identify the differences. Kohut's use of transmutation, a term borrowed from alchemy, implies a change in nature that borders on the miraculous. If nothing else, it leans toward a discontinuity between one's defining selfobjects and the emerging self-system. This I find unacceptable.

All selfobject content is absorbed into the self system for better or for worse. Its presence within the self does not unhook the self from its prior nature. The slate is not wiped clean as new selfobject content presents itself. It is, rather, taken into the self there to challenge or confirm what already resides within.

This is not to say that transformation does not happen. A self **does change** as it releases attachments and ingests the new. The critical factor, however, is the relationship taken toward the determining elements. A self may or may not come to terms with the hunger or desire which drives its life, even as it may or may not gather up (claim ownership of) its constituting factors. But to become its self, it is compelled to embrace its desires, relational legacy, and full

386

experiential matrix. As these are claimed a transformation is accomplished because the past is brought into the present with greater fullness, even as the future is anticipated through the vehicle of desire.

Self as Source of Initiative

The above formula has provided a model of the self's activity without offering particular insight as to the forces which energize this process. Virtually every explorer of self has noted some energizing factor within self ranging from simple appetite (Aristotle), to libidinal pleasure-seeking (Freud), to an inherent drive toward the object (Fairbairn).

While differing greatly around the nature and meaning of this object-hunger, most perspectives which grant self any movement at all, place this movement within the rubric of desire. Desire is the impulse which drives the birth of the self. The self, to borrow Kohut's phrase, is a "center of initiative", the thrust of which is to seek its determining objects. But why seek external objects if the self's primary impulse is to know itself?

The self as a source of initiative attempts to accomplish a particular purpose, the most central of which is to become known. Becoming known is not instantaneously given, but involves the repetitive and persistent confirmation(s) of defining objects. This necessary validation occurs throughout the life cycle, a seeking of object-encounters which match the degree or level of selfhood being sought.

The desire which governs the emergence of selfhood is not to be confused with petty neediness, although it may emerge in this form. It is rather the yearning of self for itself, the completion of its nature, the discovery of itself. This nature is not simply given, lowered from heaven, but constructed out of the mixture of self's current potentialities as carried within its historical realities.

The seeking which drives the self's efforts at finding itself will match the level of organization attained. A child will find delight in itself as it sways to music it finds pleasing, even if it has no knowledge of the structural meanings contained in the medium. A trained musician will find herself mirrored only as vastly more sophisticated levels of musical capability are reached. The common truth is that neither event would have appeal if self were not being reflected back to itself. The eternal seeking of self is for an otherness which will match, confirm, and validate the "level" or "form" of selfhood currently being lived out.

The development of self in more sophisticated ways does not necessarily eliminate the earliest forms of desire. The highest levels of artistic, intellectual, or athletic achievements can often rest upon thinly-veiled impulses of an infantile quality, whether sexual, aggressive, or narcissistic. Particularly if the earliest forms of self-hunger were not incorporated or integrated into later development, such a self risks regressing back to its unclaimed elements. In living them out self seeks to find itself.

I must return to an earlier question. In granting desire a central role, is self now understood as an evolutionary unfolding, its nature and destiny fully contained within? What place then remains for freedom, for choice, never mind the question of who should assume responsibility for this self?

Desire is not an ephemeral construct. As the primary form of engagement of subject with object it links them to one another. Therefore, tracing my desires becomes a window into my object-history even as it alerts me to new possibilities of encounter. This is not to deny that my desires can reveal forms of utter darkness and enslavement. If my object-history has generated a preponderance of suffocating and annihilating selfobjects, then my desires will reveal themselves accordingly. Our desires never lie. They both lead us to ourselves and beyond ourselves. We may choose to hide or distort these desires from ourselves or others for the sake of maintaining artificial self-states, which only enslave the self all the more.

A self's path, then, involves a choosing of itself within the object-parameters of its existence. There is no grand design for any self other than the requirement to find itself. A self can only find itself where it is, in its here and now. But its current place and current time is not an isolated monad. A self stands in continuity with its past and its anticipated future. This is the source of its joy and its terror, its freedom and its bondage. But I must push the notion of desire one step further.

From Heinz Kohut we have received the valuable contribution that active selfhood not only hungers for object confirmations, but that self seeks to ingest selfobject material for itself. Selfobject yearning, while limited by Kohut's archeological perspectives, nevertheless names the necessity for internal harmonization. The selfobject function as internal regulator balances (or upsets) the operations of self, keeping in mind the triadic nature thereof. Whether in the form of attraction or repulsion, self-soothing or self-agitation, a self will attempt to regulate itself according to its current capacities and developmental demands.

But before we leave the process factors of self a final question requires response. The attention given to desire leaves the impression that self is only defined by its activity, by the energy expended in shaping itself. How then, is the self's passivity to be understood in light of its ever-present capacity to actualize itself?

Fichte was the first to confront this question although with poor results. He attempted to shift the self toward its activity in order to undo the paralysis of static selfhood left by Hume, and all theocentric models of self. But given Fichte's need to keep self competitively overcoming its objects in order to define itself, he undercut any commitment to self's "passivity" he might have had.

I therefore wish to reframe the requirement that self be capable of suspending its activity, by reintroducing the concept of rest first found in Kierkegaard. Kierkegaard, as we recall, insists upon a state of restfulness for self even though there is nothing within the Kierkegaardian self allowing it to do so. Rest becomes meaningless when self is constantly pummeled by its polarities.

Rather, I would propose that rest refers to a self in a state of attunement, ready to receive what comes its way. Such a state of receptivity is in fact essential for any nurture or fulfillment a self might experience. Winnicott's beautiful phrase "the nursing couple" reveals a first form of such attunement in which a child and its mother are fully receptive to the stimulus emerging from the other. All levels of selfhood have this capacity within them; furthermore, without this capacity no claim can be made for a fullness to self. The radical receptivity to all Being first noted in Meister Eckhart comes much closer to the requirement that self attain a state of rest. This state of non-clinging attachment fills the self with its absolutely essential requirement: the fullness of another self.

The Phases of the Life of Self

Any talk of the "stations" which mark the life of self cannot be divorced from the truth that the unity (or fragmentation) of self along this path is dependent upon its object-experience. A self eternally seeks an otherness capable of bringing self to itself. This seeking for selfobject supply matches the level or "type" of selfhood being lived out.

Elaborate schemes have been encountered in this study as attempts at classifying the developmental stations of self. Some models such as the Aristotelian look to functional capability as the primary means of naming developmental competencies. Here, **rational** and **cognitive** capacities are given the highest value as the optimum destination for self. Mystic perspectives look to the **dissolution of boundaries** as the means of marking developmental accomplishment. Psychological paradigms generally look to the consolidation of **personal** identity as the developmental norm. The process of **individuation** is the name given to this developmental path, with the psychoanalytic scheme considering personal autonomy and creative self-directness the optimum destination, while the Jungian or Transpersonal path considers unity with Being (Self) the sought-after goal.

But perhaps the most encompassing frameworks remain the Hegelian and Kierkegaardian. Although their differences have been well traced, their developmental stations for comprehensive selfhood reveal surprising confluence. While both recognize that personal consolidation of self is important, they also share the vision that a communal substrate grounds all self-construction. Selfhood becomes meaningless when divorced from its corporate matrix. Only its connective social and relational "tissue" gives self its "substance".

Beyond the interpersonal web, however, there is a larger embeddedness for self, only visible from a particular vista. Religious paradigms have developed the necessary symbolizing frameworks to allow this reality to become known. Full selfhood cannot be approached only through the historical elements of its life but also through the encompassing, trans-historical themes which infuse its existence. Nevertheless, these too must be experientially grounded.

The grand sweep of living selfhood then, reveals three phases. The first phase concerns the birth of the self as **personal**, the second as it finds its shape in its **particular world**, the third as it **fulfills itself**.

The Personal Self

Every explorer of selfhood has envisioned a state of pre-emergent embeddedness for self. The awakening of self is never magically given, but brought about through the simultaneous arrival of the world. A subject is born hand in hand with its object(s). Physical birth is perhaps the most visible transition from embeddedness to exposure to the world, but as dramatic as it is, it is only one small occasion in a process that covers the full range of potentialities for self.

Every moment of living selfhood is in some ways an emergence, a birth. The encounter with otherness begins even in those pre-birth "experiences" which first bring the fetus to the world. The sensations of sound, movement, distress, and rest, while mediated by the maternal host, nevertheless prepare the way for full awakening.

Being born to one's self, then, is a never-ending process. This on-going impulse to find one's self is desire-driven at all levels of self, as has been consistently declared throughout this study. The key factor which shapes such desires, however, is the developmental stage which has been attained. A self emerging out of embryonic oneness experiences its first forms of object-hunger as a desire for object constancy. The persistant and faithful availability of a need-satisfying other offers a safe cocoon for a newly-emerging self. As the psychoanalytic paradigm has declared, this availability need only be "good enough"; as a matter of fact, it must contain sufficient frustration to allow some measure of internal structure-building within self.

The first developmental task to be accomplished by self, then, is for sufficient coalescing to occur to allow subsequent experience to find some ordered and safe place within the self. Conditions of chronic chaos only fragment the foundation of self, leaving it with marginal ability to claim any stability for itself.

A self wounded in this first developmental task will find its ability at boundary and structure maintenance so compromised that the threat of annihilation and collapse of self always looms. Psychotic conditions arising out of such collapsed self-structures are the most common form of a self diseased through its first object-encounters.

A second phase to the life of self is the requirement that it experience attachment with its defining object(s). To be attached is very different from being fused with one's objects. A certain measure of separation is a prerequisite for genuine attachment to occur. A self desires attachment because of the structural requirement of intimacy and engagement discussed earlier. There is no self without some form of attachment even if this attachment takes the so-called negative form of the renunciation of objects.

To be attached in self-enhancing ways nourishes the self in a manner far deeper than the equally necessary mirroring need to be discussed shortly. A self which is attached, which belongs, is warmed by this interaction because it is accepted in ways not dependent upon its particular accomplishments. A self's intrinsic acceptability is declared within attachment regardless of its capabilities and in spite of its abilities. A self which "belongs" only because of its accomplishments is a self living outside itself, hanging by the thread of productivity-maintenance.

As development continues, however, cognitive, motor, and emotional growth brings self to a new level of potential selfhood where its energy and capacities need to be validated. The well-documented narcissistic dimension of self is the name given to this ever-present need for mirroring of emerging competencies. Acknowledgement by another self is so vital that its chronic absence leaves the self vulnerable to massive self-devaluation and disorientation. Not only is the self's internal requirement to know itself thwarted if this recognition is witheld, the self can be crushed in its attempt to find some worth for itself.

Infantile hunger for a joyful response to one's self is of course transcended if such acknowledgement is forthcoming in phase-appropriate ways. However, the need to be "taken-delight-in" never departs. All stations of life contain forms of acknowledgement-hunger. Compensations and surrogate self-validations are possible, of course. Their effectiveness will nevertheless depend upon the accumulated history of recognition experienced by a self. If early validations were mixed or non-existent, then later infusions of worth often fail to soothe the ache unless, of course, the self enters into relationship with its very neediness.

Finally, personal selfhood requires consolidation of itself. Beyond all needs for cohesion, for attachment, and for recognition, lies the desire to "pull the self together". A cohesive self knows itself with a fullness only attainable as a culmination to the phases noted thus far. All aspects of its life, whether historical, emotional, or sexual are claimed and integrated into the self-system. No self accomplishes this task fully given the reality that self-knowledge is never simply given but must be arduously sought. Nevertheless, even in its incompleteness a cohesive self feels itself to be its very own self.

The Relational Self

The path of the consolidation of personal selfhood is in no way separate from relational and interpersonal themes. Every phase noted thus far is by its very nature relational. In turning to the inter-subjective arena, however, I am shifting the focus away from internal structures toward the more external social network within which selfhood moves.

Every self is embedded in a social/cultural matrix. This network of meanings, values, behaviors, and norms is the communal soil within which self either flourishes or dies. The question confronting us is not whether self will or will not have a social world, but how that world will sustain the impulses within self, or thwart them, thereby putting self at risk. We need only remind ourselves of the massive self-alienation imposed upon many Native North Americans through the cultural genocide of the prevailing culture if we have any doubts about the importance of this factor.

If the witness of Hegel and numerous other explorers is trustworthy, then **imitation** is the first form of relational selfhood. A self will adapt itself to the norms of its world largely because its own self has not yet been attained. Acquiescence is the only model of accountability known by such a self since its acceptability is dependent upon the compliance demanded of it.

A primary agenda which fuels these processes (in addition to narcissistic themes spoken of earlier) is the issue of power versus powerlessness. An emerging self is not only unaware of competing claims for allegiance, but is powerless to challenge the prevailing social order given its dependence upon it. Early forms of negation (such as a young child which hurls its "no" at the face of the parent) involve a claiming of a preliminary sense of boundary, a precursor to the establishment of internalized norms generally referred to as conscience.

A crossroads presents itself at this stage of self-development. A self will either gravitate toward conformity as its first effort at accommodating itself to the social order, or it will seek a path of more active negation called rebellion in order to consolidate its values for itself. Even conformity, however, is a stage beyond imitation, since an awareness of values has now emerged which one attempts to honor through the act of conformity. Rebellion is an equivalent attempt at finding a framework of behavior for the self only this time in more "negating" form.

The two themes of conformity and negation are the two styles by which a self will attempt to orient itself toward the sources of power in its world. Some selves therefore find their self confirmed as they acquiesce to the demands of the power-brokers of their world, while others will find their self primarily through challenging the status quo.

There is a vast arena within which these transactions occur. Sexual mores, gender identities and roles, and religious belief systems, are prime examples. In each case the social definition of acceptability will be attractive for certain emerging selves who will align themselves accordingly (conformist self). Or, conversely, a self will find itself more fully as it challenges the prevailing power and value structures of its world. Even so-called adult relationships such as husband-wife, teacher-student, employer-employee can be arranged along these power-determined lines.

While there may be some comfort found in the predictability of such arrangements it is not the final word. A fullness to relational selfhood is only attained as a self gains the capacity for increasingly nuanced response to its world. The extremes of meek conformity or strident over-againstness are unable to grant legitimacy either to the self or the social world. In negating one or the other the necessary reciprocal relation is not attained. No self can live in permanent isolation from wider meaning and value systems, just as no self can live if its only voice is to mimic the social or religious "party line".

The prevailing social order must be filtered through a self's critical capacities and affective discernments, which allows the self to sift out the incongruent and suffocating aspects of the social world. A further dialog with these elements may well need to be maintained but this does not mean that the self's life must be driven by them. To be able to challenge the values of one's world enlivens the self in that it now takes full responsibility for itself without negating or denying its world. No longer driven by the world or swallowed up by it, the self is able to live in an intentional mutuality with its social world.

The Fulfilled Self

In my definition of self I declared that self is a center of initiative which accomplishes certain purposes, the most central of which is to become known. Becoming known involves an on-going process of validation in which a self seeks confirmation from an otherness which matches the level of selfhood being sought. This eternal seeking of objects which "bring" self to itself has been mapped across a wide range of self-seeking from the earliest forms of infantile emergence out of fusion, to the highly sophisticated competencies of creative process. Such otherness supplies the selfobjects which connect the dyadic structures of self, as well as mirror the self back to itself.

Thus far, we have paid primary attention to the personal and social objects which direct self toward varying degrees of unity or fragmentation for itself. The task which remains is to demonstrate how the encounter with absolute otherness impacts self for better or for worse.[11] Rather than using the overburdened word "God" to name this otherness, I am relying upon a concept I call a **sheer defining absolute**. A sheer defining absolute covers the full range of experienceable realities from utter constriction (death) to radical openness (limitlessness), from oceanic oneness to supremely refined and nuanced differentiation. Speaking analogously, a sheer defining absolute serves the self-construct much as infinity serves mathematics and science. This is not to suggest that such an absolute only resides at the limitless "outer edges" of the self. Rather, it also names the depth dimension of the smallest bits of self-experience. The absolute is not only present as the factor of radical expansiveness for self, but the factor of supreme connectedness and fullest inwardness. The sheer defining absolute is the object of fulfillment for self.

Hegel's approach to this question, as we recall, was to posit a universal self which "gathers itself together" through the manifold forms of religiosity reflected in human experience. All religious experience, for Hegel, serves the self-discovery and self-consolidation of absolute selfhood. This proposition may or may not be persuasive, and in any case is not the approach I am advocating.

Rather than speculate upon the so-called "career" of God, I prefer to find an encompassing grounding and validation for human selfhood, which honors its deepest yearnings. My resistance to the Hegelian model centers around a subtle arrogance which creeps into all attempts at judging the adequacy of religious systems for "carrying" the self. Generally, one's own perspective or ideational framework is taken to be the norm, the supreme reflection of what self is meant to be.

I, on the other hand, wish to affirm the legitimacy of all encompassing (absolute) objects which attempt to unify and validate the self. All selves seek a viable otherness through which the worth of the self will be affirmed. All selfhood is unified for better or for worse by its operative religious object(s). Absolute Object-choice and the use that is made thereof will of course depend upon the particular history of every self and the nature of selfobject supply received. A self with limited sources of security will likely yearn for Absolute selfobject material which will correct the deficiency. Conversely, a self with a constricting selfobject legacy will likely seek an Absolute otherness which opens the horizons for the self. At the same time, if the structural dyads of self have been torn asunder through destructive experience, then the internal requirement to gather up these pieces of self will often propel such a self toward contradictory visions of itself. Yet even here, the yearning for integrity, for a sustaining center of initiative, will nudge a self toward potentially unifying absolute objects.

Does this commitment to a multiplicity of absolute objects mean they are one and the same, interchangeable even? By no means! A self steeped in an Islamic milieu, for instance, will find itself unified and validated primarily through patterns of obedience and alignment of self with a sovereign absolute object. Many a self will find great contentment therein. Yet even such a self is not static but also moving beyond itself toward a not-yet. New possibilities and new challenges present themselves with new forms of validation required. In the great melting pot of history the religious ideation(s) which feed the self are changing, even as they maintain a link to their prior inheritance.

The primary requirement, then, is to own the framework within which the self is defined. For me, as a Christian, the Christ event is normative for selfhood, the epitome of what self is and was called to be. Christ is for the Christian the supreme mirror **of the self, for the self**. In agreement with W.Paul Jones, I can declare that Christ is a double mirror, representing my self to God, and God to my self.[12]

Christ, as normative for selfhood, mirrors me to myself infusing my self with the radiance of the fullness of self. Furthermore, as was described in Chapter II, Christ "carries" my self for the Absolute, presenting my self as it were, to that supreme otherness as a self in the making. Not only is the self absolutely affirmed in this transaction, its sanctity is guaranteed. If Christ were only a one way mirror for the self then this Absolute selfobject would only beckon as a remote ideal. Rather, Christ also declares the self to be fully and eternally valid, even in its incompletion. This becomes the source of its absolute security in the midst of its manifold changeableness.

The Christian tradition has been most insistent that selfhood is in fact a house divided, perhaps even at war with itself and its truest inclinations. At first glance this division to self seems contradicted by my earlier claim that self lives in dyadic unity, organized around the four structural dyads named earlier. Granted, a self may have split off part of its structure. For instance, a self may have negated its need for intimacy by attempting to live in an exaggerated separateness. But this lopsidedness to self is not what is meant by divided selfhood.

Divided selfhood concerns the degree of bondage versus freedom actualized by every self. Selfhood is in an ongoing birthing process, of being taken beyond itself into ever new possibilities. A self may become divided from itself in two ways as it anticipates this requirement. On the one hand it can shrink from its possibilities either by being smothered by what has been, or by avoiding any option that might loosen the self from its entrenched existence. Thus is constructed an outer self detached from its authentic inclinations and deepest desires.

On the other hand, a self can be quite bold in moving toward new possibilities, seeking to find itself in their actualization. Great athletic, artistic and intellectual feats have been accomplished out of such impulses. Nevertheless, such a self can be chasing after counterfeit validations for itself. It may be seeking confirmation of some aspect of itself to the neglect of its larger requirement, namely, to find and embrace its very own self. Such a self is a false self seeking its validation in its functional capacities meanwhile missing the necessary validation of its deeper capacities.

If the model of Christ as prototype for selfhood carries legitimacy, then the fullest validation for self is found as it releases itself for another and in so doing finds itself. This is a far cry from any holier-than-thou altruism. It is a model of selfhood which does not attempt to grasp its worth, hoarding it for safe-keeping. Rather, it lets be and in releasing all claims for permanence for itself it finds it freedom and its true self.

---

1. I find welcome confirmation for my insistence that the primary energy of self is the desire to be known, in contemporary feminist scholarship such as Brock, p. 9

2. Catherine Keller, *From a Broken Web: Separation, Sexism, and Self* (Boston: Beacon Press, 1986). While Keller overstates her case in places as in her assessment of Hegel, for example, she correctly observes that the Western model of self has generally posited the other as oppositional object through which one defines oneself (Chapters 1 and 2).

3. Ibid., p.225. Keller offers four dyads as determinative for selfhood: (1) being one and being many; (2) being private or being public; (3) being body and being soul; (4) being here and being now. I wish to acknowledge the close affinity between my own first dyad and that of Keller's. Her other dyads I find somewhat wanting for the following reasons: Keller's second dyad is strangely presented as an either/or. (Note also the use of the word "poles" on p. 232). Furthermore, it mixes themes of introversion/extroversion (as styles of engaging otherness) with agendas of community vs. autonomy. The third dyad uses the unfortunate linguistic duality of "body" and "soul". These terms are too archaic and contaminated to carry the indivisible bodyself unity she affirms. The final dyad mixes spatial and temporal metaphors to affirm the experiential groundedness of self.

4. Freud held that narcissistically bound persons were quite untreatable given their seeming impossibility at forming transference relationships.

5. Ernest S. Wolf, *Treating the Self*, (New York: The Guilford Press, 1988), p. 55, 60-61

6. Keller, 1986, p. 7-46

7. Nancy J. Chodorow, *Feminism and Psychoanalytic Theory* (New Haven: Yale University Press, 1989), p. 7-19

8. I need not repeat my earlier critique of Freud other than to reaffirm the great difficulty in unifying selfhood via purely organically-driven measures.

9. The four structural dyads of self become crystallized through this cycle of satisfaction and negation.

10. See Chapter 5, p. 26. Also, G.W.F. Hegel, 1977, p.103

11. Psychoanalytic scholarship has provided a limited usefulness for exploring this aspect of self-experience. Resources such as Ana-Maria Rizzuto, *The Birth of the Living God* (Chicago: University of Chicago Press, 1979); John McDargh, *Psychoanalytic Object Relations Theory and the Study of Religion* (Lanham, New York: University Press of America, 1983); W.W. Meissner, *Psychoanalysis and Religious Experience*, (New Haven: Yale University Press, 1984); and W.W. Meissner, *Life and Faith*, (Washington, D.C.: Georgetown University Press, 1987) offer varying helpfulness. Rizzuto is limited by her severe reductionism; Meissner is limited both by Ego Psychological presuppositions along with a vision of faith development that is heavily cognitive. McDargh remains the most comprehensive of such studies. More recent efforts which demonstrate richer integration include James W. Jones, *Contemporary Psychoanalysis and Religion*, (New Haven: Yale University Press, 1991); Mark Finn and John Gartner Eds, *Object Relations Theory and Religion: Clinical Applications*, (Westport, CT: Praeger Publishers, 1992), and finally, Mary Lou Randour, Ed. *Exploring Sacred Landscapes: Religious and Spiritual Experiences in Psychotherapy*, (New York, NY; Columbia University Press, 1993).

12. W. Paul Jones, *Theological Worlds* (Nashville: Abingdon Press, 1989), p. 141

Bibliography

Ancelet-Hutache, Jeanne. *Meister Eckhart and the Rhineland Mystics*. Translated by Hilda Graef. New York: Harper Torchbooks, 1957.

Angeles, Peter A. *Dictionary of Philosophy*. New York: Barnes and Noble Books, 1981.

Augustine. The Trinity. Translated by Stephen McKenna. Vol. 45. *The Fathers of The Church*. Washington: Catholic University Press, 1963.

Blank, Rubin, and Gertrude Blank. *Beyond Ego Psychology*. New York: Columbia University Press, 1986.

Blum, Harold P. *"Theories of the Self and Psychoanalytic Theory." Journal of the American Psychoanalytic Association*. 30. (1982) 959-978.

Bostock, David. *Plato's Phaedo*. Oxford: Clarendon Press, 1986.

Brock, R. *Journey's by Heart: A Christology of Erotic Power*. New York: Crossroad Publishing, 1988.

Bultmann, Rudolf. *Theology of the New Testament* Vol. 1. Translated by Kendrick Grobel. New York: Charles Scribner's Sons. 1951.

Butler, Clark. *"Hegel and Freud: A Comparison," Philosophy and Phenomenology Research, Journey's to Selfhood, Hegel and Kierkegaard*. Berkeley: University of California Press, 1980.

Buttrick, George A. et. al. Eds. *The Interpreter's Dictionary of The Bible* Vol. 4. New York: Abingdon Press 1962.

Chodorow, Nancy J. *Feminism and Psychoanalytic Theory*. New Haven: Yale University Press, 1989.

Connell, George. *To Be One Thing: Personal Unity in Kierkegaard's Thought*. Macon, GA: Mercer University Press, 1985.

Descartes, Rene. *Discourse on Method and the Meditations*. Translated by F. E. Sutcliffe, New York: Penguin Books, 1968.

Descartes, Rene. *Principles of Philosophy*. Vol. 1. Translated by Haldane and Ross. 1931.

Descartes, Rene. *The Passions of the Soul*. Translated by E.S. Haldane and G.R.T. Ross in the Philosophical Works of Descartes Vol. 1. Cambridge: Cambridge University Press, 1931.

Doster, Kenneth. *Plato's Phaedo: An Interpretation.* Toronto: Toronto University Press, 1982.

Dourly, J.P., Jung, C.G., and Tillich, P. *The Psyche as Sacrament.* Toronto: Inner City Books, 1981.

Dunning, Stephen, N. *Kierkegaard's Dialect of Inwardness.* Princeton: Princeton University Press, 1985.

Eckhart, D.W.I. Sermon 4; cited in *Meister Eckhart: Teacher and Preacher.* Edited by Bernard McGinn. New York: Paulist Press, 1986.

Eckhart, D.W.I. Sermon 6: cited in *Meister Eckhart: The Essential Sermons, Commentaries, Treatises, and Defence.* Translated by Edmund Colledge and Bernard McGinn. New York: Paulist Press, 1981.

Edinger, Edward. *The Creation of Consciousness,* Toronto: Inner City Books, 1984.

Edinger, Edward. *Ego's and Archetypes.* Baltimore: Penguin Books, 1973.

Fairbairn, W.R.D. *An Object-Relations Theory of the Personality.* New York: Basic Books, 1954.

Findlay, J.N. *Hegel: A Re-examination.* New York: The Macmillan Company, 1958.

Fine, Rubin. *The Development of Freud's Thought.* New York: Jason Aronson Inc., 1973.

Fitche, Johann. *The Vocation of Man.* Translated by Peter Preuss. Indianapolis: Hacket Publishing Co., 1987.

Freud, Sigmund. *"Three Essays on the Theory of Sexuality" On Sexuality.* Vol. 7.   : Pelikan Books, 1986.

Freud, Sigmund. *"The Ego and the Id", On Metapsychology: The Theory of Psychoanalysis.* Vol. II, The Pelican Freud Library. Edited by Angela Richards. Translated by James Strackey. New York: Penguin Books, 1985A.

Freud, Sigmund. *"Instincts and Their Vicissitudes, On Metapsychology."* Translated by James Strachey. New York: Penguin Books, 1985B.

Freud, Sigmund. *An Outline of Psychoanalysis.* Translated by James Strachey. New York: W.W. Norton and Company, A 1949.

Freud, Sigmund. *Group Psychology and the Analysis of the Ego.* Translated by James Strachey. London: The Hogarth Press, B 1949.

Freud, Sigmund. *New Introductory Lectures on Psychoanalysis*. Translated by W.J. H. Sprott. New York: W.W. Norton and Company, 1933.

Fox, Matthew. *Original Blessing*. Santa Fe: Bear and Company, 1983.

Gardeil, H.D. *Introduction to The Philosophy of St. Thomas Aquinas*. Translated by John A. Otto. St. Louis: Herder Book Company, 1956.

Garrigou-Lagrange, Reginald. *Reality: A Synthesis of Thomistic Thought*. Translated by Patrick Cummins. St. Louis: Herder Book Company, 1958.

Goldenberg, N. *Returning Words to Flesh*. Boston: Beacon Press, 1990.

Greenberg, Jay R., and Mitchell Stephen A. *Object Relations in Psychoanalytic Theory*. Cambridge: Harvard University Press, 1983.

Guntrip, Harry. *"Psychoanalytic Object Relations Theory: The Fairbairn-Guntrip Approach"*, American Handbook of Psychiatry Vol. I 2nd ed. Edited by Silvano Arieti. New York: Basic Books Inc., 1974.

Guntrip, Harry. *Psychoanalysis Theory, Therapy, and The Self*. New York: Basic Books Inc., 1971.

Guntrip, Harry. *Personality Structure and Human Interaction: The Developing Synthesis of Psychodynamic Theory*. New York: International Universities Press, 1961.

Hartman, Edwin. *Substance Body, and Soul*. Princeton: Princeton University Press, 1977.

Hartman, Heinz, Ernest Kris, and Rudolf Lowenstein. *Papers on Psychoanalytic Psychology*. New York: International Universities Press, 1964.

Hartman, Heinz. *Ego Psychology and the Problem of Adaptation*. New York: International Universities Press, 1958.

Hegel, G.W.F. *Lectures on the Philosophy of Religion*. Edited by Peter C. Hodgson. Translated by R.F. Brown, P.C. Hodgson, and J.M. Stewart. Berkeley: University of California Press, 1988.

Hegel, G.W.F. *Phenomenology of Spirit*. Translated by A.V. Miller. Oxford: Clarendon Press, 1977.

Heidegger, Martin. *Hegel's Phenomenology of Spirit*. Translated by Parvis Emad and Kenneth Maly. Bloomington and Indianapolis: Indiana University Press, 1988.

Heisenberg, Werner. *Physics and Philosophy*. New York: Harper and Row, 1988.

Henry, Paul. *Saint Augustine on Personality*. New York: The MacMillan Company, 1980.

Homas, Peter. *Jung in Context*. Chicago: University of Chicago Press, 1979.

Hume, David. *"An Inquiry Concerning Human Understanding"*. Edited by Robert Paul Wolff. New York: New American Library, 1969.

Hume, David. *A Treatice of Human Nature* Vol. I. London: J.M. Dent and Sons Ltd., 1961.

Hyppolite, Jean. *Genesis and Structure of Hegel's Phenomenology of Spirit*. Translated by Samuel Chermak and John Heckman. Evanston: Northwestern University Press, 1974.

Jacobi, Jolande. *The Psychology of C.G. Jung*. New Haven: Yale University Press, 1973.

Jacobson, Edith. *Depression: Comparative Studies of Normal, Neurotic, and Psychotic Conditions*. New York: International Universities Press, 1971.

Jacobson, Edith. *Psychotic Conflict and Reality*. New York: International Universities Press, 1967.

Jacobson, Edith. *The Self and the Object World*. New York: International Universities Press, 1964.

Jones, Ernest. *Sigmund Freud, Life and Work* Vol. I. London: Hogarth, 1953.

Jones, J.W. *Contemporary Psychoanalysis and Religion*. New Haven: Yale University Press, 1991.

Jones, W.P. *Theological Words*. Nashville: Abingdon Press, 1989.

Jones, W.T. *A History of Western Philosophy: Kant and the Nineteenth Century*, Vol. IV. New York: Harcourt Brace Jovanovich, 1975.

Jones, W.T. *The Classical Mind: A History of Western Philosophy* 2nd. ed. New York: Harcourt Brace Jovanovich, 1970.

Jones, W.T. *A History of Western Philosophy: Hobbes to Hume*, Vol. III. San Diego: Harcourt Brace Jovanovich, 1969.

Jung, C.G. *Anion. Complete Works*, Vol. 9ii. Translated by R.F.C. Hull. Princeton: Princeton University Press, 1978.

Jung, C.G. *The Development of Personality*. Translated by R.F.C. Hull. Princeton: Princeton University Press, 1977.

Jung, C.G. *Psychological Types. Complete Works*, Vol. VI. Translated by H.G. Baynes. Revised by R.F.C. Hull. Princeton: Princeton University Press, 1971.

Jung, C.G. *The Structure and Dynamics of the Psyche. Complete Works*, Vol. 8. Translated by R.F.C. Hull. Princeton: Princeton University Press, 1969.

Jung, C.G. *Psychology and Religion: West and East. Complete Works*, Vol. II. Translated by R.F.C. Hull. Princeton: Princeton University Press, 1969.

Jung, C.G. *Psychology and Alchemy. Complete Works*, Vol. 12. Translated by R.F.C. Hull. Princeton: Princeton University Press, 1966.

Jung, C.G. *Two Essays on Analytic Psychology. Complete Works*, Vol. 7. Translated by R.F.C. Hull. Princeton: Princeton University Press, 1966.

Jung, C.G. Anion: *Researches into the Phenomenology of the Self. Complete Works*, Vol. II. Translated by R.F.C. Hull. Princeton: Princeton University Press, 1959A.

Jung, C.G. *The Archetypes and the Collective Unconscious. Complete Works*, Vol. 9. Translated by R.F.C. Hull. Princeton: Princeton University Press, 1959B.

Kainz, Howard P. *Hegel's Phenomenology, Part I: Analysis and Commentary.* ? The University of Alabama Press, 1976.

Kant, Immanuel. *Critique of Pure Reason.* Translated by F. Max Muller. Garden City: Anchor Books, 196?.

Keller, Catherine. *From a Broken Web: Separation, Sexism, and Self.* Boston: Beacon Press, 1986.

Kernberg, Otto. *Object Relations Theory and Clinical Psychoanalysis.* New York: Jason Aronson Inc., 1976.

Kernberg, Otto. *"Self Ego, Affects and Drives"* Journal of the American Psychoanalytic Association. 30 (1982) p. 900.

Kernberg, Otto. *Severe Personality Disorders: Psychotherapeutic Strategies.* New Haven: Yale University Press, 1984.

Kierkegaard, Soren. *Either/Or.* Edited by Stephen L. Ross. Translated by George L. Stengren. New York: Harper and Row Publishers, 1986.

Kierkegaard, Soren. *Either/Or.* Vol. 1. Translated by Howard V. Hong and Edna H. Hong. Princeton: Princeton University Press, 1985.

Kierkegaard, Soren. *Fear and Trembling.* Translated by Howard V. Hong and Edna H. Hong. Princeton: Princeton University Press, 1983.

Kierkegaard, Soren. *The Sickness Unto Death.* Translated by Howard V. Hong and Edna H. Hong. Princeton: Princeton University Press, 1980.

Kierkegaard, Soren. *The Concept of Dread.* Translated by Walter Lowrie. Princeton: Princeton University Press, 1957.

Kierkegaard, Soren. *Either/Or*, Vol. II. Translated by Walter Lowrie. London: Oxford University Press, 1944.

Kierkegaard, Soren. *Concluding Unscientific Postscript.* Translated by David F. Swenson and Walter Lowrie. Princeton: Princeton University Press, 1941.

Klein, Melanie. *Envy, Gratitude, and Other Works*, 1946-1963. London: The Hogarth Press, 1978.

Klein, Melanie. *Contributions to Psycho-Analysis.* 1921-1948. London: The Hogarth Press, 1948.

Klein, Milton, and David Tribich. *"Kernberg's Object Relations Theory: A Critical Evaluaton." International Journal of Psychoanalysis* 62 (1981) p. 27-43.

Kohut, Heinz. *How Does Analysis Cure.* Edited by Arnold Goldberg and Paul Stepansky. Chicago: The University of Chicago Press, 1984.

Kohut, Heinz. *Advances in Self Psychology.* Edited by Arnold Goldberg. New York: International Universities Press, 1980.

Kohut, Heinz. *TheSearch for Self*, Vol. 1. Edited by Paul H. Ornstein. New York: International Universities Press, 1978.

Kohut, Heinz. *The Restoration of the Self.* New York: International Universities Press, 1977.

Kung, Hans. *The Incarnation of God.* Translated by J.R. Stephenson. New York: Crossroad, 1987.

Lewis, H.D. *The Elusive Self.* London: The MacMillan Press, 1982.

Mahler, Margaret, and John B. McDevitt. *"Thoughts of the Emergence of Sense of Self, With Particular Emphasis of the Body Self." Journal of the American Psychoanalytic Association* 30, (1982) p. 827-848.

Mahler, Margaret, Fred Pine, and Anni Bergman. *The Psychological Birth of the Human Infant.* New York: Basic Books, 1975.

Mahler, Margaret. *"On the First Three Subphases of the Separation-Individuation Process." International Journal of Psychoanalysis*, 53 (1972) p. 333-338.

McDargh, J. *Psychoanalytical Object Relations Theory and The Study of Religion.* New York: University Press of America, 1983.

McGinn, Bernard, Ed. *Meister Eckhart, Teacher and Preacher*. New York: Paulist Press, 1986.

Meissner, W.W. *Life and Faith*. Washington D.C.: Georgetown University Press, 1987.

Meissner, W.W. *Psychoanalysis and Religious Experience*. New Haven: Yale University Press, 1984.

Moss, David M. *"Narcissism, Empathy, and the Fragmentation of Self: An Interview With Heinz Kohut."* Pilgrimage, 4, No. 1, (1976) p. 34.

Mullen, John Douglas. *Kierkegaard's Philosophy*. New York: New American Library, 1981.

Norman, Richard. *Hegel's Phenomenology: A Philosophical Introduction*. London: Sussex University Press, 1976.

Pannenberg, Wolfhart. *Anthropology in Theological Perspective*. Translated by Matthew L. O'Connell. Philadelphia: The Westminster Press, 1985.

Plato. *"Republic (514-521)," "The Dialogues of Plato."* Translated by Benjamin Jowett. Great Books of the Western World, Vol. 7. ??: Chicago, 1952.

Rangell, Leo. *"The Self in Psychoanalytic Theory." Journal of The American Psychoanalytic Association*, 30 (1982) 863-891.

Rapaport, David. *The Structure of Psychoanalytic Theory*. New York: International Universities Press, 1960.

Ricoeur, Paul. *"Two Encounter with Kierkegaard," Kierkegaard's Truth: The Disclosure of the Self*. Edited by Joseph H. Smith. New Haven: Yale University Press, 1981.

Rizzuto, Ana-Marie. *The Birth of The Living God*. Chicago: The University of Chicago Press, 1979.

Runes, Dagobert D., Ed. *Dictionary of Philosophy*. Totowa, N.J.: Littlefield, Adams and Company, 1980.

Schmidt, William. *"A Biblical Paradigm For Selfhood," Journal of Pastoral Care*, 43 (1989) p. 337-354.

Schurmann, Reiner. *Meister Eckhart: Mystic and Philosopher*. Bloomington: Indiana University Press, 1978.

Shute, Clarence. *The Psychology of Aristotle*. New York: Russell and Russell Inc., 1964.

Sertillanges, A.D. *Foundations of Thomistic Philosophy*. Translated by Godfrey Anstruther. Springfield IL: Templegate Publishers, undated.

Solomon, Robert C. *In the Spirit of Hegel*. New York: Oxford University Press, 1983.

Spitz, Rene. *The First Year of Life*. New York: International Universities Press, 1965.

Stolorow, R.D., B. Brandchaft, and G.E. Atwood. *Psychoanalytical Treatment: An Intersubjective Approach*. New Jersey: The Analytic Press, 1987.

Taylor, Charles, *Hegel*. Cambridge: Cambridge University Press, 1975.

Taylor, Mark C. *Journey's of Selfhood: Hegel and Kierkegaard*. Berkeley: University of California Press, 1980.

Te Selle, Eugene. *Augustine the Theologian*. New York: Herder and Herder, 1970.

Theissen, Gerd. *Psychological Aspects of Pauline Theology*. Translated by John R. Gaven. Philadelphia: Fortress Press, 1987.

Verene, Donald P. *Hegel's Recollections: A Study of Images in The Phenomenology of Spirit*. Albany State University of New York Press, 1985.

Walker, Nigel D. *"A New Copernicus?" The Freudian Paradigm: Psychoanalysis and Scientific Thought*, md. Edited by Mujeebur-Rohman. Chicago: Nelson-Hall, 1977.

Watson, Robert I. *The Great Psychologists: From Aristotle to Freud*. Philadelphia: J.P. Lippincott Company, 1963.

Wijsenbeekk-Wigler H. *Aristotle Concepts of Soul, Sleep, and Dreams*. Amsterdam: Adolf M. Hakkert, 1978.

Winnicot, D.W. *"The Location of Cultural Experience." International Journal of Psychoanalysis*. 48 (1967).

Winnicot, D.W. *The Maturational Process and the Facilitating Environment*. London: The Hogarth Press, 1965.

Winnicot, D.W. *Collected Papers*. New York: Basic Books, 1958.

Wolf, Ernest S. *Treating the Self*. New York: The Fuilford Press, 1988.

Woods, Richard. *Eckhart's Way*. Wilmington Delaware: Michael Glazer, 1986.

Wolf, Hans W. *Anthropology of The Old Testament*. Translated by Margaret Kohl. Philadelphia: FortressPress, 1974.

Zimmerman, Michael E. *Eclipse of the Self.* Athens, OH; Ohio University Press, 1981.

INDEX

a posterior 123
a priori 123
Absolute 89
Active reason 172
adaptation 308
affects 332
Albert the Great 89
alchemy 96
Anima 366
Animus 366
apocalypticism 48
appetite 96
    Plato 26
Aquinas 29
Aquinas, Thomas 79
archtypes 357
    Jung's theory 354
Aristotle 20, 29
Artistic religion 185
attachment 404
Aufhebung 154
Augustine 24, 69
Autism 319
Auto-eroticism 269
autonomy 93
Avorrists 79
belief
    Hegel 178
Beyond the Pleasure Principle 271
bi-polarity 101
Biblical self 44
body 79
boundary
    self development 392
breaking - through
    Eckhart's theology 100
Brentano, Franz 249
Brucke 250
Cartesian Method
    see Descartes, Rene 111
Catherine Keller 387
change
    Aristotle 30
Chodorow, Nancy 394
Christ 62, 409

Christ archtype
    Jung 371
Christianity
    Kierkegaard 230
cognition 86
collective unconscious 357
comedy 189
compliant conformist 176
Conscience 181
Consciousness
    Hegel 160
Consolidation of Individuation 324
Crucifixion 193
cultic life 186
Darwin 33
dependence-independence 166
Descartes 40, 111
    Ego 125
desire
    Hegel 164
    Plato 26
desiring desire 217
Despair 211
    Kierkegaard 208
determinism 100
dialectic 61, 132, 212
    subject - object 294
dissimilarity
    Eckhart's theology 97
dreaming desire 216
drive
    Freud 264
drives 59
    Hartmann's theory 314
    Kernberg's theory 332
    Klein's theory 283
Dualism
    Descartes 114
    Kant 127
    Plato 25
Duty
    Hegel 180
dyads
    self organizing 387
ecstatic experience 186
ego 60, 259
    anti-libidinal 290

central 291
Descartes 112
Fichte's theory 129
Hartmann 309
Jung's theory 356, 362
libidinal 290
whole 289
Ego Psychology 113, 162, 258
Hartmann 308
Ego Psychology and the Problem of
Adaptation (1939) 308
ego-identity
Kernberg 331
empathy 336
empirical ego 124
Empiricism 63
Enlightenment 194
Epic 188
Eros 272, 367
ethical selfhood 220
experience
Hegel 152
Hume 117
Kant 124
Fairbairn, R.W.A. 282
Fairbairn, Ronald 287
faith 79
Hegel 178
Kierkegaard 212, 233
Fall,The 52
feeling 81
female selfhood 392
Fichte 24
Fichte, J. G. 128
Finite-Infinite Polarity 205
flesh 47, 55
form 81
freedom 58
Freud 24, 164, 307, 390
contrast with Jung 355
Freud, Anna 281
Freud, Sigmund 113, 248
Fulfilled Self 407
function 81
God
Kierkegaard 238
God-consciousness 97
Godhead
Eckhart's theology 91
Goethe, Johann 249
Grace 101

grandiosity 297
Great Britain
Object-Relations Schools 281
Greek literature
Hegel's theory 188
Guilt
Kierkegaard 228
Guilty Man 344
Guntrip, H. 282
Hartmann, Heinz 113, 281, 307
hatching 322
heart 50
Hegel 24, 234
opposition to Kierkegaard 226
Hegel, G. W. F. 144
Heisenberg's Uncertainty Principle
163
Helmholz School 250
Hobbes, Thomas 117
human personhood 45
Hume 35
Hume, David 117
Hyppolite, Jean 153
Id 258
Id Psychology
Klein, Melanie 283
identification 262
Kernberg 331
identity 61
Descartes 119
Eckhart's theology 99
Jacobson's theory 316
immediacy 216
impingement 297
Incarnation 193
Initiative
self as source 400
instincts
Jung's theory 358
intellect 81
interiority 54
Interpretation of Dreams, The 252
Intimate self.i.Separate self 394
introjection 331
irrational principle 25
Jacobson
Edith 313
Jacobson, Edith 282
Jung 24
association to Freud 271
Jung, C. G. 353

410

Jung, C. J.
    thoughts on Fichte 128
Kant 24
Kant, Immanuel 122
Keller, Catherine 392
kenosis 102
Kernberg, Otto 282, 327
Kierkegaard 397
    Hartmann's self 310
    theory connection with Freud 267
Kierkegaard, Soren 202
Klein, Melanie 281
Knowing
    Aristotle 37
    Augustine's theory 73
Kohut, Heinz 77, 335, 390
law 59
    selfhood 54
Leibnitz 354
libido
    Freud 266
Logos 367
love 89
loving
    Augustine's theory 73
Mahler, Margaret 282, 318
masculine selfhood 392
material 101
mediate 204
mediation 397
mediator 190
Meister Eckhart 68, 88
memory
    Descartes 121
mind 82
Mind and its Relation to the Psyche-
Soma 300
monism 50
Morality
    Hegel 180
Multiple self 388
mystic paradigm 88
mysticism 88
Narcissism 267, 311, 390
    Kohut's theory 343
Nature religion 184
Negation
    Hegel 152
neoplatonic 91
Nephesh 46

New Introductory Lectures of Pscho-
analysis, The 258
non-attachment 99
nous 79
Novalis 146
nuclear self
    Kohut 343
object
    Fichte's theory 130
    Hartmann's theory 314
    Kant's self theory 123
    Kernberg 334
object-cathexes 260
Object-Relations School 283
Object-Relations Theory 167
Oedipal complex 263
Outline of Psychoanalysis, An 272
Pantheism 87
particular 76
Paul, the apostle 59
Perception
    Hegel 161
permanence 74
Persona
    Jung's theory 363
personal unconscious 357
personhood 98
Phenomenology of Spirit
    work by Hegel 156
Piaget 324
Plato 20
    Jung's Framework 354
pleasure 60
pleasure principle 172
Polarity 204
Possibility/necessity 204
practicing sub-phase 323
preconscious 258
primary process activity 254
projection 365
Psychopathology 290
pure insight
    Hegel 178
Pythagorean 30
rapprochement 323
rational principle 25
reality
    Aristotle 30
Realized Individuality 173
reflection 132
    Kierkegaard 218

relation 72
Relational Self 405
representation 63
rest 402
remembering
    Augustine's theory 73
religious selfhood 183
Resurrection 193
Revealed religion 190
Ruah 46
Schelling 146, 354
Schelling, Friedrich 249
Schlegel 146
Schleiermacher 146
Reason
    Aristotle 36
    Hegel 170
    Plato 26
Schopenhauer 354
Science of Knowledge, The
    work by Fichte 129
searching desire 217
secondary narcissism 270
secondary process activity 255
self
    immortal 80
    rational 80
    reactive
        proactive 293
    substantial 80
    synthesizing 298
self as free 99
self, self as
    true
        false
            annihilated 296
self-awareness
    Kierkegaard 209
Self-Consciousness
    Hegel 164
self-psychology 337
self-sufficiency
    Aquinas' position 82
selfhood
    triadic 53
selfobject 397
selfobjects
    Kohut 339
sensation
    Plato 23
Sense-knowing

Hegel 160
senses
    Hume 117
separation-individuation 162, 322
Shadow
    Jung's theory 365
sheer defining absolute 408
similarity
    Eckhart's theology 98
sin 60
    Kierkegaard 230
    Kierkegard 212
Singular self 388
"unhappy consciousness" 169
Positing
    Fichte's theory 131
primary narcissism 270
Rationalists 127
Rebel consciousness 177
skepticism
    Hegel 168
soul
    Aristotle 32
    Bible 46
    Plato 23
Spirit 57
    Hegel 147
    Jung's theory 359
    Plato 26
spiritual 101
stimulus-response 164
stoicism
    Hegel 168
striving
    Fichte's theory 135
subject
    Fichte's theory 130
subject-object 61
subjective idealism 63
subjectivity 87
submission-dominance 166
substance 69, 115
superego 60, 261
Symbiosis 320
Symbol
    Jungs'theory 370
synthesis 397
    Kierkegaard 203
Temporal-Eternal Polarity 207
tension arc
    Kohut 344

412

Thanatos 272
Thinking
    Aristotle 36
Topographic Model 252
Tragedy 188
Tragic Man 344
transcendent function
    Jung 374
transcendental ego 124
transference 256
Transforming Integration 399
    see Aufhebung 153
Transitional object 299
transmuting internalization 155, 340
Trinitarian formula 69
tripartite structure 60
truth
    Descartes 116
unconscious 49, 257
    Jung's theory 356
Understanding
    Hegel 162
union of opposites 62
universal 76
universal forms 21
Unmoved Mover 39
Utilitarianism 179
Validating self 389
Vocation of Man, The
    work by Fichte 134
von Hartmann, Edward
    Jung's theory 354
will 79
Winnicott, D. W. 282, 293, 397
wish 253
Wolf, Ernest 391

STUDIES IN THE PSYCHOLOGY OF RELIGION

1. James Gollnick, **Dreams in the Psychology of Religion**

2. Henry Newton Malony (ed.), **Spirit-Centered Wholeness: Beyond the Psychology of Self**

3. J. Harley Chapman, **Jung's Three Theories of Religious Experience**

4. John P. Dourley, **The Goddess, Mother of the Trinity: A Jungian Implication**

5. William S. Schmidt, **The Development of the Notion of Self: Understanding the Complexity of Human Interiority**

6. To be announced.

7. Margaret M. Poloma and Brian F. Pendleton, **Exploring Neglected Dimensions of Religion in Quality of Life Research**